Inside Multi-Media
Case Based Instruction

Inside Multi-Media
Case Based Instruction

◆

Edited by

Roger C. Schank
Northwestern University

LEA LAWRENCE ERLBAUM ASSOCIATES, PUBLISHERS
1998 Mahwah, New Jersey London

Lawrence Erlbaum Associates, Inc., Publishers
10 Industrial Avenue
Mahwah, NJ 07430

Cover design by Kathryn Houghtaling Lacey

Library of Congress Cataloging-in-Publication Data

Inside multi-media case based instruction / edited by
Roger C. Schank.
   p. cm.
  Includes bibliographical references and index.
  ISBN 0-8058-2537-1 (cloth : alk. Paper). -- ISBN
0-8058-2538-X
  (pbk. : alk. paper)
  1. Language and languages--Computer-assisted instruction.
  I. Schank, Roger C., 1946-
  P53.28.I57 1998
  418'.00285--dc21
            97-21714
            CIP

Books published by Lawrence Erlbaum Associates are
printed on acid-free paper, and their bindings are chosen
for strength and durability.

Printed in the United States of America
10 9 8 7 6 5 4 3 2 1

Contents

Preface

In 1989, I unceremoniously dragged a bunch of graduate students studying Artificial Intelligence (AI) at Yale into the wilds of the Midwest (Northwestern University) and cajoled them into working on educational software. It seemed to me that the time had come for a change in our concept of AI research. Previously, my students had built prototypes of programs that could do some clever humanlike processes on a few examples. We worked on getting computers to answer questions, translate paragraphs, make generalizations from multiple stories on the same subject, give advice on the basis of past experience and so on, but I was bothered by the fact that although all of these were exciting ventures, they lacked a certain utility. We could make the computer do certain clever acts, but the road to a really intelligent machine that could be readily usable by the general public seemed (and seems) long. While I was pondering the complex task of making AI real, a horrible thing happened—my kids went to school.

At Yale, we had been studying learning (in order to get machines to learn), so I thought I knew a little about the subject. But, everything I knew about learning seemed to be the antithesis of what the school systems of the world knew about learning. I knew, for example, that failure played a big role in learning. I knew that in order to fail one had to be trying to accomplish something in the first place. So, when I taught my kids to ride a bicycle, I expected them to become interested in issues of weight balance once they fell off, not before. Similarly, when a computer read a story and made a generalization that turned out to be wrong, we wanted it to be "interested" in making the correct generalization in the future.

In order to get a computer to have expectations about what would happen in the world that could be wrong so that it could fail and then learn, we had to program those expectations in the first place. So, we invented the idea of a script, and had computers use those scripts as the basis of their understanding of any situation. Learning meant modifying those scripts when they lacked the correct expectation of events—expectations that failed when the events did not happen in quite the way the computer thought they would.

I also programmed my kids with scripts, not by handing them ones to read of course, but by putting them in the same kinds of situations frequently enough and answering their questions when they were confused. They learned to fasten their seat belts on an airplane and to pack books in their carry-ons whenever they went on a plane by acquiring those scripts through repetition. In either case, learning took place by experiencing things, and modifying what one knew on the basis of new experiences.

Of course, this is not what happened in school at all. Subjects such as math and history were taught at school, not because the child had expressed a desire to learn them, nor because the information contained within them was useful to rectify some error they were making when they tried to do something and failed. Instead, these subjects were taught because someone somewhere mandated that they be taught. So of course my kids were bored with school, failed to understand why they needed to know any of what they were being taught, and usually forgot what they had memorized shortly after regurgitating it on a test. It was clear to me and clear to them that real learning did not take place in school but took place only in life, and that life in school was rather artificial. It crossed my mind that I could help. My students were remarkable because they were (and are) first rate computer scientists who also understood the principles of cognitive science, especially as these relate to learning. I thought it would be important to convince my students to work on making computer software that taught children in the right way rather than making more AI prototypes.

The four theses condensed in this volume were all written by students who started at Yale and finished at Northwestern University while they were working at the Institute for the Learning Sciences (ILS). They were AI people who became the vanguard of an increasing number of computer scientists who are trying to enable computers to provide powerful learning environments for children and for adults. Doing this is not a matter of simply writing a good program that enables learning. To provide powerful learning environments properly one must create programs that enable people to build programs more easily. That is, we need software tools especially meant to build learning environments.

When we arrived at Northwestern we began to consider what such tools might do. We knew why we needed the tools. All the educational software in the world was not going to be built by programmers. There are simply not enough programmers and there are a lot of things that need to be taught. On the other hand, it should be possible to build tools that can be used by subject matter experts or by any intelligent person who is working with a subject matter expert. Such tools would need to have a learning theory built inside of them, one that allowed learning-by-doing to take place and that actually prevented telling-and-testing. To build these tools we needed to identify the kinds of learning situations we expected to recur and then make those tools reflect those recurring situations.

Eight years into this enterprise we have identified eight different types of tools. We started with scripts.

A great deal of what we wish to teach people is fairly straight forward stuff. The essence of being a knowing entity is the acquisition of scripts. Humans have scripts for everything they often do in life and this includes, quite obviously, their jobs. The script class of tools are of special importance in teaching people to play various roles in life. Therefore, the nature of any script tool is fairly straightforward. The students set out to learn their role by performing the role. Intervention occurs when mistakes are made. To get the students to be able to perform a given role requires a program that understands correct and incorrect behavior within that role. The first of these tools was MOP-ED. The first version of this tool was written by Enio Ohmaye and is described in this volume. Subsequent versions of this same tool were developed by David Guralnick (Guralnick, in press) and Greg Saunders. These tools have been used in a variety of circumstances commercially.

Interpersonal behavior tools are the second class of tools. One way to enable the students to accomplish their goals within a situation that involves other people with competing goals is to create a simulated social world. Key to that world is learning to interact with other people. Especially important is attempting to convince other people of something, managing people to get them to do something, or making deals with other people that are perceived as a win for both sides. These tools have been used to produce software that teaches selling, negotiating, personnel management, and running a meeting. At the core of these tools is a program that enables a user to interact with simulated characters and that intervenes when these interactions are not working well.

Robin Burke's work (described herein) was instrumental in making the GuSS architecture that was the first version of interpersonal behavior tools. Alex Kass directed these projects and various versions were written by Eli Blevis and Kemi Jona.

Teaching planning skills is also important. To do so, situations must be created in which plans need to be made and in which the actions that embody those plans can be carried out. In a simulated world, one's decisions have effects and one needs to react to those effects and replan. But, the essence of the plan tools would not be simulation. After all, in some sense there is a simulation of one type or another in many of the tools we are proposing. Certainly, the tools mentioned previously embody simple simulations. But none of these tools attempt to teach high level planning skills or opportunistic decision making.

In a given simulated world, planning involves proposing suggestions for changes and seeing consequences of those changes, perhaps interrupted by historical realities and advice. This means that the simulated world is, itself, a subject of analysis, and so differentiates this planning tool from the others that employ simulation.

To make such a world worth thinking about, it is important to employ competing agents who can carry out plans in the same world. Thus, the essence of any planning tool is the construction and employment of those agents in a world that the user can create.

The idea behind planning, and indeed behind many of these tools, is that people should have access to a variety of cases that can help them decide what to do next on the basis of what has come before. Danny Edelson's chapter in this volume describes an early version of case-based planning. Later versions were done by Andy Fano and Sandor Szego.

We have thought about but not yet built design tools. The design of artifacts should be done for at least two reasons. First, constructing something helps one to understand it. Second, constructing something helps one to construct it in the future (or repair it). At first it seems as if these two disparate goals ought to yield tools that are in fact quite different. But further analysis reveals that most of what one would do with such a tool is the same no matter what one's end goal is. Constructing to understand may differ in terms of the level of detail of the analysis because constructing to construct can concern itself with the proper way to turn the screw, which has little import for understanding. Nevertheless, these are differences in focus, not in structure. In fact, the full notion of the comprehension of artifacts is much more a problem of design, which is the goal of the creativity tool discussed later.

We have spent a great deal of time on evidence-based reporting tools. The earliest version was in a program called Broadcast News, devised by Alex Kass (Schank & Kass, 1996). The most recent version is the Advise tool that has been devised by Kemi Jona and utilizes many of the ideas described in his chapter in this volume.

A good way to learn about issues that confront our society is to play the role of an advisor to a decision maker. When the goal of a learning situation is to encourage someone to get deeply involved in a complex issue of the day, the simplest idea is to ask him or her to read a great deal of material about it. This method is right-headed from an ideal viewpoint but totally impractical when motivation issues are taken into consideration. It is a curiosity of learning that people are more fascinated by information they have discovered for themselves than they are by information that they have simply been told to read. Furthermore, it makes a great deal of sense to ask students to come to a conclusion about a situation and argue for that conclusion, than simply to ask them to write a term paper about the subject. The latter method may work well enough with a highly motivated student, but it does not work well at all with someone who really does not care about a situation.

One very good way to teach history then, is to make the history more real by having the student play the role of an advisor to a real decision made in the historical period under discussion. To make this more interesting, a great many materials need to be made available so the student can discover what he or she needs, get curious about asking more questions and be able to find answers to those questions. This is the goal of the Advise tool.

The Advise tool is primarily concerned with teaching cases, and therefore owes some of its history to the work of Danny Edelson. The student should learn what has happened and how that event took place. The student should be able to identify the issues that surrounded the events that have taken place. And, central to this tool, the student needs to reason about the events, coming to a decision about what should be done. This tool should provide a framework in which a student learns to make an argument based on the rules of evidence that would be convincing to the person he is supposed to be advising. The emphasis of this tool, therefore is on reasoning rather than history. Teaching history is important, but reasoning about events and their consequences dominates what is taught in any use of this tool.

At ILS we have built a relatively simple decision program called Advise the President. The essence of that program is the ASK system that it employs (Ferguson, et al. 1992). In the Advise tool, while a "gather data" phase is important, the actual teaching takes place in "report" and "criticize" phases. Thus, it is important for these programs to provide the possibility for detailed criticisms of reasoning processes used and for supporting evidence cited.

We have also built a more complex version called Broadcast News (Kass, et al., 1994). In that program a student plays various roles in the production of a television news program, culminating in the making of a videotape of a day's news. The

Broadcast News program does not have any real relation to the Advise the President program. That is, they were built in different ways by different people for different purposes. Nevertheless, they are very similar structurally. Although the role played by the student in Broadcast News is not advisory, the student nevertheless issues a report. That report is criticized for its news appropriateness rather than its reasoning, but the structure of "gather data", "report", "criticize" is nevertheless maintained. The whole idea of this class of tools is to allow a variety of programs to be built that are structurally similar yet are quite different in what they teach.

Another type of tool that has received considerable attention at ILS is what we call the investigate and decide tool (INDE). In the Advise tool, the essence of the learning is in the content area (typically history as taught by cases) and in the domain of reasoning and logical argumentation. Experts are not likely to be subject matter experts. Instead, experts who can help students learn to reason from data observed should predominate. Experts on the particular style of a report would also be used. In the INDE tool, the emphasis is quite different. Here the expertise is on methodology, and content experts predominate. The goal here is less to teach reasoning than to teach the details of reasoning about a particular domain.

In order to learn about particular content areas, one needs to delve into them in some detail. It is wrong to imagine that a few hours spent on any subject is likely to make one much of an expert on that subject. If we were to spend a few hours on the Cuban Missile crisis we would presumably wind up knowing something about that situation, but we would not necessarily have become experts at history or on the creation of foreign policy. If we wanted to concentrate on teaching the particulars of a domain rather than on teaching one to reason within a somewhat randomly chosen domain, we would want to concentrate on the methodologies that are solely applicable to that domain.

The emphasis of INDE programs is on the analytical methods used in a given field. Typically these would include certain ways of obtaining data, instruction on how to understand that data, and various forms of analysis of that data.

The Sickle Cell program (Bell, et al., 1994) built at ILS is an example of what later became the INDE tool (Riesbeck, et al., in press). In that program, a student had to understand what evidence might be available, determine how to get that evidence, get it, and interpret it and analyze it. Along the way, many experts from the field were called on to help the student perform various tests, interpret the results of those tests, and then draw conclusions from those tests. In subsequent uses of the initial version of this tool, many other programs were built, each drawing on the Sickle Cell program. They all had a similar structure and the teaching contained within them came from domain experts who knew about the initial problem, the tests involved with solving that problem, and the interpretation of those test results.

ILS has also been building a class of tools that we call the RUN tools. Early version were built by Ray Bareiss and John Cleave (Cleave, unpublished). The latest version is due to the work of Brendon Towle. All these tools seek to help one understand an environment by living it.

We live in a world of complex institutions. Some of these institutions have been designed, some have simply evolved, and others are an amalgamation of initial design and reactions and adjustments to real world conditions. To appreciate history and to comprehend why things are the way they are, or to begin to think about how to effect change, it is a good idea to try to manage such an institution. Naturally, it is not practical to put someone in charge of the police department in order to facilitate his or her understanding of the issues that the police must deal with. Nevertheless, the idea is sound. One could learn a great deal from such a vantage point. The purpose of any program built with a Run tool is to give the user an understanding of the conflicting goals that need to be resolved, and the tradeoffs that need to be made in the life of a complex organization. Such programs allow the student to run the organization over a hypothetical period of time, making decisions and coping with their consequences. The goal of the student is to successfully run the organization. The goal of the program is to introduce sufficient complexity so the student will have to make hard decisions and will have much to think about. In the end, the hope is that the student will have learned something about decision-making. Furthermore, the student should have come to an under-standing of the processes that take place in such an organization. Finally, the student should have become aware of cases that typify various situations and should be able to draw on these to make conclusions about what should be done.

A creativity tool has never been worked on but it is a part of the set of tools we are describing. It is the theoretical analog of the design tool. The idea is to attempt to figure something new to do given an array of materials. The design tool is more or less the same thing except that the given materials are intended to result in some known final structure. For creativity, the idea is to be inventive.

Making something work out that is seemingly impossible is a good way to foster creativity. The idea in this tool is to put the students in a situation that seems hopeless and have them flail around until they come up an idea. Critical to the process here would be the issues of explanation and adaptation, which is where the "teaching" would take place.

Teaching reasoning under uncertainty, creativity, speculative reasoning, and so forth requires a program that understands all possible suggestions in a micro-world. Thus, the problem is building a program that can actually understand inventions made within its domains. This is, of course, a complex task.

In summary we have two broad classes of tools we envision for creating educational environments. We have comprehension tools that teach reasoning (Advise), analysis (INDE), creativity, and organizational structure (Run). An analogous set of tools that are intended to teach performance rather than compre-hension are the scripts, interpersonal themes, design, and planning tools.

The fact that these tools relate so strongly to the ideas set out in Schank and Abelson (1977) is not random. In that volume we discussed that in order for computers to become intelligent they must have the ability to comprehend the world around them and that world consists of humans who were involved in scripts, plans, goals, and themes. Understanding a human situation meant understanding what background assumptions humans were bringing to that situation. Computers needed to learn scripts because people were using scripts implicitly when they described a situation, and explicitly when they performed in a situation. People need to learn scripts in order to process the world around them and in order to function in that world. It follows therefore, that a good teaching environment would include methods of teaching scripts, both comprehending them and performing them. Thus, if we want to build high quality software for instruction of children or adults, we must ascertain what scripts need to be learned and teach them in a learn-by-doing fashion.

This same argument applies for anything we want to teach. We must teach what people need to help them comprehend and to help them perform. Typically instruction focuses on what people need to know, but the knowledge we are talking about is quite implicit. Doing implies knowing how to do but that knowing is implicit. The goal of this work is to make software that allows people to practice the things they will really do in life.

So, when I dragged all my students out of AI and into education I was not doing anything all that traumatic. We are still working on the same ideas, but in a new, more practical, and more important context. The theses contained in this volume were the beginning of that effort.

Deep appreciation goes to my assistant, Heidi Levin, for her careful, patient, and tenacious efforts in preparing this material for publication. Her work included editing the original versions of the chapters, as well as wielding her administrative skills to turn an array of manuscripts from various parties into one cohesive book. Without her invaluable skills this work surely would not have been completed. Jarret Knyal, a senior graphics programmer at ILS, rendered essential help in preparing the program screens included in each chapter. Dave Guralnick lent his technical expertise for a chapter review.

The work of the individual authors was supported in part by the Defense Advanced Research Projects Agency, monitored by the Air Force Office of Scientific Research under contract F49620-88-C-0058 and the Office of Naval Research under contract N00014-90-J-4117, by the Office of Naval Research under contract N00014-89-J-1987, and by the Air Force Office of Scientific Research under contract AFOSR-89-0493; by a grant from the IBM Program for Innovative Uses of Information Technology in K–12 education, and by the Defence Advanced Research Projects Agency monitored by the Office of Naval Research under contract N00014-01-J4092. The work described here was conducted at the Institute for the Learning Sciences at Northwestern University. ILS was established in 1989 with the support of Andersen Consulting.

REFERENCES

Bell, B., Bareiss, R., & Beckwith, R. (1994). *Sickle cell counselor: A prototype goal-based scenario for instruction in a museum environment* (Tech. Rep. No. 56). Evanston, IL: Northwestern University, Institute for the Learning Sciences.

Cleave, J., (1998). *A storyline-based approach to developing management goal-based scenarios.* Unpublished doctoral dissertation. Northwestern University, Evanston, IL.

Ferguson, W., Bareiss, R., Birnbaum, L., & Osgood, R. (1992). *ASK systems: An approach to the realization of story-based teachers* (Tech. Rep. No. 22). Evanston, IL: Northwestern University, Institute for the Learning Sciences.

Guralnick, D. (1997). *An authoring tool for procedural task training* (Tech. Rep. No. 71). Evanston, IL: Northwestern University, Institute for the Learning Sciences.

Kass, A., Dooley, S., Luksa, F., & Conroy, C. (1994). Using broadcast journalism to motivate hypermedia exploration. *Educational Multimedia and Hypermedia Annual, 1994.*

Riesbeck, C. K., & Dobson, W. D. (in press). Authorable critiquing for intelligent educational systems. *Proceedings of 1998 International Conference on Intelligent User Interfaces 1998.*

Schank, R., & Abelson, R., (1977), Scripts, Plans, Goals, and Understanding. Hillsdale, NJ: Lawrence Erlbaum Associates.

Schank, R. & Kass, A., (1996). A goal-based scenario for high school students. *Communications of the ACM, 39*(4) 28–29.

Simulation-Based Language Learning: An Architecture and a Multi-Media Authoring Tool

Enio Ohmaye
Apple Computer, Inc.

CHANGES IN FOREIGN LANGUAGE INSTRUCTION

Introduction

The goals of foreign language instruction have shifted considerably in the last 100 years. At the turn of the century, learning languages was primarily an intellectual exercise for the well educated (Richards & Rodgers, 1986), having nothing to do with communicating with others. Learners studied the structure of languages, memorizing long lists of words and their translations, and focusing on rules of grammar. Given this view of language, it is not surprising that the skills students developed were useless in real-life interaction.

This situation has changed over the last century. Language instruction is now primarily concerned with developing communicative competence—the ability to interact with others in a foreign language. Current methods emphasize interactions, both as a goal and as a means to learning, and try to give students experiences that prepare them to perform in real life. Naturalistic methods, as methods that replicate real-life experiences are referred to, try to expose students to a target culture and engage them in realistic interactions.

Nevertheless, although the goal and methods of language instruction have changed—now we want people to learn how to interact, and people learn by interacting with others—classroom instruction still falls short of preparing students to perform in real life. The reason is that, despite the concern with real-life performance (better theories) and a more pragmatic approach (classroom instruction), the problem that has always afflicted language instruction remains: lack of resources.

Language acquisition depends heavily on interactions with native speakers, and native speakers are hard to come by. Regardless of the method of instruction or how well intentioned teachers are, without native speakers to interact with, instruction often falls back on practices that are useless in real life. In addition, interactions always occur in a larger cultural context, and students need access to this context. During inter-actions, the physical and social context provide important cues that are integral parts of the process of communicating. Even when native speakers are available, bringing the target environment into the classroom is dif-ficult.

Individual instruction and feedback are also scarce commodities. To be motivated to learn, students have to work on problems that are relevant to them. Instead, classroom instruction forces every student to participate in uninteresting group dialogues; because they must wait their turn to interact with the teacher, students have limited individualized feedback. When instruction does not address the specific needs of a student, the student will likely look out the window and mechanically repeat whatever he or she has to say. In contrast, interacting one on one forces people to exchange information, express feelings, and perform social transactions. Unless students address personal needs by engaging in interactions that are meaningful to them, the information conveyed is irrelevant. Unfortu-nately, in the typical classroom, teachers cannot give each student suffi-cient individual attention.

Due to the lack of adequate resources, classroom instruction still pro-vides limited (a) interactions with native speakers, (b) access to the target culture, and (c) individual attention and feedback. Despite the improved methods of language instruction, students still do not get the chance to develop the skills necessary to interact in a foreign language. Proficiency tests that emphasize language structure further aggravate this problem by discouraging teachers from searching for adequate solutions and en-couraging students to focus on rules and memorization that have little to do with interacting in real life.

Technology Can Help

Ideally, students should learn by living in the target environment, inter-acting with native speakers, being immersed in the target culture, and receiving intense individual instruction and feedback. Because this is not always possible, however, an alternative solution is to bring those expe-riences to the student. This is what early language laboratories tried to do, by using instructional materials such as tape recorders, audiovisual materials, and/or videotapes.

Traditionally, laboratory material has been noninteractive. This is problematic because, to learn to interact, interactivity is essential. Watching others passively (e.g., going to see French movies three times a week) does not really teach much. The unfortunate consequence of this limitation is that, instead of providing the much-needed experiences, technology has been perpetuating ineffective educational practices. Tape recorders have been drilling students in patterns out of context, videos have been keeping students in passive roles, and multiple-choice computer programs have been testing students on memorized grammar rules. Technology can be used more effectively.

This is where multi-media and artificial intelligence come in. Short of importing a lot of native speakers, computer-based simulations are the closest we can get to living in a target culture. Given the plummeting cost of hardware, computer-based multi-media simulations of real life can be the ideal playground for language learning. Simulations can give students much-needed interactions with native speakers, access to the target culture, and individualized attention. It is even conceivable that, in certain situations, simulations could be better than real-life experiences.

To be used properly, however, technology must simulate those elements of the environment that promote language acquisition. Simply simulating conversations, for example, is not enough: That would be like throwing an apprentice mechanic into an auto shop with cars to fix and no tools, instruction, or guidance. Instead, we must consider the student's needs, the problems he or she will confront in real life, the type of guidance and information he or she requires, and the tools needed to accomplish the task.

In addition, and very important, in order to design language learning environments, we need to consider how people acquire languages, the conditions that are necessary for learning, what motivates people to learn, and the resources and experiences they need to develop communication skills. This requires the combination of content expertise (second language acquisition research), theories of learning (educational research and cognitive science), and issues of motivation and tutoring systems design (psychology and intelligent tutoring systems).

When we consider these issues of language acquisition, education, learning, and motivation, it becomes clear that certain design principles should guide the development of computer-based language learning environments. For example, knowledge is always a product of the activity, context, and culture in which it is used (Brown, Collins, & Duguid, 1989). Consequently, language should always be presented in the context in which it is used in real life. The environment provides the conditions for applying and organizing knowledge. Also, because students learn best when they are using language as a tool to achieve their goals, the goal of their interactions must always be meaningful and clearly defined. Moreover, students need to have control over the environment so that they can address their own needs and explore their own learning strategies. In terms of feedback, second language research shows that correcting grammar mistakes does not help much. Experience with intelligent tutoring systems raises some problems with interface design. For instance, because computers do not understand facial expressions, a common way to express communication breakdowns, simulations must provide users with alternative means of expressing the same information. These design principles are discussed later in this chapter.

A Solution: Dustin

Dustin, a multi-media language learning environment, addresses problems afflicting classroom instruction in foreign languages and incorporates the principles mentioned earlier. Dustin allows students to interact with and observe native speakers in the target culture while providing them with tools and individual instruction and feedback. The program helps foreign employees of Andersen Consulting who are coming to the United States for 3 weeks of intensive training in St. Charles, Illinois. Dustin helps these new Andersen employees minimize their problems understanding and interacting with Americans by exposing them to the St. Charles environment before they arrive.

To bring a student into the simulated environment, Dustin starts by introducing him or her to the experiences he or she will face in the simulation, which include typical events during a trainee's first 24 hours in the United States. The introductory video shows a sample of the tasks the student will face at O'Hare Airport and in St. Charles, establishing the context of the experiences that lie before him or her. The tutor assigns tasks, gives individualized instruction to the student, and helps him or her interact with native speakers. Whenever the student is unable to perform a task, or gets stuck somewhere, the tutor either gives some instruction or shows an example of someone else performing the same task, letting the student model the correct behavior. Figure 1.1 shows the tutor intervening after the student refused to turn in his passport a number of times.

Dustin later gives the student a guided tour of the St. Charles facility, throwing him or her into interactions and showing him or her examples. Under normal conditions, the tutor sequences the tasks for the student, following a storyline that reflects the experiences of a typical trainee. However, the student can also take control over the environment, choos-

FIG. 1.1. The tutor intervenes.

ing what to do and what to watch. If a task is uninteresting to the student it can be skipped or if it is so complex that the student wants to revisit it, he or she can do so by simply choosing to repeat it. Overall, Dustin includes 16 tasks in 9 different scenarios—4 additional tasks in the room-mate scenes accommodate either male or female students. All tasks involve achieving goals that require interacting with native speakers who work in St. Charles. Dustin provides a number of tools to assist the student during his or her tasks (e.g., a dictionary, translations, a transcript of the simulated conversation, a recorder).

More than just implementing simulations of dialogues, Dustin implements an environment in which students learn from experience. Instead of transmitting information to the student, Dustin engages the student in realistic tasks and gives him or her the support (i.e., tutor, tools, help, examples) necessary for him or her to learn experientially. As suggested later, Dustin's architecture can be used to teach other well-scripted skills (e.g., teach other languages, train bank tellers, receptionists, and even auto mechanics). A more detailed description of an interaction with Dustin is described later.

Implementing Dustin. Implementing systems that respond to a large number of events, organize a large number of scenarios in different ways, provide contextualized help, simulate dialogues, and provide remediation when needed requires complex knowledge representation structures. In addition, the complexity of these knowledge networks increases rapidly with size, and maintaining such knowledge networks can be a nightmare.

In working with Dustin, we found it impossible to maintain its complex networks of information without adequate tools to help organize and visualize them. Networks consisting of knowledge structures such as the one in Fig. 1.2, from an early implementation of Dustin, become hard to maintain. Their intricate interdependencies and connections are difficult to visualize even when a small number of structures is involved. Solving this problem required the development of an authoring tool to implement Dustinlike, interactive social simulations. The solution introduced here, MOPed, based on an artificial intelligence model of memory organization proposed by Schank (1982), enabled us to organize, reuse, contextualize, visualize, and understand the information in Dustin. More than a tool to organize and maintain knowledge, MOPed helps developers understand complex information by providing visual aids to improve readability and mechanisms to contextualize data.

The idea underlying MOPed's memory organization scheme is simple. MOPed is based on the idea of having a memory structure whose only function is to organize other memory structures (Schank, 1982)—like having a sheet of paper on which to organize Post-its. The basic unit in

```
(in-package "USER")

(SOF SCE-REC-CHECK-IN
:NAME SCE-REC-CHECK-IN
:DESC "Check in"
:REQUIRED-P T
:WATCH-TEXT "Watch John Harrison check in"
:WATCH-SCRIPT SCR-REC-CHECK-IN
:NEXT-TASK (TASK OPT SCE-REC-CHECK-IN)
:DO-TEXT "Go to the reception desk and check in"
:DO-AGENT A-KELLEY
:SUCC-TEXT "Good! Now, go to your room and meet Scott."
:SUCC-TASK (TASK DO SCE-ROO-MEET)
:FAIL-TEXT "Let's watch something simpler"
:FAIL-TASK (TASK ?COMPUTE ?NEXT)
:OPT-TEXT "Can you check in at the reception desk?"
:OPT-YES-TASK (TASK DO SCE-REC-CHECK-IN)
:OPT-NO-TASK (TASK ?COMPUTE ?NEXT)
:GOAL-TEXT "Try to check in"
:GOAL-OK-TEXT "You've already checked in. Leave"
:GOAL-TEST (DONE-P D-REC-CHECKIN)
:GOAL-SAY ""
:EXAMPLES NIL
:PLAN (SCE-REC-GREET SCE-REC-PURPOSE SCE-REC-NAME SCE-REC-
    PACKAGE SCE-REC-THANK)
:DIALOGS "d-rec-checkin")
```

FIG. 1.2. A knowledge representation structure in an old version of Dustin.

this scheme, a memory organization packet (MOP), serves as a sheet of paper, and the simpler memory structures serve as Post-its. Figure 1.3 shows a MOP that organizes the events in the Immigration scene at O'Hare International Airport.

The simpler memory structures, or Post-its, can be things like a tutor message, 😈 Watch Maria go thro... or a video clip, 📺 (V) O'hare/Immigration. When connected to each other, as in Fig. 1.4, they indicate that Dustin should display a tutor message saying, "Watch Maria go through Immigration," and then show a video clip in which Maria interacts with the Immigration officer.

MOPed allows the same knowledge representation and visualization scheme to organize everything in Dustin. It organizes Dustin's storyline with its 16 tasks; in each task, it organizes tutor messages, video clips,

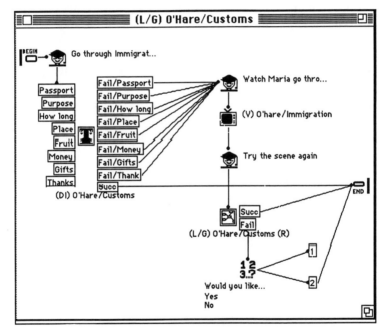

FIG. 1.3. A MOP: Going through immigration at O'Hare International Airport.

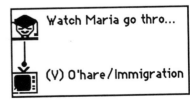

FIG. 1.4. Post-its connect.

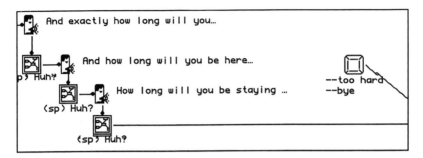

FIG. 1.5. Responding to a series of HUH?s.

and dialogues; in each dialogue, it organizes the simulated interactions, speech patterns, help messages, and button handlers. Figure 1.5 shows a small portion of a simulated dialogue.

In addition to helping visualize information, MOPed allows us to reuse existing MOPs. For example, a MOP like the one in Fig. 1.6, which occurs in many dialogues, can be re-used instead of re-created. When the MOP "(sp) I need to" (Fig. 1.6) is used inside another MOP (see Fig. 1.7, p. 9), it appears as a Post-it. The MOP is not copied into the MOP in which it appears; instead, the Post-it only points to it, avoiding duplication of existing structures. The MOP in Fig. 1.7 parses sentences beginning with, for example, "I am trying to" and "find. . . ."

MOPed also simplifies the development of templates for lessons. Determining the sequence of events in each lesson (i.e., tutor messages, simulations, examples, remediation, interventions) involves a process of approximation that usually involves numerous code changes. In earlier versions of Dustin, without MOPed, creating these lesson templates in-

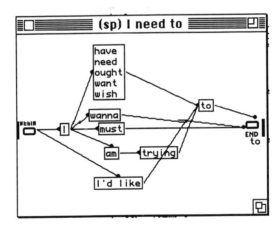

FIG. 1.6. A MOP: Ways of saying "I need. . . ."

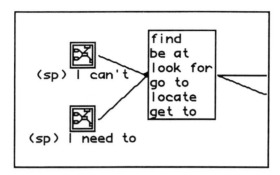

FIG. 1.7. Using a MOP inside another.

volved code modification and recompilation. With MOPed, simple object manipulation (e.g., dragging, deleting, connecting Post-its) does the job. In addition, once a template is created, it can be copied through simple copy/paste operations. In fact, most of the lessons in Dustin were copied from a few original templates.

MOPed is a tool to organize, visualize, contextualize, and reuse knowledge structures. One way of thinking about MOPed, from a developer's perspective, is as a tool with which to organize messages exchanged by objects in an object-oriented environment. In most object-oriented environments, few tools help developers organize and understand the interactions between the messages that objects exchange. This is what MOPed does. It is described in greater detail later.

LANGUAGE LEARNING

Language Teaching Methods

The following overview of methods of instruction begins at the end of the 19th century with the grammar–translation method, and ends at the end of the 20th century with the natural approach. Over the last century, there has been a significant increase in cross-cultural interactions in the world, and language teaching has become concerned with communication rather than with intellectual exercise. During this period, methods have evolved from a structural, noncommunicative approach to a very different interactionist, communicative approach. Each method addressed specific needs in particular contexts and contributed information that helped define the goal of language instruction today and the main problems in achieving that goal.

Grammar–Translation.   In the 19th century, given the limited opportunities for contact with foreigners, people studied foreign languages either to read foreign literature (mainly Latin, a language no longer spoken) or to develop intellectually through the mental discipline involved in studying a foreign language (Richards & Rodgers, 1986). During that time, grammar–translation combined the influence of German scholarship with methods used to teach Latin. In this method, language was viewed as a set of symbols and rules, and language learning was synonymous with memorization of these symbols and rules. Grammar–translation emphasized the study of grammatical rules and translation exercises, and typically students acquired extensive knowledge about the language, but no competence in using it interactively (Finocchiaro & Brumfit, 1983).

In grammar–translation, the student (a) listens to explanations of grammar rules, (b) memorizes bilingual lists of words that contain the vocabulary needed for the day's exercises, and (c) practices the grammar rules and vocabulary on a given reading selection. These exercises consist of translating sentences to and from L1 (the source language) and L2 (the target language), with L1 being the medium of instruction.

Implicitly, grammar–translation assumes that mastering languages depends on conscious knowledge of grammar. Heavily influenced by the idea that language learning is a good mental exercise, teachers present rules of grammar abstractly and then force students to practice their application in selected readings; students learn grammar deductively. The linguistic knowledge imparted includes types of sentences (e.g., declarative, interrogative), vocabulary organized by parts of speech (e.g., verbs, nouns), and endings (e.g., genitive, accusative, nominative). Accuracy is important, and translation exercises measure student performance.

Vestiges of grammar–translation still inhabit contemporary college textbooks in the form of long word memorization lists, emphasis on grammar rules, and translation exercises. One of the main reasons these features have survived is that, although painful for students, they are convenient for teachers. Grading is easy. Although still practiced, grammar–translation today has no advocates; no one in the field defends its utility or theoretical foundations (Richards & Rodgers, 1986). The method addresses literary needs of literary people. Sessions are usually boring, and the pressure for accuracy often causes anxiety. No attempt is made to teach students to interact, and what they learn from grammar–translation is of little use on the streets of a foreign city. Grammar–translation is a prime example of "learning about a language," rather than "how to use a language."

Direct Method.   As written communication gave way to oral communication, due to increased opportunities for interaction among Europeans, the direct method emerged. The direct method evolved, in the 1920s, almost as a reaction to the grammar–translation method. Instead of focusing on written language, it focused on spoken language; instead of translating everything, it presented everything in the target language. Instead of teaching grammar explicitly, it expected students to learn grammar inductively. However, although successful with certain populations, most notably through the Berlitz school, the direct method proved inadequate for use in schools.

In the direct method, teachers defer written language for months and even years, and teach oral skills first. They focus on pronunciation and grammatical accuracy, and are particularly strict about exclusively using the target language. As described in Richards and Rodgers (1986), according to Gouin and colleagues, precursors of the method, people should learn L2 (second or other language) in the same way that children learn L1 (first language). The most important characteristic, they proposed, is that "a foreign language [can] be taught without translation or the use of the learner's native tongue if meaning [is] conveyed directly through demonstration and actions." It was Franke, a psychologist, who provided the theoretical justification for a monolingual approach. For Franke, students learned best by using language actively because there is a direct association between forms and meaning in the target language (Richards & Rodgers, 1986). In the direct method, everything happens in the target language—translating is taboo. Teachers introduce every new word through pictures, pointing, and mime, or through associations of ideas. Sentences are sequenced according to their grammatical structure, and teachers ask questions about the structure of the language to help students extract grammatical knowledge. The direct method emphasizes (a) aural-oral skills, (b) exclusive use of the target language, (c) teaching of grammar inductively, and (d) accuracy—errors are corrected in the classroom.

The direct method met with success with highly motivated, paying students who found language learning intrinsically motivating. However, although successful with this population, through private institutions such as Berlitz, which could hire good teachers who were native speakers, the method proved problematic in secondary schools. It depended heavily on native speakers and on the teachers' skills, rather than on more readily available resources, such as textbooks. In practice, it also proved counterproductive in its dogmatic rule that forbade the use of L1, leading to many wasted hours of mime and actions trying to explain a single new word. In overemphasizing the importance of using only the target language, Sauveur and other proponents overlooked important factors, such as extent of exposure, the artifacts in the environment, and the quality of the experience that were not captured by the simple absence of the native language (Richards & Rodgers, 1986). Also, the requirement that sentences be sequenced according to their grammatical structure imposed an unrealistic sequencing of input, making it hard for teachers to contextualize the use of language. After studying artificial sentences like "La plume de ma tante est sur le bureau de mon oncle" (Finocchiaro & Brumfit, 1983, p. 5), students had difficulty applying them to real-life situations. As Finocchiaro described it, "all statements used were related to the classroom. Teachers did not generally think of students using language beyond the classroom. Any connection with real life was expected to come later and was not the business of the school." Its theoretical foundations were weak, and the direct method was soon perceived as the product of amateurism (Richards & Rodgers, 1986).

Although based on good intuitions about naturalistic learning, the direct method's dependence on intensive resources was incompatible with the means of most schools. Certainly, its extremist stance on sequencing material according to grammatical structures and its dogmatic position on forbidding translations contributed to its demise. However, its major problem was the lack of resources. The skilled teachers required by the method were costly and beyond the means of the typical school classroom. These practical issues, documented in the Coleman Report (Coleman, 1929), triggered the direct method's decline. After studying the state of foreign language instruction in the United States, Coleman published a report that attacked the importance given to spoken language. He argued that teaching conversational skills was impractical given the restricted time for foreign language instruction in schools, and, considering the limited skills of teachers, instruction should focus on reading and grammar involved in simple readings. Conversation skills for secondary students in the United States were perceived as irrelevant, and between the two World Wars, language instruction reverted once again to focus on reading, writing, and grammar (Finocchiaro & Brumfit, 1983; Richards & Rodgers, 1986).

Audiolingual Method. When the United States entered World War II, the need for oral proficiency increased dramatically (Richards & Rodgers, 1986). For 2 years, the army trained soldiers in German, French, Italian, Japanese, and other languages to prepare interpreters and code-room assistants. Fifty universities provided 8-hour-a-day intensive courses. The intensity of contact during these courses proved to be effective and convinced applied linguists of the value of both intensity and the oral-based approach. When the war was over, the United States emerged as an international power. With its new role came a need to train Americans in foreign languages and to train foreigners in English.

For the first time in history, a method—audiolingualism—would combine theories of language learning with those coming from other fields—namely, linguistics and psychology. Another innovative aspect of audiolingualism was the use of technology. For the first time, technological artifacts other than textbooks played a major role in instruction. Tape recorders and audiovisual materials contributed extensively and constituted an important part of instruction. Without native speakers to serve as informants, students used tapes of native speakers, with feedback coming from recording and listening to one's own output.

Audiolingualism had a strong impact on language learning because it addressed a strong demand for oral proficiency and combined widely accepted theories of language and learning. Its main concern is oral proficiency, its foundation drill and practice—mimicking and memorization (mim-mem). Because errors are thought to result from interference from the native language, they are always corrected in the classroom. Teachers dominate the classroom activities; students have a reactive role. Addressing students' personal interests (e.g., talking about dating) is against the model and strongly discouraged.

In summary, audiolingualism is a combination of structural linguistic theory, aural-oral procedures, and behavioristic notions of learning, with tape recorders and audiovisual materials playing central roles in audiolingual courses. Audiolingualism relies on oral drills and practice of dialogues memorized through repetition. The linguistic syllabus contains items of phonology, morphology, and syntax that are taught in the order of listening, speaking, reading, and writing. The assumptions of audiolingualism are that (a) foreign language learning = other learning, (b) we learn from experience, and (c) language learning is mechanical habit formation. Audiolingualism rejects the analytical model of the grammar-translation method in favor of mimicry and memorization, and rejects the model of exposure, usage, and absorption of grammatical structures of the direct method in favor of grammar as the starting point (Richards & Rodgers, 1986).

Audiolingualism began to fall into disfavor when Chomsky (1959, 1966) rejected its theoretical foundation, structural linguistics, and behavioristic learning in favor of the more mentalistic theory of transformational generative grammar. Chomsky proposed that language is an innate aspect of the mind and postulated a language-processing module. Contrary to Skinner's view, that language behavior is equal to other behaviors, Chomsky's view is that language is separate from other behaviors and so is learned differently; humans have a language-acquisition mechanism, and sentences are not imitated and repeated but rather generated from competence. Chomsky showed that behaviorism and structural theories did not account for creativity and uniqueness of individual sentences.

The combination of technology and scientific theories in audiolingualism was an attractive innovation, and for a long time its overall impact camouflaged the weaknesses of the method. Today, pattern practice is still used to proceduralize knowledge but it is now considered artificial and useless. Drills are boring; what students memorize often has little application in real life. Students parrot incomprehensible material, but while they become good at parroting, they develop no communication skills. Motivation is curtailed by the fact that students are not allowed to discuss topics that are interesting to them. Instead they are forced to stick to the topic of the day; the emphasis on mastering patterns, and not on communication, makes interest fall rapidly. Grammatical sequencing forces unrealistic dialogues and, because production is supposed to be error-free, students usually feel anxious in the classroom. Although significantly better than grammar–translation, audiolingualism also falls short of preparing students to perform in real-life situations.

A Need for Change

The fall of audiolingualism left a void, generating a renewed interest in teaching grammar deductively (i.e., teaching rules and then how to apply them). Chomsky's more mentalistic view of human language capabilities, and his notion that "competence precedes performance," provided a rationalization for a way of teaching that was much more amenable to the factory model of schooling, which was becoming prevalent at the time. One method based on Chomsky's theory, the cognitive-code method, for instance, shifted back to teaching rules—students learned about the language before, and separated from, learning how to use it. Such rationalization was, in fact, a distortion of what Chomsky had proposed. Chomsky did not defend that competence involved explicit knowledge of language structure, but only that the development of the necessary knowledge structures, conscious or unconscious, preceded performance. At any rate, despite its theoretical interest, cognitive-code had a relatively small impact on second language instruction.

An increasing interdependence among European countries eventually prompted instruction to focus on communicative proficiency, rather than mastery of structures. In 1973, Wilkins proposed that, instead of describing language through traditional concepts of grammar and vocabulary, language should be described through a system of meanings that underlie the communicative use of language. Wilkins described two types of meaning: notional categories (e.g., time, sequence, quantity, location) and communicative functions (e.g., requests, denials, offers). He published a complete description of his view in *Notional Syllabuses* in 1976. Wilkins motivated a new definition of language compatible with the view of language as a tool for communication and language learning as the development of communicative competence. *Language competence* was redefined in the following way: (a) Language is a system for expression of meaning, (b) the primary function of language is interaction and communication, (c) the structure of language reflects functional and communicative uses, and (d) the primary units of language are functional and communicative.

A number of methods emerged whose goal was to develop communicative competence. Psychologist James Asher (1977) created total physical response (TPR), in which the student responds to imperative statements through actions. For example, the teacher says, "Touch your face" and the student touches her face. Speech is delayed until comprehension has been internalized. When a student displays readiness to talk, he starts engaging in verbal interactions. The method has had some success in basic-level instruction, and has received support from theorists who believe that acquisition is comprehension-based (comprehension precedes production). TPR's major advantage lies in helping students feel less threatened because they do not have to produce language for a few months.

Another method, silent-way (Gattegno, 1972, 1976), was based on Bruner's (1962) distinction between expository and exploratory (hypothetical) learning. Gattegno's silent-way uses minimal modeling; the teacher models the pronunciation and intonation at the beginning of the class, and then guides students during the exercises by using colored rods that help indicate intonation, stress, and so on. Despite its claims, in practice, this method does not differ significantly from other methods such as audiolingualism, which emphasize accurate reproduction of sounds and sentences.

Natural Approach.　Terrell (1977, 1981, 1982) proposed a method based on naturalistic principles observed in second language acquisition studies. The natural approach develops communicative competence by using language in communicative situations without grammatical analysis, drilling, or grammatical theory. Unlike the direct method, the natural approach de-emphasizes teacher monologues, repetition, formal question and answer, and accuracy of production. Rather, it emphasizes exposure, emotional preparedness, and listening before producing.

Terrell received the support of, and later joined forces with, Krashen, a theorist who had proposed an ambitious model of second language acquisition (SLA; Krashen & Terrell, 1983). This alliance solidified the position of the natural approach in the field of SLA. Krashen and Terrell rejected the view of grammar as a central component, and argued that language teaching methods should be based on theories of learning, not on the structure of language. They emphasized meaning and the greater importance of words over grammar—grammar is subordinate to lexicon. Language is a vehicle for communication of messages, and acquisition takes place only when people understand messages in the target language. Procedures used in the classroom do not differ from those of other methods, but the underlying theory changes the emphasis.

Krashen's (1982, 1985) theory of language learning, the monitor model, described in a series of papers and books, provides the theoretical rationale for the approach. Krashen claimed that the model is an empirically grounded theory of SLA. The monitor model is extensively discussed in the literature (Krashen, 1985; McLaughlin, 1978). The model is based on five hypotheses, described by Krashen (1985) as follows:

1. The Acquisition/Learning Hypothesis

There are two independent ways of developing ability in second languages. "Acquisition" is a subconscious process identical in all important ways to the process children utilize in acquiring their first language, while "learning" is a conscious process that results in "knowing about" language. (p. 1)

2. The Natural Order Hypothesis

We acquire the rules of language in a predictable order, some rules tending to come early and others late. The order does not appear to be determined solely by formal simplicity and there is evidence that it is independent of the order in which rules are taught in language classes. (p. 1)

3. The Monitor Hypothesis

This hypothesis states how acquisition and learning are used in production. Our ability to produce utterances in another language comes from our acquired competence, from our subconscious knowledge. Learning conscious knowledge serves only as an editor, monitor. We appeal to learning to make corrections, to change the output of the acquired system before we speak or write. (p. 1)

4. The Input Hypothesis

The input hypothesis claims that humans acquire language in only one way—by understanding messages, or by receiving "comprehensible input." We progress along the natural order (hypothesis 2) by understanding input that contains structures at our next "stage"—structures that are a bit beyond our current level of competence. . . . We are able to understand language containing unacquired grammar with the help of context, which includes extra-linguistic information, our knowledge of the world, and previously acquired linguistic competence. (p. 2)

5. The Affective Filter Hypothesis

Comprehensible input is necessary for acquisition, but it is not sufficient. The acquirer needs to be "open" to the input. The "affective filter" is a mental block that prevents acquirers from fully utilizing the comprehensible input they receive for language acquisition. . . . This occurs when the acquirer is unmotivated, lacking in self-confidence, or anxious, when he is "on the defensive," when he considers the language class to be a place where his weaknesses will be revealed. The filter is down when the acquirer is not concerned with the possibility of failure in language acquisition and when he considers himself to be a potential member of the group speaking the target language. (p. 3)

The principles underlying this model are that: (a) the goal of learning is to develop communicative skills, (b) comprehension precedes production, (c) production emerges when the learner is ready, (d) acquisition is central—not learning, and (e) affective filter must be low.

The natural approach emphasizes oral communication skills based on a student's needs. It is designed to create low affective filter, provide extensive exposure to vocabulary, and pay no explicit attention to grammar. Lessons are not organized around a grammatical syllabus. Activities are borrowed from other methods, such as the direct method; but during question-and-answer sessions, the teacher tries to minimize anxiety by not requiring the student to speak until he is ready. Instead, students are allowed to respond by using body language or, less compulsively, their native language—emphasis is on communication, not form. Talking slowly and clearly, the teacher leads the student through interactions requiring simple yes/no responses first, then progressing to word answers, and finally to full sentences. Activities focus on meaningful communication, not on form; teachers do not correct errors in form. The method does not introduce any novel procedure, but instead uses familiar activities in a framework that emphasizes comprehensible input in an environment that minimizes anxiety and maximizes self-confidence.

The purpose and nature of these activities are to: (a) supply comprehensible input to facilitate acquisition, (b) ensure that the learner does not feel anxious, (c) restrict grammar instruction, (d) correct errors only in learning, not in acquisition, (e) let teacher use only L2 and let student use L1 or L2, (f) include grammar work only in homework, and (g) talk about ideas, perform tasks, and solve problems.

The learner does not *try* to learn, but instead engages in meaningful activities that require language. The teacher serves as a source of input, manages the environment, and coordinates activities. Unlike the cognitive or habit-drill approaches, the natural approach prepares students to communicate with native speakers in real-life situations. Unlike any single predecessor, the natural approach addresses a wide number of issues: readiness for production, the role of affect, the role of monitoring processes, sequence of learning, the role of nonverbal communication, and the distinction between learning and acquisition. It brings us back to the resource-intensive approach of the direct method, except now it can count on technological resources that may compensate for the still limited availability of native speakers and exposure to the target culture. Unlike the direct method, the natural approach addresses a widespread need and rests on a more mature theoretical foundation.

The State of Language Teaching

The natural approach sits at the end of two major trends in language instruction. The first trend shows a shift away from teaching grammar toward teaching interactive skills. In the predominant view of language at the turn of the century, the structuralist view, language was a system of structurally related elements, and the goal of language learning was to master these elements. In this view, language competence is synonymous with grammar competence. Grammar–translation and audiolingualism derive from this view of language.

Later, the structuralist view gave way to the functional view. In this view, language is a "vehicle for the expression of functional meaning," and the emphasis is on communicative, rather than grammatical, features of language. Wilkins' (1976) *Notional Syllabus* marked the beginning of a communicative-competence movement that influenced methods referred to as *functional-notional methods*. According to the functional view of language, *proficiency* is the acquisition of discourse competence—the ability to understand and produce coherent text.

Recently, the notion of communicative competence has evolved to an interactional view, in which language is a tool for the "realization of interpersonal relations and the performance of social transactions between individuals" (Richards, 1990; Richards & Rodgers, 1986; Rivers, 1987a). Language is about performing transactions to have needs met and establishing and maintaining relationships. Proficiency, in the interactional view, is the ability to produce and recognize appropriate language in context. Instead of emphasizing any aspect of the language, the interactional view emphasizes how language is used in the target environment to perform social transactions—the view promotes sociolinguistic competence.

Naturalistic Learning. Another trend in language teaching shows a shift away from academic instruction toward more naturalistic ways of learning—toward instruction that is more conducive to sociolinguistic competence. The main purpose of learning languages is no longer to read books in a foreign language or to seek intellectual development, but to do business and exchange ideas in an international community. The goal of language instruction is to teach people how to interact and perform social transactions using language. When developing methods such as the direct method, silent-way, natural approach, and total physical response, researchers attempted to capture the qualities of natural settings (e.g., type of interactions, physical surroundings, cultural idiosyncrasies) and based their methods on notions of naturalistic learning (e.g., how children learn, what happens during immersion, how our bodies interact with language).

In developing naturalistic methods, theorists assumed that the process of acquiring language is the same for L1 and L2, although the conditions are different. When learning L2, the learner's internal condition is different because he or she has already acquired a great amount of knowledge, cultural background, and motor skills, and does not need to relearn what he already knows. The external conditions are also different in that those with whom the learner interacts expect him to act his age, imposing constraints on the interactions they have; for example, motherese (i.e., simplified language) is restricted between adult speakers. However, whether we are learning L1 or L2, we learn by interacting with people in the process of achieving goals. We acquire knowledge about the language inductively, from examples, rather than through the memorization of decontextualized rules. These naturalistic methods are all based on a principle described later.

The Problems. This idea of capturing naturalistic language use and learning and trying to bring them into the classroom is not new; it has inspired teaching methods since the 19th century. In France, C. Marcel (1793–1896) proposed child language learning as a model for language teaching, the Englishman T. Prendergast (1806–1886) observed that children use contextual and situational cues to interpret utterances, and Gouin (1831–1896) developed a language teaching method based on his observations of children's use of language (Richards & Rodgers, 1986). Today, the shift toward naturalistic instruction is gaining strength because we are getting better at capturing those qualities of natural settings that are essential for language acquisition. We have also come to understand that the principle underlying naturalistic learning is that we learn language by using it as a tool to perform social transactions.

However, naturalistic and all other methods face a pervasive problem: the teacher. Despite the evolution of theories and the wider spectrum of variables taken into account, all methods become heavily dependent on this one central figure. In fact, it is not exactly the teacher who is the problem, but the lack of resources that causes problems attributed to the teacher. In the hands of a good teacher, the natural approach is likely to help students prepare for real-life interactions; without a good teacher, and good teachers who are native speakers are hard to come by, learning is hindered. The main problems are: (a) limited interactions with native speakers, (b) limited exposure to the target culture, and (c) limited individual instruction and feedback.

If the purpose of language instruction is to help the student develop sociolinguistic competence, interactions with native speakers are a crucial part of the learning process. Rivers (1987b) argued that, "If communication of messages in the target language is the goal, then interaction must be present from the first encounter with the language" (p. xiv). We learn by doing or, in other words, we learn to use language by using it. Authentic use of language, which forces the student to use what he knows, create messages, and organize knowledge in his head, is an essential part of the learning process. This means that the student should learn by interacting with hotel receptionists, cab drivers, scientists, business executives, or whomever he or she is likely to meet in real life. To be effective, this practice must address the immediate interests of the student.

When interacting with each other, people take into account the context and extralinguistic cues associated with the message they hear. The physical surroundings and the precise context of a social transaction help people understand and organize the language being used. Authentic conversations always happen within a larger context that supplies elements essential to the interaction. In the classroom, students are limited to practicing situated dialogues (e.g., asking for directions to the YMCA) in unsituated physical contexts (e.g., not in New York, but inside a classroom), which forbids allusion to concrete referents. Again, limited resources makes bringing this contextual information into the classroom almost impossible.

Compounding this problem, students are often forced to engage in activities that may be of interest to the group, but are not always relevant to the individual. If a student is preparing to go to school in England, he or she should expose him or herself to the speech patterns he or she will encounter there. Students like to participate in activities that address their concerns; they want to practice in situations similar to those they will encounter in real life. The problem is that letting each student choose a target culture requires much more than a single teacher can give.

In summary, although we know what students need to learn languages, classroom instruction lacks the resources needed to prepare students to perform in real life. These resources are teachers, native speakers, and physical surroundings. All are necessary for the student to learn languages by engaging in interactions with native speakers in interesting activities that are situated in and contextualized by its real-life surroundings while receiving individualized feedback and instruction.

TECHNOLOGY IN LANGUAGE LEARNING

Although not always explicitly stated in most language-instruction methods, technology has been playing a significant role in exposing students to target cultures. An increasing reliance on materials such as audiovisuals, videotapes, multi-media, and, more recently, computers brings some of the missing resources and experiences into the classroom and language laboratory. Although technology can perpetuate bad practices, there are also many ways it can be used to solve existing problems.

Until recently, technology was noninteractive, thus unsuitable for addressing many of the issues raised in the previous section. However, computers provide interactivity, and consequently can provide individualized instruction and feedback, letting students take control and pursue their interests. Computers can help compensate for the shortage of teachers and native speakers, while addressing each student's interests and exposing him or her to a target culture.

This section traces the increasing use of technology in language learning, which, not surprisingly, parallels very closely the trends in language instruction. Each new application of technology, usually accompanying a particular method, contributes insights into what works and what does not. From tape recorders used in audiolingual methods to multi-media simulations used in naturalistic methods, each has features that give us a sense of direction. The trend that becomes apparent, as we follow the development of technological solutions to language learning problems, seems to point toward building simulations in which students learn by interacting with people. Extrapolating, it is argued here that simulations should not only replicate situations, so that they can be used as tools in naturalistic methods, but that they should incorporate naturalistic notions. More than serving as simple tools, simulations can be implementations of innovative methods of language learning. The next sections show how audiovisual materials, computers, multi-media exploratory environments, and multi-media simulations have been used in language instruction.

Audiovisual

Language teaching has relied heavily on records, tapes, slides, films, and videos. During the 1960s, for example, tape recorders introduced not only a new type of presentation, but also a new type of feedback: Students could record and listen to themselves. This technology was at the core of the audiolingual method of instruction. Later, TV and videos brought to the classroom extralinguistic elements of conversations that were not captured by tape recorders (e.g., gesticulation, physical surroundings, facial expressions). This ability to capture extralinguistic cues suited the emerging "naturalistic" methods of language instruction.

For the past 30 years, audiovisual material has been exposing students to foreign languages and cultures. Videos have not only captured essential aspects of foreign environments, but have also delivered entire language courses. Today, on a regular basis, TV networks broadcast a number of language courses. For example, engaging teachers, native speakers, and authentic surroundings merge in courses for Japanese, *Let's Learn Japanese;* Italian, *Buon Giorno Italia;* and French, *French in Action.*

French in Action. The most complete of these courses, *French in Action,* developed at Yale University, (1987) combines textbooks, cassette tapes, and 42 videotapes containing the core of the course. In the videos, an enthusiastic and captivating teacher guides the student through the experiences of a group of French people going about their lives in France. Shot in France with native actors, *French in Action* introduces the student to characters and follows them through the day.

> The objective of *French in Action* is total language teaching through planned immersion—the presentation of French language and culture in a way that simulates the experience of actually being in France. . . . Above all, it makes [students] aware that the acquisition of a language does not merely entail learning grammatical structures but depends on a complex system of verbal and non-verbal communication, gestures, looks, attitudes, behavior, intonation, and cultural conventions and assumptions. (Yale University, 1987, p. vii)

French in Action incorporates many of the ideas found in current models of language teaching. Its interesting story and well-designed scenarios, and the charisma of the teacher and actors are hard to match under ordinary classroom conditions. Besides, *French in Action* includes an enormous amount of cultural information in its 42 videotapes. The major problem with *French in Action* is that the student does not engage in interactions. In the practice modules, the student repeats lines and records utterances, using tape recorders, as in the audiolingual method. Exposure is there, but the interaction essential to learning is missing. This is a limitation of the technology. Video technology is limited by its noninteractive nature, which forces students into passive roles. For language learning, passive exposure is ineffective. Language acquisition is a by-product of interactions.

Computers

One potential solution to this interactivity problem is to use computers. Unlike videos, computers can exchange information with the student and give feedback that is essential for language acquisition. Microcomputers, which became widespread in the early 1980s, seemed to provide the interactivity missing in audiovisual efforts, and were thus a welcome innovation. The first attempts at using computers, however, were disappointing. Unfortunately, computers did not mesh with multi-media back then. Instead of using computers to complement videos, designers used them to implement outdated structural and behavioristic models of instruction. Instead of building on currently available technology and adding interactivity to videos, they added interactivity to textbooks. As a result, the first computer-assisted language learning (CALL) systems did little more than provide vocabulary lists and administer multiple-choice tests. These early systems helped teachers grade but did not help students learn. Instead of adapting computers to address language learning problems, developers adapted their solutions to technology.

As an example of this reverse thinking, one of the reasons Alan and Pamela Maddison (1987) defended transformational grammar as a useful approach was that it was "suitable to computers." Transformational grammar, they argued, could be used to teach students to "generate a large number of acceptable utterances and how to understand them." They explained that "if the rules are adequate, the computer can be used to generate kernel sentences and carry out transformations; and to match sentences generated by the students" (Maddison & Maddison, 1987, pp. 20–31). They were defending pattern practice based on the fact that computers can use transformational grammar to implement it. They were adapting needs to the constraints of technology.

This type of thinking led to the development of computer-based word lists, sentence lists, dictionaries, and translation programs, and systems that focused on grammar, verb conjugation, and other structural aspects of language that ostensibly suited the computer. Multiple-choice tests and fill-in-the-blank exercises, typical of classroom tests and textbooks, were also computerized. In general, the only beneficiaries at this stage were teachers, who no longer had to grade papers. These systems perpetuated bad practices, and students gained very little from them.

The strong initial influence of structuralism, behaviorism, and technological limitations led many teachers to see computer-based instruction as synonymous with outdated paradigms. Many of those genuinely interested in helping students develop communicative competence were discouraged by early CALL programs. Fortunately, a few went on to devise new and better ways of using the available technology. Two examples of this work are described next.

Supplementing Classroom Activities. At the University of Delaware, Braun and Mulford (1987) introduced computer-assisted instruction as part of a radical restructuring of the entire first-year French curriculum. They threw away grammar drills, reliance on textbooks, and the language laboratory, "with its mindless repetitions," and replaced them with active learning of oral French with inductive acquisition of grammar, a writing workshop, and a computer classroom.

In the classroom, Braun and Mulford used a modified version of total physical response (TPR), obtaining good results after short 40-hour terms. During the first few weeks, students act out commands without producing speech. Grammar accuracy is acquired gradually, and this method usually leads to better comprehension than audiolingualism. When students finally begin to produce, they find the transition to production exciting and are surprised at themselves. From then on, vocabulary introduced through TPR is used in role-playing activities. At the end of the 14-week term, students have a basic stock of adverbs, prepositions and articles, conjunctions, and noun-adjectives, in a total vocabulary of about 400–500 words (Braun & Mulford, 1987). Outside the classroom, homework helps students review classroom activities; a writing workshop helps them think about the things they learned in class through questions, reviews, quizzes, dictations, and completion of stories; and computer programs help them with vocabulary and verbs.

Two computer programs (located on machines in a computer classroom) work on verb forms and vocabulary. In the verb form lessons, the less interesting of the two, the computer asks the student to conjugate a verb in a certain tense (e.g., Verb: "Parler," Tense: "Passé Composé") and then provides feedback according to the student's answer. The more interesting vocabulary lessons involve sight, hearing, and touch. Unfortunately, these are not all available at the same time; the student has to choose one format: picture, audio, or word arrangement. In the picture format, a picture appears on the screen, and the student has to fill in the corresponding word in a sentence-completion exercise. In the audio format, a sentence appears on the screen with a word missing while the complete sentence is played over the headphones. The student types in the missing word. Although this format was expected to be the most promising, it was the word arrangement format, in which students organize and memorize words, that proved most popular. In word arrangement, 16 words appear on the screen, and the student reorganizes them anyway she wants (e.g., moving them within a window), usually placing them on the screen according to an imaginary story with the words serving as signposts. Once done rearranging, the student sees the words replaced with their translations into English. When she is ready, the program begins the recall exercise. Only the initial letter of the French words reappear, and the student has to retype them.

Despite its simplicity, this program helped students reinforce the vocabulary used in class, serving as a useful complement to classroom activities. When properly positioned within a larger context, even simple text-based applications may be effective to address specific language learning needs. Such programs might be useful as submodules of larger computer-based language learning environments.

A Microcomputer Game in French Culture and Civilization. In many cases, the impact of a CALL program depends more on how it is used than on its design. In 1983, Betje Klier developed a game, "Poker Pari," to be used in a contest among high school students who gathered annually at the Texas French Symposium (1987). Klier had noticed in class that "students regarded as a treat any activity dealing with culture and civilization." Klier decided to exploit their interest in culture and civilization along with game elements high school students liked. Poker Pari gives points for correct single-stroke answers to multiple-choice language, culture, and civilization questions. Thirteen topics compose a deck of cards. The computer, an Apple II Plus, selects seven topics at random and presents questions one at a time. The student has the option of rejecting two topics; the system imposes no time constraints.

The most interesting aspect of this game, as it turns out, is the way it is used. Klier decided that students would compete in teams, and that proved to be a good idea. Students found playing as a team more fun, and were motivated to work with their friends to prepare against their opponents and other schools. The system served as a catalyst for learning. It pulled students together in a cooperative learning environment, in which they discussed and helped each other understand and memorize the topics in the system.

Over 3 years of personal interviews, Klier found that the objectivity of judging, the possibility of getting easy questions, the potential of avoiding topics not desired, and the novelty of the activity motivated students to prepare for the contest. Students said that playing in a team (a) intensified their feelings of success, (b) helped them remember answers they associated with experiences with team members, and (c) made it more fun. Students asked to play "unofficially" after their game scores had been posted because they wanted to see if they could achieve a higher score.

Although interesting, Poker Pari's game qualities do not qualify it as a good language learning environment. The amount of information it exchanges with a student is severely limited by its text-based, multiple-choice nature. Nevertheless, Poker Pari exemplifies one of the best ways in which we can use technology: as a catalyst. Peer acceptance and pressure are major factors in learning, particularly in language learning, and Poker Pari threads students together in collaborative activities.

Multi-Media Exploratory Environments

As language teachers became more competent with computers and tools, like Hypercard, they began to use graphics, sound, and text combined with intuitive interfaces to give students access to words and phrases in more useful ways. At the same time, multi-media was becoming accessible, and hypermedia systems began to offer computer-driven interactive video. Interactive video disc (IVD) allowed a good degree of control over the material, giving students the ability to address individual needs; in the classroom, the IVD exploratory environments enabled teachers to adjust the material dynamically to address immediate interests.

After the initial crop of text-based CALL programs, it was becoming clear that language learning systems had to integrate audio and visual information. Visual information was shown to assist in comprehension, inference of meaning, and inference of connections between sentences (Doughty, 1991). Videos also depicted authentic language usage, provided visual and aural information, and allowed access to extralinguistic cues and interesting scenarios. Combined with computers, videos enabled the creation of interactive multi-media systems that enabled (a) user involvement and participation, (b) self-paced learning and user control, (c) audiovisual teaching and learning, (d) immediate feedback, and (e) tracking and affordability (Slaton, 1991).

Instead of just presenting information in videos, interactive multi-media allows students to select desired topics to address their own needs. Multi-media systems re-purpose video discs and organize them into maps and lists of topics, allowing students to use them as navigational tools to explore the target environment.

The Zarabanda Notebook. One of these multi-media navigational tools is The Zarabanda Notebook (Underwood, 1991). The Notebook is based on a 25-episode soap opera called "Zarabanda," produced by the BBC in 1973 for teaching Spanish. "Zarabanda" is the story of Ramiro, a mechanic, who goes to the city to seek his fortune. Shot in real locations with native speakers, "Zarabanda" is rich with linguistic and cultural information.

The goal of the Notebook is to organize the information in "Zarabanda" so that students can see and hear information in the repurposed video at both the language and the story level. Developed in Hypercard, the Notebook has a number of maps: Ramiro's room, The Village, and Maps for each scene. In the room map, the user can click on objects or other maps. Clicking on the book, for instance, starts an introductory video clip; clicking on Ramiro's girlfriend's picture starts a brief textual and graphic presentation of the cast of characters for the first episode. Clicking on camera icons shows a still frame of the characters.

The student can play a segment with or without a transcript, play single lines, and play single lines with English translations appearing momentarily on the screen. The Notebook also includes listening comprehension exercises, in which the program turns off the video portion of the scene so that the student concentrates on the sounds. A transcript of the dialogue

appears with some words missing, which are listed on the right-hand side of the screen. As the dialogue is played, the student has to click on the missing words in the proper sequence. Mistakes are signaled with a gong sound, and the student can stop and go to other activities.

This type of exploratory system, usually using repurposed video discs, makes watching more interesting by giving some control to the student. Other examples of exploratory systems include the Japanese, "Good-bye this year's love," and the French, "Dans le Quartier St. Gervais." The Japanese version, developed by Michio Tsutsui from MIT, is based on a video drama taken directly from Tokyo broadcast television, which was re-edited into segments for comprehension exercises. "Good-bye this year's love" also includes slide files of cultural events, maps, and art. The French version, developed as part of a project called "Direction Paris," explores a neighborhood in Paris, showing people who live and work there. It is a hypermedia system with many sequences including slides, videos, and slides with text. "Dans le Quartier St. Gervais" organizes information through a system of three indices: (a) topic (issues such as gentrification), (b) maps (selected areas and sequences about those areas), and (c) foot-tour of the neighborhood (MIT, 1990).

In most cases, exploratory systems are used to assist in classroom instruction. Students explore the environment while trying to collect information that is used later in classroom activities. As a stand-alone language learning environment, however, exploratory systems do not have the necessary type of interactivity that simulations have.

Multi-Media Simulations

Despite its advantages, IVD was still not enough. Having the control to navigate at will in the target environment is an important aspect of the learning process. But watching a social interaction is very different from participating in one; controlling information is not the same as exchanging information. Hence, the major problem remained unsolved: To learn how to interact, one must interact. In social interactions, people are never passive; instead, they use language as a means to establish and maintain relationships by constantly exchanging information. Interactions involve feedback, clarification of statements, and extralinguistic exchanges that are essential in social transactions. This song and dance, necessary in performing social transactions, is never necessary when simply controlling information in exploratory systems.

To help students develop communicative competence, programs are needed that give students not only conversations to watch, but also conversations in which to participate. When Krashen (1985) said, in his input hypothesis, that we acquire language by being exposed to comprehensible input, he did not mean to say that, by watching French TV all day, we will become proficient in French. Exposure to comprehensible input must occur in contexts in which we can make sense of what we hear and in which we negotiate meaning by interacting with people, even if not using language. What we need is to simulate the target environment. By simulating it, we give students a chance to participate in face-to-face interactions with foreigners.

Athena Language Learning Project. At MIT, a number of programs have been developed that focus on developing communicative compe-tence, some of which focus on interactions (i.e., they simulate conversa-tions). The goal of MIT's Athena Language Learning Project (ALLP) is not mastery of the grammatical and syntactic code, but the ability to understand language in a culturally authentic and task-centered situation (Lampe, 1988; Morgenstern, 1986; Murray, 1987, 1990). In the short run, the goals are to implement simple interactions based on matching and anticipated responses. The long-term goal is to build full simulations that will occur within stories that provide a natural link to classroom activities.

MIT stresses communication and interaction in what it calls "Language Learning Through Interaction via Software." It is firmly grounded on the interactional notion of competence—in other words, that "language learn-ing takes place in an interactional context in which the learner expresses, interprets, and negotiates meaning with other interlocutors" (Mor-genstern, 1986, p. 25). "Language is not 'presented' as an abstract, static, and closed system, but is experienced as dynamic interplay." Dialogues are essential. "Language is seen as a negotiable system of meaning, ex-pressed and interpreted via the social interaction of reader and text, or between speakers culturally coded situations rather than on a closed system of formal lexical and grammatical rules" (Murray, 1990, p. 22).

One of the aspects that the ALLP is working on is the natural language processing module. The quality of a simulation depends on effective interpretation of the input accompanied by appropriate responses. Effec-tive interpretation depends on how well the system processes input (Mor-genstern, 1986). Most systems currently available have limited input ca-pabilities through multiple-choice or keywords. Artificial intelligence techniques may give the illusion that the program understands the input (typed, not speech), so that learners develop command of the language by interacting with simulated interlocutors.

This emphasis on communication and natural language processing has guided the development of a number of prototypes at MIT. Prototypes developed or being developed include versions for French (*Direction Paris: Part I: A la rencontre de Philippe, Part II: Dans le Quartier St. Gervais*), Spanish (*No Recuerdo*), Japanese (*Good-bye this year's love*), and German (*LINGO*).

Two of these systems, *A la rencontre de Philippe* (MIT, 1990) and *No Recuerdo* (Morgenstern, 1986), both include interesting features that make them worth mentioning. *A la rencontre de Philippe* does not use natural language, but it implements interesting exploratory features; *No Recuerdo* is not yet fully implemented, but it will use natural language to implement simulations of interactions.

DESIGN ISSUES

Mirroring the trends in language instruction, computer-based language training has been moving away from passive presentation systems toward systems that simulate real life. Most existing systems implement limited interactions, usually simply allowing students to navigate and watch interactions. Ideally, however, authentic simulations could be used to give students individualized exposure to a target culture and engage them in active interactions with native speakers. If properly designed, these simulations can help students develop language skills by interacting with others as they would in real life, acquiring language as a by-product of performing social transactions in the target culture.

What Is So Good About Living in Japan?

"Living in Japan is the best way of learning Japanese"

If I move to Japan, Japanese immediately becomes the vehicle of every social transaction, the instrument of my survival, well-being, and social acceptance. I need to eat, conduct business, earn money, interact with others, feel accepted in the community, express frustration, convey sadness and loneliness, and find companionship; all of this is heavily dependent on my knowing the language. I can use alternative means of communication (gesticulation, pointing, and mime), but I definitely need language to say something like, "Express delivery please." I go at it with an insatiable thirst. I ask people to help me; I hang onto phrases as if my life depends on them; I buy books, dictionaries, tapes, and translating machines; I hire a private tutor; take classes; ask friends to teach me; watch TV; read the papers. People correct me or restate what they thought I wanted to say, showing me the right way of saying things; they get angry, making me realize that something is wrong; they frown, making it clear that I did not make sense. I expose myself to situations in which I have to interact with native speakers. I drink, eat, and breathe the culture 24 hours a day, paying attention to its customs and social protocols, afraid of committing gaffes. The language becomes so important in my life that I almost can't help learning it.

Obviously, a number of elements contribute to learning in the Japan experience. The person is highly motivated to learn Japanese to go about his life. Language is crucial, and the drive to survive and prosper stimulates learning. The goals that the individual wants to achieve in the target culture affect his role in the environment. He spends 24 hours a day immersed in the target environment, hearing, seeing, and interacting with people who use only Japanese to communicate. The student is exposed to the context in which language is used, including physical, social, and task settings as they occur in real life. He participates actively, engaging in interactions that require the use of language. These interactions force the student not only to recognize words, but also to recall and adapt knowledge to the situation. He receives help. Native speakers, or tutors, correct errors or suggest better ways of saying things, and the environment is fortuitous in that it provides referents that assist in communication. The way people react, their behavior, provides the learner with essential feedback to adjust behavior. The student tries to understand patterns of the language, questions how words are used and what they mean in different contexts; in other words, he engages in analysis and reflection. When communication breaks down, due to insufficient competence or performance variables, he uses extralinguistic means of communication that help smooth social interactions. When at a loss for words, he resorts to tools like dictionaries, recorders, and translating machines. The social context and the interactions with others elicit emotions, affect, that influence learning, and the personality of the individual influences the degree of exposure and his willingness to try things out. Finally, different people use different learning strategies because they learn in different ways. Table 1.1 (p. 31) provides a summary of the variables that influence language acquisition when living in the target culture.

These variables cover a wide range of phenomena—from tools in the environment to characteristics of the learner. Organized in groups, they address four important elements of real-life experiences: (a) situations (e.g., context and behaviors), (b) student (e.g., goals, motivations), (c) interactions (e.g., sequence of events, freedom of choice), and (d) resources (e.g., tutor, books, etc.). See Table 1.2 (p. 32) for a summary of the aspects of the environment that each variable addresses.

The following sections discuss each of these four elements (i.e., situations, student, interactions, resources) and the problems involved in simulating real life using current technology. A set of principles for the design of simulations is defined and used to develop the simulation described later.

The Situations

If we capture the context in which interactions occur and the behavior of the people we are simulating, we provide the student with a chance to expose him or herself to a target culture, comprehensible input, and

TABLE 1.1
Variables That Influence Language Acquisition in Natural Settings

Variable	Description	How It Influences Learning
Motivation	Highly motivated. Personal needs have to be met; language is a powerful tool to satisfy them.	The more goals depend on language, the more motivated student will be.
Goals	Survive, make friends, establish oneself, thrive.	Dependency on language proficiency affects other variables.
Immersion	Completely immersed, 24 hours a day.	Extent of exposure is thought to have a stronger impact than age.
Context	Native speakers, target culture and environment, real-life situations.	Higher relevance of language used in real life for real-life purposes.
Active participation	Engage in interactions continuously.	Forces retrieval and adaptation of existing knowledge structures.
Help	People help, friends help, tutor helps.	Nonthreatening situations foster exploration, and corrections help eliminate errors.
Behavior/feedback	The environment is fortuitous, people give feedback all the time.	Crucial for fine-tuning language skills.
Analysis and reflection	Study the language, think about the culture and social protocols.	Detect patterns in the language, build abstractions that enable transfer.
Extralinguistic communication	Gesticulation, mime, pointing, facial expressions.	Helps handle communication breakdowns. Eases interactions.
Tools	Use dictionary, tape recorder, translating machines.	Artifacts help us with specific problems.
Affect	Emotions influence learning and interaction with the environment.	Fear, threat, and security influence openness to exploration and learning.
Personality	Traits determine student's relationship with the environment.	An outgoing person will have more exposure and willingness to experiment.
Learning strategies	Tricks used to learn the language.	Personal learning styles, cognitive strategies.

interactions with native speakers. How well we capture the social and physical settings in which something occurs and how well we capture the way people react to utterances determine how much the student can gain from the simulation.

Context (Social/Physical). Language must be presented in context as it is used in real life. The situated learning literature articulates how context helps us learn. Brown, Collins, and Duguid (1989), arguing for

TABLE 1.2
Variables That Influence Language Learning and
How They Relate to Aspects of the Environment

Variables	Shape
Context Behavior/feedback	Situations
Motivation Goals Analysis and reflection Affect Personality Learning strategies	Student
Immersion Active participation Extralinguistic communication	Interactions
Help Tools	Resources

the importance of teaching knowledge in context, noted that, "knowledge is situated, being in part a product of the activity, context, and culture in which it is developed and used." Activity, concept, and culture are interdependent, they argued, and learning in context allows us to offload part of the cognitive task onto the environment. We offload part of the task by leaving it up to the environment to give us the cues with which to retrieve a piece of knowledge. The environment provides the student with conditions for applying and organizing knowledge, by showing how a piece of knowledge is used in a larger context (Collins, 1988).

This means that simulations should re-create the social and physical contexts in which language is used. Because the environment provides the keys to index knowledge in our heads, language must be presented in context. For example, if the task is to prepare American students for life in a Japanese university, the program must simulate conversations that occur in Japanese universities, with Japanese students, speaking the way they speak in real life. Ideally, it should also expose the Americans to the same physical surroundings, social setting, and tasks they will face at the university.

Perception (Audiovisual). Most of the contextual information described earlier is perceived either visually or aurally. In real life, we observe the way people walk, gesticulate, or move their lips when they talk. The visual, aural, and contextual cues involved in interactions all assist learning.

An example that illustrates the importance of visual and aural cues in learning was given by T. Gallwey (1991) during a talk in Chicago. Gallwey suggested teaching someone how to say the word *uncoordinated* by explaining:

> You round your lips and open your mouth until your lips are about half an inch from each other, place the tip of your tongue behind your lower teeth where the teeth meet the gums, lower the middle of your tongue so that the inside of your mouth forms a wide chamber, now release a puff of air and vocalize from the middle of your throat for about a third of a second. This will take care of the "U" in *uncoordinated*. Now immediately after vocalizing, raise the back of your tongue until it touches the back of the palate, completely obstructing the passage of air. It is this closing of the channel that stops the vocalization. We have now done the entire "UN" part of the word.

The complete description of the word *uncoordinated* fills about one page. Such a long description makes the student aware of the complexities of uttering the word *uncoordinated*, but it is not the way people produce speech; there is not enough time to think of all these rules.

Also, as shown experimentally, visual information is more effective than other types of memory. An example that illustrates its effectiveness was given by Alan Kay during a conference in Chicago. Kay pointed out that while flipping TV channels we can recognize a movie we have seen before after seeing only a few seconds of it. What is more impressive, we can also remember what is going to happen next. Visual information provides powerful cues with which to retrieve information. Whenever applicable, simulations should always provide visual and aural information.

Behavior. Although replicating the context of interactions is important, the value of simulations lies in replicating the behavior of people. The way people act provides feedback that is essential for language learning. For example, an angry tone of voice tells us that we should change something or maybe apologize. People's reactions to what we say help us adjust our own behavior and correct our knowledge structures. People in the simulated environment must react authentically to students' utterances.

As Rivers (1987a) put it,

> Interaction involves not just expression of one's own ideas but comprehension of those of others. One listens to others; one responds (directly or indirectly); others listen and respond. The participants work out interpretations of meaning through this interaction, which is always understood in a context, physical or experiential, with nonverbal cues adding aspects of meaning beyond the verbal. All of these factors should be present as students learn to communicate: listening to others, talking with others, negotiating meaning in a shared context . . . communication there must be—interaction between people who have something to share. . . . Through interaction, students can increase their language store as they listen to or

read authentic linguistic material. . . . In interaction, students can use all they possess of the language—all they have learned or casually absorbed— in real-life exchanges where expressing their real meaning is important to them. They thus have experience in creating messages from what they hear.

The Student

If we manage to simulate the context of the interactions and the behavior of people, we have captured an important portion of the living-there experience. But, as important as this may be, it is not enough to guarantee learning. It is what the student *does* that promotes learning. The tasks that the student performs determine how much he or she will learn, how motivated he or she will be to learn, and how useful the simulation will be to address his or her real-life needs. The level of proficiency the student achieves depends heavily on his or her reasons for wanting to learn the language and the learning strategies he or she uses. Simulations cannot directly control either of these. However, on the one hand, simulations can define the role of the student and the goals he or she will pursue in ways that address his or her reasons and, on the other hand, simulations can provide tools that assist with his or her learning strategies.

Roles/Goals. Language acquisition is heavily influenced by the needs of the individual, and students learn by getting involved in performing tasks that are relevant to them. The role the student plays in the simulation must be the role that he or she is practicing for in real life. The student must participate actively, not reactively. Active participation forces recall and adaptation of knowledge structures. Students engage in more than just recognition tasks; they learn by building knowledge structures (Papert, 1976, 1987).

To involve a student in simulated situations, we must come as close as possible to replicating real-life roles. One way to do this is to establish goals that are closely related to a student's goals in real life. Goals must be meaningful to the student. Language is a means to achieving a goal, not the goal itself. The role that a person plays in a social context is intimately tied with the goals he or she pursues. To the extent that the simulation addresses his or her real-life goals, the student will be motivated to interact with the simulation.

In a study on motivation, Malone (1981) found that "the single feature of computer games that correlated most strongly with preference was whether or not the game had a goal." According to a study by Morozova, Malone said, motivating goals have the following qualities:

- Using the skill being taught was a means to achieving the goal, but it was not the goal in itself

- The goal was part of an intrinsic fantasy
- The goal was one with which readers could identify

Morozova's study shows that learners acquire skills better when they focus on achieving goals than they do when focusing on learning the skill. In language learning, this means to focus on the message, not on its structure. In fact, the shift in language instruction away from grammar toward communicative skills is based on the fact that people learn language better when they are concerned with communicating messages, instead of with the language.

To engage the student in the simulated activities, the goals in the simulation must be closely related to the goals of the student in real life. If the simulation helps the student acclimate to an American university, for example, then goals should include things like registering for classes, dropping/adding courses, getting on meal plans, moving into a dorm, and getting a student ID.

Interaction: The Student and Situations

In real life, we are not always free to engage in interactions with others. Social norms, limited resources, and personality traits constrain what we can do. Although simulations do not replicate all the advantages of living in a target culture, they offer the advantage of relaxing these constraints that real life imposes on our interactions with others.

Before discussing how interactions should happen in simulations, it is important to note that we cannot control how much time a student spends playing with a simulation. Immersion studies conducted in Canada have shown that the amount of exposure to a target language (for which length of residence is an index) is one of the most important factors in determining the level of linguistic skill achieved (Harley, 1990). Unfortunately, we have little control over this variable because the student chooses the amount of time he or she wants to spend in the simulation. Unlike real life in a foreign country, once the student switches off the computer, everything reverts to the source language and culture.

However, because simulations allow us to remove some constraints imposed by real life, simulations offer advantages that may replace quality and intensity for quantity of exposure. First, we can sequence the events in ways that optimize learning (sequencing). Second, students can choose what to do, and even do things repeatedly, which is not always possible in real life (exploration). Third, simulated environments are nonthreatening, giving students a chance to engage in interactions without the emotional constraints of real life (threat).

Sequence of Events.   Given that we can simulate context and behaviors, and involve students in roles that are meaningful to them, we need to address one more problem: determining how things should happen in the simulated environment so that students learn. For teaching to be effective, we must first prepare students to acquire some new knowledge or skill, then help them acquire and organize the new information in memory, and finally make them use it (Schank, 1991a). In order for students to be prepared, they must be curious to learn something new. Curiosity arises when students realize that their knowledge is incomplete, inconsistent, or unparsimonious (Malone, 1981). In other words, they realize they need to learn something when they fail (Schank, 1982, 1991a). Because it is not always clear what constitutes a failure, the system must prepare students by establishing this condition for them, either by intervening in a conversation or simulating authentic behavior that indicates a failure to communicate (e.g., the simulated person frowns or says "I don't understand you"). Hence, the first task a computer-based learning environment has is to place students in a situation of interest and wait for an indication that the students need information they do not have. When the students realize their failure, they will be interested in acquiring new information.

Once the student is ready to acquire new knowledge, we present him or her with an example. Because failure always occurs in the context of trying to perform some social transaction, the example is always of someone else successfully performing the same social transaction. As described previously, this has to be done in a way that conveys all the necessary cues to help him or her retain and organize the information (i.e., providing physical context, social context, and audio/aural information). Later, to ensure that the information is correctly assimilated, we force the student to use the knowledge in a situational simulation. Performance in the simulation provides feedback to the student and lets the system detect further failures. If the student fails again, the task he or she is pursuing might be too difficult. If possible, the system should break it down into more manageable portions and reapply the sequencing described previously.

Exploration: Let the Student Choose.   The structure proposed earlier should not be taken as a motion for rigidity. The student should have control over what to do in the simulated environment. Freedom of choice enables individualized instruction. The student gets to do what he or she wants and when he or she wants to do it. No longer does he or she have to comply and pay attention to things that other students are interested in but that are irrelevant for him or her. The student is provided with the means of controlling his or her experiences.

Threat. How the student feels, which is largely determined by personality traits, has a strong impact on learning. For example, introverts and extroverts relate differently to the demands of the environment. Simulations can work as a social buffer, enabling less socially adventurous learners to engage in conversations with strangers without feeling threatened. Exactly how affect influences language acquisition, however, is the subject of a long debate among second language theorists. A dialogue between two theorists, Krashen and McLaughlin, captures the state of the field when it comes to the role of personality traits and affect in language acquisition.

Krashen (1982, 1985) postulated that individuals learn language through exposure to comprehensible input. However, individuals exposed to the same amount of comprehensible input may acquire different levels of proficiency. Krashen proposed that this difference is due to an affective filter. The learner must be open to the input; the affective filter is a mental block that prevents all input from being processed. This filter is usually up when the learner is unmotivated, anxious, defensive, or lacking self-esteem; the filter is down when the learner is not afraid of failing and feels he belongs in the target group.

McLaughlin (1987) argued that the problem with Krashen's affective filter hypothesis is that "there is no research evidence to support a causal relationship between these personality variables [self-consciousness, vulnerability, and insecurity] and language learning. Indeed, research on individual differences in second language learning has proven to be a methodological Armageddon. It is extremely difficult to show any relationship between personality factors and language learning." However, McLaughlin did not deny that affect seems to play an important role. He used the lack of supporting evidence to argue against Krashen's "affective filter hypothesis," but acknowledged that "most researchers in the field of second-language acquisition would admit that affective variables play a critical role."

The consensus seems to be that affect does play a critical role. As Seliger put it,

> Since language is used in social exchanges, the feelings, attitudes, and motivations of learners in relation to the target language itself, to the speakers of the language, and to the culture will affect how learners respond to the input to which they are exposed. In other words, these affective variables will determine the rate and degree of second language learning. (cited in Bebee, 1988)

Most researchers believe that extroverted, self-confident people are better learners. People with these characteristics are usually more willing, or open, to trying things out—they are less afraid of relating to other people.

Consequently, they engage in interaction more often than shy people, who lack self-esteem.

Simulated environments are nonthreatening. The nature of the instrument—simulations—helps high-filter individuals feel at ease and comfortable when playing with others. Regardless of how realistic our model of the world turns out to be, the student knows that the simulated agent's reactions need not be taken personally. The only case in which a simulation can become threatening is if it is used to evaluate the learner or keep records of interactions. We should avoid this. These negative aspects of real life need not be transferred into the simulation. The reason the student plays with a simulation is that he or she wants to interact with foreigners in a foreign language; the motivation is intrinsic. It is up to the student to choose what to focus on, what he or she thinks is important for him or her to know, and so on. Imposing external punishment or rewards on the student only lowers intrinsic motivation (Lepper & Greene, 1978; Malone, 1981). We should not keep information that can be used to evaluate the student.

Resources

The only remaining elements that we need to capture in the simulated environment are resources—tools that provide cognitive assistance. In real life, a number of resources facilitate or assist in learning. Books, dictionaries, and people help us cope with the target culture. In simulations, a number of new tools such as transcripts of conversations, subtitles, and translations can be added. Also, tools that help students reflect and practice language patterns, such as tape recorders, should also be provided.

Tutor. Simply being thrown in an environment where a second language is used is insufficient for learning to occur. Immersion has its limitations. Universal, nonverbal means of communication may help us survive, but to learn a language we need to properly socialize, and for that we need help.

Apprenticeship, the most popular model of instruction until the 19th century (Collins, Brown, & Newman, 1989), is based on the idea that skills used to be learned by working with an expert. The apprentice sits at the feet of the master and learns through a process of observation, practice, and coaching. The student observes the master performing a task, tries to do it himself, and receives help from the master. Both the master and the task provide the necessary feedback for the student to monitor his performance.

In simulations, we need to give the student someone who can assist him in these social transactions—a tutor. Good tutors share three characteristics. First, they do not correct grammar. There is no evidence that correcting grammar is helpful or necessary in language acquisition (Terrell, 1977). Learners in natural settings acquire grammar even if incorrect speech is accepted in the initial stages of language acquisition. Moreover, it is almost impossible for a beginner to be able to carry on a conversation without errors.

Second, a good tutor provides constructive feedback. Malone (1981) argued that, to be educational, feedback should be constructive: "In other words, the feedback should not just reveal to learners that their knowledge is incomplete, inconsistent, or unparsimonious, but should help them see how to change their knowledge to become more complete, consistent, or parsimonious" (p. 364). Although the tutor should not intervene at the grammatical level, it should intervene when the student is not saying the right thing at the right time. If the student asks for something without first greeting the other person, for example, the tutor should intervene and suggest that the student greet first. Other types of interventions can occur when aiding the student in making decisions that give him or her control over the environment (e.g., Are you hungry? Do you want to meet someone?). The student's choice will determine the course of his or her experiences in the simulated environment.

Finally, a good tutor provides means for the student to interact with it. It is not always possible for the tutor to detect what kinds of problems the student is having. Student models, or inferences based on a student's input, enable us to detect cognitive problems; the interactions will provide the necessary information to infer the state of the student. But to individualize instruction, a tutor needs both cognitive and affective feedback. If a task is too easy, the student will be bored. There is no way for the system, based solely on the input, to determine whether the student managed to accomplish the task because he or she is overqualified for it or if his or her knowledge is just about enough at that level of difficulty. In real life, the student shows boredom on his or her face. In the simulation, we need alternative ways to detect boredom. This means the tutor must handle common problems that students face, and the system must provide the student with the means to communicate the most common states to the tutor (e.g., bored, not knowing what to do, not knowing what to say).

Problems: Limitations of Technology

Although simulations are ideal for language learning, ideal simulations are not yet feasible. Technology, as it currently stands, is still limited, and a number of problems have to be addressed. The major problem has to do with communicating with a computer—a problem that is best explained by an example. The student is able to absorb a large amount of information coming from the computer, through video and audio, but the computer has narrow channels of communication to get information from the student. Does the fact that computers do not process facial expression, speech, tone of voice, body language, gesticulation, focus of attention, and blankness in the eyes mean that we cannot simulate interactions with people? If the agents in the environment cannot detect the student's reactions, can they interact at all with the student?

Conceptual Feedback. Here is one solution. In an article about reflection, Collins and Brown (1988) described different levels of feedback that can be given to a student who is learning a swing in tennis. At the level with highest physical fidelity (i.e., replay), the student performs a forehand, and then the system video tapes him or her and plays it back side by side with a video of an expert performing the same swing. The student has an accurate view of what he or she is doing. At another level (i.e., abstracted replay), the computer records the critical features of the motion, and a reflective material is taped to critical points, such as the racquet and body joints, so that the student is able to focus on the important aspects of the swing and compare it to the expert's motion at a different level of abstraction. Here the student is not distracted by the way he or she looked in comparison with the pro. This second type of feedback lacks physical fidelity but it has conceptual fidelity. It extracts the information that is important in that context.

Now turn this around. We may be unable to have physical fidelity when conveying information to the simulated environment, but we can have conceptual fidelity of feedback—as long as the environment allows us to express what we need to express (e.g., through an "I am crying" button). Until computers become able to process body language and tears, we can resort to conceptual feedback for the purposes of interaction. The next question is, what kind of conceptual feedback?

Lepper and Chabay (1985) argued that truly personalized instruction must be individualized along motivational and cognitive dimensions. This means that, when interacting with a student, as when teaching mathematics, we need to know more than whether the student is getting the correct answer. We need to know whether he or she is bored and whether the whole thing is above his or her head. Perhaps the student would prefer to be working on something else. Interactivity means having the student's states affect the environment. The system must provide means for the student to convey these states to the computer. Because the system cannot detect it from the input all the time, the student communicates it by pushing a button or some other active means. As discussed earlier, the student must be able to communicate both cognitive and affective states to the simulated people.

Natural Language

The limited speech-recognition capability of current technology is another problem for language learning. Development of oral proficiency is heavily dependent on feedback from listeners; in the natural setting, almost all interactions are based on oral communication. To provide the same amount of feedback and style of interactivity, language learning systems will have to incorporate speech recognition. This is a limitation of current technology that we need not rationalize. It would certainly be preferable to have full-blown speech-recognition capabilities.

Oral proficiency develops from a combination of input, feedback, and reflection. We hear a speech pattern a number of times until we grasp its meaning and sound. At some point, we try to use it in some context, and receive feedback that means either that we did not pronounce it correctly or that it did not make sense in the context in which we used it, or both. We then reflect on the experience and make necessary adjustments. The part of the process that current technology does not allow us to provide is feedback on pronunciation. Other than that, computer-based environments can give the student a wealth of input (e.g., videos of people using language and interacting with each other in many different real-life contexts). Using a natural language interface (i.e., typed input), the system can provide feedback indicating that something said did not make sense in the specific context. Computers can also provide innovative tools to help the student reflect on his or her oral performance by giving feedback (by recording the student's speech and playing it back, and/or showing graphical representations of speech [spectrographs] and intonation [pitch tracking]).

The Silent Period. To determine in what conditions either limited speech-recognition capabilities or natural language interface would be useful, we need to determine under what conditions feedback on pronunciation plays no significant role in language learning. Research shows that, in natural settings, learners go through a silent period during which they listen carefully to input and produce little output (Richards & Rodgers, 1986). During this period, learners interact with others by using simple expressions, such as "yes," "no," and pointing. In the long run, people who use this learning strategy acquire better oral proficiency than people who engage in speech production early on. This phenomenon seems to be attributable to the fact that such learners develop more acute aural discrimination before they engage in production. Table 1.3 summarizes the desirable characteristics discussed in this section.

TABLE 1.3
Desirable Characteristics of Computer-Based
Language Learning Environments

Variable	Desirable Characteristics	Shape
Context/perception	(1) Present language in context, as it is used in real life.	Situations
	(2) Provide visual and aural information.	
Behavior/feedback	(3) People in the simulated environment must react authentically to student utterances.	
Role	(4) The role the student plays in the simulation is the role he or she is practicing for in real life. The student participates actively, not reactively.	Student
Goals	(5) Goals must be meaningful to the student. Language is a means to achieving the goal, not the goal itself.	

Sequence	(6) Engage in interactions
	    If fail, then show an example
	      Try again
	      If fail, break the task down into smaller parts
	    If succeed, move on
		Interactions

Exploration	(7) Let the student have control over what to do in the simulated environment.	
Threat	(8) Do not keep scores. Do not evaluate. Do not keep records.	
Tools and tutor	(9) Provide tools for addressing communication problems (e.g., dictionary, transcript of conversations, etc.).	Resources
	(10) Provide tools for analysis and reflection (e.g., recorder).	
	(11) Help student perform social transactions.	
	(12) Do not correct grammar.	
	(13) Provide constructive feedback.	
	(14) Provide means for the student to interact with the tutor.	
Conceptual feedback	(15) Provide means for the student to express important cognitive and affective states to the stimulated people and to the tutor. Provide means of communicating common states (e.g., Huh?).	Problems
Natural language	(16) Use natural language interface (assist/facilitate spelling).	

DUSTIN—A LANGUAGE LEARNING ENVIRONMENT

Based on the principles outlined earlier, I designed an architecture for computer-based language learning systems called Role Playing in Social Simulations (RPSS). When using RPSS systems, students practice for real-life performance by rehearsing in a simulated environment. In this environment, they interact with native speakers while playing the roles for which they are preparing themselves in real life. Students receive guidance from a tutor, who determines the tasks they have to accomplish and provides help when needed. Students have access to a number of supporting tools, and can control how they navigate in a space of tasks and examples. For the sake of clarity, instead of describing features of the RPSS architecture out of context, this section explains them in the context of a session with an implementation called Dustin.

The Components

Any simulation can be divided into three major components: (a) what it simulates (real-life situation), (b) how it simulates it (mechanism), and (c) how it looks to the student (interface). Figure 1.8 depicts these three components and how they relate to each other. In the description that follows, the interface and real-life situation become apparent to the reader. For now, the mechanism described later remains transparent.

The Real-Life Situation

Andersen Consulting employees from around the world come to the firm's educational center in St. Charles, Illinois, for training. Typically, these newcomers have had training in English as a second language, but have had little or no exposure to native speakers. They can read and write fairly well, and usually perform well on tests. However, once in the United States, they have difficulty performing simple tasks, such as going through immigration and checking into a hotel—difficulties that derive mostly from their lack of exposure to the target environment.

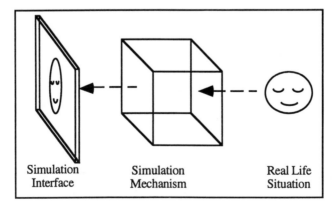

| Simulation
Interface | Simulation
Mechanism | Real Life
Situation |

FIG. 1.8. Simulations can be divided into three major components.

Dustin simulates the situations these newcomers confront during their first day in the United States. The simulation begins at O'Hare Airport, where the students must go through immigration and find transportation to St. Charles, and continues through a number of activities during a day in St. Charles, where students check in, meet their roommates, get food, go to classes, and engage in similar tasks facing trainees in St. Charles.

Newcomers use Dustin on a one-on-one basis before coming to the United States. The version described here was developed for, and installed in, the firm's office in Madrid. To place yourself in the proper context, imagine yourself in the Madrid office of Andersen Consulting, as an employee who has just been hired by the firm. You know English from a few years of English classes in high school, and you have passed a test in English proficiency (grammar/vocabulary). You will soon leave for training in St. Charles.

Exhibit 1.1 shows Dustin's introductory screen. The left column shows system actions, and the right column shows student actions. The picture in the center is a snapshot of the screen the student sees when using Dustin. These boxes should be read from left to right; the sound transcribed in the left column (system action) is played before the student action is shown in the right column. At this point, the student clicks on the central screen to start the system. As each new feature of Dustin appears, the text indicates the design principle that the feature addresses. Principles are italicized and are numbered according to Table 1.3.

(2) *Provide visual and aural information.*

The "screen" area (see Exhibits 1.2, p. 45, and 1.3, p. 46) shows the window into the simulated environment. It is here that the simulation

Exhibit 1.1

provides visual information, accompanied by audio. Physical surroundings, extralinguistic cues, and behaviors are captured and conveyed through this window.

(1) *Present language in context, as it is used in real life.*

The system places the student in the same contexts he or she will face when arriving in the United States (Exhibits 1.2, 1.3 and 1.4). The physical

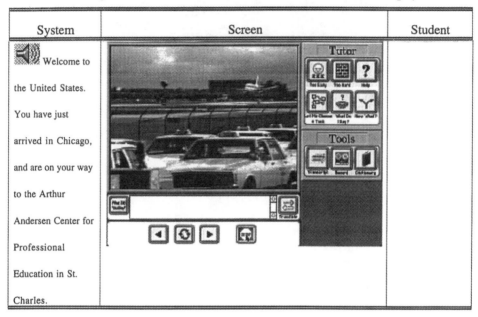

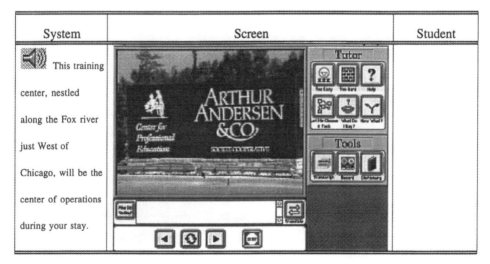

Exhibit 1.2

System	Screen	Student
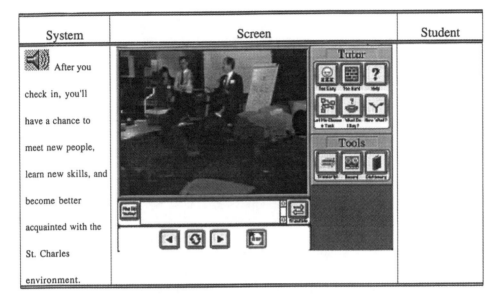 After you check in, you'll have a chance to meet new people, learn new skills, and become better acquainted with the St. Charles environment.		

Exhibit 1.3

surroundings and the people he or she will see in the simulation are those the student will see in real life. Every situation involving the use of language mirrors how it is used in real life. Soon the student will be introduced to his or her first task: go through immigration at O'Hare Airport (Exhibit 1.5, p. 47).

System	Screen	Student
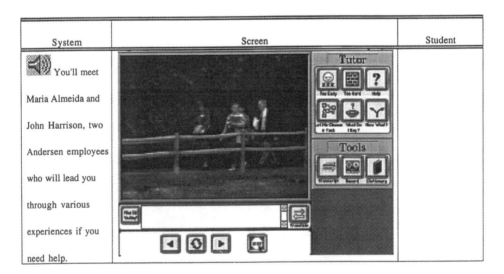 You'll meet Maria Almeida and John Harrison, two Andersen employees who will lead you through various experiences if you need help.		

Exhibit 1.4

System	Screen	Student
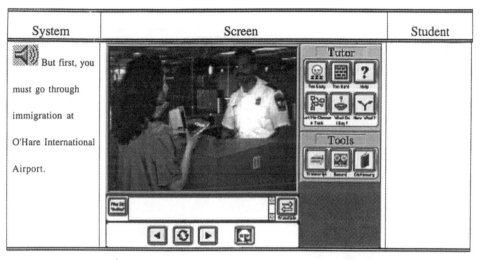 But first, you must go through immigration at O'Hare International Airport.		

Exhibit 1.5

The interface language is an option in the menu bar, through which the user can change the labels of the buttons and the introduction to his or her native language. The rest of the simulation is always in English, regardless of the choice of interface language. Tutor interventions always appear in the middle of the screen (Exhibits 1.6 and 1.7, p. 48). The tutor will appear often to direct the student, provide hints, offer choices, and give feedback.

(4) *The role the student plays in the simulation is the role he or she is practicing for in real life. The student participates actively, not reactively.*

The tutor places the student in the proper context by assigning her tasks, tasks that always involve interacting with someone. The goals in these interactions are well defined, and are basically the same as the ones he or she will pursue when he or she comes to the United States for training. Going through immigration is the first task—the student has to interact with the immigration agent to enter the country (Exhibit 1.8, p. 49).

Translations are always available (Exhibits 1.9, p. 49, 1.10, and 1.11, p. 50). The student is not allowed to "turn on" translations because we want to encourage reliance on the target language, but they are always, at most, a couple of steps away.

(15) *Provide means for the student to express important cognitive and affective states to the simulated people and to the tuor. Provide means of communicating common states (e.g., Huh?).*

The student expresses confusion through the HUH? button (Exhibit 1.12, p. 57). In real life, we can just frown to let people know we are confused. In simulations, the student has to translate his or her frowning into an input that is understandable to the computer. The solution adopted in Dustin is to provide buttons through which the student communicates

System	Screen	Student
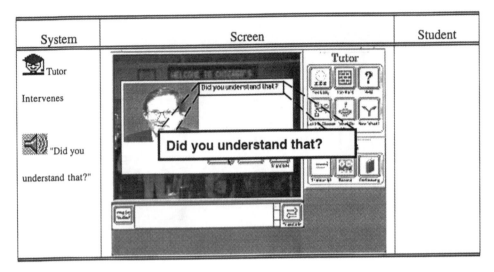		

Exhibit 1.6

System	Screen	Student
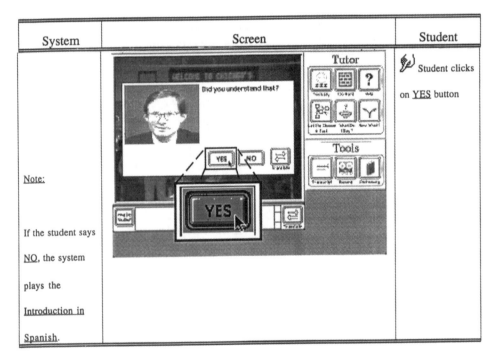		

Exhibit 1.7

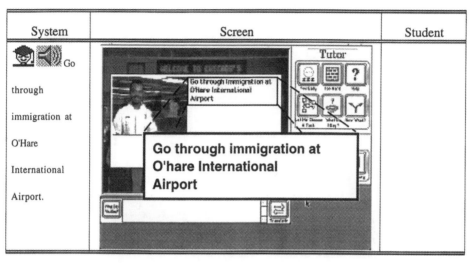

Exhibit 1.8

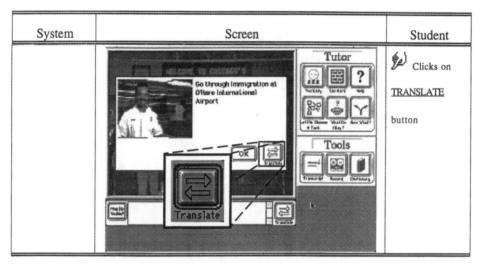

Exhibit 1.9

these states. When interacting with simulated people, the student can either use the HUH? button to express lack of understanding, like frowning, or the BYE button, which indicates that, as far as the student is concerned, he or she is done with the task. Other buttons allow the student to communicate cognitive (e.g., Now What?) or affective states (e.g., Too Easy → I'm bored).

Although most interactions are language-based, some are best represented by actions, such as handing over a passport. In Dustin, whenever

System	Screen	Student

Exhibit 1.10

System	Screen	Student

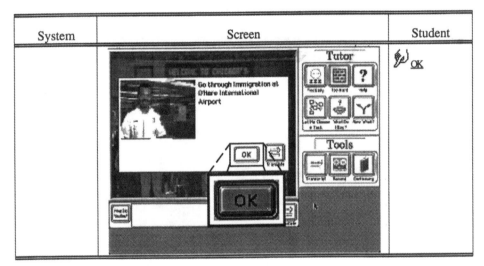

Exhibit 1.11

the student has to pay for something or transfer an item he or she has the option of physically dragging the object to the simulated agent (Exhibit 1.13, p. 52), instead of just saying "Here it is." This type of tool is effective in creating TPR systems, in which students react to input by performing actions. Object manipulation in computer-based environments can cover a wide range of interactions, and can serve as a metaphor for a wide number of tasks. Simulations of this kind might prove useful for beginners who are developing comprehension skills in a TPR style of apprenticeship.

System	Screen	Student

Exhibit 1.12

(3) *People in the simulated environment must react authentically to student utterances.*

The student was being uncooperative in this task (Exhibit 1.14, p. 53), and the simulated agent reacted as he would in real life (Exhibit 1.15, p. 54). First, the student tried to give the agent money, then refused to give him the passport, and later persisted in refusing. Immigration agents are always polite and usually refer problem passengers to their supervisors, but, like any human being, they react emotionally to annoying questions, and become impatient if the conversation is not progressing satisfactorily. Dustin captures such reactions and uses them accordingly in the simulated interactions.

One reason this is important is that, when interacting with others, people often engage in nonstandard behavior as a way to determine what is acceptable and what is not. During one of our test sessions with 25 foreign employees, misbehaving was common among people using the simulation. They refused to do things, tried to pick up women in the simulation and often tried to push people to their limits. One reason they do this is that they want to test the limits of the system. Another more interesting reason is that simply knowing what is right is not enough. People like to test the limits of acceptable conduct as a way to develop adequate models of how they should interact. Simulations have to account for this type of behavior.

(11) *Help student perform social transactions.*

The student's uncooperativeness is getting her into trouble. The tutor, one of the most important resources available to the student, helps her refocus on the task at hand (Exhibit 1.16, p. 54). The tutor will reappear a number of times playing different roles. In this case, it is simply guiding

System	Screen	Student
Note: Another tool: the text for the sound just heard appears. Translation is also available. Tools are discussed later.	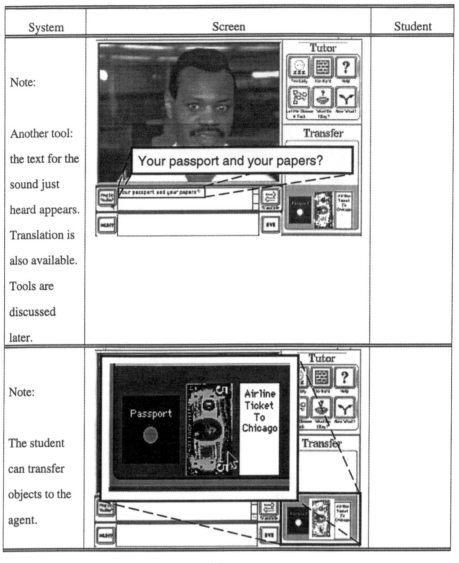	
Note: The student can transfer objects to the agent.		

Exhibit 1.13

the student so she accomplishes the task she was given (i.e., go through immigration; Exhibit 1.17, p. 55).

(14) *Provide means for the student to interact with the tutor.*

The student interacts with the tutor to ask for help (Exhibit 1.18, p. 55). This button, What Do I Say?, allows the student to communicate a state that would otherwise have to be inferred from the actions of the student—an inference that is not always feasible. Other buttons serve similar purposes (see Fig. 1.9, p. 56):

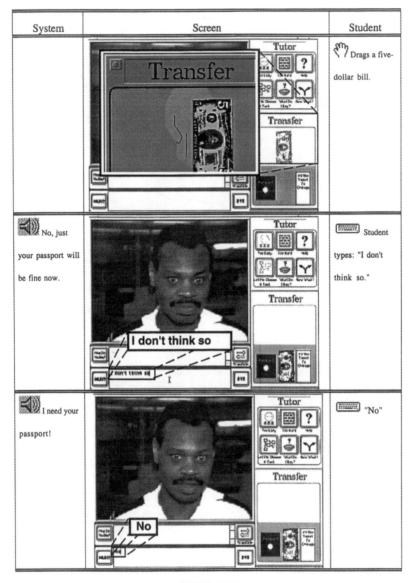

System	Screen	Student
	Tutor — Transfer	Drags a five-dollar bill.
🔊 No, just your passport will be fine now.	Tutor — Transfer — I don't think so	⌨ Student types: "I don't think so."
🔊 I need your passport!	Tutor — Transfer — No	⌨ "No"

Exhibit 1.14

1. *Too Easy/Too Hard*: The system selects the next task, depending on
   the circumstances under which the student presses these buttons.
   It may be a simpler task, watching an example of the current task,
   a hint, or passing control over to the student.
2. *What Do I Say?*: The tutor suggests things to say. Tutor suggestions
   may include inappropriate utterances.

System	Screen	Student

Exhibit 1.15

System	Screen	Student

Exhibit 1.16

3. *Now What?*: Instead of telling the student how to achieve a goal, it explains to the student what is expected of him or her. It serves as a reminder of what the current task is.

(16) *Use natural language interface (assist/facilitate spelling).*

In Dustin, the major means of interacting with simulated agents is through typed input in natural language—the student types in the lower

System	Screen	Student
I need your passport.		Drags the passport.

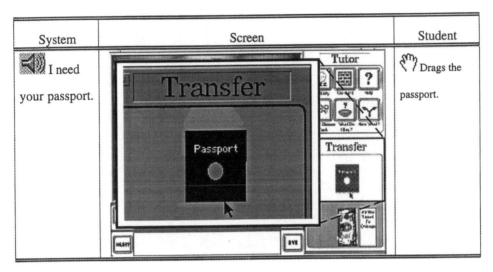

Exhibit 1.17

System	Screen	Student
What is the purpose of your visit today?		What do I say?

Exhibit 1.18

box on the screen (Exhibit 1.19, p. 56). The input is checked for spelling (a spellchecker offers alternatives for misspelled words) and then processed by the simulation mechanism. This mechanism determines how the agent will respond. Using natural language forces the student to recall, instead of simply recognizing, the knowledge needed to perform a social transaction (see Exhibits 1.20, p. 57, and 1.21, p. 58). The use of typed English was possible in Dustin because employees who are coming to the

FIG. 1.9. Tutor buttons in Dustin.

System	Screen	Student
	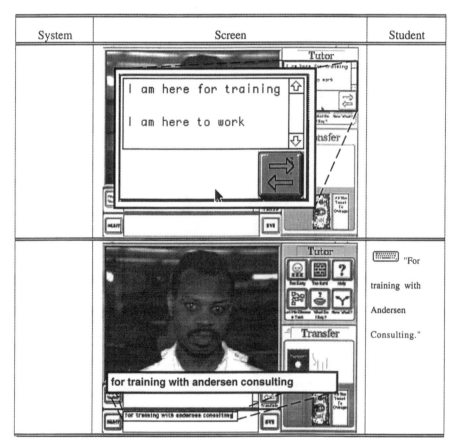	

Exhibit 1.19

System	Screen	Student
🔊 Exactly how long will you be in the United States?	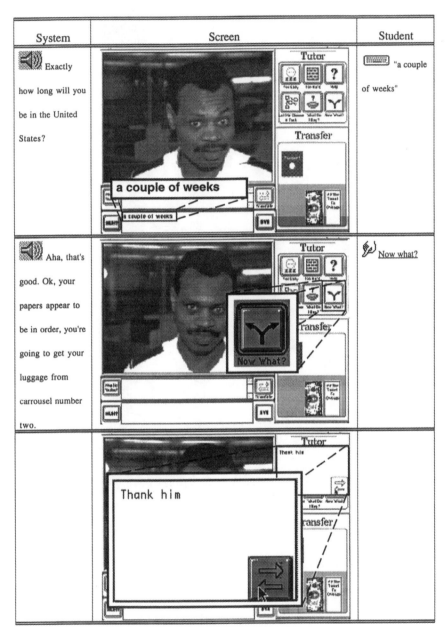 a couple of weeks	⌨ "a couple of weeks"
🔊 Aha, that's good. Ok, your papers appear to be in order, you're going to get your luggage from carousel number two.		Now what?
	Thank him	

Exhibit 1.20

System	Screen	Student
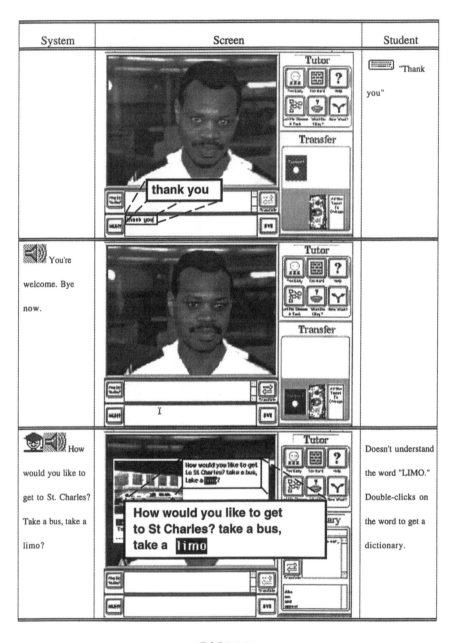		"Thank you"
You're welcome. Bye now.		
How would you like to get to St. Charles? Take a bus, take a limo?		Doesn't understand the word "LIMO." Double-clicks on the word to get a dictionary.

Exhibit 1.21

training in St. Charles have had training in English as a second language. They all know how to write in English.

(9) *Provide tools for addressing communication problems (e.g., dictionary, transcript of conversations, etc.).*

Many of the resources available in real life can be easily implemented in computer-based systems (see Fig. 1.10). In Exhibit 1.22, the student does not understand a word, and decides to look it up; simply double-clicking on the word calls up the dictionary entry for that word. When sound is available, the student can listen to how a word is pronounced.

FIG. 1.10. Dustin tools.

System	Screen	Student
Note: Dictionary allows Translation & Sound playing.(Say).	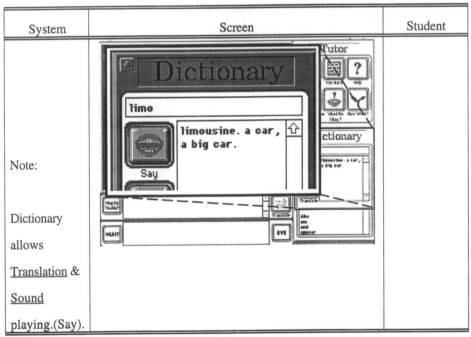	

Exhibit 1.22

Two other tools appeared earlier: subtitles and translations. When interacting with the tutor, the student can request translations; when interacting with simulated agents, the student can request subtitles for utterances heard and also translations for those utterances. In Fig. 1.11, the button "What Did You Say?" displays the utterance in text form, and "Translate" translates it into the source language.

(10) *Provide tools for analysis and reflection (e.g., recorder).*

A recorder can be used to record and compare the user's pronunciation with that of the native speakers in the simulation. While watching an example, the student can record his own voice and then replay the line in the example for comparison.

(5) *Goals must be meaningful to the student. Language is a means to achieve the goal, not the goal itself.*

The system always tells the student to perform tasks that will be relevant to the student's needs in real life. Here (Exhibit 1.23, p. 61), the student has to find a way of getting to St. Charles. All the tasks the student pursues in the simulation depend on language and occur in the student's real life.

(6) *Engage in interactions*
    If fail, then show an example
     Try again
     If fail, break the task down into smaller parts
    If succeed, move on

The student may observe someone else performing a task. If the student cannot perform a social transaction, Dustin shows her an example of someone else performing the same transaction, which is what happened here (Exhibits 1.24, p. 62, 1.25, p. 63, and 1.26, p. 64). The student watches Maria trying to get a bus to go to St. Charles. He or she can pause, go back, repeat, and skip lines in the dialogue. Once she is done watching the example, the simulation returns the student to the simulation (see Exhibits 1.27, p. 64, 1.28, p. 65, 1.29, p. 66, and 1.30, p. 67).

(7) *Let the student have control over what to do in the simulated environment.*

If the student is not satisfied with what the system is telling her to do, he or she can choose a task (Exhibit 1.31, p. 68). He or she can jump to any scenario and either watch someone else or do the task him or herself.

FIG. 1.11. Dialogue box.

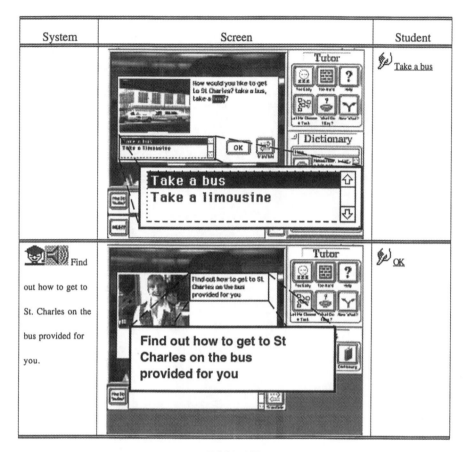

Exhibit 1.23

This is an important feature, as discussed earlier, because it allows students to address their own interests. The task selector in Dustin is organized by physical location. Once the student chooses a location, the tutor gives choices for tasks to perform in that particular scenario (Exhibit 1.32, p. 69).

(13) *Provide constructive feedback.*

The student did not exactly do something wrong in Exhibit 1.33 (p. 70), but people respond better if we greet them first. The tutor provides this information in order to sensitize the student to the fact that she skipped an important part of the social protocol. Once the student does that, the receptionist is noticeably more friendly (Exhibit 1.34, p. 70). Not conforming to social protocols may lead to uncomfortable interactions in real life. When the student forgets to greet someone, or uses language that comes across as rude, the tutor intervenes with some explanation of the correct thing to say in such circumstances.

System	Screen	Student
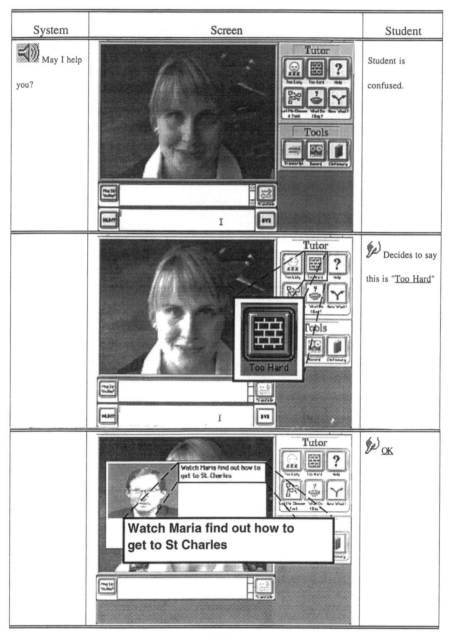 May I help you?		Student is confused.
		Decides to say this is "Too Hard"
		OK

Exhibit 1.24

System	Screen	Student
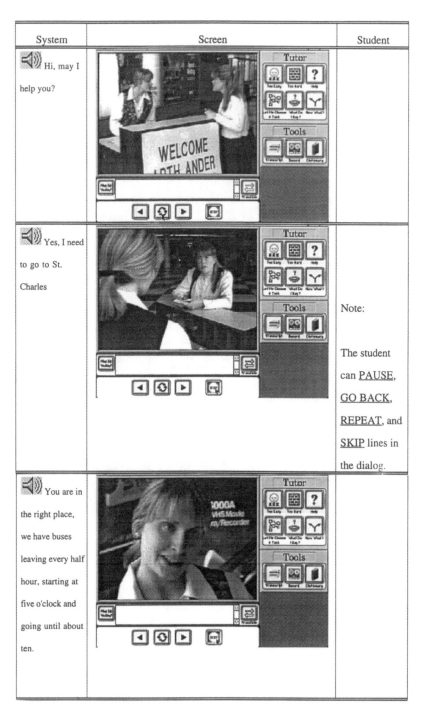 Hi, may I help you?		
Yes, I need to go to St. Charles		Note: The student can PAUSE, GO BACK, REPEAT, and SKIP lines in the dialog.
You are in the right place, we have buses leaving every half hour, starting at five o'clock and going until about ten.		

Exhibit 1.25

System	Screen	Student
• • •  Thank you very much.		

Exhibit 1.26

Exhibit 1.27

(12) *Do not correct grammar.*

Instead of criticizing what the student said, "I register," which would focus attention on structure, the tutor simply suggests a better way to express the desire to register. Instead of correcting grammar, the tutor suggests a correct way to convey the message (Exhibit 1.35, p. 71).

(8) *Do not keep scores. Do not evaluate. Do not keep records.*

The system does not keep scores, does not evaluate, and does not keep records. Students use Dustin because they are interested in performing well when they get to St. Charles. They need no extrinsic forces to motivate

System	Screen	Student
	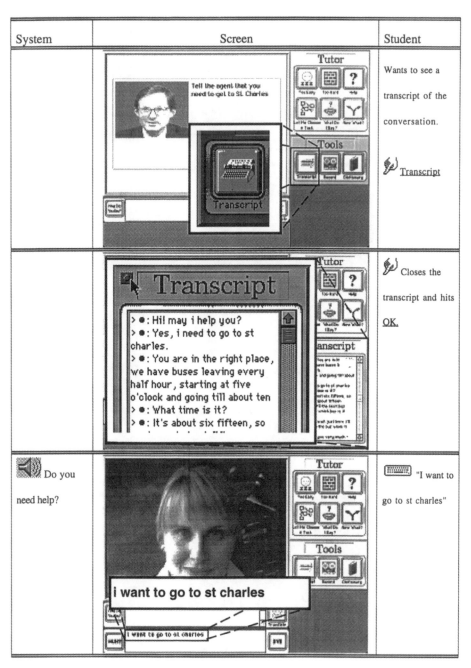 Tutor ... Tell the agent that you need to get to St Charles ... Tools ... Transcript	Wants to see a transcript of the conversation. Transcript
	Tutor ... **Transcript** > ●: Hi! may i help you? > ●: Yes, i need to go to st charles. > ●: You are in the right place, we have buses leaving every half hour, starting at five o'clock and going till about ten > ●: What time is it? > ●: It's about six fifteen, so	Closes the transcript and hits OK.
Do you need help?	Tutor ... Tools ... **i want to go to st charles**	"I want to go to st charles"

Exhibit 1.28

65

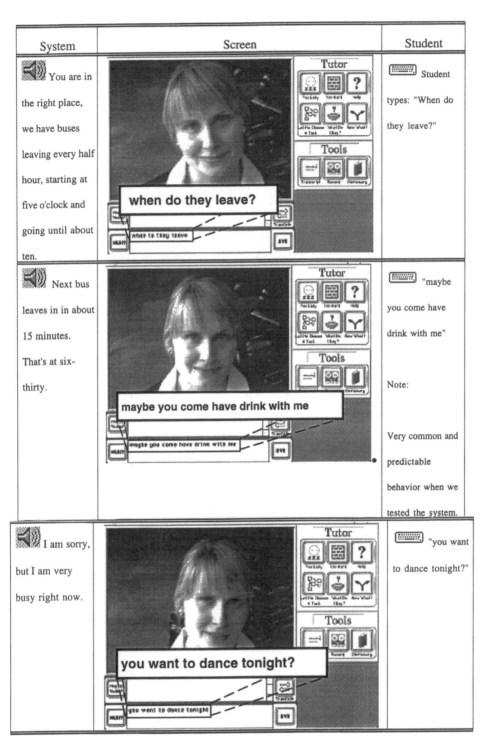

Exhibit 1.29

System	Screen	Student
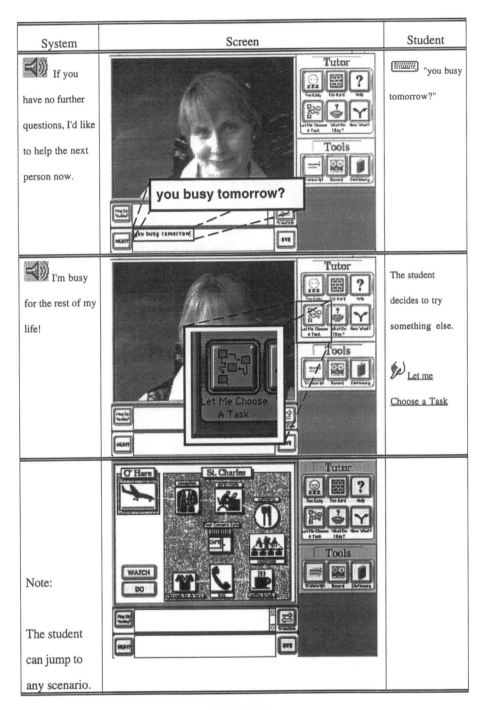 If you have no further questions, I'd like to help the next person now.		"you busy tomorrow?"
I'm busy for the rest of my life!		The student decides to try something else. Let me Choose a Task
Note: The student can jump to any scenario.		

Exhibit 1.30

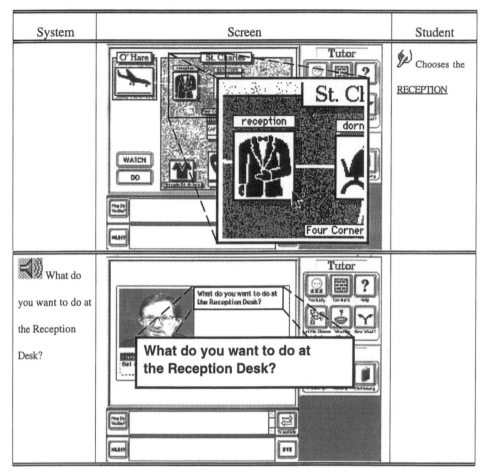

Exhibit 1.31

them to do well (Exhibit 1.36, p. 72). Exhibit 1.37 (p. 73) illustrates some of the tasks available for the scenarios shown in Fig. 1.12 (p. 73).

THE RPSS ARCHITECTURE

What Exactly Is Dustin?

Dustin implements an interactionist view of language, focusing on communication and social transactions, in a naturalistic environment in which students learn a language by using it as a tool to perform social transactions. Dustin gives learners interactions with native speakers through simulated dialogues, letting students engage in interactions that are al-

System	Screen	Student
	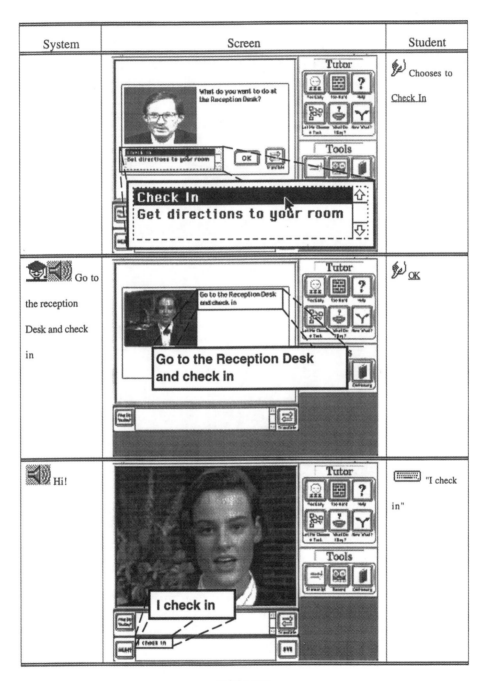	Chooses to Check In
Go to the reception Desk and check in		OK
Hi!		"I check in"

Exhibit 1.32

69

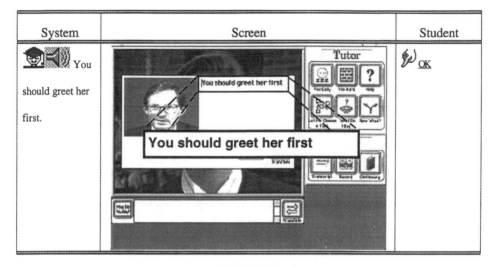

Exhibit 1.33

Exhibit 1.34

ways situated in the context of achieving some goal in the target culture. Dustin gives learners exposure to the target culture, letting them explore the same environment they will face in real life. Audio and video give students access to extralinguistic information, and the interface allows them to communicate through extralinguistic means (e.g., handing over a passport). Dustin gives learners individual instruction and feedback. The tutor intervenes whenever the student is having problems, and stands

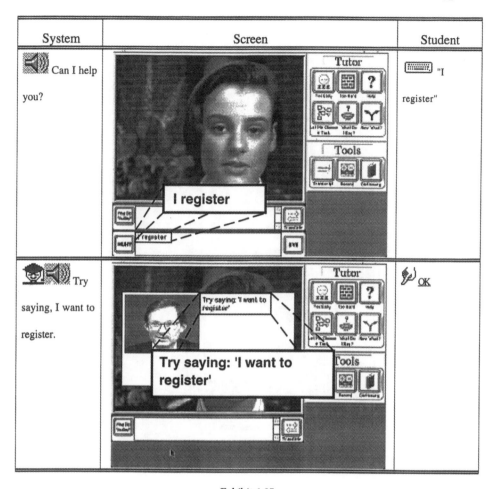

System	Screen	Student

Exhibit 1.35

by (i.e., tutor window) ready to provide him or her with information necessary to complete tasks. If the student is having problems, Dustin provides remediation, working according to the student's needs and interests.

Dustin also observes the principles outlined earlier, taking into account characteristics of the (a) situation, (b) student, (c) interactions, and (d) resources that contribute to learning. Table 1.3 lists these principles. Dustin combines (a) a tutor, (b) simulations, (c) examples, and (d) tools in a model of instruction that, instead of transmitting information to the student (which characterizes traditional instruction), helps students learn by doing. Dustin engages the student in interactions and helps him or her learn in the process of performing situated tasks. Instead of feeding

System	Screen	Student

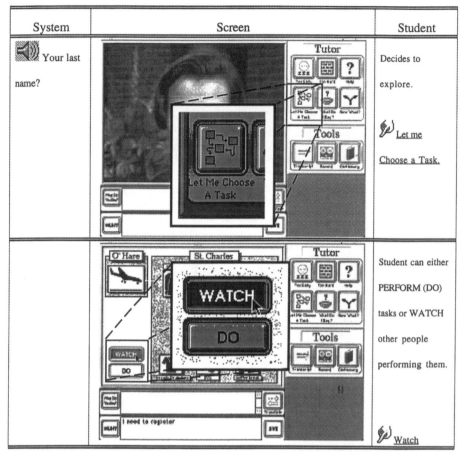

Exhibit 1.36

information, Dustin coaches the student through the process, establishing an apprenticeship relationship with the student (Brown, Collins, & Duguid, 1989; Collins, 1988; Collins, Brown, & Newman, 1989). The important implication of this apprenticeship model is that the function of teaching ceases to be one of transferring knowledge. Rather, it engages the student in situated tasks while providing the support and modeling necessary to promote experiential learning.

Language learning is a prime example of skills that, in real life, we learn through apprenticeship. This apprenticeship model has given way to the traditional schooling model, not because of ineffectiveness, but because of its resource-intensiveness. Apprenticeship requires individualized attention and access to the target environment, and these resources are in short supply. Fortunately, as technology brings the resources necessary

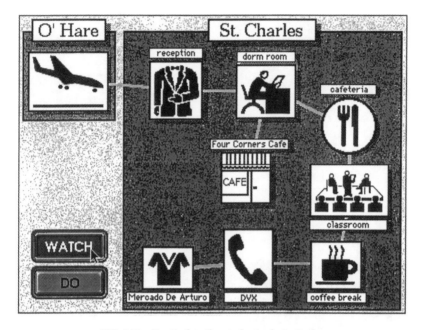

FIG. 1.12. Dustin lets the student select a task.

Going through Immigration
at O'hare

Getting a bus to go
to St. Charles

Exhibit 1.37 *(Continued)*

Requesting a Limo to
go to St. Charles

Checking In at St. Charles

Asking for directions

Meeting a Roommate

Inviting the roommate to eat

Getting breakfast at the
cafeteria

Exhibit 1.37 *(Continued)*

Getting a sandwich at

Four Corners Cafe

Listening to Instructions

in the CAPS class

Helping a friend who

arrived late for class

Meeting people

Leaving a DVX message

Buying a T-shirt at

Mercado de Arturo

Exhibit 1.37

to language learning, so does it bring those resources necessary to implement this more effectively through a resource-intensive model of instruction (Collins, 1988).

This section discusses Dustin's architecture (RPSS) in more detail. It starts by describing its components and its model of instruction and then discusses what is good and bad about Dustin, also comparing it to other systems. Finally, it suggests some future applications of Dustin-like systems.

Dustin's Components

The RPSS architecture has four major components: tutor, examples, simulation, and tools. The student is always either (a) receiving guidance from the tutor, (b) participating in a conversation, (c) watching other people, or (d) consulting some tool. Figure 1.13 depicts these major components and their functions, which are described in more detail next.

Tutor. Throughout our lives, other people help us acquire language. Our parents, teachers, colleagues, and peers are constantly coaching us. In Dustin, the tutor embodies this coach figure. The tutor assigns tasks and makes sure that the student follows norms of good communication. After giving assignments, the tutor guides the student, helping with hints and providing feedback.

The tutor came into existence as a by-product of the demands imposed by principles such as "Provide constructive feedback" and "Help the student perform social transactions," which called for a guiding figure. To understand the importance of a coach, we need to reiterate the importance

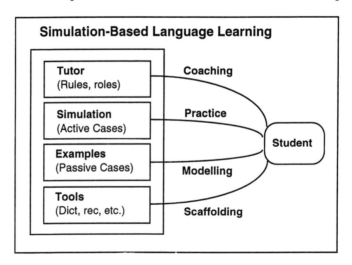

FIG. 1.13. Components of the RPSS architecture and their functions.

of goals. As discussed earlier, goals are one of the most important keys to situate knowledge because having a clear goal helps learners organize knowledge and understand feedback. Instead of relying on external sources to establish these goals, Dustin provides the goals to the student. It provides motivation for each task with clear goals, helping the student organize information by setting the conceptual context in which the task occurs.

Simulation. Simulations are at the core of Dustin's architecture; all other components support the student during interactions. The purpose of Dustin is to prepare learners to perform in real life; it does so by engaging students in interactions with those people they will encounter in real life. By interacting in the simulation, the student uses his or her knowledge and receives essential feedback to fine tune his or her skills. He or she becomes accustomed to the target environment and, because the tutor provides a clear goal for each setting, learns exactly what to do in each situation.

Examples. We need exposure to meaningful input to learn (Krashen, 1985; Schank, 1991b). In Dustin, the tutor guides the student to see relevant scenes, or the student roams around eavesdropping, so to speak, on other people's conversations. Through observation, learners develop a conceptual model of a task before executing it. The idea that people learn from examples, or modeling, is defended by both second language theorists (e.g., Krashen's input hypothesis) and artificial intelligence (AI) theorists (e.g., Schank's case based reasoning). In the AI view, cases are contextualized by goals and the circumstances in which they occur, tying back to the role of the tutor. All the examples in Dustin show people using language in the context of pursuing a goal, which is described in advance by the tutor. This way, the student indexes the information in the example by the goals that it helps to achieve—the context and the goal become indices for retrieving information.

Tools. Learners use dictionaries, recorders, and other tools to help them develop communication skills. Computers are particularly good for implementing memory aids, translations, guidebooks, and a variety of feedback tools. They empower students by complementing their knowledge, and computer-based simulations can accommodate a large number of these cognitive tools. Dustin implements a number of them, including a dictionary, transcripts, translations, and a recorder.

Dustin's Model of Instruction

Dustin's model of instruction—apprenticeship—resembles the way children learn with their parents. Parents serve as coaches (e.g., "go ask your aunt if you can have a cookie"), provide examples (e.g., "say, may I have a cookie?"), serve as test bed for interactions (e.g., "try saying it to me, let me see if you can"), and often assist children in interactions with others (e.g., "no, not *oo*kie, *coo*kie").

The apprentice receives personalized attention and engages in tasks that are always compatible with his level of competence. The expert helps at critical points and serves as a source of information. The typical process of learning in the apprenticeship model (Collins, 1988) involves observation, coaching, practice, and scaffolding (i.e., holding the learner's hand until he is ready to perform alone). In Dustin, the student acquires skills by working with a master (tutor → coaching) who provides the necessary guidance in performing tasks in a specific context (simulation → practice). When the apprentice needs information, the tutor exposes him to the necessary information (examples → modeling), and Dustin holds the apprentice's hand until he can do it on his own (tools → scaffolding).

This type of apprenticeship, originally used to teach physical skills, but adapted to teach cognitive skills, is resource-intensive and rarely cost-effective (Collins, 1988). Providing individual attention and practice to each apprentice requires resources that are rarely available, not unlike the current problem in language instruction. However, as in language instruction, technology allows us to go back to resource-intensive models of teaching (Collins, 1988; Collins, Brown, & Newman, 1989), enabling us to provide personalized attention and expose students to tasks at their level of competence.

Instead of transmitting information, the cognitive apprenticeship model (Collins, Brown, & Newman, 1989) has been used successfully by researchers and educators to teach reading (Palincsar & Brown, 1984), writing (Scardamalia & Bereiter, 1985), and math (Schoenfeld, 1983, 1985). A brief description of the characteristics of the cognitive apprenticeship model reveals the parallel between this model and the RPSS model. The most salient characteristics of apprenticeship are (a) situated learning, (b) modeling and explaining, (c) coaching, (d) reflection, (e) articulation, and (f) exploration (Collins, 1988). Situated learning means that learners acquire knowledge used in real tasks; Dustin engages the student in exactly those situations that he or she will face in real life. Modeling is providing examples, showing either a process or an expert performance; Dustin has at least one example for every task it tells students to perform, allowing students to observe a native speaker and integrate what happens with why it happens. Coaching is giving personal attention; Dustin's tutor helps address individual difficulties at critical times, guides students through social interactions, and provides feedback when appropriate. Reflection allows students to study what they did, compare to others, abstract from their knowledge, and compare their knowledge to abstractions; Dustin provides a recording tool, allowing students to compare their speech to that of others in the simulation. Articulation helps students make implicit knowledge explicit—making knowledge more available, and comparing structure and encouraging insight; Dustin's help here is limited; this limitation is discussed later in this chapter. Finally, exploration allows students to try out different things, helping them learn how to set achievable goals, form and test hypotheses, and make discoveries; Dustin lets students have control over the tasks they perform and observe.

The cognitive apprenticeship model is of interest in the context of RPSS systems because it provides a metaphor that integrates RPSS' components, functions, and ideas. Although some of the theories presented earlier explained parts of Dustin, this metaphor connects Dustin's components. The interactionist/naturalistic view explains the need for interactions in authentic situations (i.e., practice); Krashen's input hypothesis and case based reasoning explains the need for examples (i.e., modeling); work on intrinsic motivation shows the need for clearly defined goals and constructive feedback (i.e., coaching). The apprenticeship metaphor clarifies the role of the tutor as an expert guide who provides help and reveals the need for scaffolding (i.e., tools) to help students walk on their own. More important, it connects all these components and functions.

In AI terms, Dustin's way of teaching contrasts with methods that teach rules rather than cases. Much of language instruction is based on structural teaching strategies that try to teach rules apart from the cases from which they derive and apart from the context in which they are used. The context from which a rule derives is what indexes the rule; Dustin teaches these cases, not the rules, relying on inductive acquisition of grammar. Word games, syntactic structures, conjugation of verbs, and agreement are just a few of the labels under which decontextualized rules are organized and taught in classical language instruction. Structural strategies encourage the creation of a mapping between the source language, one's native language, and the target language—the language one is trying to learn. Dustin uses language as a tool for achieving goals in specific situations. Instead of encouraging the creation of a mapping function between two languages, it encourages the creation of a mapping function between a goal to be achieved in a certain context and the language that is necessary to achieve that goal.

What Is Good About Dustin?

A number of elements contribute to learning in the Dustin experience. The user is highly motivated to learn English to go about his or her life when he or she gets to St. Charles. Language is crucial, and the drive to learn and perform well is high. The goals the individual wants to achieve in St. Charles motivate his or her role playing in the simulation. He or she spends a period of intense immersion in the target environment, hearing, seeing, and interacting with people who use only English to communicate. The student is exposed to the context in which language is used. This includes physical, social, and task settings as they occur at O'Hare and in St. Charles. He or she participates actively, engaging in interactions that require the use of language. These interactions force the student to recognize words and recall and adapt knowledge to the situation. He or she receives help. Simulated native speakers and Dustin's tutor correct errors or suggest better ways of saying things, and the environment is fortuitous in that it provides referents that assist in communication. The way people react—their behavior—provides the learner with essential feedback to adjust behavior. The student tries to understand patterns of the language, and questions what words mean in different contexts; in other words, he or she engages in analysis and reflection. When communication breaks down, due to insufficient competence or performance variables, the learner uses extralinguistic means of communication (e.g., the HUH? button, dragging objects) that facilitate social interactions. When at a loss for words, he or she resorts to tools like dictionaries, recorders, and translations. The social context and interactions with others elicit emotions—affect—that influence learning. Finally, different people use different learning strategies because they learn in different ways.

Field Tests and Future Challenges.   Dustin helps. Twenty-five foreign trainees from Japan and Spain, who tested an early version of Dustin, thought that the program would have helped them improve their ability to interact with people in O'Hare and St. Charles, and that the exposure to the St. Charles environment prior to their coming to the United States would have put them more at ease in that environment. Exposing themselves to the people they eventually will meet in real life, listening and interacting with them in the simulated setting, generates a sense of familiarity with the place and the personnel in St. Charles. The informal data collected from these subjects show that Dustin helps students familiarize themselves with the target environment as well as the speech patterns of native Chicagoans. Trainees get used to the particular accent of those people working in St. Charles and O'Hare, and Dustin prepares trainees to face the impact of the first 24 hours in the St. Charles culture.

Some Problems With Dustin

Although the comments received so far have been enthusiastic, these preliminary data have also pointed out some problems not solved in Dustin, which are discussed next.

Situated Learning and Transfer. The implementation of Dustin described here is large enough to guarantee its scalability, which means that implementing a larger version would pose no technical problems. However, to compare and extrapolate the embedded knowledge to other situations, learners need a larger number of similar, but not identical, examples. Students benefit from exposure to variations on themes (e.g., different ways of greeting, different people greeting, people greeting in different situations), and Dustin has too limited a number of variations. Trainees reported that, although useful to prepare them to interact with people in St. Charles, Dustin was too limited to help them interact in other settings. Dustin needs more cases.

This is a problem that has been pointed out in apprenticeship (Collins, 1990). Students acquire knowledge in a particular context and have difficulties transferring the knowledge to other domains. To address this problem, besides being exposed to more cases, students may need help abstracting from the particular situation. Collins (1990) suggested that this can be done through articulation and reflection. *Articulation* involves an effort to integrate pieces of information gained from particular situations, thinking about how what one knows in one context relates to the knowledge needed in other situations. For example, following a scene in a Japanese restaurant, the tutor could ask, "Why do you think he is taking off his shoes?" The current version of Dustin does not encourage or demand this type of thinking from the student. *Reflection* involves looking back at what one did, trying to analyze one's performance or compare it to others. To help the student reflect, Dustin could ask the student questions like, "Why did he get upset? Did you miss something?" Here again, Dustin does not explore this type of reflection. It would not be hard to implement these features; in fact, the idea of adding cultural notes to explain such things, suggested by a number of users, would come as a perfect model after articulation and reflection questions.

Exploring Learning Strategies. Dustin does not explore learning strategies, special tricks that people use to learn a language (e.g., using visual imagery to understand new information, classifying words according to their meaning, associating phrases with body language). Technology offers a great potential for supporting learning strategies with tools that would not be available otherwise. For example, imagine someone who likes to stand in front of a mirror and observe himself as he imitates someone, associating speech and intonation with facial expression. To explore this strategy, we could provide tools for him to videotape himself, allowing him to see himself as he would in a mirror, and to play back and compare his performance with that of others. Dustin supports some learning strategies by allowing students to have control over the environment, letting them explore it according to individual preferences. However, Dustin does not provide any tool that directly explores any particular learning strategy.

Exploring the Social Context. I have not explored the social context in which Dustin is used. It is a mistake to think that how a system will be used in a larger social context is a problem that lies outside the scope of its design. In fact, how a system is used in a larger context may well be the best feature of a given system. Dustin was designed as a stand-alone system, making it less threatening than the typical real-life environment. But in doing so, I missed the opportunity to explore competition, cooperation, argumentation, and other social forces that promote learning. The potential to explore these social factors was obvious during sessions in which more than one user tested Dustin at the same time. They consistently engaged in discussions about the scenes, talking about how to handle simulated situations, generating hypotheses together, laughing, and encouraging each other to try out things. To properly use RPSS systems, these sociopsychological factors must be considered. Peer pressure and other social factors are extremely important in learning; so far, Dustin leaves out this significant element of the learning process.

I Want to Belong. Finally, Dustin may not be good for learning that depends heavily on affect. One instance of this dependence occurs when students want to learn a language in order to feel accepted in the community. Research shows that learners' attitude toward the target culture and language influences language acquisition. Dulay, Burt, and Krashen (1982) showed that the level of proficiency achieved is influenced by whether a learner simply wants to use language for utilitarian reasons (e.g., a Hispanic uses English to go shopping, but Spanish for social interactions), to integrate in the target society (i.e., participate in the life of the target culture), or to identify himself with the social group (i.e., belong to the target culture). The research shows that the desire to belong leads to higher proficiency. I believe that the RPSS architecture helps those with utilitarian motives. These people seek to develop repetitive, well-scripted interactive skills; in these situations, RPSS systems can simulate most of the interesting cases. However, there are limitations in using RPSS systems to promote integration and identification because these involve complex interactions that depend heavily on affect. Unlike real people, simulations cannot truly satisfy the learner's need for affection.

What Is RPSS Good For?

Dustin was designed to address a specific problem: to help foreign trainees of Andersen Consulting coming to St. Charles for the first time. The model of instruction that it incorporates, however, can be used in other domains. The interface may have to be changed to fit new domains, but the overall architecture, including simulations, models, tutor, and tools, stays the same. The following suggests some applications for RPSS systems. With superficial changes, RPSS can be used to promote experiential learning through apprenticeship in a variety of domains.

Teaching Other Languages. Dustin can teach other languages; nothing in it makes it applicable to teach only English. The small prototypes we built, using the same architecture, to teach Japanese (going to a Japanese restaurant), Spanish (going to a snack bar), and French (meeting people) posed no adaptation problems. Given its design, we had no difficulty developing a French version for Americans, and it would be perfectly possible to implement a simulation of a business negotiation in Japan to help Brazilians. Besides changing the content of the simulation, we only have to change button labels and translations to accommodate different source languages.

Other Apprenticeships. RPSS can teach auto mechanics. Imagine an auto mechanic undergoing apprenticeship with a master mechanic. A customer comes with a problem (e.g., "the engine is stalling when in idle"), and the master throws the student in a simulation: "fix it." Because computers allow object manipulation, it is possible to replicate the parts of an engine. Instead of interacting in English, the learner interacts by manipulating parts of the engine, disassembling, testing, and inspecting components. As in Dustin, the tutor intervenes by either asking information-loaded questions ("What makes an engine choke?") or giving hints ("Something seems to be missing in the carburetor").

This simply expands the TPR style of instruction. In TPR (Asher, 1977), students learn languages by responding physically to input. Here, students learn by interacting not only with simulated people, but also with simulated systems. Computer-based environments are particularly suited for this type of simulation, and using Dustin in this example would require only simple changes. Instead of typing "I want to register," for instance, moving objects would generate messages like "carburetor removed." The RPSS architecture may prove useful for training in which students learn by interacting with physical systems (e.g., computers, engines, circuits).

Communication Skills. RPSS develops communication skills. Learning a language is learning *what* to say and *when* to say it to achieve a *goal* in a specific *culture*. Language is a tool for communication and cannot be separated from the situations in which it is used. Learning a language is learning that a hostess in a Japanese restaurant will welcome you with the word *Irashaimasse* while bowing to you and that the proper response on your part is to nod ever so gently to acknowledge her courtesy. Language learning entails learning about goals and the communication skills necessary to achieve them in a specific culture. Notice, however, that learning how to be a bank teller is similar. Learning how to be a bank teller is learning a new way of interacting with people—it is learning a new language, a new culture, and the goals associated with the role. This means that the same RPSS architecture can teach people to perform roles in any situation that requires individuals to learn what to say and when to say it to achieve a goal in a specific culture. If we wanted to train bank tellers, we would simulate bank customers trying to close accounts, transfer money, and so on. Instead of the tools that help students deal with language problems (e.g., recorder), we would include tools that assist bank tellers (e.g., a calculator). The overall architecture would remain the same.

In summary, RPSS systems teach people how to perform well-defined roles (e.g., bank tellers, customer representatives, receptionists, auto mechanics, Immigration officers). Dustin-like social simulations improve performance by allowing learners to play roles in authentic simulations. For example, RPSS systems can train people in every role in the St. Charles environment (e.g., receptionists, cafeteria attendants, etc.). As long as the roles involve predictable interactions, RPSS provides an unusually engaging environment. Knowledge is situated and tasks are always directed at the learner's level of competence.

What Next? Ookie? No, Cookie. One of the aspects of Dustin that people enjoyed and that has great potential to be explored is object manipulation (e.g., dragging money and passport). In the Lithuanian version of Dustin, for example, before we were able to type in a response, we could understand and respond to input by manipulating objects or pushing buttons. The TPR method of instruction (Asher, 1977) encourages the development of comprehension before production—an approach that has shown to be very effective—and interacting through object manipulation may prove very useful for this style of teaching. Besides, relative to the amount of effort involved, this type of interaction usually conveys more information than typing in natural language.

Combined with Dustin's infinite patience, this TPR approach may enable us to implement effective language learning environments for beginners. Using object manipulation, or even using limited speech recognition (more like noise recognition), we can have a mother say to us, "Do you want the milk or the cookie?", to which we may respond, "oooooggggiiieee" or point to the cookie. She then responds, very supportively, "ok, here's your CCCoookkkiiieee." This type of interaction is essential for learners to develop good sound discrimination, which determines later degree of competence. Interactions through manipulations, with the help of an infinitely patient mother, may enable us to explore Krashen's notion of language acquisition through exposure to comprehensible input, while capturing some of the great things about mothers—the best language teaching systems around.

Conclusion

This section discussed the components, functions, and ideas that went into the design of Dustin. As described previously, Dustin borrowed from second language-acquisition research, educational research, psychology, cognitive research, and intelligent tutoring systems (see Fig. 1.14). The difficult part of integrating all these influences lies in translating them into concrete features. For example, it is never clear how a design principle such as "provide extralinguistic means of communication" translates into interface elements. Even with something as simple as "provide constructive feedback," it is not clear how and when we should do so. Should we interrupt? Should we wait until the student interacts with the tutor?

Solving these problems is a generate-and-test process. We cannot avoid the sometimes painful process of iterating through a number of versions, removing and putting back features, until they begin to converge into a

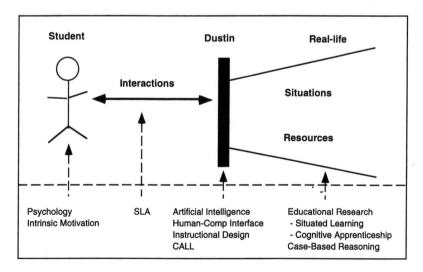

FIG. 1.14. Elements involved in language acquisition.

graspable version of the metaphor we had in mind. During the many Dustin iterations, we were always surprised by how unintuitive our intuitively obvious solutions were—a problem that is pervasive in software design, and that can be solved, most of the time, through an obsession with listening to users.

The most ubiquitous problem I faced as a developer was that of having to fight the tendency, my own and of other members of the Dustin project team, to be driven by technology rather than the problem at hand. It took a conscious effort to abide by the principles we had in mind and avoid including features that would not have contributed to language learning. For example, despite our knowledge about the ineffectiveness of structural approaches, we were constantly tempted to implement games to engage students in vocabulary building and grammar exercises. The technology was so conducive to this type of solutions that they attracted us like gravitational fields, tempting us to focus on language structure. Despite our views, we would come up with word association and multiple-choice exercises that were frontally opposed to our design philosophy (i.e., experiential learning through apprenticeship, with a heavy focus on interactive skills). It was easy to see why so many systems end up perpetuating these practices.

Implementing Dustin was the other major problem we faced. Organizing information in Dustin posed difficulties that taught us a number of lessons about knowledge representation (i.e., existing formalisms sent us in the wrong direction for a while), scaling up, contextualizing data, and reusing knowledge structures. The complexity of this problem warrants more detailed discussion, and its solution, a cognitive tool called MOPed, deserves a thorough description. This is the topic of the next section.

MOPed—AN AUTHORING TOOL

A Problem . . . A BIG Problem

Dustin responds to a large number of buttons, organizes 20 scenarios, uses a natural language interface, and maintains a complex network of tasks, including remediations and alternate paths. It organizes the 20 scenarios in three ways (i.e., by storyline, goals, locations); in each scenario, it organizes simulated dialogues, vignettes, and tutor interventions. Each simulated dialogue encodes goals, speech patterns, agent responses, tutor interventions, button handlers, contextualized help messages, and default behaviors. Processing these items involves inheriting behavior, handling defaults, sequencing actions, backtracking, and handling user-initiated events. Controlling processes and organizing, understanding, and manipulating knowledge structures in a system like Dustin are tasks whose complexity increase rapidly with size. Without adequate tools, implementing only a couple of Dustinlike scenarios may still be attainable, but scaling up is extraordinarily difficult.

In early implementations, Dustin encoded information in structures like the one shown in Fig. 1.15 (do not try to understand it; it is shown only to exemplify obtuse representations). This structure, which organized part of the reception scene, contains tutor messages, some help messages, and the steps in the simulated dialogue (i.e., the steps in a plan). It also contains links that interlace it with other structures. With 40 tasks to arrange and link, it was extremely hard to visualize where a task fit in the larger picture.

This cryptic syntax filled all levels of representation in Dustin. To run dialogues, Dustin parsed input into an elaborate internal representation and then used it to trigger rules like the ones shown in Fig. 1.16 (p. 88). Updating large sets of rules in a rule-based system can be confusing. In the case of Dustin's dialogues, even going from three simulated dialogues to just twice as many was a frustrating effort. Dustin encoded dialogues

```
(in-package "USER")

(SOF SCE-REC-CHECK-IN
:NAME SCE-REC-CHECK-IN
:DESC "Check in"
:REQUIRED-P T
:WATCH-TEXT "Watch John Harrison check in"
:WATCH-SCRIPT SCR-REC-CHECK-IN
:NEXT-TASK (TASK OPT SCE-REC-CHECK-IN)
:DO-TEXT "Go to the reception desk and check in"
:DO-AGENT A-KELLEY
:SUCC-TEXT "Good! Now, go to your room and meet Scott."
:SUCC-TASK (TASK DO SCE-ROO-MEET)
:FAIL-TEXT "Let's watch something simpler"
:FAIL-TASK (TASK ?COMPUTE ?NEXT)
:OPT-TEXT "Can you check in at the reception desk?"
:OPT-YES-TASK (TASK DO SCE-REC-CHECK-IN)
:OPT-NO-TASK (TASK ?COMPUTE ?NEXT)
:GOAL-TEXT "Try to check in"
:GOAL-OK-TEXT "You've already checked in. Leave"
:GOAL-TEST (DONE-P D-REC-CHECKIN)
:GOAL-SAY ""
:EXAMPLES NIL
:PLAN (SCE-REC-GREET SCE-REC-PURPOSE SCE-REC-NAME
   SCE-REC-PACKAGE SCE-REC-THANK)
:DIALOGS "d-rec-checkin")
```

FIG. 1.15. Reception scenario described in incomprehensible language.

```
;;; Rules for CASHIERS
;;; ------------------
;;; (clear-agent-rules a-cashier)

(rule "Hi, object please ---> ATRANS & Anything else?"
  a-cashier '(,c-inf-obj-sta ,c-req-obj)
  :prec t
  :exec ((tell ?other ?self c-que-obj-nee-mor)
   (atrans ?other ?self (second (agent-just-heard ?self)))))

(rule "Objects, please ---> ATRANS & Anything else?"
  a-cashier c-req-obj
  :prec t
  :exec ((tell ?other ?self c-que-obj-nee-mor)
   (atrans ?other ?self (agent-just-heard ?self))))

(rule "Objects ---> ATRANS & Anything else?"
  a-cashier c-obj
  :prec t
  :exec ((tell ?other ?self c-que-originate-nee-mor)
   (atrans ?other ?self (agent-just-heard ?self))))

(rule "How much is x? ---> $"
  a-cashier c-que-obj-pri
  :prec t
  :exec ((tell ?other ?self c-inf-obj-pri)))

(rule "Hi, how much is x? ---> $"
  a-cashier '(,c-inf-obj-sta ,c-que-obj-pri)
  :prec t
  :exec ((tell ?other ?self c-inf-obj-pri)))
```

FIG. 1.16. Rule-base for dialogues (absurd!).

in if–then rules that said: "If he asks you out and you have heard that before, then get upset and say that you are very busy," or "If you ask him how long he'll be in the country and he says more than one year, then negate interlocutor's goal," or "If you ask him how long he'll be in the country and he says less than a year, then confirm interlocutor's goal." The problem with this type of representation is that it gets very confusing very fast, and sometimes adding 20 new rules has unpredictable effects. I confronted a major problem: understanding the data.

Solution (MOPed)

The solution to the problem evolved from combining the (a) need for a uniform representation with (b) a simple visual artifact and (c) a model of memory organization borrowed from AI research. Although different processes in Dustin used different formalisms (e.g., rules for dialogues, framelike structures for tasks, and plans for sequences of utterances), all levels of knowledge representation shared characteristics. Common patterns appeared everywhere. For instance, students make mistakes when interacting with agents, and these mistakes are similar across levels. At the word level, students misspell words. They misplace, omit, transpose, and add unnecessary characters. Similarly, at the sentence level, they misconstruct sentences by misplacing, omitting, transposing, and adding unnecessary words. The same error pattern appears at the dialogue and scenario levels.

However, these common patterns were not restricted to errors. Two other recurring patterns involved inheritance of behavior and reuse of knowledge structures. Inheritance of behavior occurred in handling both dialogues and help messages. In a dialogue, if a rule was not available for, say, receptionists, Dustin would inherit rules from the set of rules for humans, following an ISA hierarchy. Similarly, when trying to help the student, Dustin would inherit help from higher levels of abstraction if help was not available at the current level, following another hierarchy. Although their representation schemes differed, both cases shared the same mechanism. However, the reuse of structures occurred everywhere. For example, the same speech pattern (e.g., ways of saying thanks: "thanks," "thank you," "I appreciate that") could appear in a number of dialogues. When the student says "thanks" after checking in, for example, the receptionist says, "You're welcome." However, if he says it before even greeting her, the tutor takes over, saying, "You should greet her first." These are two completely different outcomes based on the same speech pattern. In such cases, we should not have to re-create the same structure to handle each one, and Dustin frequently required re-using existing structures. These similarities across levels of representation seemed to suggest that a single formalism could represent all processes in Dustin.

We stumbled on a simple, yet powerful, artifact. Two members of the team working on Dustin went to St. Charles to collect data. They visited 25 locations and identified 45 tasks that students commonly face in St. Charles. When they returned from St. Charles, I asked them to explain to me how those 45 tasks occur in an employee's typical day. Their explanation sounded like this:

They can go to the cleaners early in the morning before breakfast, or they'll have to wait until the second break in the afternoon. They go to the cafeteria for breakfast, lunch, and dinner, but they can also go to the Four Corners Cafe, but the cafe is closed from 2 PM until 6 PM. . . .

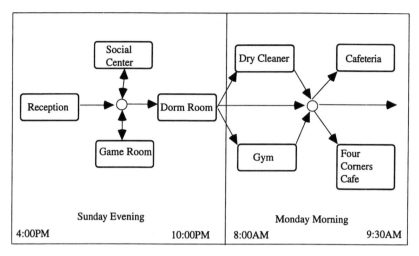

FIG. 1.17. St. Charles—A big sheet of paper with Post-its.

After listening for 10 minutes, I could not understand what they were saying anymore. At that point, we resorted to a simple artifact. I asked them to take a big sheet of paper, a stack of Post-its (i.e., sticky pieces of paper), and drawing material, and to create a visual representation of what they were trying to say. They came up with a comprehensible graph that looked like the one in Fig. 1.17. Using paper, Post-its, and pen made it easy to understand tasks in St. Charles. It seemed that the same idea could help us understand the rules in the dialogues, the interactions between the tasks, the tutor interventions, and so on.

MOP—Memory Organization Packet

A knowledge structure called MOP (Memory Organization Packet), suggested by Schank (1982) as a basic unit in a model of human memory, provided the building block for a powerful representation scheme and manipulation tool. Building on this basic unit, we developed a tool that made it possible to implement and use the visual aid described earlier at all levels of representation in Dustin and address the problems of inheritance and re-use of knowledge structures. Furthermore, it provided an excellent mechanism to contextualize information, encode predictions, and organize hierarchies.

To understand how MOPs served as a building block and to understand a few important ideas behind MOPs, we have to go back to the notion of scripts introduced by Schank and Abelson (1977). A *script* is a structure that describes an appropriate sequence of events in a particular context. For example, when we go to a restaurant, we follow a script: sit, read the menu, select, order, eat, pay, say thanks, and leave. Knowing the restaurant script helps us understand events such as the waitress giving us a bill and saying, "I'll take it when you're ready." In addition, it helps us know that, following that, we should pay, say thanks, and leave.

The next logical question following the work on scripts was: How are scripts stored in memory? Schank (1982) proposed an answer to this question in a model called *dynamic memory*. The dynamic memory model introduces structures (i.e., MOPs, TOPs, meta-MOPs) and processes that account for understanding, reminding, cross-contextual reminding, indexing of information, and learning. This section concentrates on MOPs.

To understand the main problem that MOPs address, we return to the saying-thanks example mentioned earlier. There are hundreds of situations in which we need to express gratitude. In the restaurant script, for example, we say thanks after we pay the bill when we are getting ready to leave. When we do so, where is the knowledge about ways of saying thanks coming from? Where is it stored? Assuming that we know a dozen or so ways to express gratitude (e.g., thanks, thank you, thanks a lot, thank you very much, I appreciate that, *muchas gracias*, etc.), would these be stored with the restaurant script? Is it the case that with each script we have stored in memory (e.g., dentist, registering for classes, going to the movies) we store a separate instance of the saying-thanks information? Most likely not. We can expect that what we know about saying thanks may apply in numerous other circumstances, and memory would be too redundant if it stored recurring information separately for each situation. Therefore, Schank (1982) proposed that these large scripts get broken down into smaller, sharable units (e.g., the restaurant script is broken up into distinct pieces—the ordering part, the eating part, the paying part, and the saying-thanks part). The most important corollary of this is: "There must be some memory structures available whose job is to connect other memory structures together." This is the key to MOP-based memory.

What Is MOPed?

Besides being a way to organize and maintain knowledge, MOPed is an artifact that helps developers understand complex networks of information. It accomplishes that by providing visual aids to improve readability and grouping information to help contextualize data. In an environment based on objects that process messages, MOPed organizes the messages that objects exchange. It is a message organizer that handles defaults, inheritance and backtracking, and that supports data sharing. Other tools (e.g., Smalltalk, CLOS) define objects and how they handle messages, whereas MOPed focuses on the messages they send to each other. By providing a visual representation of how messages interconnect, MOPed reifies interactions, making explicit the behavior of objects across time.

A MOP, the basic unit in the MOPed scheme, is like a sheet of paper. It holds symbols (or even other pieces of paper) or other MOPs, combining and organizing them according to certain conventions. One of these conventions is that MOPs have markers—Post-its—showing where they begin and end (i.e., ▣, ▣). When processing a MOP, the MOPed engine starts at the BEGIN Post-it and either follows arcs or searches from left to right and from top to bottom until it reaches an END Post-it. MOPs can also have entry, ▣, and exit, ▣, Post-its. The difference between these and BEGIN/END is that they affect the way MOPs appear inside other MOPs. For instance, a MOP with two exit points, ▣, one labeled *fail* and another labeled *succ*, looks like this, ▣⌈Fail⌉⌊Succ⌋, inside another MOP. Its behavior depends on what connects to its entry and exit points. BEGIN, END, IN, OUT, and the MOP Post-it, ▣, which includes another MOP inside a MOP and whose appearance varies with the number of entry and exit points, are the most idiosyncratic Post-its in MOPed.

All other Post-its simply contain messages for the objects that they symbolize: ▣ _ Video, ▣ simulated agent, ✔ flag setter, ◈ flag tester, ▣ randomizer, and ▣ tutor.

When creating a MOP, we simply choose Post-its from the palette shown in Fig. 1.18 and place them anywhere inside the MOP (see Fig.

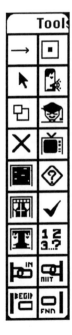

FIG. 1.18. Palette.

1.19). We can also copy and paste parts of other MOPs using existing templates to create new ones. To determine processing order, we either create arcs between Post-its or place them up or down in the MOP, keeping in mind that processing proceeds from left to right and from top to bottom.

One useful feature of MOPed is that it supports embedded MOPs, which helps group and contextualize information. Another important feature is that we can re-use MOPs without re-creating them. For example, suppose we create a MOP that encodes what the immigration agent says when he does not understand an input (see Fig. 1.20).

In the course of a conversation, whether the agent is asking for the passport, the extent of a person's stay, or telling her what to do next, if the student says something incomprehensible, like "Capoeria e' de matar," the agent will react the same way (by saying "Pardon me?"). Whenever

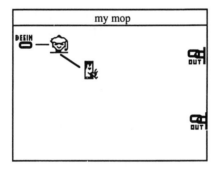

FIG. 1.19. Creating a MOP.

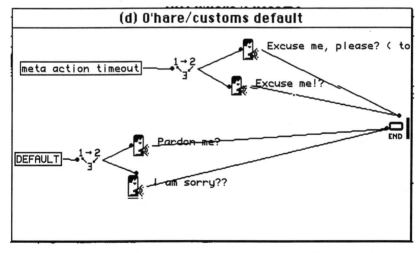

FIG. 1.20. A MOP that is reused in four other MOPs.

he does not understand an input, regardless of the context, his reaction is the same. Therefore, we do not have to re-create the structure that encodes this behavior (Fig. 1.20, p. 93) for each subdialogue. This also holds for speech patterns or other dialogues that reappear in other MOPs. Reiterating, MOPs are like big sheets with information; whenever we use a MOP inside another, we simply leave a Post-it saying, "here we use the Customs/Default MOP." At run time, the engine accesses the real thing, does the job, and releases it for further use. This allows Dustin to use the same structure without duplicating it.

This scheme organizes knowledge at all levels of Dustin. From scenarios down to speech patterns, including tutor messages, simulations, button handlers, help messages, and examples, everything is organized by MOPs. Button handling and help messages are contextualized through the embedding mechanism, which also supports another important feature. If the current MOP does not have a handler for a button, the system tries to inherit the handler from the MOP above it. More precisely, it goes up the run-time hierarchy in which that MOP appears until it finds a handler for that button press.

What Is MOPed Good For?

When creating a sizable system involving intricate interactions among agents, contextualized processing of buttons, help, and input, with information organized in complex sequences and hierarchies, we need tools to help understand the data. Scaling up without them is impossible. As a visualization tool, MOPed helps show how elements of the system interact. Even the simple if–then rules used in dialogues, which associate input patterns to output, are much easier to understand when expressed as a graph with meaningful icons and grouped into embedded units. Icons make it easy to determine who is doing what at any point in the system. They help show how and when a help message becomes active and when a button handler is used. By looking at how data are spatially organized inside a MOP, one can quickly determine the order in which the system parses input, what patterns it accepts, what keywords it looks for, and exactly in what order it does that. Furthermore, one can readily grasp how a particular subdialogue fits into a larger context, including the consequences of failing to perform that subdialogue. At the scenario level, it gives one immediate information on what scenarios are available and how scenes and tasks relate to each other. As a visualization tool, MOPed expands one's ability to grasp and understand complex knowledge structures.

As an organization tool, MOPed helps contextualize information. Consider the following situation. When the student types, "Hello, how are you?", the engine tries to find Post-its in the currently active MOP that parse that message. If successful, it triggers a response (e.g., the agent says, "Fine thanks"). This way of handling messages is analogous to using an if–then rule: if input is x, then do y. However, the advantage MOPed offers over common rule-based systems is the contextualization of rules. Humans use predictions to understand what they hear, and MOPs encode these predictions. When parsing an input, only those rules that are relevant in that context are active. They are based on the predictions encoded in the MOPs. This contextualization mechanism constrains search and allows the system to move up the hierarchy to find handlers for input that the current MOP cannot handle—a search upward that is also always contextualized by higher level structures. Because we do not have to consider all the rules in the system, the search space is drastically reduced. Moreover, because every event in Dustin is a message, search space is reduced across the board. Contextualization has helped encode authentic reactions; by constraining the search space, it has enabled realistic response times—simulated agents never take more than a second to respond to the student.

As a manipulation tool, MOPed simplifies the task of creating complex information networks by reusing existing structures and copying parts of existing templates. Once a lesson is developed, it can be copied and used elsewhere. In fact, all scenarios in Dustin derive from a single template. Furthermore, MOPed assists in handling these structures. A specialized editor lets the developer update structures and provides searching tools for finding relevant constructs. As opposed to the changes in earlier versions of Dustin, changes with MOPed become immediately active. Combined with the re-use and template capabilities, this dynamic updating saves considerable coding time. Additionally, the use of entry and exit points in MOPs makes it possible to tailor shared structures to particular situations, making it easier to create generic structures.

At its core, MOPed is very simple. It is an editor that allows users to create, link, and store big sheets of paper with Post-its. They may point to MOPs or contain messages. Post-its contain only three slots of information: content, type, and position. The type determines how the engine handles it and that can differ significantly. However, as far as the editor is concerned, there are only six types of Post-its: (a) LEAF, (b) IN, (c) OUT, (d) BEGIN, (e) END, and (f) META. Meta Post-its simply point to other MOPs. On top of these six basic types, the developer can define any number of Post-its. This is where MOPed's flexibility lies. The user can define not only his own Post-its, but also associate methods to handle them and icons to represent them. For each new Post-it, he can assign a symbol or an icon and simply map it onto one of the six basic types.

MOPed needs improvements. To be a complete authoring environment, it must integrate tools that help developers build interfaces and object behaviors. As a knowledge manager, it can improve the way it handles data. The current implementation loads all data in memory, making changes during a session immediately activated. However, at the end of a session, changes have to be saved so that they can be reloaded in the next session. Storing data on disc makes this step unnecessary. As a knowledge manipulation tool, the editor needs to be extended to help define classes of objects and their behaviors and maybe include some predefined methods. Finally, as a processing mechanism, the MOPed engine needs standard processes, automatically incorporating the common processes identified as more simulations are developed.

CONCLUSION

One of Dustin's important contributions is that it addresses those problems afflicting classroom language instruction. Students need interactions with native speakers, exposure to the target culture, and individual attention. Dustin incorporates all of these elements in its simulation-based learning architecture. But Dustin also brings a new degree of realism to computer-based instruction, introducing a new class of simulations. The centerpiece of Dustin's architecture is a combination of visual and aural information with an interface design that creates realistic imitations of real-life interactions. These simulated interactions convey linguistic, extralinguistic, and contextual information; engage students; and bring into play social factors that are important in learning. By introducing this new generation of simulations, Dustin takes us a step closer to bringing real-life experiential learning to computer-based environments.

In addition, whereas Dustin contributes a design, MOPed helps build it. MOPed provides the blueprint and building blocks for creating Dustin-like, simulation-based learning environments.

Dustin gives students access to tools and experiences, coupled with a degree of control and safety that are not available in real life. At the press of a button, the student can eavesdrop on other people's conversations, ask for a transcript of any utterance, get translations for sentences, get a tool to record and play back utterances, or jump into another conversation. By clicking on a word, he or she can bring up a dictionary that pronounces, explains, and translates the word. Also at his or her fingertips is a cooperative tutor, ready to give hints and guidance whenever necessary and intervene with constructive comments when something is done wrong. All these resources and experiences come at no threat and are completely under the student's control. He or she can explore them according to his or her own needs, determining the amount of help that he or she receives and the kinds of experiences that he or she has, and he or she can address particular interests at his or her own pace. Overall, Dustin is an environment rich with information, experiences, and tools to promote language acquisition.

The central element of this rich environment is the simulation of interactions. To promote learning, interactions must be authentic, and their verisimilitude determines their effectiveness. Simulations must look and feel realistic enough that students suspend disbelief and engage in experiences that lead to learning. To make simulations seem realistic, Dustin combines multi-media technology with a number of interface solutions that incorporate essential elements of ·discourse (Clark & Schaefer, 1989). Discourse involves verbal exchanges, extralinguistic means of communication, and a common ground composed of objects, concepts, and goals, which constitute integral parts of discourse. Dustin incorporates these elements by using a natural language interface (i.e., in lieu of verbal communication), conceptual feedback buttons through which users convey extralinguistic information (e.g., Huh?, Bye), and a common set of objects that the user can manipulate (e.g., money, passport). In addition, the conceptual ground, including the goals of the interlocutors, is always carefully defined by the tutor.

Information captured by audio and video contributes to Dustin's realism. Simulated agents look, talk, and behave like real people and even react emotionally to annoying behavior. They are always in the physical context in which they operate in real life. The end result is a simulated interaction that feels real; Dustin creates the illusion that we are interacting with a real person. Interacting with others is an important part of language learning because we learn by using language in meaningful interactions and interacting with others brings into play social factors that strongly influence learning.

As a learning environment, Dustin introduces a number of innovations. Interactive simulations using natural language and object manipulation, coaching through individual instruction and feedback and supporting tools combine to create an apprenticeship environment in which students learn experientially. Dustin merges a high degree of interactivity with visual and aural information in a new class of language learning environments. Most important, Dustin captures the realism essential to motivate and promote experiential learning, introducing a new look and feel to computer-assisted instruction.

To be useful to others, learning architectures must be accompanied by a blueprint, building blocks, and tools with which to build them. Dustin's architecture includes complex simulations and an intricate network of structures that is difficult to maintain without adequate tools. MOPed, the authoring tool, provides the mechanisms, templates, and knowledge manipulation tools to help implement Dustinlike systems. The templates already implemented in Dustin serve as building blocks to create the next versions of simulation-based learning environments, and the existing dialogues help developers think about how to capture behaviors in future implementations. Dustin shows what we can do with realistic simulations, and MOPed shows exactly how to do it.

Most AI systems work on just a few examples (McDermott, 1981; Schank, 1991b). The reason, described earlier, is that the systems are complex and their complexity increases geometrically relative to size. They are difficult to maintain, and this difficulty generally means that, above a certain size, usually two or three examples, we can no longer understand what is going on inside the systems. The interdependencies among the underlying knowledge structures become intractable. One unfortunate consequence of this problem is that AI systems are often incomprehensible to others, sometimes even to the developer, and researchers cannot build on each other's work (McDermott, 1981).

However, AI scientists should be accountable for their computer-based experiments in the same way that psychologists and physicists are accountable for theirs. These researchers have to document their experiments in such a way that results can be replicated, allowing others to test and build on their knowledge. Similarly, if we are to build on AI's mistakes and findings, we need a clear definition of what computer-based experiments do and how they do it. The burden lies on the developer who should always help others understand and manipulate what they invent. In AI, McDermott (1981) pointed out, researchers get away with building theories on experiments that they did not really run—"Only a preliminary version of the program was actually implemented." They pontificate without even running the experiment and, in those rare cases in which they indeed implement the experiment, usually build such cryptic systems that we end up having to take their word for it.

Truth maintenance systems, networks of frames, and temporal reasoning involve complex knowledge networks that become hard to understand and maintain as they increase in size. Our inability to scale them up says something about the limits of our comprehension, showing exactly where humans need help. It clearly shows the threshold beyond which humans cannot grasp the complexity of intricate networks of information. For example, if expert-systems researchers had thought of maintainability from Day 1, they would have discovered the need to help users contextualize, re-use, visualize, and prioritize rules. The resulting effort would have made them either give up on the idea of using production systems or come up with some clever knowledge organization schemes. Either way, they would have saved AI a lot of bad press.

What happens instead is that AI researchers suffer clarity phobia, fearing that to expose the guts of their programs is to show that they do not do AI at all. Instead of encouraging simplicity, this fear reinforces the creation of cryptic representations, which perpetuate the obscurity of AI programs. But to make progress, researchers must understand each other's work. Consequently, if the systems we build are so complex that we would not understand them without tools, then building tools to help others and ourselves understand and manipulate them becomes an important part of developing powerful systems.

MOPed clarifies what Dustin does and how it does it. After a 10-minute demo of the tool, anyone can see exactly how Dustin works—the patterns of speech that it understands, those that it does not, when it cheats, how it cheats, how much processing it does with a button press, how things are hard-coded, and how they are not. Instead of building a complex, incomprehensible system for which I could claim AI feats, we developed a tool that completely exposes Dustin, empowering users to grasp and maintain the complex information embedded in simulation-based learning environments.

MOPed is certainly not the solution to all problems. However, it stands for an important function in AI: to extend intelligence. We have built a complex, simulation-based learning environment, Dustin; unavoidably, Dustin involves complex networks of information—networks so complex that we cannot understand them with the naked eye. MOPed explores the computer's potential for creating cognitive extensions and empowers us to understand more than we normally can.

REFERENCES

Asher, J. (1977). *Learning another language through actions: The complete teacher's guide book* (2nd ed.). Los Gatos, CA: Sky Oaks Productions.

Bebee, L. M. (1988). *Issues in second language acquisition.* New York: Newbury.

Braun, T. E. D., & Mulford, G. W. (1987). Computer-based instruction as a supplement to a modern French curriculum. In *New developments in computer-assisted language learning* (pp. 137–154). New York: Nichols.

Brown, J. S., Collins, A., & Duguid, P. (1989). Situated cognition and the culture of learning. *Educational Researcher, 18*(1), 32–42.

Bruner, J. (1962). *On knowing: Essays for the left hand.* Cambridge, MA: Harvard University Press.

Chomsky, N. (1959). A review of B. F. Skinner's Verbal behavior. *Language, 35*(1), 26–58.

Chomsky, N. (1966). Linguistic theory. In J. P. B. Allen & P. Van Buren (Eds.), *Chomsky: Selected readings* (pp. 152–159). London: Oxford University Press.

Clark, H. H., & Schaefer, E. F. (1989). Contributing to discourse. *Cognitive Science, 13*, 259–294.

Coleman, C. A. (1929). *The teaching of modern foreign languages in the United States.* New York: Macmillan.

Collins, A. (1988). *Cognitive apprenticeship and instructional technology* (Report No. 6899). Cambridge, MA: BBN Laboratories.

Collins, A. (1990). *Generalizing from situated knowledge to robust understanding.* Unpublished manuscript.

Collins, A., & Brown, J. S. (1988). The computer as a tool for learning through reflection. In H. Mandl & A. Lesgold (Eds.), *Learning issues for intelligent tutoring systems* (pp. 1–18). New York: Springer-Verlag.

Collins, A., Brown, J. S., & Newman, S. E. (1989). Cognitive apprenticeship: Teaching the crafts of reading, writing, and mathematics. In L. B. Resnick (Ed.), *Knowing, learning, and instruction: Essays in honor of Robert Glaser* (pp. 453–494). Hillsdale, NJ: Lawrence Erlbaum Associates.

Doughty, C. (1991). Theoretical motivations for IVD software research and development. *CALICO Monograph Series, 2,* 1–15.

Dulay, H., Burt, M., & Krashen, S. (1982). *Language two.* New York: Oxford University Press.

Finocchiaro, M., & Brumfit, C. (1983). *The functional-notional approach.* New York: Oxford University Press.

Gattegno, C. (1972). *Teaching foreign languages in schools: The Silent Way* (2nd ed.). New York: Educational Solutions.

Gattegno, C. (1976). *The common sense of teaching foreign languages.* New York: Educational Solutions.

Harley, B. (Ed.). (1990). *The development of second language proficiency.* Cambridge, England: Cambridge University Press.

Klier, B. (1987). A microcomputer game in French culture and civilization. In *New developments in computer-assisted language learning* (pp. 69–77). New York: Nichols.

Krashen, S. D. (1982). *Principles and practice in second-language acquisition.* Oxford: Pergamon.

Krashen, S. D. (1985). *The input hypothesis: Issues and implications.* London: Longman.

Krashen, S. D., & Terrell, T. D. (1983). *The natural approach: Language acquisition in the classroom.* Oxford: Pergamon.

Lampe, D. R. (1988). Athena MUSE: Hypermedia in action. *The MIT Report,* pp. 4–12.

Lepper, M. R., & Chabay, R. W. (1985, April). *Intrinsic motivation and instruction: Conflicting views on the role of motivational processes in computer-based education.* Invited address to the biennial meeting of the Society for Research in Child Development, Toronto.

Lepper, M. R., & Greene, D. (Eds.). (1978). *The hidden costs of reward.* Hillsdale, NJ: Lawrence Erlbaum Associates.

Maddison, P., & Maddison, A. (1987). The advantages of using microcomputers in language teaching. In *New developments in computer-assisted language learning* (pp. 20–31). New York: Nichols.

Malone, T. W. (1981). Toward a theory of intrinsically motivating instruction. *Cognitive Science, 4,* 333–369.

McDermott, D. (1981). Artificial intelligence meets natural stupidity. In J. Haugeland (Ed.), *Mind design.* Cambridge, MA: MIT Press.

McLaughlin, B. (1978). The monitor model: Some methodological considerations. *Language Learning, 28*(2), 309–332.

McLaughlin, B. (1987). *Theories of second-language learning.* London: E. Arnold.

MIT. (1990). *Project Athena Visual Computing Group.* (Available from Ben Davis, MIT)

Morgenstern, D. (1986). Simulation, interactive fiction and language learning: Aspects of the MIT Project. *Bulletin of the CAAL,* pp. 23–83.

Murray, J. H. (1987). Humanists in an institute of technology: How foreign languages are reshaping workstation computing at MIT. *Academic Computing,* pp. 34–38.

Murray, J. H. (1990). *The Athena Language Learning Project.* (Available from Janet H. Murray, MIT, Department of Humanities, Athena Language Learning Project)

Palincsar, A. S., & Brown, A. L. (1984). Reciprocal teaching of comprehension-fostering and monitoring activities. *Cognition and Instruction, 1,* 117–175.

Papert, S. (1976). *Mindstorms: Children, computers, and powerful ideas.* New York: Basic Books.

Papert, S. (1987). Microworlds: Transforming education. In T. W. Lawler & Y. Masoud (Eds.), *Artificial intelligence and education* (Vol. 1). Norwood, NJ: Ablex.

Richards, J. C. (1990). *The language learning matrix.* Cambridge, England: Cambridge University Press.

Richards, J. C., & Rodgers, T. S. (1986). *Approaches and methods in language teaching: A description and analysis.* Cambridge, England: Cambridge University Press.

Rivers, W. M. (1987a). Interaction as the key to teaching language for communication. In W. M. Rivers (Ed.), *Interactive language teaching.* Cambridge, England: Cambridge University Press.

Rivers, W. M. (1987b). Preface. In W. M. Rivers (Ed.), *Interactive language teaching.* Cambridge, England: Cambridge University Press.

Scardamalia, M., & Bereiter, C. (1985). Fostering the development of self-regulation in children's knowledge processing. In S. F. Chipman, J. W. Segal, & R. Glaser (Eds.), *Thinking and learning skills: Research and open questions* (pp. 563–577). Hillsdale, NJ: Erlbaum.

Schank, R. C. (1982). *Dynamic memory: A theory of reminding and learning in computers and people.* Cambridge, England: Cambridge University Press.

Schank, R. C. (1991a). *Case-based teaching: Four experiences in educational software design* (Rep. No. 7). Evanston, IL: Institute for the Learning Sciences.

Schank, R. C. (1991b, Winter). Where's the AI? *AI Magazine.*

Schank, R. C., & Abelson, R. (1977). *Scripts, plans, goals and understanding: An inquiry into human knowledge structures.* Hillsdale, NJ: Lawrence Erlbaum Associates.

Schoenfeld, A. H. (1983). Problem solving in the mathematics curriculum: A report, recommendations and an annotated bibliography. *The Mathematical Association of America,* MAA Notes, No. 1.

Schoenfeld, A. H. (1985). *Mathematical problem solving.* New York: Academic Press.

Slaton, A. (1991). How to get started in interactive videodisc: A user's perspective. *CALICO Monograph Series, 2,* 25–29.

Terrell, T. D. (1977). A natural approach to second language acquisition and learning. *Modern Language Journal, 61,* 325–336.

Terrell, T. D. (1981). *The natural approach in bilingual education.* California Office of Bilingual Education.

Terrell, T. D. (1982). The natural approach to language teaching: An update. *Modern Language Journal, 66,* 121–132.

Underwood, J. (1991). Interactive videodisc as hypermedia. *CALICO Monograph Series, 2,* 63–71.

Wilkins, D. A. (1973). The linguistic and situational content of the common core in a unit/credit system. In *Systems development in adult language learning.* Strasbourg: Council of Europe.

Wilkins, D. A. (1976). *Notional syllabuses.* Oxford: Oxford University Press.

Yale University. (1987). Instructor's guide. *French in Action: A beginning course in language and culture—The Capretz method—Instructor's guide, 1.*

2

Learning From Stories:
An Architecture for Socratic
Case Based Teaching

Daniel C. Edelson
Institute for the Learning Sciences,
Northwestern University

The case based teaching architecture[1] is a novel architecture for computer-based learning environments that is designed to enhance learning through the presentation of cases (Burke, 1993; Edelson, 1993; Schank, 1991). Building on theories from cognitive science and observations of effective teachers, the case based teaching architecture takes advantage of artificial intelligence (AI) programming techniques and multi-media technologies. This chapter explores the case based teaching architecture through a discussion of Creanimate, an early implementation of the case based teaching architecture. It is an interactive learning environment that draws on a library of video clips to teach elementary school-age students about animal adaptation. Creanimate is an example of a specific form of the case based teaching architecture called the Socratic case based teaching architecture. This architecture uses thought-provoking questions to engage students in active learning. The primary research goal of the Creanimate program has been to develop technologies for the implementation of the case based teaching architecture and demonstrate the ability of the architecture to engage learners. This research is designed to pave the way for future research on the validity of the theories of learning and understanding that underlie the architecture and its educational effectiveness.

---

[1]To distinguish the specific approach to computer-based learning environments presented in this chapter from teaching with cases in general, this approach is referred to as the *case based teaching architecture*, rather than the more general *case based teaching*.

The first two sections of this chapter introduce the case based teaching architecture with its supporting theories and the Creanimate system. The next two sections discuss the implementation of the two central components of a case based teaching system: the task environment and the storyteller. Specifically, they describe the dialogue manager that conducts the question-and-answer dialogues in Creanimate's task environment and the reminding strategies and indexing vocabulary that were used to implement Creanimate's storyteller. The final three sections place the case based teaching architecture in the context of other research in the learning sciences, present the results of studies conducted with Creanimate in public school settings, and discuss the strengths, limitations, and future directions of this research based on the experience gained through the implementation and testing of Creanimate.

THE CASE BASED TEACHING ARCHITECTURE

Two pedagogical principles underlie the case based teaching architecture. They are:

Active learning. Effective learning takes place when students are engaged in the active pursuit of tasks that provide them with both motivation and opportunities for learning.

Learning from cases. When opportunities for learning arise, students should be provided with cases that will help them learn from their situations.

The principle of *active learning* demands that a student be actively engaged in a personally meaningful task. A meaningful task provides both a motivation for learning and a context for interpreting and retaining new knowledge. The principle of *learning from cases* recognizes that reasoning from cases is an important element of human reasoning, and that the acquisition of cases is a prerequisite for effective case based reasoning. The case based teaching architecture is based on the observation that a great deal of learning, both formal and informal, comes from hearing stories and cases. In the case based teaching architecture, a student's active learning is augmented by just-in-time teaching in the form of relevant cases. When combined, cases provide a way to supplement the learning that a student can achieve through activity, and active learning provides a meaningful context for learning from cases. The goal behind the case based teaching architecture is to achieve benefits from combining active learning with learning from cases beyond what either can offer in isolation.

A case based teaching system supports these goals through two inter-dependent components: the task environment and the storyteller. The task environment provides a student with an engaging, motivating activity. The storyteller[2] monitors the task environment, looking for opportunities to present cases that will help students to learn from their interactions with the task environment. An effective task environment is constructed so that it exposes students to a variety of situations that provide valuable experience with the subject matter. An effective storyteller is able to recognize opportunities for learning that arise in the course of a student's interactions with the task environment and capitalize on those opportunities by presenting cases that will help the student learn from his or her situation. To achieve this goal, a storyteller must have a sufficiently wide range of cases to cover the opportunities for learning that may arise in the task environment. In addition, these cases must be indexed in such a way that the storyteller can locate appropriate cases to present to a student based on its observations of the student's actions.

In this architecture, the task environment helps a student understand the underlying structure of the domain, and the storyteller provides the student with cases to support that structure. These two forms of knowledge complement each other. The framework for the domain that the student learns from the task environment and the cases that the student gains from the storyteller mutually reinforce each other in the student's memory.

In practice, the construction of case based teaching systems is both an art and a science. Creating engaging task environments that are motivating, challenging, and interesting is in many ways an art, whereas developing systems that can present cases to help students learn draws on the science of AI. When humans teach with cases and stories, they rely on two critical skills: the ability to recognize an opportunity to present a case or a story, and the ability to identify the right one to tell to suit that opportunity. Reproducing these two important human qualities is the primary technical challenge of case based teaching.

Why Teach With Cases?

Parents and teachers often tell stories to convey lessons. Teaching with stories and learning from them occurs naturally and unconsciously. Stories are but one form that cases take in human learning. Professional schools, such as business, law, and medical schools, have employed cases in their teaching for decades with approaches such as the case method (McNair, 1954; Redlich, 1914; Reed, 1921), case based instruction (Williams, 1992),

---

[2]Because of the similarity between the retrieval and presentation of cases in a case based teaching system and human storytelling, the module that performs this process is called a *storyteller*.

and problem-based learning (Barrows, 1986; Barrows & Tamblyn, 1980). For the purposes of this chapter, a *case* is a description of a specific incident or observation that can be used to convey one or more lessons. Cases are useful in instruction to the extent that they can provide a learner with material for drawing generalizations and with precedents that are useful for reasoning about novel situations. Cases can be distinguished from rules and generalizations by their descriptive, as opposed to prescriptive, nature and their specificity. Cases describe situations, whereas rules and generalizations provide prescriptions for and observations about situations. However, cases can be used in teaching to support rules and generalizations and provide the raw materials for deriving prescriptions. Traditionally, cases have been conveyed orally and in writing, but multi-media technologies now provide for case presentation through film, graphics, and animation.

Support for teaching with cases comes from the theory of case based reasoning (Kolodner, Simpson, & Sycara-Cyranski, 1985; Riesbeck & Schank, 1989; Schank, 1982). This theory argues that many situations are too complex for people to deal with by reasoning from first principles. Instead, they reason using previously stored cases. Researchers have observed evidence of people using case based reasoning in practical situations in a wide variety of problem-solving domains (Klein, 1988; Kolodner, 1991; Ross, 1989). Because complex subjects require case based reasoning, it is important to teach those subjects in a way that will assist the natural process of case based reasoning. Although the prevalence of the case method in professional education reflects this recognition, much of K–12 and undergraduate education does not.

To be an effective case based reasoner in a particular domain, an individual must have a library of cases to draw on and enough understanding of the domain to evaluate a case's relevance to specific situations. Thus, to support case based reasoning, it is important to help students acquire cases to reason with. In considering how students are able to acquire cases from learning interactions, it is important to recognize the central lesson of constructivism—that knowledge is not absorbed by learners in the form in which it is presented to them. Rather, knowledge is constructed by them through a process that is heavily influenced by their prior understanding and the context in which they are constructing it. Therefore, the process of learning from cases must be viewed as a construction process, in which the cases that students retain in their memory are a reflection of the actual cases they are exposed to in a learning interaction, their prior knowledge and experience, and the situation in which the construction process takes place.

Students can effectively gather cases through either first- or secondhand experience. In schools, firsthand experience has traditionally been provided by laboratories, demonstrations, role playing, simulations, and other hands-on activities. These experiences are important for helping students develop personal case libraries. However, firsthand experience is not always feasible or even advisable, so cases can be provided secondhand through storytelling or other forms of presentation. To the extent that learning from case presentation resembles firsthand experience and observation, case based teaching enables students to build personal case libraries using the same natural learning process that they use when learning from experience.

Although experience and direct presentation are both effective for providing cases to students, combining firsthand experience with case presentation can improve on either by itself. One advantage of the case based teaching architecture is that it provides students with an opportunity to mix experience with cases. In a learning situation in which students gain both experience and cases, the cases can go beyond what the students can experience firsthand. Cases can reinforce students' experiences and help students understand their experiences. However, effective teaching must be more than just the presentation of cases. It must help students organize the memory structures in which they retain cases effectively.

Learning From Cases in Context

To perform case based reasoning effectively, a person must have a sufficiently large library of cases that covers an adequate variety of situations. The accumulation of such a library is one of the goals of human learning in natural settings. For example, one of the things that people do when they start a new job is to observe their boss as much as possible. They do so to build a case library of situations in which their boss has acted, so that they will be able to predict how he or she will act in future situations. However, having a large library with wide coverage is not sufficient in and of itself. It is also necessary to have the case library organized, or indexed, so that appropriate cases can be retrieved at the moment when they are most useful. For example, an employee who organizes his observations of his boss according to the weather will have a case library of his boss' behavior that is less likely to be usefully indexed than that of an employee who indexes his observations of the boss according to the latest sales reports. According to the theories of case based reasoning, cases in memory are organized according to features that describe situations in which the case may be useful. The collection of features that label a particular case is called an *index*. A case library is only as useful as the indexes that organize the cases. If cases are stored under irrelevant or incorrect features, then the reasoner will not be able to retrieve those cases when they might be useful in the future.

Because of the need for an appropriately indexed case library, case based teaching must attend to the issue of how students will develop appropriate indexes for the cases in their memories. When people learn from experience, they pay attention to the circumstances in which an experience occurs. This context helps individuals store experiences as cases in their memories. The context provides learners with features that they can use to index cases. When they find themselves in situations that have features that match the context of the earlier experiences, they are able to retrieve the earlier case to help decide how to act in the new situations. When teaching with cases, the context in which a case is conveyed provides the learner with features for indexing that case, just as when someone is learning from experience. Effective case based teaching takes advantage of context to help the learner index cases effectively in his or her own memory. For example, if a student makes a mistake in solving a problem, that mistake establishes an important context for the student to hear a case that will help him or her avoid that mistake in the future. The features that characterize the student's current situation, the problem the student is working on, and the mistake the student made all form the basis for indexes to that case. If the learner indexes that case in memory based on this context, he or she will be able to retrieve the case in similar situations in the future. Having retrieved it, the learner will be able to avoid making the same mistake or recover from it if he or she repeats it. Thus, the context in which a learner hears a case provides features that help him or her to index it effectively. A well-indexed case can be retrieved when it becomes useful for dealing with novel situations.

In summary, one of the most compelling reasons to teach with cases is the role that these cases can play in supporting case based reasoning. Case presentation is an important supplement to firsthand experience in providing people with cases to reason with, especially when firsthand experience is impossible or impractical. Effective case based teaching requires more than just the simple presentation of cases. The cases presented to a student must cover a wide enough range of situations and be presented in a context that helps the student: (a) construct meaningful representations of the cases in memory, and (b) index these cases appropriately for future use.

CREANIMATE: A CASE BASED TEACHING SYSTEM

Creanimate is a case based teaching system that teaches children about biology. It was conceived partially in response to the way students are currently taught about animals in schools. Children are fascinated by animals, yet they too often find school biology boring and dry. What turns fascination into distaste so effectively? Too many schools leave the elements that make science compelling out of the teaching of science, and they replace them with the memorization of disconnected facts. The Creanimate project is designed to put the enjoyment that accompanies real scientific inquiry into an effective educational experience. As a research project, Creanimate was designed to explore the challenges of implementing the case based teaching architecture. As an educational system, Creanimate has three central pedagogical goals: (a) provide students with an engaging interaction; (b) teach students the explanation questions that are central to the subject of animal adaptation; and (c) help students develop their own personal case libraries of animals, organized in a way that will help them use cases to reason about other animals.

An Overview

Creanimate is designed to help elementary school-age children learn about animal adaptation. Specifically, it focuses on the relationships among the physical features of animals, the way they act in the wild, and how their features and actions enable them to survive. It does so by inviting a student to create his or her own animal by taking an existing animal and changing it in some way. Hence, the name *CreANIMate* is obtained by combining the words *create* and *animal*. Following the students' choice of an animal, Creanimate engages them in dialogues in which they consider the ramifications of the modifications to their animals. For example, a student might ask for a fish with wings or a bear that can dance. In response, Creanimate might ask how the fish will use its wings or what good it might do a bear to dance. Creating a new animal is an inviting task for children because it offers them the opportunity to be imaginative. This fact has been recognized by many others in both commercial and experimental systems that allow users to create their own animals (Coderre, 1988; Karakotsios, 1992; Resnick, 1991; Travers, 1988). Inventing a new animal is compelling to children because it rewards their natural inclination to push beyond the limits of the world around them.

Following in an instructional tradition dating back to Socrates, Creanimate helps students learn from their animals by posing thought-provoking questions. It raises questions about the implications of students' modifications to their animals, and discusses possible answers with students. For example, a student could ask for a fish with wings. The program might respond by asking how the student's fish will use its wings. In the ensuing discussion, the student could propose answers (e.g., to fly), or ask the program to suggest answers (e.g., to dance, keep cool). After discussing an answer, students have the opportunity to commit to that answer for their animals or consider other answers. Because the answers to Creanimate's questions usually entail making additional changes to a student's animal, they typically give rise to new questions. As a result, the student and the computer pursue an ongoing dialogue in which the student proposes a modification to an animal, Creanimate raises questions about that modification, the student resolves those questions by making new modifications, and the system raises new questions about the new modifications. For example, after considering several possibilities, a student might decide that his or her fish should use its wings to help it fly. The addition of flying to a fish raises new questions for the student to consider, such as what other modifications the fish would require to fly, and how flying might help the fish to survive.

To help the student in the consideration of answers to its questions, Creanimate presents video clips of animals in the wild. These video clips are the cases stored in Creanimate's case library. In presenting these cases, Creanimate capitalizes on the powerful impact of video. Nature is full of dramatic and surprising animal adaptations, and no medium captures this better than film. In the course of answering questions about their animals, students see dramatic video clips that show concrete examples of the answers to those questions. For every answer discussed, Creanimate attempts to locate relevant video clips from its library. For example, in one session, a student who asked for a bee with a big nose answered the question "What will it use its big nose for?" with, "so it can suck up honey." Creanimate responded: "I think that might work. Elephants use their big noses to suck up liquids. I have an interesting video about that. If you like baby elephants, then you'll love this video. Would you like to see that?" The student then saw a video clip showing a young elephant and its mother using their trunks to drink and to bathe themselves. In this interaction, Creanimate showed a video clip to confirm that a student's answer can be supported by an example of animal behavior in the wild. In other situations, Creanimate shows video cases for other reasons, such as to suggest answers to questions, show interesting similarities, and show surprising exceptions to general rules. In the event that a student proposes an answer that Creanimate cannot verify, the storyteller responds with a video clip that shows the student's answer in some other context. For example, if a student requested a fish that used its wings to dig holes, the program would respond: "I don't know any animals that use their wings to dig holes. However, I can show you some things that animals use to dig holes. For example, meerkats use their paws to dig holes. Would you like to see that?" Creanimate helps students resolve questions about animal adaptation by presenting them with vivid cases. These memorable cases are designed to help students develop the ability to apply the natural process of case based reasoning for thinking about animal adaptation.

Creanimate in Action

The best way to introduce the Creanimate system is to show it in operation. This section presents an annotated, extended transcript of the system in use. The program has an appealing, colorful interface that allows students to express themselves through a combination of mouse clicks and typing. Figure 2.1 shows a sample screen from the program. The top portion of the screen is devoted to the program's output. The text in this section may include explanations, invitations to view video, and questions for students. The middle section of the screen is used for student input. Students respond to the system by clicking on the options provided in this section. Students may enter their own text by selecting an option containing an ellipsis and completing the phrase with their own text.[3] The picture at the lower right shows the animal that the student is working on. When Creanimate offers a student the opportunity to see a video, the picture of the student's animal is replaced by a single "preview" frame from the clip. Along the bottom edge of the screen are user control buttons that allow students to exert control over their interactions by skipping ahead, backing up, obtaining additional information, or starting over with a different animal. The following paragraphs walk through a transcript recorded during the session of a fourth-grade girl using Creanimate in a trial involving 23 students at a Chicago-area public school.

Choosing an Animal

The first step in the program is selecting an animal. The student is presented with a list of animals and modifications from which to choose. These options were selected according to criteria that included the interests of children as determined by surveys, diversity of the animals and modifications, and the available video. A student may request an animal or modification that is not on the list of options by clicking on "A . . ." or "Something else," instead of the listed animals or modifications and entering their answers in free text.

Because of practical limitations, when students type in their own animals or modifications, they are not able to see a picture of the animals they create, and the storyteller may not have as many relevant video clips as it does for the options on the list. Ideally, there would be many more choices available or just free entry. However, with only 1 hour of video available in early versions of the system, it was necessary to provide choices to ensure a fruitful dialogue for the student. As the system's knowledge base and video library grow, the choices could be increased or replaced.

---

[3]The natural language parser is based on the DMAP architecture (Martin, 1989, 1990). It is described in Fitzgerald (1992, 1995).

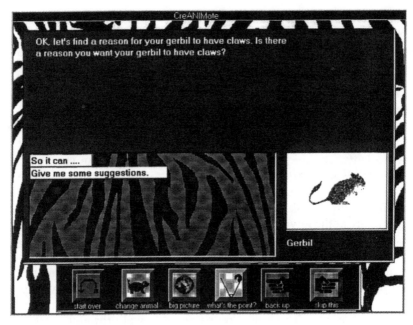

FIG. 2.1. A sample screen from the Creanimate program.

If you could create a new animal by taking an existing animal and changing it some way, what would you make? (Pick one animal from the list on the left and one change from the list on the right.)

A Fish (pike)   With a big nose.
A Frog   With a beak.
A Bear   With wings.
A Bee   That can dance.
A Butterfly   That can hide.
A Dog   That can hunt.
A Bird (robin)   That can fight.
A ...   Something else.

The student selected "A . . ." from the list on the left, typed in "monkey," and then selected "with wings" from the list on the right.

Student: A *monkey* with wings[4]
Unfortunately, I don't have any pictures of a monkey, so you will

---

[4]In the transcripts in this chapter, portions of the input that were typed by the student appear in italics. The remainder was input by selecting an option on the screen with the mouse. For brevity, the choices presented to the user have been omitted in many cases. Except where noted in transcripts or footnotes, all inputs and outputs appear exactly as they appeared on the screen.

```
not be able to see the animal you make. We can still talk about it
though.
Student: Go on.
```

If the student had selected an animal from the list provided, the program would have shown the student a large picture of her unmodified animal in a box labeled *Before* with a picture of a question mark in a box labeled *After*. This is designed to set up the goal of seeing what the modified animal will look like.

Incidental Remindings

```
Actually there are mammals that have wings. For example, fox bats
have leathery wings.
Is that something you would like to see?
Student: No
```

When the system's case library includes an animal with an unexpected feature that is similar to the animal the student wants to create, it gives the student the option of seeing a video about it. In this case, the storyteller was reminded of another mammal with wings. These incidental remindings are designed to challenge learners' generalizations and broaden their experience of the exceptions to general rules.

The system immediately responds to the student's proposal by posing a question about that animal.

```
If your monkey is going to have wings, that should help it to do
something. Why would you like your monkey to have wings?
   So it can . . .
   Give me some suggestions.
Student: So it can fly away from its enemys
```

The dialogue manager selected the question "Why have wings?" after determining that the system's video library includes clips that show ways that animals use wings. The questions that the system asks are intended to help students learn the basic relationships that underlie animal behavior. In this case, the question emphasizes that animals use their features to perform actions. The student selected "So it can . . ." and typed in "fly away from its enemys [*sic*]."

Example Cases

The computer determines from its knowledge base that flying is a reason for having wings, and then locates the best video in its library to show wings used for flight. This example case is used as a way to confirm the student's answer and provide case based reinforcement for the knowledge in the student's memory. Because the program is only prepared to talk about basic actions (e.g., flying, smelling, biting) in answer to this particular question, the dialogue manager ignores the student's mention of getting away from enemies. The program will return to the higher level question of why flying might help the monkey to survive later, if the student sticks with flying. The student asks to watch the video:

```
That's a good idea. White breasted sea eagles use their feathered
wings to help them fly.
Do you want to see that ?
Student: Yes
[VIDEO: "Sea Eagle Catches Fish"]
```

This particular video shows a dramatic scene of a white breasted sea eagle pouncing on a fish nearly as big as itself and carrying it away. Because the case library contains several videos about wings being used to fly, the storyteller offers another one to the student. She chooses to view it. As soon as the student refuses a video on a particular subject, the dialogue manager moves on to the next step in the dialogue.

```
White breasted sea eagles are not the only animals that use their
wings in order to fly. For example, black skimmers have wings to
help them to fly. I have a great video about that.
Would you like to see that?
  Yes.
  What other videos can I see?
  No.
Student: Yes
[VIDEO: "SKIMMER SKIMS"]
[Program error⁵ deleted]
```

Committing to an Answer

Once the student has seen examples that illustrate her answer for how her monkey might use its wings, she has the opportunity to commit to that answer. If she commits, she will go on to other questions about her monkey with wings. Otherwise, she can consider other uses for wings. Because flying is the most obvious use for wings, the portion of the dialogue up to this point does little more than reinforce knowledge the student already has. When students go on to consider other uses for wings that Creanimate knows about, such as keeping cool, swimming, and

---

[5] Because of an error at this point, the program incorrectly offered the student the same video about the black skimmer over again. She declined.

performing mating dances, the opportunities for learning become much richer.

```
So, your monkey could have wings to fly. Why would you like your
monkey to have wings?
   To fly
   Show me more reasons.
Student: To fly
Ok, your monkey will have wings so that it can fly.
```

If the student had selected one of the seven animals that the program originally suggested, she would see a predrawn picture of her animal with its wings at this stage. Instead, she sees a drawing of a pile of bones in a workshop next to a sign saying, "Under Construction."

A Second Question

Now that the student has decided what her monkey will do with its wings, the program raises a new question: "What other changes will be required for it to be able to fly?" This question emphasizes that many actions require a combination of different physical attributes.

```
In order to fly, animals must be able to keep themselves in the air.
Let's talk about how your monkey will keep itself up in the air.
Having wings is not enough for your monkey to keep itself up in the
air. It needs more.
How else do you want to change your monkey so it can keep itself
up in the air?
   Give it . . .
   Make it . . .
   Give me some suggestions.
Student: Give me some suggestions.
```

Rather than answer the question, the student asks the program to give her some suggestions.

Cases to Provide Suggestions

When students ask for suggestions, the program design assumes that they are doing so because they do not know any answers to the current question. This constitutes an opportunity for learning. Rather than simply tell the student an answer, Creanimate provides the answer through a case. In this example, it proposes larger wings. Because of the structure of Creanimate's knowledge base, it treats combinations of features that enable an animal to achieve an action as aggregate features. Creanimate's knowledge base contains several combinations of animal size and wing size that enable flying, such as small animals with small or medium-size wings, and medium-size animals with large wings. (Monkeys fall into Creanimate's category of medium-size animals.) Currently, however, Creanimate's knowledge representation contains no way to represent the negative relationship between size or weight and flight, or the manner in which wing size can compensate for overall size in enabling flight. All aggregate features are treated as if the subcomponents of the features work together toward the enablement of an action. Therefore, the program proposes large wings to the student in an admittedly awkward manner, by proposing the combined feature of large wings and medium size, as if size contributed to, rather than conflicted with, flight. Limitations such as these in Creanimate's knowledge representation, their impact on the system's effectiveness, and proposed solutions are discussed in a later section.

```
Large wings and medium size can work together to help an animal to
keep itself up in the air.
Your monkey already has medium size.
Swainson hawks use their large wings and medium size to help them
keep themselves in the air.
I have a good video about that. They had to be up in the air in
order to film this video.
Is that something you would like to see?
Student: Yes
[VIDEO: "SWAINSON HAWK HUNTS"]
```

The Swainson hawk video is followed by an offer to see another medium-size animal with large wings.

```
Swainson hawks are not the only animals that keep themselves in the
air by using their large wings and medium size. For example, Canada
geese also use their large wings and medium size to help them keep
themselves in the air.
This is a good video.
Do you want to see that ?
Student: No
What would you like to add to your monkey so it can keeps [sic]
itself up in the air?
  Large wings
  Show me more ways.
Student: Large wings
OK, your monkey will use its large wings to help it keep itself up
in the air.
```

User Control Buttons

After committing to large wings, the student goes on to consider how the monkey will be able to steer while it's flying. In the course of this portion of the dialogue, she takes advantage of one of the user control buttons provided by the program. As illustrated in Fig. 2.1, at the bottom of the Creanimate screen are buttons that allow the student to skip ahead, back up to a previous screen, see a transcript of the interaction to the current point, start a new animal, and ask, "What's the point?" In the midst of her discussion about steering in flight, the student clicks the "What's the point?" button. Creanimate's response to this button is to provide the student with a rationale behind the computer's most recent output:[6]

```
You already said you wanted to add wings to your monkey, but it
still can't steer in flight. We need to make another change.
Having wings is not enough for your monkey to steer in flight. It
needs more.
How else do you want to change your monkey so it can steer in flight?
. . . [Discussion and videos of feathered tails deleted] . . .
What would you like to add to your monkey so it can steers [sic]
in flight?
```
Student: [Button Press: What's the point?]
```
It is your decision what to give your monkey so it can steer in
flight. You can choose now or see more ways to change it and decide
later.
```
Student: Go on.

Similarity in Case Retrieval

In this extended discussion, the student resolves the issue of how her monkey will steer and then deals with the question of how flying will help it to survive. She requests that it fly to "get away from enemys [sic]." When the system is unable to understand her input, she selects "flee predators," a behavior that Creanimate knows about, from a list of options.

```
Let's see if we can find a reason for your monkey to fly.
Can you think of a reason for your monkey to fly?
```
Student: So it can get away from its enemys
```
I did not understand that. Try picking one of the choices below.
Chase its mate              Drink
Eat                         Fight for its mate
Fight for its young         Flee predators
Grasp vegetation            Ingest food
Migrate                     Migrate from cold
Pounce on its prey          Process food internally
Pursue its prey             Scare predators
Run away from its enemies   Search for its prey
Remove competition for food Steal food
```

---

[6]Portions of the dialogue have been omitted for brevity.

```
Remove competition for their mates
Student: flee predators
That's a good idea. Monkeys could fly to help them to flee preda-
tors.
There are other animals that flee predators, only they don't fly.
Frogs are one example. They leap so they can flee predators.
Would you like to see a video about that?
```

Interestingly, in the prior interchange, the storyteller was unable to locate a video about flying to flee predators, but it was able to locate a video about frogs that leap to flee predators and offered that instead. The ability to use this sort of similarity in case retrieval enables the Creanimate storyteller to get maximum utility out of the cases in its library.

Eventually, Creanimate exhausts its questions about flying, but the student chooses to stick with her monkey and add a new characteristic.

```
That's all I can think of for now. You can either add something
else to your monkey or try another animal.
Student: Add something else to my monkey
   . . .
How would you like to change your monkey?
Student: So it can fight
```

In the remaining portions of the dialogue, the student considers the questions of why and how her monkey will fight. She resolves the former question by having it fight for its mate, and the latter by having it kick other animals.

In this 45-minute dialogue, the student considered six questions about her animal and viewed seven videos. She was unusual in the length of time she devoted to one animal. Most of the 23 public school fourth graders in the study in which she participated chose to switch animals after one or two questions, and saw slightly more videos (7.8 videos per session on average). The student in this transcript never used the "Start over" button to start a new animal, whereas students overall used it an average of 1.3 times per 45-minute session.

The Status of Creanimate

Creanimate is a working prototype that has been tested successfully in a variety of settings. The study of Creanimate in a fourth-grade classroom from which the preceding transcript was drawn is described in a later section. The most recent version contains 140 indexed video clips totaling 60 minutes. It conducts dialogues about six different types of questions, each focusing on a different relationship among the physical features, actions, and behaviors of animals. The knowledge base includes over 200 animals and over 1,000 different characteristics of animals. Included in this knowledge base is the information that allows Creanimate to construct natural English sentences and understand students' typed input. Tests of the program indicate that students can use the current prototype for at least 3 hours without exhausting its capabilities. Although it has received considerable use, Creanimate remains a prototype system. The vocabulary and accuracy of its natural language understanding module has been increased as a result of data gathered in use. However, during an early study, unacceptable parses (situations in which the system misunderstood a student's input or the parser asked the student to repeat the input because it was unable to generate any parse at all) made up 17% of all typed input (n = 146 inputs; Fitzgerald, 1995). Because of the system's strategies for recovering from failures to parse input, such as asking students to try again or to select their answer from a list, this level appears to be tolerable while still less than optimal. Due to the relative simplicity of Creanimate's knowledge representation, some of its language and explanations are unnatural. Finally, bugs and inaccuracies remain in both the code and the system's knowledge base that are visible in a majority of students' transcripts. These bugs result in behavior that is often not noticeable to the user, but occasionally disrupts the flow of the interaction because the program appears incoherent or incorrect.

THE TASK ENVIRONMENT

The next two sections turn to an examination of the elements that are necessary for effective case based teaching systems and how Creanimate incorporates those elements. This section is devoted to the task environment and the next to the storyteller. An effective task environment gives a student the opportunity to learn in the course of pursuing goals that are natural to him or her. Some examples of designs for effective task environments include simulations, problem-solving, design, and diagnosis environments. Four criteria for effective task environments are (Edelson, 1993):

1. *Opportunities to form and explore hypotheses.* Active learning demands that students have the opportunity to learn by building their own understanding and refining it in response to experience. A task environment must give the student chances to form, express, test, and revise hypotheses. In Creanimate, the student's choice of an animal to create serves the role of expressing a hypothesis. Students explore their

"hypotheses" by considering questions about how their hypothetical animals might survive.

2. *Opportunities for learning.* The task environment must be constructed in a way that students experience opportunities to extend their understanding as a result of interacting with it. Opportunities for learning often arise in the form of expectation failures (Schank, 1982). In Creanimate, opportunities for learning arise from the questions posed by the system and the responses offered by students. Creanimate's questions can point out gaps in students' understanding or offer opportunities to enhance their existing understanding with novel cases.

3. *Authenticity.* A task environment must be authentic both to the student and the world. It must be authentic to the student in that it must interact with the student's personal goals. It must be authentic to the world in that the knowledge and skills that a student gains through experience with the environment must be encountered in a context that is consistent with the way they will be encountered and employed in the real world (Brown, Collins, & Duguid, 1989; Schoenfeld, 1992). Authenticity to the student's goals ensures that the student will have the motivation to engage and learn. Authenticity to the world increases the likelihood of a student being able to apply what he or she learns in settings that arise naturally. Creanimate's authenticity to the student comes from the nature of the task. Children find the opportunity to invent new animals naturally engaging. Creanimate's authenticity to the world comes from the process that students go through in discussing their designs. The questions that students consider in Creanimate are authentic to the questions that biologists ask in explaining animal adaptation.

4. *Motivation.* The key to active learning is appropriate motivation. To be motivating, a task environment should provide sufficient challenge, curiosity, control, fantasy, satisfaction, and relevance (Keller, 1983; Lepper & Hodell, 1989; Malone, 1981). Creanimate attempts to motivate students through the inventive nature of the task, the challenge of the questions the system poses, its responsiveness to the student, and the drama of the video clips.

Any specific task environment must address these criteria in a way that is appropriate for the subject matter it is designed to teach, for the learners who will use it, and for the environment in which they will be using it. In Creanimate, the task of designing a new animal was selected to be engaging for the target age group. The central activity, a dialogue that focuses on open-ended questions, was selected to suit the nature of the subject matter and the pedagogical goals of the system, as well as to provide ample opportunities for learning from cases.

The Creanimate Task Environment:
Socratic Case Based Teaching

As the extended transcript presented earlier illustrates, questioning is at the heart of Creanimate's dialogues. In this respect, it follows in the tradition of two early intelligent tutoring systems, SCHOLAR (Carbonell, 1970a, 1970b) and WHY (Stevens & Collins, 1977). Because it conducts question-and-answer dialogues with students, Creanimate's variant of the case based teaching architecture is called the Socratic case based teaching architecture. Creanimate's dialogues respond to a student's proposed animal with questions that expose important issues for the adaptability of that animal. Although the dialogue manager does not employ all of the techniques that have been associated with Socratic-style teaching (Clancy, 1987; Collins & Stevens, 1983), it adheres to the Socratic tradition of encouraging a student to make hypotheses and then leading the student through an exploration of those hypotheses with thought-provoking questions.[7] The dialogue manager's responses to a student's proposed animal capitalize on the student's investment in the animal to introduce the student to the issues involved in animal adaptation. Students' interest in their own animals serves as a natural motivator to engage them in the process of answering the explanation questions that apply to their animals. These explanation questions also provide a context for presenting example cases that supply appropriate answers. The remainder of this section explores Creanimate's Socratic dialogue manager in detail. First, it presents reasons for teaching with questions; second, it describes the dialogue cycle that provides the underlying framework for Creanimate's Socratic-style dialogues.

Why Teach With Questions?

Although cases can play an important role in instruction, they are but one of the tools at an effective teacher's disposal. Questions are another. Creanimate uses questions to help establish a context for learning from cases. These questions provide important information to assist a student in developing a representational framework for the subject matter and in indexing the information in cases. However, Creanimate uses questions for two additional reasons. First, asking questions is a way to model a behavior for students to learn. Second, questions can serve as motivators in a learning interaction.

---

[7]It has been pointed out that questions ascribed to Socrates were not typically open ended; they were yes-or-no questions. The use of the name Socratic case based teaching is supposed to reflect the spirit of Socratic teaching, not the exact technique employed by Socrates.

Questions to Support Representation and Indexing

The primary reason for teaching with questions in the Socratic case based teaching architecture is that questions can teach students the critical relationships among the important concepts in a particular field. Although we usually think of expertise as being the knowledge of a lot of answers, the ability to ask good questions is at least as important to expertise. Knowing the right questions to ask is an important element of expertise because it permits the expert to deal with unfamiliar situations. What differentiates an expert from a novice in any domain is knowing the questions to ask to begin to understand novel phenomena. For example, if a geologist is presented with an unfamiliar land formation, he or she will know the right questions to ask to start constructing an explanation for how that formation was created. Explanation, the central process of understanding, alternates between asking questions and constructing plausible answers. With respect to learners, the Chi et al. (1989) studies of students engaged in teaching themselves from textbooks identified questioning as a skill that distinguishes between good and poor learners in such self-teaching situations. But where do these questions for understanding come from? The questions that one asks in the process of explanation in any domain derive from knowledge of the basic relationships that underlie that domain. These questions, called *explanation questions* (Schank, 1986), express the relationships that tie concepts in the domain together.

The explanation questions for a field are important because they express the relationships with explanatory power in that field. Someone who understands the explanation questions for a particular subject will use the relationships they express to organize his or her knowledge about that subject. For example, a naturalist's knowledge would likely be organized around the relationships between physical features and their uses, and between animals' actions and their goals. Therefore, teaching students the explanation questions in a domain is the same thing as teaching them the important relationships that underlie that domain. Once learners understand the important relationships that tie concepts together in a domain, they can use those relationships as the basis for indexing cases in their memories. Using this framework, they can further extend their understanding by both asking explanation questions and organizing their observations according to the relationships that the questions express.

Teaching the explanation questions underlying animal adaptation is a central pedagogical goal of Creanimate. Although an individual can understand the relationships within this subject area at ever-increasing levels of sophistication, the Creanimate project has identified five initial explanation question categories:

1. *Why feature?* The *Why feature?* explanation question attempts to connect an animal's physical feature with some action that the feature supports. For example, "Why do cheetahs have long legs?"

2. *How action?* The *How action?* explanation question explores the same relationship as *Why feature?* However, *How action?* takes an action performed by an animal and looks for the features that are necessary to perform that action. For example, "What does an eagle have to help it to fly?"

3. *Why action?* The *Why action?* explanation question attempts to connect an action performed by an animal with some survival behavior. It assumes that the actions that animals perform enable them to survive in some way. For example, "Why do female alligators dig holes?"

4. *How behavior?* The *How behavior?* explanation question is the reverse of *Why action?* It starts with a survival behavior and seeks actions that enable an animal to achieve that behavior. For example, "How do chimpanzees get food?"

5. *Why behavior?* Behaviors can be performed for more than one reason. For instance, finding shelter can be in the service of both keeping warm and avoiding danger. Therefore, the fifth category of explanation question is *Why behavior?* For example, "Why do bears fight?"

These five explanation question categories correspond to the relationships among three different conceptual categories: features, actions, and behaviors. These basic concepts and the relationships between them can provide a student with a solid groundwork to understand animal adaptation. The goal of the Socratic dialogues in Creanimate is to ask questions in a way that will help students develop an understanding of adaptation according to these relationships.[8] This understanding will enable students

---

[8]One of the risks of Creanimate's approach to teaching animal adaptation is that it may lead students to develop a view of evolution that is inconsistent with the accepted scientific view (i.e., they may develop an intentional or Lamarckian view of evolution). Creanimate is built around the assumption that a view of animals as being adapted to survive in their environment is an important step toward understanding evolution, the process by which the adaptations developed. Creanimate is designed to teach about the adaptedness of animals without focusing on the evolutionary process. As such, its dialogue is based on the assumption that the attributes that animals possess all serve a survival function. Although it is not accurate to say that features are developed through evolution to serve particular functions, it is fair to generalize that, as a result of evolution, animals have features and perform actions that serve particular survival functions. It is an assumption of Creanimate, albeit an untested one, that focusing on the issues of evolution before establishing a strong grounding in adaptation would be a mistake, but that with such a grounding in adaptation established, developing a sophisticated understanding of the evolutionary process will be more likely. The issue of misconceptions about evolution is further complicated in

to index cases of animal adaptations using these relationships, and to ask appropriate questions as they continue to learn on their own. In the construction of the Creanimate system, these five explanation questions and three conceptual categories formed the basis for the indexing vocabulary and reminding strategies of the storyteller, as well as the knowledge representation used by the dialogue manager.

Modeling Questioning and Motivating Active Learning

Beyond the primary goal of teaching the central relationships of a domain, the Socratic case based teaching architecture also asks questions to model the desirable behavior of question asking and to motivate active learning. As was stated earlier, the ability to ask good questions is fundamental to the processes of learning and understanding. Recent work in education (e.g., Collins, Brown, & Newman, 1989) has advocated modeling as a way to help students develop desired behaviors. Modeling consists of demonstrating a behavior for a student as a means to help the student learn the behavior. This has been identified as an integral step in apprenticeship learning (Collins et al., 1989). Both Collins and Stevens (1983) and Brown and Palincsar (1989) have described the effective use of modeling to teach questioning in inquiry teaching and reciprocal teaching, respectively. Admittedly, the cognitive apprenticeship approach advocated by Collins et al. (1989) includes coaching, scaffolding, articulation, reflection, and exploration, in addition to modeling. Also, it is not clear that students will respond to a computer as a model in the same way they will respond to another person. Therefore, one of the issues to be addressed in empirical studies of the Socratic case based teaching architecture is whether the modeling of questioning by a computer in the context of the case based teaching architecture can be effective in teaching appropriate questioning behaviors. (Initial studies, described in a later section, failed to show a significant change in questioning behaviors among fourth graders as a result of using Creanimate.)

A final reason for asking questions is to motivate the student to be an active learner. Responding to a question provides a student with an

---

Creanimate by the design goal of using everyday language and avoiding stilted constructions. For example, in the extended transcript in the previous section, the dialogue manager says, "White breasted sea eagles are not the only animals that use their wings in order to fly. For example, black skimmers have wings to help them fly." Stating that "black skimmers have wings to help them fly" could imply that black skimmers evolved wings to fly. However, this wording is characteristic of the way that people discuss adaptation in ordinary conversation, and was chosen for its naturalness over other more accurate, but less natural-sounding, constructions.

opportunity to think independently and creatively. Thought-provoking questions can prove particularly effective in computer-based learning environments that are self-paced and free of social pressure. Questions activate students in two important ways. They encourage students to form their own hypotheses, and they evoke curiosity. Each of these can be especially effective in combination with the presentation of cases.

A thought-provoking question gives students the opportunity to construct their own hypotheses. Forming their own hypotheses is important because it increases students' investment in their own learning process, and gives them a perspective from which to learn. Commitment to hypotheses provides students with the motivation to attend to and consider relevant information. In addition, hypotheses give learners a frame of reference for evaluating additional information.

Good questions evoke curiosity. Curiosity, in turn, is a dramatic motivator for learning. The trigger for curiosity is an individual's recognition of a gap or inconsistency in his or her understanding. This is what Schank (1982) called an *expectation failure*. The expectation failure and ensuing curiosity that result from an effective question represent an opportunity for learning. A teacher or learning environment that is able to respond to a student's curiosity in a way that helps the student fill the gap or repair the inconsistency is able to capitalize on that opportunity for learning. The Socratic case based teaching architecture is designed to capitalize on the opportunities for learning from cases that arise from questions.

The Dialogue Cycle

The Creanimate task environment employs explanation questions in a Socratic-style dialogue with the goal of achieving the learning benefits described earlier. These dialogues are implemented through the dialogue cycle. The dialogue cycle provides a framework for the discussions between student and computer in Creanimate. Each dialogue starts with an explanation question and proceeds through the consideration of answers to that question. Within this framework, however, dialogues vary according to the responses of individual students.

The Origin of the Dialogue Cycle

The dialogues in Creanimate have their origins in an experiment conducted in 1987. In this "reverse Turing" or "Wizard of Oz" test, seventeen 11- and 12-year-old children were told that they were testing an unfinished computer program. However, instead of using a program, the children were conversing through a terminal with a professor of biology at a terminal in an adjoining room.[9] The goal of this experiment was to gather information about how children would respond to a program like Creanimate and what they might say. In addition, the conversations provided an important human model for Creanimate to emulate. The following is a brief example of a dialogue with an 11-year-old girl from this experiment:

> **Professor:** Okay! I really enjoy talking about kangaroos! Is there something special you would like your kangaroo to do, or to have? Or do you want to ask a question?
> **Student: would want it to have a colorful body**
> Professor: That sounds attractive! How might a colorful body be an advantage to the kangaroo?
> **Student: it would be able to blend in to things to hide from danger.**
> **Professor:** Excellent idea! You are talking about colors to hide the animal.
> Many animals have that kind of coloration!
> In a way the kangaroo has that kind of coloration—it is fairly drab, and its surroundings are also fairly drab. Some other animals have very bright colors.
> I am thinking of a couple of examples: the "robin red breast" is a small bird. At certain times of year, the feathers on the chests of the males turn red. . . .

An analysis of the transcripts from this experiment revealed that most of the conversations followed a simple, but effective, pattern. This conversational pattern consisted of (a) the student asking for a modification, (b) the professor asking a question about that modification, (c) the student proposing an answer to the question or asking the professor for assistance, and (d) the professor presenting a case that related to or provided an answer to the professor's question. Using this pattern as a model, the dialogue cycle in Creanimate was developed, enabling the program to produce dialogues that bear a strong resemblance to these human examples.

The Steps in the Dialogue Cycle

The steps in Creanimate's dialogue cycle are shown next with examples drawn from a student's dialogue.

1. Pose Explanation Question
That's a good idea, is there a reason you want your frog to fight?

---

[9]The experiment described in this section was conducted by William Purves at Harvey Mudd College. Additional transcripts from these experiments appear in Edelson (1993).

```
2. Get answer from student or knowledge base.
Student: So it can protect its self [sic]
3. Present example case (if available)
```
That's a good idea. Bees protect themselves by fighting enemies.
Would you like to see that?
```
4. Allow student to commit to the answer.
```
So, your frog can fight to protect itself.
You can commit to that now, or we can look at some other reasons
why animals fight and you can decide later.
Why would you like your frog to fight?
```
   To protect itself
   Show me more reasons
Student: To protect itself
```

These four steps are repeated as the student proposes or the dialogue manager suggests different answers. Once the student commits to an answer (Step 4), the current dialogue terminates and a new dialogue is initiated. Because of the variety of places in the cycle that the storyteller can intervene and the range of responses that students can make, the four steps of the dialogue cycle shown earlier are simply the skeleton of a dialogue. Actual dialogues are more elaborate and varied than the simple dialogue cycle. For example, if a student provides an answer to a question that is not consistent with the dialogue manager's knowledge base, the system offers the student the opportunity to digress from the discussion of the current explanation question to see video clips of his or her answer. This "unverifiable answer" reminding strategy is discussed in the next section.

The dialogue cycle is managed by the Socratic dialogue manager. This dialogue manager is supported by a large knowledge base about animal adaptation. The knowledge base includes information for natural language understanding and generation; the dialogue manager is able to translate responses typed in by students into an internal representation (Edelson, 1993; Fitzgerald, 1995) and then evaluate the correctness of a student's answer with respect to the program's own knowledge base. Using this evaluation, the dialogue manager generates an appropriate response to the student in informal English by using the natural language-generation information in its knowledge base to complete template sentences (Edelson, 1993). In practice, this simple dialogue cycle gives rise to a wide range of student interactions. Its open-ended questions and responsiveness to students' answers are designed to give students a large sense of control over their own learning interactions. The dialogue cycle enables students to formulate their own hypotheses in response to open-ended explanation questions, and provides opportunities for them to learn from relevant cases that respond to these hypotheses.

In summary, the Creanimate task environment conducts question-and-answer dialogues with students. The questions serve two goals: to teach explanation questions, and to activate the learner. Modeled on a human teacher, the Socratic dialogue manager is able to conduct open-ended question-and-answer dialogues using a simple, but flexible, dialogue structure.

THE STORYTELLER: INDEXING AND REMINDING

This section moves from the task environment to the storyteller. The goal of the storyteller in a case based teaching system is to harness the reminding process to help students learn from their interactions with the task environment. To retrieve cases when they are appropriate, the storyteller must have a well-organized case library and strategies for searching that library that suit the particular opportunities for learning that occur in the accompanying task environment. The central issues for the design and construction of a storyteller are:

1. *Case selection.* Case selection is the process of compiling a case library to be used by the storyteller. As a fundamental requirement, a storyteller must have a sufficiently large library of cases to cover the range of opportunities for learning that can occur in the task environment.

2. *Communication with the task environment.* A storyteller must have a means of bidirectional communication with the task environment, which will allow it to effectively monitor the student's interactions and intervene when it sees the opportunity to present a case.

3. *Indexing scheme.* An indexing scheme is a method for labeling cases in memory so that the storyteller can recognize situations in which they are relevant. To be effective, the indexing vocabulary must be sufficiently expressive to cover both the range of cases in the storyteller's library and the range of opportunities for learning from cases that occur in the task environment.

4. *Reminding strategies.* Reminding strategies are algorithms used by a storyteller to search its case library and locate appropriate cases to present. The input to a reminding strategy is a description of a situation in the task environment, and the output is one or more cases that are relevant to that situation. Reminding strategies must be able to search the case library in a computationally efficient fashion to retrieve stories in a timely manner.

5. *Presentation of cases.* Once the storyteller has identified a case to present, it must be able to present it in a way that engages students and helps clarify the relevance of the case to the current situation.

In any case based teaching system, the resolution of these issues is partially determined by the design of the task environment and the character of the cases that make up the storyteller's library. Thus, in the Creanimate system, the storyteller was designed to suit a task environment that conducts Socratic-style dialogues. Of the issues described earlier, the two that were the primary foci of the Creanimate researcher effort were indexing and reminding. The issues of indexing and reminding are discussed separately in this section, although in practice they must be resolved in tandem because of their interdependence.

Reminding Strategies

A reminding strategy is a procedure for identifying a story to tell in a particular context. Although being reminded is usually thought of as a passive event (i.e., something that happens to you), reminding appears to be the result of active processes monitoring observations coming in from the outside world and matching those observations against cases in memory (Schank et al., 1990). Teaching requires a set of specialized procedures for retrieving cases to serve pedagogical goals. The reminding strategies in the storyteller of a case based teaching system serve this function. Reminding strategies monitor the progress of a student in the task environment and use features that describe the student's situation to identify stories that can help the student to learn from that situation. Different case based teaching systems will have particular reminding strategies that suit the subject being taught, the nature of the task environment, and the educational goals of the system.

The reminding strategies for any particular task environment must correspond to the types of opportunities for learning that arise in the task environment. Some educational reminding strategies include retrieving stories that correct misconceptions, give advice, provide warnings, or present examples. Although there are undoubtedly reminding strategies that are useful across a wide range of teaching settings, certain settings and pedagogical goals require special-purpose reminding strategies. For example, Kass et al. (1993/1994) described a system that uses a social simulation (GuSS) to teach salespeople the skills necessary to sell products and services. This system uses the following 10 reminding strategies: demonstrate risks, demonstrate opportunities, demonstrate alternative plan, warn about optimism, warn about pessimism, warn about assumption, reinforce plan, warn about plan, explain plan of another, and explain perspective of another. These strategies are clearly specialized for a system that teaches a student how to construct and execute plans. They focus on the process of developing a plan. Burke and Kass (1992) pointed out that their strategies differ from the reminding strategies in Creanimate because the latter focus on the ramifications of design decisions, whereas those in GuSS focus on the process by which an individual makes decisions. As this example shows, reminding strategies differ with the subject matter and structure of the task environment.

Creanimate employs several reminding strategies, each of which serves a specific pedagogical objective. Each strategy places particular demands on the information available in the indexes that label cases in the program's memory. Creanimate's reminding strategies fall into two categories: example and incidental. Example remindings display examples of the issues that arise in the course of a discussion. Incidental remindings present cases that relate tangentially to the current focus of the discussion. The specific types of example and incidental remindings employed by the Creanimate storyteller are displayed in Table 2.1. Example cases provide students with concrete examples of the abstract principles that arise in the course of dialogues. These examples are intended to enlarge a student's personal case library of animal adaptations. Example remindings reinforce the structure of the domain provided by the dialogue manager's explanation questions.

In addition to example remindings, the Creanimate storyteller employs two types of incidental remindings. They are called *incidental* because they digress from the central point of the discussion to present interesting sidelights. These sorts of digressions are, in fact, characteristic of good teachers. Good teachers are able to broaden students' exposure and increase their interest without sacrificing the main point of a discussion. The two types of incidental remindings generated by the Creanimate storyteller are similarity-based and expectation-violation remindings. The similarity-based reminding strategy is designed to retrieve a case that is similar to an immediately preceding case, but is also different from it in an interesting way. Similarity-based remindings help students draw appropriate generalizations, and they introduce them to things they might not see in other contexts. The second form of incidental reminding, the expectation-violation reminding, retrieves cases that violate students' likely expectations. This reminding strategy uses the element of surprise to introduce students

TABLE 2.1
The Reminding Strategies in Creanimate

Example Remindings	Incidental Remindings
Correct answer	Similarity-based
Unverifiable answer	Expectation-violation:
Suggest answer	Only-rule
	No-rule
	All-rule

to uncommon phenomena. Although the example reminding strategies provide the foundation for the discussion of explanation questions, the incidental reminding strategies pepper the discussion with relevant, interesting digressions. Together they are designed to provide the student with a dialogue that resembles a natural human discussion.

Example Reminding in Creanimate

Example remindings are the bread and butter for the Creanimate system, just as they are for any teacher. In the following transcript, the dialogue manager asks the student an explanation question of the category *Why feature?* in response to his request for a bear with a big nose, and responds to the student's answer with an example reminding:

```
.  .  .  What would you make?
Student: A bear with a big nose.
If your bear is going to have a big nose, that should help it to
do something. Why would you like your bear to have a big nose?
Student: So it can smell good
That might work. Tapirs have big noses to help them to smell.
This next video is really hilarious. I like this one because it has
strange animals in it. Is that something you would like to see?
Student: yes
[VIDEO: "TAPIR SMELLS"]
```

In this transcript, the student responded with an answer that the system evaluated as correct. In other words, it was able to determine from its knowledge base that there is at least one animal with the combination of attributes in the student's answer—in this case, a big nose to smell effectively. When a student provides a correct answer to an explanation question, the storyteller employs the example reminding strategy in an attempt to identify a case that provides an example to support the student's answer. In the prior transcript, it located a video about a tapir using its large nose to help it smell. The ability to perform example remindings requires that an index describe the questions and answers that a case exemplifies.

To account for the three types of answers that students may give to explanation questions, the Creanimate storyteller uses three varieties of the example reminding strategy. In addition to the correct answer reminding strategy, shown earlier, there is an unverifiable answer reminding strategy and a suggest answer reminding strategy. The unverifiable answer reminding strategy is employed when the student provides an answer that the dialogue manager cannot verify according to its knowledge base. An unverifiable answer reminding shows the student an example of a question for which the student's answer would have been

correct. In the following transcript, the student proposes smelling as a
reason for his animal to have a beak. The dialogue manager is unable to
verify from its knowledge base that beaks are used to smell, so it employs
the unverifiable answer reminding strategy to locate a story that shows
something that is used to smell.

```
OK, Let's find a reason for your bear to have a beak. Is there a
reason you want your bear to have a beak?
Student: So it can smell better
I've never heard of any animals that have beaks to smell, but there
are some other ways that animals smell.
For example, pikes smell. Pikes use their nostrils to help them to
smell.
I have an interesting video about that. I like this one because it
has mean fish in it.
Would you like to see a video about that?
Student: yes
[VIDEO: "Pikes smell"]
```

The third form of example reminding, the suggest answer strategy, is
employed when a student chooses not to answer an explanation question
and asks the computer to suggest an answer instead. In response, the
program suggests an answer in the form of an example, as in the following
transcript:

```
We need a reason for your dog to fly. Is there a reason you want
your dog to fly?
Student: Give me some suggestions
Canada geese fly. They fly to migrate from the cold. I have a re-
ally good video about that. Would you like to see it?
Student: Show me a video
[VIDEO: "GEESE MIGRATE"]
```

Similarity-Based Remindings in Creanimate

One of the risks of teaching with examples is that students may miss
the opportunity to make generalizations from the specific examples they
see. Therefore, a case based teaching system should assist students to
form generalizations at the appropriate levels of abstraction. The strategy
that Creanimate uses to help the student form appropriate generalizations
is called *similarity-based reminding*. In similarity-based reminding, the system retrieves a case that illustrates the same basic principle as a previous
example, but is sufficiently different to allow the student to form an
appropriate generalization. The following example of a similarity-based

reminding can be initiated by a student's request for a tortoise that could run fast:

```
Cheetahs run fast. Do you know why cheetahs run fast? (I have an
impressive video about that. )
Student: So they can catch other animals.
That is right. Would you like to see that?
Student: yes
[VIDEO: Cheetah Pursuing Prey]
```

Similarity-Based Reminding

```
That reminds me of a cool video. Fishing bats also move fast in
order to get food. Only, instead of running fast to pursue their
prey, they fly to pounce on their prey. Would you like to see that?
Student: yes
[VIDEO: Fishing Bat]
```

In the example reminding in this transcript, the program presents a video of a cheetah that runs fast to pursue its prey. To help the student generalize and enrich his or her repertoire of cases, the program presents a similarity-based reminding about an animal that moves fast to get its food, but flies instead of running. To perform similarity-based reminding, the system must be able to identify cases that are similar, but not identical, to the given example. This is done by searching through its knowledge base and looking for videos that share an abstraction with the preceding example. In this case, the descriptions of the action in both videos share the abstraction: *move fast to hunt*. In addition to assisting with the process of generalizing, similarity-based remindings also serve to broaden student exposure and hopefully increase their curiosity.

Expectation-Violation Remindings in Creanimate

Surprise is a great motivator for learning. When some expectation that you have is violated by an experience or observation, you become surprised and are motivated to understand why your expectation was not met. This is what Schank (1982) called *failure-driven learning*. Expectation failures promote learning as well as interest. The reminding strategy called *expectation-violation reminding* capitalizes on surprise to provoke interest on the part of a student while also broadening his or her exposure. To present videos that violate students' expectations, the system must have knowledge of what sorts of things students are likely to believe. This information is added to the knowledge base during the indexing process. Expectations take the form of generalizations, such as "Mammals do not fly." This particular generalization leads to the following expectation-violation reminding:

```
If you could create a new animal by taking an existing animal and
changing it some way, what would you make?
Student: A dog that can fly
Actually some mammals do fly. For example, fishing bats fly. I have
a cool video about that. Would you like to see that?
Student: yes
[VIDEO: Fishing Bat]
```

Part of the index for the fishing bat video contains the information that the bat violates the expectation that mammals do not fly. When the student asks for an animal that violates the same expectation (in this case, a dog that can fly), this matches the expectation violation in the video, and the program gets reminded of that video.

All three reminding strategies capitalize on a student's current context to present a case that is directly relevant at that moment. The cases that a student sees respond to an action or answer that the student has made in the course of his session. The responsiveness of the reminding strategies is designed to enhance students' motivation. The cases retrieved by the reminding strategies provide concrete cases to illustrate the current discussion, promote appropriate generalizations, and widen students' exposure. Each of these, in turn, can promote curiosity and trigger additional inquiry. However, to facilitate these reminding strategies, a storyteller must have an appropriately indexed library of cases.

Indexing

In the course of a dialogue, a case based teaching storyteller examines indexes in its case library to retrieve cases that are relevant to a student's situation. To support effective case retrieval, the indexing vocabulary must be expressive enough to describe the range of storytelling situations that arise in the task environment. An index must capture enough information about a case that the storyteller can identify situations to which the case applies.

An index is neither the complete representation of a case, nor is it necessarily the summary of a case. The role of an index is to describe when and how a case should be told. Therefore, an index may make no reference to the contents of the case, but may instead describe the sorts of settings in which the case is appropriate. For example, a case based teaching system that uses a simulation to teach firefighters must contain a case about a previous fire that climbed up through the walls of a building without any visible flames and burst out several floors above firefighters.

The index for that case would not necessarily describe anything about the contents of the case. Instead, the index would describe situations in which the case is relevant. For example, the index would indicate that the case applies to situations in which a student acts as if a fire is under control without checking the walls. Through its communication with the task environment, the storyteller would be able to identify when the student firefighter is in the situation described by the index, and the reminding strategies would find and present this case.

An index in a case based teaching system is typically a structured data representation implemented in the form of slots and fillers. The set of slots that makes up an index for a particular case library provides the structure of the index, and the allowable filters comprise the indexing vocabulary. Just as with reminding strategies, the structure and contents of indexes are determined by the educational goals of the system, the structure of the task environment, and the nature of the subject matter. The structure of indexes and the indexing vocabulary must be developed together with the reminding strategies to ensure that the indexes contain all of the information required by the reminding strategies. In addition, indexes must be structured in a manner that allows for the implementation of the reminding strategies using efficient algorithms.

In Creanimate, a student's situation—for the purposes of reminding— can be described by the explanation question under consideration, the most recent output by the system and the student's response, and the cases and explanation questions that the student has already seen. Therefore, the explanation questions that structure the dialogues also determined the structure of indexes. Similarly, the relationships expressed by the explanation questions and the conceptual categories to which they refer determined the indexing vocabulary. Using the indexing vocabulary within the structure provided by indexes, an indexer is able to describe the concepts and relationships that appear in a particular video. This information allows the reminding strategies to recognize situations in which that particular video is appropriate for presentation to a student.

The Indexing Vocabulary in Creanimate

Although the primary role of the indexing vocabulary in a case based teaching system is the support of indexing and retrieval, the indexing vocabulary in Creanimate also plays a critical role in supporting the dialogue manager. The representation language that provides the indexing vocabulary also enables the dialogue manager to draw the inferences about animal adaptations necessary to manage its open-ended question-and-answer dialogues. The indexing vocabulary in Creanimate supports four major activities of the storyteller and dialogue manager:

- Case retrieval (storyteller)
- Dialogue initiation (dialogue manager)
- Evaluation of student responses to questions (dialogue manager)
- Communication (between dialogue manager and storyteller)

To support these activities, the Creanimate indexing vocabulary is capable of expressing both the specific information about cases required by the reminding strategies of the storyteller and the general information about animal adaptation employed by the dialogue manager in conducting dialogues. These capabilities are provided by the Creanimate knowledge representation language, implemented as a semantic network. It is designed not only to support the indexing requirements of the storyteller and the inferencing requirements of the dialogue manager, but to provide the ability to generate and interpret natural language.

The structure and content of indexes must derive from the educational goal of the system. As discussed earlier, helping students to understand explanation questions and store their knowledge with respect to these explanation questions is a central pedagogical goal of Creanimate. Therefore, determining the appropriate explanation questions was the first step toward developing a representation and indexing vocabulary. The choice of explanation questions determined which types of concepts and relationships were required for the knowledge representation. For example, historically, the first explanation question implemented in Creanimate was *How action?* (e.g., "How would you like to change your tortoise so it can run fast?"). This explanation question reflects an educational goal that students recognize that every action an animal performs requires a set of enabling physical features. Furthermore, students should know the particular features required for particular actions. To present knowledge to the student in this form, Creanimate must have its knowledge organized in the same fashion.

In this manner, each explanation question used by the Socratic dialogue manager establishes important requirements for the Creanimate knowledge representation. For instance, the implementation of *How action?* required that the knowledge representation include a vocabulary to describe the physical features and actions, and the different ways that actions can depend on physical features. In addition, it has to provide a way to associate a particular feature with a particular action for a particular animal. In implementing the *How action?* dialogue, these requirements gave rise to the knowledge structures called *features, actions,* and *feafuns,* described later. The implementation of this explanation question also influenced the structure of indexes. For the storyteller to retrieve cases that are relevant to a discussion of the *How action?* explanation question, the indexing vocabulary has to be able to indicate that a particular case illustrates the use of one or a set of physical features to support an action.

The Creanimate indexing vocabulary is composed of two classes of representational structures: objects and relationships. Objects are used to represent individual concepts, such as animals, features, and actions. Relationships link two of these objects together in a structured relationship so that they can be associated with an animal. For example, a relationship may associate a physical feature and an action to a particular animal that uses the feature to perform the action. The object classes in Creanimate include:

Features. Physical characteristics of animals (e.g., beak, claws, fur, small size).

Actions. Activities of animals that are performed using features (e.g., running, swimming, biting, scraping).

Behaviors. High-level, goal-directed activities of animals (e.g., hunting, fleeing predators, attracting a mate).

Animals. Specific animals or abstract categories of animals (e.g., cheetah, raptor, pike, mammal).

Phys-obj's. Physical objects other than animals that are found in the world (e.g., plant, rock, seed).

Objects are represented in Creanimate as nodes in hierarchical networks with links to other objects. Objects are connected to other objects of the same type through a variety of abstraction and packaging hierarchies. For example, behaviors may be connected to other behaviors by *part-of, achieves,* and *isa* relationships. Objects are connected to objects of other types in ways that indicate how they relate to each other in the natural world. For example, actions are connected to the behaviors that they support, the features that are required to perform them, and the animals that perform them.

The Creanimate indexing vocabulary contains three primary relationships. They connect objects together in the following ways:

Feafuns. A feafun connects a physical feature to an action that it is used to perform (e.g., *long legs in order to run fast*). The name *feafun* is an abbreviation of "feature for a function."

Plans. A plan connects an action to a behavior that it supports (e.g., *run fast in order to pursue prey*).

Bplans. A bplan connects a lower level behavior to the higher level behavior that it supports (e.g., *pursue prey in order to hunt*).

Relationships are used to tie features, actions, and behaviors together and associate them with a particular animal. For example, the animal *giraffe*

possesses the feafun *long neck in order to reach*. These relationships correspond directly to the explanation questions that the system poses. For
instance, the questions "What feature could an animal use to reach for
food?" and "Why might an animal have a long neck?" are both answered
by the feafun *long neck in order to reach*.

In addition to the primary relationships listed earlier, Creanimate contains a special kind of relationship called a *rule*. Rules are used to support
the expectation-violation reminding strategy.

> *Rules.* A rule encodes a common generalization (e.g., "No fish have
> wings") that is known to have exceptions.

Rules differ from the other relationships in Creanimate, in that the information they encode is not true under all conditions. Rules are used to
capture generalizations that students are likely to believe for the purposes
of expectation-violation remindings. However, every rule in Creanimate
has at least one significant exception that is illustrated by a case in the case
library. The role of a rule in the storyteller is to trigger expectation-violation
remindings about an exception to that rule. The process by which relationships and objects are added to the indexing vocabulary proceeds from (a)
a taxonomy of the questions that are critical to an understanding of the
subject matter to (b) a set of relationships that correspond to those questions
to (c) a set of basic concepts that are connected by these relationships.

The Structure of Indexes

An index in Creanimate is implemented as a frame with slots and
values. The values are drawn from the indexing vocabulary. Each index
describes the attributes and activities of one animal that appears in the
video clip. Any particular video clip may have several indexes. Thus, a
clip about a robin chasing a cat away from a nest full of chicks might
have three indexes: one for the robin, one for the cat, and one for the
chicks. Figure 2.2 shows an index for a case about a woodpecker using
its beak to probe for insects. This index is relatively simple; more elaborate
indexes can be found in Edelson (1993).

The slots in indexes are divided between primary and secondary slots.
The primary slots describe an animal and the attributes that it displays
in the video clip. The secondary slots serve pragmatic requirements of
the storyteller. The primary slots in an index are: *animal*, an animal that
appears in the case; *features*, the features used by the animal in the case;
actions, the actions performed by the animal in the case; *behaviors*, the
behaviors achieved by the animal in the case; *feafuns*, the feafuns demonstrated by the animal in the case; *plans*, the plans demonstrated by the

```
(DEFFRAME index woodpecker-pecks-woodpecker
  :animals ([animal red-cockadoo-woodpecker]
  :features ([feature small-beak])
  :behaviors ([behavior search-for-insects])
  :actions ([action peck])
  :feafuns ([feafun :feature [feature small-beak ]
      :action [action peck ]
      :abstraction
        feafun :feature [feature beak]
        :action [action pierce]]])
  :plans ([plan :action [action peck ]
      :behavior [behavior search-for-insects ]
      :impact ([impact askable])
      :abstraction
      [plan :action [action pierce]
      :behavior [behavior get-food]]])
  :story [story woodpecker-eats]
  :impact ([impact cool ] [impact slow-motion])
  :rating 8
  :video ((101001 102500 (disk 'nat-and-brit) "A")))
```

FIG. 2.2. An index for a video that shows a woodpecker using its beak to peck at a tree in search of insects.

animal in the case; and *expect-viols*, the general expectations about animal adaptations that are violated by the case. The *animal, features, actions*, and *behaviors* slots are bidirectional slots that link indexes directly to objects in the knowledge representation. The secondary slots in an index—the *story, video, rating,* and *impact* slots—assist the storyteller in locating clips on a laserdisc, deciding which clips to show first, and preparing textual descriptions of clips to introduce them.

The Use of Indexes by Reminding Strategies

The reminding strategies in Creanimate are implemented as searches through abstraction hierarchies. Because indexes are linked to animals, features, actions, and behaviors by bidirectional links, the reminding strategies are able to locate relevant cases by searching through hierarchies of these objects and then retrieving indexes that are linked to them. This is made possible by the hierarchical knowledge representation that makes up the indexing vocabulary. As an example, consider the following transcript showing an *example reminding*:

```
OK, let's find a reason for your frog to have wings. Is there a
reason you want your frog to have wings?
Student: So it can fly
That's a good idea. White breasted sea eagles use their feathered
wings to help them to fly.
```

```
Would you like to see that?
Student: Yes
[VIDEO: "Sea Eagle Catches Fish"]
```

In this transcript, the explanation question is, "Why have wings?", and the student's answer is, "so it can fly." Once the dialogue manager has verified that flying is a reason that animals have wings, the correct answer reminding algorithm initiates a search for an example case. This search is guided by the relationship that results from combining the current explanation question and the student's answer. When the student in the prior transcript gave the answer *to fly*, the storyteller combined them into the following feafun representing *wings in order to fly*: [feafun :feature [feature wings] :action [action fly]].

To be an appropriate correct answer reminding, an index must contain this feafun, which is called the *target concept*. To find a case that contains the target concept, the Creanimate storyteller searches down abstraction hierarchies, starting from one of the values in the target concept. The goal of this search is to find an index that contains the target concept or a specialization of it. The principle behind the example reminding algorithm is: A case about the specialization of a concept is an example case for the concept. Therefore, a case about a feafun that is a specialization of *wings in order to fly* is an example case for *wings in order to fly*. To retrieve the prior example case, the correct answer reminding strategy starts with the feature *wings* and searches down abstraction links for features associated with cases. Each time it finds a feature that appears in a case, it checks to see if the index for the case contains a feafun that matches the target concept. The abstraction hierarchy beneath the feature *wings* is shown in Fig. 2.3.

As the reminding algorithm traverses this hierarchy, it looks for indexes that match the prior feafun. When it reaches *feathered wings*, it finds the index for the sea eagle case that appears in the earlier transcript. The index for this case contains the following feafun: [feafun :feature [feature feathered-wings] :action [action fly]]. Because this feafun is a specialization of the target concept *wings in order to fly*, the example reminding algorithm recognizes this case as an example of the current concept, and thus it presents it to the student. Of course, another index that contained a further specialization, such as *large wings in order to soar*, would also be an appropriate reminding.

The correct answer reminding strategy described here is the simplest of the reminding strategies. Other reminding strategies use different information and pursue different search algorithms through the system's knowledge base. For example, the similarity-based reminding strategy employs a search algorithm resembling spreading activation, which starts from a description of the most recent case and examines similar cases to

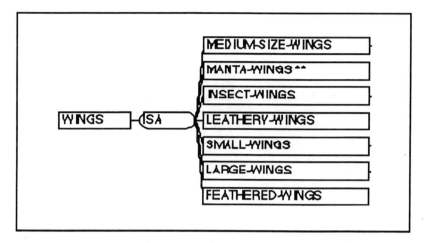

FIG. 2.3. A portion of the abstraction hierarchy of features beneath the feature *wings*. Parent objects (abstractions) appear to the left and children (specializations) to the right.

see whether they meet the criteria for a similarity-based reminding. The expectation-violation reminding strategies employ search algorithms that are similar to those used by the prior example reminding strategy. However, they focus on the information contained in the *expect-viols* slot in indexes. The algorithms used to implement these reminding strategies are described in detail in Edelson (1993).

The Coverage of the Indexes in Creanimate

The most recent Creanimate knowledge base includes 206 indexes. However, the prototype version tested in the study described later had access to only 60 minutes of video, which limited it to 135 indexes. The indexes in Creanimate cover a wide range of birds, mammals, fish, reptiles, and amphibians. Creanimate is able to get a great deal of coverage out of the clips that it possesses because each clip can be used in several different contexts. To maximize the value of clips, versatility is emphasized in the case-selection process. The versatility of a clip is determined by the number of animal attributes that can be recorded in an index for that clip. For example, an index with five different features can be retrieved to illustrate five different *Why feature?* dialogues by the example reminding algorithm. The average index in Creanimate includes at least two different values for each type of animal attribute (i.e., more than two features, two actions, and two behaviors). Because actions and behaviors can be used in both *how* and *why* dialogues, the average index can be used to illustrate discussions of at least eight different explanation questions.

Indexing and Reminding for Socratic Case Based Teaching

In presenting Creanimate's indexing scheme and reminding strategies, this chapter has described their specific implementation for the Creanimate system. However, the approach presented here is a general one for the support of Socratic case based teaching. Once the explanation questions for a subject area have been determined, these explanation questions can be used to establish the structure of indexes and the nature of the indexing vocabulary in the same way that the five basic explanation questions and three conceptual categories from animal adaptation were used to construct the indexing scheme in Creanimate. The reminding strategies employed by Creanimate's storyteller (e.g., example reminding, similarity-based reminding, and expectation-violation reminding) can be directly applied to Socratic-style dialogues for any subject matter. The construction of additional Socratic case based teaching systems will likely lead to the development of new reminding strategies, especially as systems are developed to deal with subject matter of greater complexity and subtlety than that of Creanimate.

THE CASE BASED TEACHING ARCHITECTURE IN CONTEXT

The development of the case based teaching architecture is taking place in an environment of increasing attention on the learning sciences. This research on the case based teaching architecture has important ties to other methods for teaching with cases, other research on artificial intelligence in education, and other developments in technology in education.

The Case Based Teaching Architecture and the Case Method

The case based teaching architecture has much in common with the case method of instruction that is commonly employed in business schools, law schools, and other professional education (McNair, 1954; Williams, 1992). Both the case based teaching architecture and the case method share an emphasis on learning from cases and a recognition of the importance of a learner's development of a personal case library. However, the case based teaching architecture focuses on a specific element of teaching with cases—the presentation of cases in response to opportunities that arise in the course of learning interactions. As it is commonly practiced, the case method employs cases to establish the context for a discussion or problem-solving episode. Within the context of a case, students might discuss interpretations of the situation or present solutions to posed problems. Instead of focusing on the use of cases to establish such a context, the case based teaching architecture focuses on the presentation of cases that respond to a student's context within a task environment. This recall and presentation of cases in response to learning interactions is by no means unique to the case based teaching architecture; indeed, it is an important element of the case method as it is practiced in many settings.

The Case Based Teaching Architecture and Intelligent Tutoring Systems

With few exceptions, research on intelligent tutoring systems (ITSs) has not focused on the use of cases in instruction. Two notable exceptions are Clancy's (1987) GUIDON system, which used a case method approach to teaching medical diagnosis, and Ashley and Aleven's (1992) approach to teaching the appropriate use of precedents in legal reasoning. Instead, the primary focus of most ITSs has been on student modeling and diagnosis. The goal of the ITS approach is to respond intelligently and dynamically to the needs of a student by representing expert and novice understanding for the particular domain and inferring the student's understanding from limited information. The use of rule-based representations generally restricts the applicability of the ITS approach to domains that lend themselves to such representations—primarily formal domains, such as algebra, physics, and computer programming.

One of the goals of the case based teaching architecture is to extend beyond well-structured domains by adopting a case based approach to the challenge of responding to students' needs. The case based teaching architecture aims to reduce the amount of representation and inference necessary to track the student while increasing the richness of the communication with students through the presentation of cases. The criterion for intervention in an ITS is typically, "Can the system infer that the student is lacking a particular rule, fact, or skill?" The case based teaching architecture reduces this criterion for intervention to, "Is a case relevant to the student's situation?" This is done by using cases with content rich enough that a student will profit from the case in that situation, regardless of the exact state of the student's knowledge. By reducing the reasoning requirements of the system to reasoning about the student's situation in the task environment, and not the student's knowledge, the case based teaching architecture is designed to widen the range of subjects that can be taught by computer-based systems.

In addition to attempting to reduce the burden of inference, the case based teaching architecture also addresses the issue that Wenger (1987) called *knowledge communication*. Because most ITSs are rule-based systems, and have at their heart a model of a student as a rule-based reasoner, the form that their communication usually takes with students is rules. In contrast, the case based teaching architecture is designed to support case based reasoning through the presentation of cases in context.

The Case Based Teaching Architecture and Goal-Based Scenarios

A recent strand of research in educational technology that is closely related to the case based teaching architecture is directed at implementing the goal-based scenario (GBS) framework (Schank, Fano, Bell, & Jona, 1993/1994). A GBS provides a context in which a learner pursues a set of authentic goals and increases his or her understanding of a particular subject matter through the activities that lead to the achievement of these goals. The implementation of the GBS framework on a computer takes the form of a learn-by-doing environment in which a user acquires a particular set of skills and knowledge by adopting a role in a simulated scenario. Implemented GBSs on the computer include Broadcast News (Kass, Dooley, Luksa, 1994), a system that teaches high school students about political science and current events by enabling them to assemble a television news show; Sickle Cell Counselor (Bell, Bareiss, & Beckwith, 1993/1994), a museum installation that teaches about Sickle Cell disease by allowing the user to play the role of a genetic counselor for couples concerned about passing on Sickle Cell disease to their children; and Human Resources Management (Acovelli & Nowakowski, 1994), a module of a corporate training system on business practices that teaches about human resources management by allowing the learner to play the role of a manager.

The core of the GBS framework is a carefully selected scenario that provides students with the motivation and opportunities to learn. Schank et al. (1993/1994) presented a detailed specification of the features that are necessary for an effective scenario. In this respect, the GBS framework represents an important approach to the construction of effective, engaging task environments. The framework is broad enough to encompass a wide range of strategies for responding to the opportunities for learning that arise as a student participates in the scenario. Presenting cases as a response to student actions fits within the GBS framework, as do coaching, outcome-driven simulation, and direct tutorial intervention. Therefore, the case based teaching architecture and the GBS framework are overlapping approaches. The GBS framework provides recommendations for effective task environments that could be used within the case based teaching architecture, and the case based teaching architecture provides a mechanism for capitalizing on opportunities for learning through case presentation that can be used within the GBS framework.

EXPERIENCES WITH CREANIMATE

This section turns from the theoretical and implementation issues of Creanimate and the case based teaching architecture to its use. Formal evaluations of Creanimate were conducted in two suburban Chicago public schools. The primary test site was a mixed-socioeconomic status (SES) elementary school, where Creanimate was used by 23 fourth graders. The secondary test site was a summer school program, where Creanimate was used by 15 students in fifth through eighth grades. In both sites, students had the opportunity to use the program for three sessions of approximately 45 minutes over a 2- to 3-week period. Because of the mixed age group in the sample, the secondary test site was used more for software testing than for design evaluation. However, our observations in the secondary test site confirmed our expectations about the target age group for Creanimate. Although students beyond fourth or fifth grade enjoyed Creanimate, it did not appear to sustain their attention as it did for younger students. For this reason, the results in the remainder of this section describe only the primary (fourth-grade) site.

The studies of Creanimate were designed to examine three central questions: Did the software succeed in engaging students? What patterns of use emerged among students? Did the use of Creanimate have any impact on question asking and reasoning with cases by students within the animal adaptation domain? The studies to examine the third question, on learning outcome, yielded no results of statistical significance, and thus are not discussed in this section. However, they are discussed in the following section as part of the discussion of future evaluation. Because the studies described here represented the first time the software received extended use by children, they were an occasion for bug identification and repair, and for enhancement of the natural language parser. Consequently, the software was modified significantly both in the course of and following these evaluations.

The Setting

The primary study site was a mixed-SES, racially mixed elementary school in suburban Chicago. Detailed demographic information about the particular students was not available. However, they were primarily from lower SES working-class backgrounds. There were 12 girls and 11 boys. Nineteen of the 23 students were African American. All students reported previous experience with computers, but half had never used a mouse before.

Students were called out of regular class activities one or two at a time to use Creanimate for 45 minutes, approximately once a week for 3 weeks. Each student used Creanimate three times. The study was conducted in a small room adjoining the classroom that was equipped with four computers. The version of Creanimate they used runs on an IBM PS/2 computer connected to a laserdisc player. Video was displayed directly on the computer screen, and students wore headphones so they would not disturb each other. Researchers were present at all times to teach students how to use the equipment, answer any questions, and respond to technical problems. The students' sessions were clearly affected by the prototype nature of the software. A careful reading of the students' transcripts reveals parsing problems and buggy output in virtually every transcript. Most errors, such as grammatical errors in the system's output, did not appear to disrupt students. However, students were occasionally frustrated by the parser, confused by its incomplete or inaccurate understanding of their input, or puzzled by apparently incoherent or incorrect output.

Student Engagement

In the primary test site, with few exceptions, the students used the system for as long as we would allow them—40–45 minutes—at all three sessions. Five of the nearly 70 sessions at the primary site were terminated early because of persistent technical problems. Typically when the researcher announced that a session was over, students would ask to continue beyond the allotted time. This was not permitted because of the limited time available for all the students. At the end of every session, students were asked if they wanted to come back and use the program again the following week. All students responded positively.

All of the students' sessions were observed by researchers who kept notes about both student and program behavior. It was evident from these observations that students found the software engaging. Research notes recorded that many students laughed and exclaimed at the videos, carefully composed answers to questions, and begged to use the program for "just 2 more minutes." They often tried to draw a researcher or student sitting at a neighboring computer into their session. The observations also recorded that, although students were engaged, they were not necessarily engaged in ways that completely met with the designers' expectations. Some students did not appear to be reading the questions the program posed. Others appeared to read them, but not to be interested in answering them. Some students seemed to find the questions compelling, and devoted a great deal of attention to answering them. However, some of these same students then showed little or no interest in viewing the videos that were offered in response to their answers. Some students found ways

TABLE 2.2
Student Opinions on Various Aspects of Creanimate

	Creating an Animal	Answering Questions	Watching Videos	How the Program Looks	User Control Buttons	Using the Mouse
Mean	4.22**	3.10*	4.12**	4.25**	3.58*	4.14**

Note. Students were asked how they felt about different elements of the program, and were asked to choose from *dislike alot, dislike, neutral, like,* or *like alot.* Their responses were coded from 1 to 5, with *dislike alot* being 1 and *like alot* being 5 ($N = 20$). Means followed by double asterisks (**) are significantly higher than those with a single asterisk (*) in paired t tests ($p < .05$).

to view videos without ever answering questions, and several chose to view the same video over and over again. One girl, a dancer, asked for a butterfly that could dance at the beginning of all three of her sessions, and consequently watched the same videos showing animals dancing in all three sessions.

After the students' first session with Creanimate, they were interviewed about how they liked different aspects of the program. Because approximately half of the students were using a mouse for the first time, they were also asked how they liked using the mouse. The rating of the mouse was designed to serve as a baseline comparison. The average rating for all aspects of the program was positive (Table 2.2 and Figure 2.4).

The program's appearance, the act of creating an animal, using the mouse, and watching videos received higher ratings than the user control

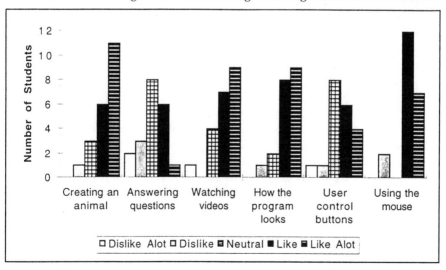

FIG. 2.4. Frequency of student responses to the question of how well they liked specific aspects of Creanimate.

buttons and answering questions. There was no significant difference between the means of the higher rated four features and the lower rated two. However, in a pairwise comparison, ratings of answering questions and of the user control buttons were significantly lower than the ratings of the other features ($p < .05$ for all comparisons). The lower rating of the user control buttons may reflect the limited amount of use these buttons received. Answering questions also received a lower rating—lower than the mean rating of watching videos by 1.12 [$t(19) = 6.319$, $p < .0001$] and the mean rating of creating an animal by 1.22 [$t(19) = 3.340$, $p < .01$]. Students' relatively low rating of how they liked answering the program's questions is also reflected in the use patterns described later, where some students' transcripts revealed a clear tendency to avoid the answering of questions. Although the average student rating of answering questions is still positive (between neutral and good), the low rating relative to other aspects of the software indicates that a closer examination of the motivational aspects of these questions may be necessary.

In the students' interview responses and researchers' observations, there is significant evidence that the students found Creanimate engaging. However, the observations raised questions about the nature of their engagement, which were further examined through an analysis of the use patterns that appeared in their transcripts.

Patterns of Use

Following the observation that students were responding to different aspects of the program in different ways, an analysis of their interactions was performed to identify specific patterns of use and quantify the prevalence of the various use patterns (Cleave, Edelson, & Beckwith, 1993). All the students' interactions with Creanimate were recorded in transcripts that captured every action of both the software and the student. For this study, more than 60 transcripts were analyzed, excluding only the 5 transcripts from sessions that were significantly abbreviated because of technical problems. To facilitate analysis, student–computer interactions were coded into categories such as those shown in Table 2.3. Because transcripts varied significantly in the number of events (58–247, $M = 120$) per session, the percentage of total events for each category was used in the analysis, rather than the number of events.

An analysis of the correlations of the frequency of particular events in student transcripts revealed an interesting result about the relationship between answering open-ended questions and watching videos. There was a negative correlation between typing text in response to questions (as opposed to selecting an answer from a menu) and watching videos when they were offered ($r = -.60$, $p < .01$). This indicates that students who were

TABLE 2.3
A Sample of the Categories of Student Actions
Used in Coding Creanimate Transcripts

Category	Action
BACKUP	Student pressed "Back up" button.
COM-PLAN	Student completed a dialogue about an explanation question for a plan.
EQ-PLAN	Student began a dialogue about an explanation question for a plan.
IN-EQ <text>	Student input an answer for an explanation question posed by the program.
NO-VIDEO	Student responded "no" to an offer to see a video.
SUGGEST	Student selected "Give me some suggestions" in response to an explanation question.
VIDEO	Student selected "yes" in response to an offer to see a video.
WHAT	Student selected "What other videos can I see?" in response to an offer to see a video.

Note. The coding system included 59 event categories (Cleave et al., 1993).

motivated to respond to questions were less likely to watch videos. Conversely, students who chose to ask the program to tell them the answers to questions, instead of entering their own answers, were more likely to watch videos ($r = .53, p < .01$). This unexpected result could have important implications for the success of Socratic case based teaching systems, if interest in question-and-answer dialogues does not correlate with interest in video cases. However, this result may only be a limited reflection of individual preference because the analysis considered each event category as a percentage of all events. Therefore, an increase in one event category, such as question answering, must be accompanied by a decrease in some other event category. Further research will be necessary to clarify this result.

To better understand the overall patterns of use, a cluster analysis was performed on the event counts, using Euclidean distance and a furthest neighbor technique.[10] Z scores of the variables representing the count of each event as a percentage of all events were used in the cluster analysis to balance events that occurred more frequently (e.g., watching a video) with events that occurred more rarely (e.g., completing a dialogue). The cluster analysis produced five clusters of users, which have been given the names *balanced users, video avoiders, compliant users, video hoppers,* and *resisters.*[11] Representative transcripts from these groups are included in the appendix.

---

[10]An average linking between groups technique produced the same results.

[11]In a previous analysis (Cleave et al., 1993), balanced users were called *writers,* compliant users were called *model users,* video avoiders were called *dominators,* and resisters were called *artists.* Subsequent analysis of the clusters has led to the new names, which better reflect the attributes of these users.

The characteristics that distinguish groups were students' preference for typing responses or asking for suggestions, amount of video they watched, and tendency to exert control over the flow of the dialogue or follow the program's lead. Table 2.4 and Fig. 2.5 show the frequency of certain events, expressed as an average of the total events, both by cluster and for all students.

Analyzing the clusters based on field notes and transcript events, the following characterizations of cluster members were developed:

1. *Balanced users* ($n = 4$). The balanced users took advantage of the greatest range of the features offered by the software. Balanced users stand out as the group that typed in answers to questions more than any other group; but, with the exception of video hoppers, they also watched the most video clips. When they typed responses, their answers were significantly longer than those of the other groups. Finally, unlike compliant users, who also answered questions and viewed videos in large numbers, balanced users took advantage of opportunities to exert control, and were persistent in their efforts to express themselves in free text. They commonly typed in second and third answers after the parser failed to understand an initial input.

TABLE 2.4
Mean for Selected Transcript Events Shown for All Users and by Cluster

Event Category	All Users	Video Hoppers	Video Avoiders	Balanced Users	Compliant Users	Resisters
Completed a dialogue	4.6	4.7	4.7	4.7	7.3	2.5
	(2.1)	(0.3)	(1.3)	(0.9)	(1.6)	(0.9)
Watched a video	17.1	29.3	10.4	18.9	16.3	18.1
	(7.4)	(2.4)	(5.4)	(4.6)	(3.6)	(7.6)
Typed in an entry (not	8.7	3.3	10.0	11.7	8.8	7.4
including an animal)	(2.8)	(1.7)	(1.2)	(1.8)	(1.8)	(1.8)
Selected "Give me some	5.4	10.2	4.9	5.3	6.0	4.0
suggestions"	(2.8)	(1.3)	(1.5)	(1.6)	(2.6)	(3.0)
Took a tangent from a	2.8	1.4	3.5	3.5	1.3	3.3
dialogue	(2.2)	(0.8)	(2.4)	(1.1)	(1.6)	(2.6)
Replied "no" to an offered	7.7	3.0	13.4	8.0	7.0	5.3
video	(4.3)	(0.3)	(3.9)	(2.6)	(3.0)	(2.1)
Pressed "Start over" button	2.7	0.3	2.4	1.7	1.4	5.0
	(2.5)	(0.3)	(1.7)	(1.5)	(1.0)	(2.6)
Said "Tell me" or "I don't	1.6	6.6	1.4	1.0	1.2	1.0
know" to a question	(1.9)	(1.0)	(1.2)	(1.7)	(1.0)	(0.8)
Entered own animal or	1.8	0.6	1.1	0.8	1.7	3.3
modification	(1.6)	(0.6)	(0.7)	(1.0)	(1.2)	(1.6)

Note. The events are expressed as the average of total events per transcript. Standard deviations appear in parentheses.

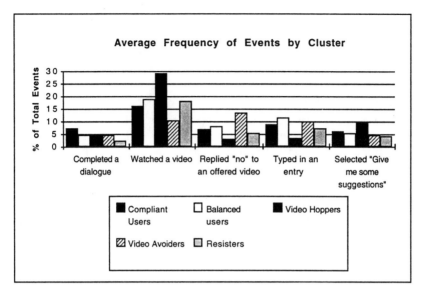

FIG. 2.5. A graph of the average frequency of selected events by cluster.

2. *Video avoiders* ($n = 5$). The cluster analysis showed video avoiders and balanced users to be the two most similar groups. The primary difference is that video avoiders watched fewer videos, the fewest of any group, and declined offers to view videos more than any group. Like balanced users, video avoiders showed a preference for typing in responses, rather than asking for suggestions. After balanced users, video avoiders typed input and entered a second input when the first was not understood more often than any other group. However, they were the group that was most likely to type in answers that Creanimate could not understand, and to give unverifiable answers leading to tangent dialogues about the unverifiable answers. Video avoiders also exerted more control than balanced users, using the "Skip this" button more than any other group. Unlike resisters, however, they tended to exert control within the confines of the dialogue, using "Skip this" to move around within a dialogue. Resisters tended to use the "Start over" button to begin a completely new dialogue.

3. *Compliant users* ($n = 5$). Like balanced users, compliant users were characterized by balance in their use of the program. However, as a group, they were distinguished by their minimal efforts to control the dialogue and their lack of persistence in response to failures by the parser to understand their answers. Their transcripts often read as if they were trying to cause the least trouble for the program. They answered questions an average amount of times, but they asked for suggestions, instead of typing answers, slightly more often than average. Unlike balanced users

or video avoiders, they rarely tried a second time when the parser could not understand their input. In contrast to the other groups, compliant users appeared to have the completion of dialogues as a goal. They generally declined opportunities to take tangents from the central dialogue, and they completed dialogues almost twice as often as any other group. Compliant users saw an average number of videos.

4. *Video hoppers* ($n = 2$). Video hoppers seem to be motivated to watch videos at the expense of all the other aspects of the program. The two video hoppers each saw 48 and 52 videos across their three sessions—more than twice the average for all students, which was 23.5. Their transcripts reveal strategies that allowed them to navigate between one video and the next in the shortest possible time. As a result, they input text the least of any students, averaging 6 text inputs over all three sessions, compared with an average of 12 for all students.

5. *Resisters* ($n = 7$). Members of the resister cluster can only be characterized as not accepting or not understanding the basic structure of the Creanimate dialogues. Their failure to comply with the program's normal flow is illustrated by the fact that they rarely completed dialogues (half the class average) and used the "Start over," "Skip this," and "What's the point?" buttons more than any other students. Although resisters had the lowest number of successful parses, they were the most likely to choose their own animal (e.g., shark, lion, panther, boar, horse, koala) instead of the suggested animals, and they had the highest number of responses that were anthropomorphic (e.g., "boxing gloves," "bonnet," "do the mc hammer," and "kick someone's butt"). Field notes record that resisters were motivated by the act of creating an animal more than the other students, and were frustrated by the inability to see their animal right away or draw it themselves. One student, when asked why he wanted a particular feature, ignored the computer's prompt, "So it can . . . ," and typed in, "I want to see my animal." In answer to an interview question about how the student would change the program, one resister said, "Put the animal on the screen and show changes immediately." Another said, "[I want a] picture of the changed animal," and a third requested animations of the created animals. Resisters watched an average number of videos, but, with the disjointed nature of their dialogues, their attitude toward videos probably most resembles that of the video hoppers. The resisters appeared, as a group, to respond to the idea of creating an animal and even to seeing the video, but not to participating in Creanimate's dialogues.

The cluster analysis provides reason for encouragement and discouragement about Creanimate and teaching with cases. The balanced users, video avoiders, and compliant users (14 of 23 students) appeared to respond positively to the question-based dialogue structure. Similarly, all but the video avoiders (18 of 23) appeared to respond positively to the video cases. However, the video avoiders (5 of 23), video hoppers (2 of 23), and resisters (7 of 23) appeared to respond negatively to one or more central elements of the program. The existence of the balanced user and compliant user clusters shows that a significant number of students respond to Creanimate's combination of the dialogue structure with video cases. However, the video avoiders, video hoppers, and resisters raise questions about the relative value of a Socratic case based teaching system like Creanimate to a user who does not fully engage with either the dialogue or the video cases. The evidence from observations, interviews, and transcript analysis—that all of the students found Creanimate engaging, but that different individuals responded to different elements—raises the significant question of how differences in engagement impact learning outcomes. The theory of the importance of cases in context that underlies this research would predict that neither engagement with just cases nor with just the dialogue would lead to an understanding that is as well developed as that which would result from engagement with both. Students who only engage with the video would be expected to develop poorly indexed case libraries, and those who only engage with the dialogue would be expected to develop a framework for understanding that is not well supported by cases. Further examination of these issues requires additional research.

STRENGTHS, LIMITATIONS, AND FUTURE DIRECTIONS

The preceding sections detailed the theory, implementation, and use of Creanimate, and the case based teaching architecture. This section turns to a discussion of the strengths and limitations of this work, with an emphasis on directions for future research to address these issues.

The Creanimate system is an attempt to put the case based teaching architecture into practice. Its primary research goal was to develop a framework for the presentation of educational cases in the context of an engaging task environment. The Socratic case based teaching architecture embodied by Creanimate is such a framework. This architecture provides for a question-and-answer dialogue between the computer and a student that establishes a context for learning from video cases. The indexing scheme and reminding strategies enable the storyteller to capitalize on opportunities for learning that arise in the course of a dialogue with relevant cases from its video library. The construction of Creanimate, a system encompassing over 200 video clips and capable of engaging fourth grade students for over 2 hours, represents an important level of success for this design and engineering effort.

However, the initial success of this particular implementation effort only emphasizes the importance of further research on the case based teaching architecture. Three areas in particular stand out. First, additional work is necessary to develop architectures for more sophisticated and engaging task environments. Second, the architecture must be generalized to allow for the application of the case based teaching architecture to a broad range of domains. Finally, additional experience and evaluation is necessary to investigate the impact of case based teaching systems on students' understanding and abilities. Although additional experience and evaluation is possibly the most important of the three areas, the technology is still quite immature, and it would be a mistake to be overly influenced by the lack of demonstrable, positive learning outcomes at the early stages of this technology's development. For that reason, it may be necessary to continue development and testing of the technology for quite some time on the strength of the pedagogical theory, before robust empirical results to support the theory become available.

Engagement

Although the development of Creanimate was a significant effort and its initial use provided reason for encouragement, clear limitations are evident in its ability to engage students in active learning. The most significant limitations in the Creanimate task environment's engagement of the student are the: (a) reactive role of the learner in the dialogues, (b) limited flexibility of the dialogues, (c) lack of a clearly articulated goal for the student, and (d) passive role of the student with respect to the video cases.

First, although the question-and-answer dialogues that the Creanimate dialogue manager is capable of conducting provide for rich learning opportunities and a great deal of student control, they fall short of the truly engaging active learning that is the goal of the case based teaching architecture. Although they give a learner room to propose hypotheses and give direction to an interaction, they place the student in a reactive, overly passive position. Rather than having the option to ask questions him or herself, the student is placed in the position of responding to questions posed by the computer. This reactive role falls short of the truly active learning that is the goal of the case based teaching architecture.

Second, compared with both human conversation and other styles of human–computer interaction, the dialogues are limited in their flexibility. At any point in a Creanimate dialogue, a student has a fixed number of options for responding that will result in predetermined and predictable responses by the computer. Question-and-answer discussion can be an extremely efficient mechanism for establishing and capitalizing on opportunities for learning, but other mechanisms that allow students to interact more directly with subject matter are often more engaging. For example, design, modeling, and simulation environments can provide richer, more motivating active learning opportunities. Without needing to discard Socratic-style dialogue as one aspect of the interaction, Creanimate as a case based teaching system could be made significantly more engaging if students had the ability to construct their animals through a direct manipulation interface and to observe their creations interacting with a simulated environment. In fact, other efforts to teach biology through design have focused on this construction and simulation approach (Coderre, 1988; Resnick, 1988, 1991; Travers, 1988).

Such an approach would help resolve the third major limitation listed earlier: the lack of a clearly articulated goal for the student. In the current implementation of Creanimate, students are invited to create a new animal without any indication of what objectives are being served by creating the animal. Only through the questions asked by the dialogue manager do students get the idea that they are creating an animal to consider how it might survive. Some students did not expect to be asked the sorts of questions that the dialogue manager posed, and they were clearly put off by them. Many of these students—members of the resister group in the cluster analysis—had a primary goal of viewing and interacting with their invented animal—a goal that is poorly supported by the current implementation. These students, a significant percentage of the users in the study, perceived the dialogue as an interference to their preferred goal of interacting with an onscreen representation of their animal. A task environment that created a novel animal adapted to survival in the wild and also gave the student the opportunity to manipulate and observe that animal in a simulated habitat would prove more engaging.

Within such an enhanced task environment, the Socratic dialogue manager could take its place as one of the mechanisms by which a student receives feedback and experiences opportunities for learning. The dialogue manager might respond to certain student actions as one element of this richer environment. In such an integrated system, the storyteller architecture would also be enhanced to respond to opportunities for learning that arise through students' interactions with other elements of the task environment. The development of richer task environments such as these is part of the research being conducted on GBSs at the Institute for the Learning Sciences (Schank et al., 1993/1994). One of these GBS environments, the Artifact Construction GBS, will allow a student to construct an object through a direct manipulation interface and receive feedback about the invention through a simulation.

The fourth limitation of Creanimate's Socratic case based teaching architecture—to engage the student in active learning—lies at the borderline between the task environment and the storyteller. The problem is that, in the current implementation, students' exposure to cases is essentially passive. Students watch a video and, at most, are asked to answer a simple question about it (e.g., "Now do you know why sage grouses dance?" [*So they can . . .* , *Show me the video again, What other videos can I see?*]). Creanimate never asks a student to reason in any meaningful way with the cases he or she sees. For example, students could be asked to relate cases they have seen together in various ways. Such additional reasoning could both expand and reinforce the indexing in a student's memory that resulted from the initial viewing of the case and the context in which it was viewed. In addition, observations revealed that video clips often raised questions in students' minds. Because Creanimate could not accept such questions, students typically asked anyone who happened to be in the room. In the current architecture, these questions are lost. Yet they represent powerful opportunities for learning because they are generated by the students.

Currently, Creanimate's ability to engage students comes from the questions it poses and the videos it presents. Adding a more active, less reactive task environment, and encouraging students to reason more deeply with the cases, could greatly enhance the program's ability to engage students in active learning.

Sophistication of Subject Matter

Beyond its ability to engage, the Socratic case based teaching architecture, as it is instantiated in the Creanimate system, is also limited by its ability to deal with complexity in the subject matter. This limitation is a direct result of its knowledge representation. The relative simplicity of Creanimate's knowledge representation was an intentional choice motivated by the priority of producing a functional system in a relatively short period of time. However, with additional effort, the knowledge representation and indexing scheme could be extended to account for many issues of animal adaptation that it is currently unable to deal with effectively. These issues include conflicts among animal attributes (e.g., weight interfering with flying and fur interfering with keeping cool), effects of habitat, developmental stages of animals, and activities involving multiple animals (e.g., communication, conflict, nurturing).

An example of the knowledge representation's current limitations is revealed in an earlier transcript in this chapter. In that transcript, the student created a monkey with wings. After she had given her monkey wings, the program asked her what other features the animal would require to be able to stay aloft. The dialogue manager's goal is to ensure that the student's animal has one of the combinations of body size and wing size that it knows are sufficient for flying. The student can achieve an appropriate balance by making an animal smaller, if the animal is altogether too large, or by making sure that the wings are the right size for the animal's size (e.g., large wings for medium-size animals, medium-size or small wings for small animals). The system also knows about hollow bones as a feature that makes it easier to fly, but hollow bones are not factored into the consideration of wing size. A good representation to handle the relationship between wing size and body size would be able to represent that larger wings are necessary for larger animals because the wings compensate for the fact that large size interferes with flying. However, the current representation can only account for the fact that particular combinations of features allow an animal to perform a particular action, not the possible negative or positive interactions between the individual features and the action. Thus, it simply knows that medium body size and large wings, or small body size and small wings, are two combinations of features that enable an animal to stay aloft. Furthermore, it assumes that all of the features in a combination work to support the action. Thus, the dialogue manager makes a statement such as, "Medium size and large wings can work together to help an animal to keep itself up in the air." Because the actual relationship between wing size and body size is compensatory, it would be better if the dialogue manager said, "Large wings can enable an animal with medium size to keep itself up in the air." The Creanimate knowledge representation would need to be extended to support this additional level of sophistication. Such an enhancement would by no means push the state of the art of knowledge representation, but it raises the question that haunts any knowledge representation effort: How good does the representation need to be to be good enough?

With an extension of its knowledge representation and inferential capabilities, Creanimate could conduct dialogues about a wider range of explanation questions, as well as handling students' answers and generating explanations with a greater degree of sophistication. The quality of the interaction and the opportunities for learning that would result would clearly be improved as a result of such an extension. One would expect a similar improvement in learning outcomes. It is also likely that a more sophisticated knowledge representation, and the resulting more sophisticated dialogues, would provide opportunities for reminding strategies designed to illustrate forms of subtlety that are currently beyond Creanimate's repertoire. Although the power of Creanimate is clearly limited as a result of the simplicity of its knowledge representation, the solution to this limitation is relatively straightforward. Extending the knowledge representation, indexing scheme, and inferential capabilities is definitely possible within the conventional techniques of symbolic artificial intelligence employed by Creanimate.

Generalization of the Architecture

At this early stage, it is difficult to say with any certainty how effectively the Socratic case based teaching architecture will generalize beyond Creanimate in terms of educational effectiveness. However, from the technical point of view, an important strength of Creanimate's architecture is that the underlying structure is not tied in any way to the specific domain of animal adaptation. Accommodating a set of explanation questions for a different domain, along with the knowledge representation and inferences they would require, could be done with simple modifications to Creanimate's current infrastructure. Likewise, the indexing scheme and reminding strategies are domain-independent, and could be applied with minimal adaptation to new knowledge bases. The biggest effort involved in such an adaptation would be to take those elements of the dialogue manager and reminding strategies that are currently defined procedurally and transform them to a declarative representation. This would allow nonprogrammers to specialize the inference and search routines to suit the idiosyncrasies of specific domains.

The key to resolving the technical issues associated with applying the Socratic case based teaching architecture and the expanded architecture described earlier will be the development of software engineering tools to support the process. The processes of developing a knowledge representation, defining inference rules to pose questions and evaluate students' answers, collecting and indexing a case library, and, in the case of the expanded architecture, creating a direct manipulation interface and simulation environment are time- and labor-intensive processes. Furthermore, they can require quite specialized training and expertise. To move this technology beyond its current prototype stage will require the development of tools that reduce the time and degree of programming expertise required to implement a case based teaching system. The development of Creanimate began to resolve this problem with the creation of a knowledge representation and indexing tool that allowed a nonprogrammer to create the entire knowledge base and case library, and has been used subsequently to develop other knowledge representations for other systems. This tool is described in Edelson (1993).

The question of which domains are appropriate for the architecture remains open. It is easy to think narrowly about how to extend Creanimate and consider other domains where students can learn by considering new inventions in the way they do in Creanimate. These domains include design and engineering, where the creation of objects is a defining characteristic of the domain, but also other domains, like animal adaptation, where design is not the ordinary way to approach the domain, but can provide valuable opportunities for learning. These domains are not limited to the sciences. For example, designing a government or religion as a way to study political science or comparative religions are applications of this approach that have been discussed. However, beyond these relatively "near transfer" applications of the Socratic case based teaching architecture to learning through design are tasks such as planning, problem solving, and diagnosis, all of which lend themselves to the use of explanation questions and cases as a means to explore the implications of decisions.

Evaluating the Architecture

The research reported here has focused primarily on the technological issues of instantiating the case based teaching architecture. Obviously resolving these issues is on the critical path of developing effective case based teaching systems, but the ultimate goal of this research is not the development of new technologies, but providing effective educational interactions. Therefore, the evaluation of the impact of case based teaching systems must be an element of this research. As stated earlier, however, the inability to demonstrate positive learning outcomes while the technology is still immature should not be taken overly seriously. The risk of throwing the baby out with the bath water is great in weighing early assessments too heavily, especially when the theories on which the architecture is based are as compelling as the theories of case based reasoning. These cautions aside, it will be important to address the evaluation of the case based teaching architecture seriously, and to expand on the results of the studies reported here.

The success of the case based teaching architecture, or any educational interaction, depends critically on motivating the learner to expend effort and attention on the interaction. The goal of the case based teaching architecture is to provide the student with an intrinsic motivation that will engage him or her in active learning within the task environment. For that reason, evaluating the motivational aspects of the architecture has been the first priority. The studies described earlier provided valuable information about the differences in the ways students responded to Creanimate. These studies need to be extended to gather information about differences between age groups, genders, and other individual characteristics that often prove to be significant in educational settings. Student motivation and engagement will also need to be reevaluated as the architecture is enhanced and applied to other subject matters. Even over the month that Creanimate was in use by the fourth graders in the primary site, the system was enhanced—the parser vocabulary in particular. These improvements had a clear effect on students' transcripts, as the number of failed parses dropped significantly, and students were able to express themselves more freely.

After motivation and engagement, the next priority for evaluation must be learning and attitudinal impact. Educational interactions influence the state of students' understanding and abilities, and their attitudes about subject matter, learning, and themselves. Having a beneficial effect on all of these is the goal of any educational innovation. Evaluating this effect is as complicated as understanding and attitudes are themselves. In the case of Creanimate and its case based teaching architecture, the learning objectives are relatively clear, whereas the attitudinal objectives are less well specified and are probably best characterized as a desire to foster an excitement about science and an appreciation of scientific activity as open ended and creative. The learning objective of Creanimate is to provide students with a framework for understanding animal adaptation as expressed by the explanation questions employed by the system, and a case library of animals, their attributes, and activities, which will help students reason about animal adaptation in novel situations.

As part of the studies conducted at the primary study site described previously, an evaluation designed to highlight any impact on questioning and the use of cases in explanations was conducted. In particular, we investigated students' questioning and explanation behaviors when presented with unfamiliar animals. In pre- and posttests before their first and after their third session with Creanimate, students were given line drawings of eight exotic animals that were selected to be unfamiliar to fourth graders. For four of these drawings, they were asked to generate questions about the animals, and for four they were asked to answer specific explanation questions and provide justifications for their answers. The hypothesis being explored was that students, as a result of using Creanimate, would ask more explanation questions about the relationships among physical features, actions, and behaviors, and that they would refer more often to cases of other animals in their explanations. Our analysis of their answers yielded no statistically significant results.

The lack of measurable positive outcomes on the question task appears to be at least partially a result of a ceiling effect. The use of fourth graders in this initial study was based on a combination of preliminary testing and practical constraints. Maximum learning benefits from Creanimate might actually be expected to appear in students much younger. The current lower age limit for use of Creanimate is determined by the reading and writing abilities of the user. There is also the possibility that, for both tasks, the students' sessions were either too brief or too widely spaced to yield measurable outcomes for these two tasks. Therefore, two immediate next steps would be to repeat these evaluations with younger students and with an intervention that provided for longer or more closely spaced interactions with the software. It may not be true that more contact time is necessary, but just that the frequency or duration of that contact be increased. However, it may be true that the limitations of the current system discussed previously are sufficient to prevent Creanimate from having the desired learning impact. In that case, the desired measurable outcomes of the case based teaching architecture may not appear until the technology is sufficiently advanced to fulfill its promise. It is worth noting that there are other learning outcome measures that are not consistent with the objectives of the architecture that might yield immediate results. These outcomes include recall of facts about animals and their attributes for the animals a student discussed with the system, and the video cases he or she viewed.

A topic for evaluation of learning outcomes that was not anticipated prior to the studies described here is the impact on learning of the different patterns of use that were observed. These patterns of use appear to be a reflection of persistent individual differences among students. The implications of these differences could range from: (a) the differences represent styles of use, but have no influence on learning and attitudinal outcomes; to (b) Creanimate or the Socratic case based teaching architecture are not appropriate for certain students because they derive no significant positive outcomes from using it; to (c) Creanimate and Socratic case based teaching is appropriate for all students, but different students derive different sorts of benefits from their use of it. In either of the latter two cases, additional research would be necessary to see if it is possible to redesign the system to enhance the learning of all students. The examination of these questions will require further investigation of students' patterns of use to see whether these initial findings are robust and apply across different ages and characteristics of students. These results will then need to be combined with the results of learning outcome studies to identify interactions.

From the foregoing discussion of the strengths and limitations of Creanimate, it is clear that, as an educational program, Creanimate has its share of flaws. However, it is important to remember that the primary goal of this research has been to explore the computational challenges of implementing the case based teaching architecture. Even if the Creanimate program never reaches its potential as an educational system, future work that addresses the limitations in technology discussed here should enable the case based teaching architecture to achieve that potential in other domains. This future research should also continue to attempt to address the motivational, attitudinal, and learning impacts of the approach.

CONCLUSION

According to theories of case based understanding and learning, the case based teaching architecture offers enormous promise as a means to combine two effective instructional techniques: active learning and learning from cases. The development of such an architecture has been made possible by important advances in artificial intelligence, cognitive science, and multi-media technology. The Socratic case based teaching architecture is a specific form of case based teaching that takes advantage of the power of questions to establish opportunities to learn from cases. As a prototype of a Socratic case based teaching system, Creanimate is a first step in the exploration of the case based teaching architecture. The development of Creanimate required technological solutions to the problems of Socratic-style dialogue management, indexing schemes for large case libraries, and the development of reminding strategies. In the development of a working prototype that incorporates over 200 cases and a knowledge base that includes over 1,000 animals, physical features, actions, and behaviors, this design and engineering research has been successful. On the pedagogical front, the initial experiences with the Creanimate system in public school environments demonstrated the power of such systems to engage students at the same time that these experiences raised important questions about the nature of that engagement and the learning that results. Hopefully, further technological developments, combined with additional experience, will pave the way for systems that expand the case based teaching architecture.

ACKNOWLEDGMENTS

I would like to thank Alex Kass and Andrew Fano for helpful comments on earlier drafts of this chapter. The data analysis for the evaluation studies was performed by John Cleave with Richard Beckwith. In addition to the author, the Creanimate development team included Bob Kaeding, Riad Mohammed, John Cleave, Will Fitzgerald, Diane Schwartz, Ken Greenlee, and Ian Underwood. This research was conducted under the supervision of Roger Schank. William Purves of Harvey Mudd College provided expert consultation on the biology domain. This research was supported by a grant from IBM through their Program for Innovative Uses of Information Technology in K–12 Education, and by the Defense Advanced Research Projects Agency monitored by the Office of Naval Research under contracts N00014-91-J4092 and N00014-90-J4117. The National Geographic Society and the Encyclopaedia Britannica Educational Corporation provided video footage for experimental use in Creanimate.

The Institute for the Learning Sciences was established in 1989 with the support of Andersen Consulting.

REFERENCES

Acovelli, M., & Nowakowski, A. (1994). The business practices course: Self-study learning reengineered. *Educational Technology, 34*(9), 21–27.

Ashley, K. D., & Aleven, V. (1992). Generating dialectical examples automatically. In *AAAI-92: Proceedings of the tenth national conference on artificial intelligence* (pp. 654–660). San Jose, CA: AAAI Press/MIT Press.

Barrows, H. S. (1986). A taxonomy of problem-based learning methods. *Medical Education, 20*, 481–486.

Barrows, H. S., & Tamblyn, R. (1980). *Problem-based learning: An approach to medical education.* New York: Springer.

Bell, B., Bareiss, R., & Beckwith, R. (1993/1994). Sickle Cell Counselor: A prototype goal-based scenario for instruction in a museum environment. *The Journal of the Learning Sciences, 3*(4), 429–454.

Brown, A. L., & Palincsar, A. S. (1989). Guided, cooperative learning and individual knowledge acquisition. In L. B. Resnick (Ed.), *Knowing, learning, and instruction: Essays in honor of Robert Glaser* (pp. 393–451). Hillsdale, NJ: Lawrence Erlbaum Associates.

Brown, J. S., Collins, A., & Duguid, P. (1989). Situated cognition and the culture of learning. *Educational Researcher, 18*(1), 32–42.

Burke, R. (1993). *Representation, storage and retrieval of tutorial stories in a social simulation.* Unpublished doctoral dissertation, Northwestern University.

Burke, R., & Kass, A. (1992). Integrating case presentation with simulation-based learning-by-doing. In *Proceedings of the fourteenth annual conference of the Cognitive Science Society* (pp. 629–634). Hillsdale, NJ: Lawrence Erlbaum Associates.

Carbonell, J. R. (1970a). AI in CAI: An artificial intelligence approach to computer-assisted instruction. *IEEE Transactions on Man-Machine Systems, 11*(4), 190–292.

Carbonell, J. R. (1970b). *Mixed-initiative man-computer instructional dialogues.* Unpublished doctoral dissertation, Massachusetts Institute of Technology.

Chi, M. T. H., Bassok, M., Lewis, M. W., Reimann, P., & Glaser, R. (1989). Self-explanations: How students study and use examples in learning to solve problems. *Cognitive Science, 13*, 145–182.

Clancy, W. J. (1987). *Knowledge-based tutoring: The GUIDON program.* Cambridge, MA: MIT Press.

Cleave, J. B., Edelson, D. C., & Beckwith, R. (1993, April). *A matter of style: An analysis of student interaction with a computer-based learning environment.* Paper presented at the 1993 annual meeting of the American Educational Research Association, Atlanta, GA.

Coderre, B. (1988). Modeling behavior in Petworld. In C. Langton (Ed.), *Artificial life* (pp. 407–419). Reading, MA: Addison-Wesley.

Collins, A., Brown, J. S., & Newman, S. E. (1989). Cognitive apprenticeship: Teaching the crafts of reading, writing, and mathematics. In L. B. Resnick (Ed.), *Knowing, learning, and instruction: Essays in honor of Robert Glaser* (pp. 453–494). Hillsdale, NJ: Lawrence Erlbaum Associates.

Collins, A., & Stevens, A. L. (1983). A cognitive theory of inquiry teaching. In C. M. Reigeluth (Ed.), *Instructional-design theories and models: An overview* (pp. 247–278). Hillsdale, NJ: Lawrence Erlbaum Associates.

Edelson, D. C. (1993). *Learning from stories: Indexing and reminding in a case-based teaching system for elementary school biology.* Unpublished doctoral dissertation, Northwestern University.

Fitzgerald, W. A. (1992). *Direct memory access parsing in the Creanimate biology tutor.* Unpublished manuscript.

Fitzgerald, W. A. (1995). *Building embedded conceptual parsers.* Unpublished doctoral dissertation, Northwestern University.

Karakotsios, K. (1992). *SimLife* [Computer program]. Walnut Creek, CA: Maxis.

Kass, A., Burke, R., Blevis, R., & Williamson, M. (1993/1994). Constructing learning environments for complex social skills. *The Journal of the Learning Sciences, 3*(4), 387–428.

Kass, A., Dooley, S., & Luksa, F. (1993). *The Broadcast News Project: Using broadcast journalism as a vehicle for teaching social studies* (Tech. Rep. No. 40). Evanston, IL: Institute for the Learning Sciences, Northwestern University.

Keller, J. M. (1983). Motivational design of instruction. In C. M. Reigeluth (Ed.), *Instructional-design theories and models: An overview of their current status* (pp. 383–434). Hillsdale, NJ: Lawrence Erlbaum Associates.

Klein, G. A. C. (1988). How do people use analogies to make decisions? In J. L. Kolodner (Ed.), *Proceedings: Case-based reasoning workshop (DARPA)* (pp. 209–218). San Mateo, CA: Kaufmann.

Kolodner, J. L. (1991). Improving human decision making through case-based decision aiding. *AI Magazine, 12*(2), 52–67.

Kolodner, J. L., Simpson, R. L., & Sycara-Cyranski, K. (1985). A process model of case-based reasoning in problem-solving. In A. Joshi (Ed.), *Proceedings of the ninth international joint conference on artificial intelligence.* Los Altos, CA: Kaufmann.

Lepper, M. R., & Hodell, M. (1989). Intrinsic motivation in the classroom. *Research on Motivation in Education, 3*, 73–105.

Malone, T. (1981). Toward a theory of intrinsically motivating instruction. *Cognitive Science, 4*, 333–369.

Martin, C. (1989). Case-based parsing. In C. K. Riesbeck & R. C. Schank (Eds.), *Inside case-based reasoning* (pp. 319–352). Hillsdale, NJ: Lawrence Erlbaum Associates.

Martin, C. E. (1990). *Direct memory access parsing.* Unpublished doctoral dissertation, Yale University, New Haven, CT.

McNair, M. P. (Ed.). (1954). *The case method at the Harvard Business School: Papers by present and past members of the faculty and staff.* New York: McGraw-Hill.

Redlich, J. (1914). *The common law and the case method in American university law schools* (Bulletin No. 8). New York: The Carnegie Foundation for the Advancement of Teaching.

Reed, A. Z. (1921). *Training for the public profession of the law* (Bulletin No. 15). New York: Carnegie Foundation for the Advancement of Teaching.

Resnick, M. (1988). LEGO, logo, and life. In C. Langton (Ed.), *Artificial life* (pp. 407–419). Reading, MA: Addison-Wesley.

Resnick, M. (1991). Animal simulations with *Logo: Massive parallelism for the masses. In J. A. Meyer & S. W. Wilson (Eds.), *From animals to animats: Proceedings of the first international conference on simulation of adaptive behavior* (pp. 534–539). Cambridge, MA: MIT Press.

Riesbeck, C. K., & Schank, R. C. (1989). *Inside case-based reasoning.* Hillsdale, NJ: Lawrence Erlbaum Associates.

Ross, B. H. (1989). Some psychological results on case-based reasoning. In K. Hammond (Ed.), *Case-based reasoning: Proceedings of a workshop on case-based reasoning* (pp. 144–147). San Mateo, CA: Kaufmann.

Schank, R., Osgood, R., Brand, M., Burke, R., Domeshek, E., Edelson, D., Ferguson, W., Freed, M., Jona, M., Krulwich, B., Ohmaye, E., & Pryor, L. (1990). *A content theory of memory indexing.* Technical Report No. 2, Institute for the Learning Sciences, Northwestern University.

Schank, R. C. (1982). *Dynamic memory.* New York: Cambridge University Press.

Schank, R. C. (1986). *Explanation patterns: Understanding mechanically and creatively*. Hillsdale, NJ: Lawrence Erlbaum Associates.

Schank, R. C. (1991). *Case-based teaching: Four experiences in educational software design*. Technical Report No. 7, Institute for the Learning Sciences, Northwestern University.

Schank, R. C., Fano, A., Bell, B., & Jona, M. (1993/1994). The design of goal-based scenarios. *The Journal of the Learning Sciences, 3*(4), 305–346.

Schoenfeld, A. H. (1992). Learning to think mathematically: Problem solving, metacognition, and sense-making in mathematics. In D. A. Grouws (Ed.), *Handbook of research on mathematics teaching and learning* (pp. 334–370). New York: Macmillan.

Stevens, A. L., & Collins, A. (1977). The goal structure of a Socratic tutor. *Proceedings of the National ACM Conference* (pp. 256–263). New York: Association for Computing Machinery.

Travers, M. (1988). Animal construction kits. In C. Langton (Ed.), *Artificial life* (pp. 421–442). Reading, MA: Addison-Wesley.

Wenger, E. (1987). *Artificial intelligence and tutoring systems: Computational and cognitive approaches to the communication of knowledge*. Los Altos, CA: Kaufmann.

Williams, S. M. (1992). Putting case-based instruction into context: Examples from legal and medical education. *The Journal of the Learning Sciences, 2*(4), 367–427.

APPENDIX: SELECTED TRANSCRIPTS

This appendix contains selected portions of transcripts for the clusters that were identified in the analysis of patterns of use among students. The transcripts were selected to be illustrative of the features that distinguish the particular clusters.

Video Hoppers

The following portion of a transcript is characteristic of the two video hoppers. The student never types in any input, watches one of the video clips three times in a row, and uses the "What other videos can I see?" option to see all the available video clips.

We need a reason for your frog to dance. Is there a reason you want your frog to dance?

So it can . . .

Give me some suggestions.

Student: Give me some suggestions.

Bees dance. Do you know why bees dance?

So they can . . .

Show me a video.

What other videos can I see?

Skip this.

Student: What other videos can I see?

Which would you like to see next?

bee

ostrich

crowned crane

whooping crane

gull

Student: Ostrich.

Do you know why ostriches dance?

(I think this video is funny.)

So they can . . .

Show me a video.

Skip this.

Student: Show me a video.

VIDEO: "OSTRICH DANCES"

Now, do you know why ostriches dance?

So they can . . .

Show me the video again.

Tell me.

Student: Tell me.

Ostriches dance to attract their mates.

That last video made me think of another one. This one is pretty good. I like this one because it has ferocious animals in it.

Bears also get mates. Only, instead of dancing to attract their mates, they swat to fight for territory.

Is that something you would like to see?

Student: Yes.

VIDEO: "BEARS MAULING EACH OTHER"

Ostriches are not the only animals that dance in order to attract their mates. For example, crowned cranes also dance to attract their mates.

This is a colorful video. This video also has funny looking birds in it.

Do you want to see that?

Student: What other videos can I see?

I can show you videos about all of these animals that dance.

Which would you like to see first?

crowned crane

whooping crane

gull

Student: Crowned crane.

VIDEO: "CRANE DANCES"

Whooping cranes also dance to attract their mates.

I have a cool video about that. This has frantic dancing in it.

Would you like to see that video again?

Student: What other videos can I see?

Which would you like to see next?

  whooping crane

  gull

Student: Whooping crane.

VIDEO: "CRANES DANCE"

Gulls also dance to attract their mates.

This next video is really funny.

Would you like to see that again?

Student: No.

So, ostriches dance to attract their mates. Your frog could dance to attract its mate, too. Do you know how frogs currently attract their mates?

  They . . .

  I don't know.

Student: I don't know.

Frogs attract their mates by croaking.

So, a frog might dance to attract its mate. Why would you like your frog to dance?

  Attract its mate.

  Show me more reasons.

Student: Show me more reasons.

Well, that's the only reason I know for dancing, but I know about some things that are like dancing. Maybe one of them will give you a reason you'll like for your frog to dance.

Barking is like dancing, because they are both ways that animals send signals.

Hyenas bark. Do you know why hyenas bark?

(I have an interesting video about that. This video also has lions in it.)

  So they can . . .

  Show me a video.

  Skip this.

Student: Show me a video.

VIDEO: "HYENAS AND LION"

Now, do you know why hyenas bark?

  So they can . . .

  Show me the video again.

  Tell me.

Student: Show me the video again.

VIDEO: "HYENAS AND LION"

Now, do you know why hyenas bark?

Student: Show me the video again.

VIDEO: "HYENAS AND LION"

Now, do you know why hyenas bark?

Student: Tell me.

Hyenas bark to warn their friends about danger.

Video Avoiders

Video avoiders were characterized by their higher than average rejection of offers to view video clips. In this portion of a transcript, the student declines five video clips in the course of discussing two explanation questions.

Student: A bear that can dance.

Picture: Bear.

How do you want to change your bear so it can dance?

Student: Give it something new.

Ok, what should we give your bear to help it dance?

Give it . . .

Make it . . .

Give me some suggestions.

Student: Give it *human legs*.[12]

That's a good idea. Sage grouses use their legs to help them dance.

Is that something you would like to see?

Student: No.

So, your bear could use legs to help it dance.

You can commit to that now, or we can look at some more ways animals dance and you can decide later.

What would you like to give it?

Legs.

Show me more ways.

Student: Legs.

Before we change your bear's legs, we should look at what its old legs were good for.

Bears have legs to help them to wade.

I think this video is great.

Do you want to see that?

Student: No.

Let's look at another reason for your bear's old legs. Bears have forelegs to help them to wrestle.

---

[12]The parser misparsed the student's input as "legs" because the knowledge base lacked a specific form of legs corresponding to "human legs."

I have an interesting video about that. This video also has ferocious animals in it.

Would you like to see that?

Student: No.

OK, your bear will use its new legs to help it dance.

Student: Go on.

Let's see if we can find a reason for your bear to dance. Can you think of a reason for your bear to dance?

Student: Give me some suggestions.

Bees dance. Do you know why bees dance?

(This next video is really amazing.)

  So they can . . .

  Show me a video.

  What other videos can I see?

  Skip this.

Student: Skip this.

Sage grouses dance. Sage grouses dance to compete for the attention of a female.

This is a hilarious video.

Would you like to see a video about that?

Student: No.

Ostriches dance. Do you know why ostriches dance?

This next video is really funny.

Student: Skip this.

. . .

Button Press: SHOW ANIMAL

Button Press: SKIP THIS

We can do any of the things listed below. Which would you like to do next?

See why other animals dance

  Add to my bear

  Start a new animal

  Continue where I was

Student: Add to my bear

Student: A bear with wings

Picture: Bear

Actually there are mammals that have wings. For example, fox bats have leathery wings.

Is that something you would like to see?

Student: No.

We should come up with a reason for your bear to have wings.

Why would you like your bear to have wings?

Student: So it can *fly*.

That's a good idea. White breasted sea eagles use their feathered wings to help them fly.

Do you want to see that?

Student: No.

So, your bear could have wings to fly. Why would you like your bear to have wings?

To fly.

Show me more reasons.

Student: To fly.

Resisters

Resisters appeared to either not understand or not accept the basic flow of Creanimate. Characteristic of resisters was frequent use of the "Start over" and "Skip this" buttons, and of anthropomorphic changes for their animals. In this transcript, the student resisted the system's offer to make one change at a time, by asking for two changes at once, and then asked for a butterfly that could emulate a popular musician and dancer, MC Hammer.

> **Student: A butterfly that can fight.**
> *Picture: Butterfly.*
> That's a good idea, is there a reason why you want your butterfly to fight?
> *Button Press: BACKUP*
> How would you like to change your butterfly?
> So it can . . .
> Give it . . .
> So it is . . .
> **Student: So it can *dance and fight*.[13]**
> *PICTURE: Butterfly*
> How do you want to change your butterfly so it can dance?
> Change its . . .
> Give it something new.
> Use its current . . .
> Give me some suggestions.
> **Student: Give it something new.**
> Ok, what should we give your butterfly to help it dance?
> Give it . . .

---

[13]Because the dialogue manager can only deal with one modification at a time, it ignores "and fight."

Make it . . .

Give me some suggestions.

Student: Give it *MC Hammer legs*.[14]

That's a good idea. Sage grouses use their legs to help them dance.

Would you like to see a video about that?

Student: No.

So, your butterfly could use legs to help it dance.

You can commit to that now, or we can look at some more ways animals dance and you can decide later.

What would you like to give it?

Legs.

Show me more ways.

Student: Legs.

OK, your butterfly will use its new legs to help it dance.

We need a reason for your butterfly to dance. Is there a reason you want your butterfly to dance?

So it can . . .

Give me some suggestions.

Student: So it can do the MC Hammer.

Compliant Users

Characteristic of the compliant user cluster was a willingness to follow the lead of the program. In this segment from the transcript of a compliant user, the student asks the system to suggest an answer to the explanation question and then chooses to use the first suggestion she sees for her animal.

Student: A Butterfly with a beak.

Picture: Butterfly

Actually there are animals other than birds that have beaks.

For example, octopuses have curved beaks.

Would you like to see that?

Student: Yes.

VIDEO: "OCTOPUS SPAR"

OK, let's find a reason for your butterfly to have a beak. Is there a reason you want your butterfly to have a beak?

So it can . . .

Give me some suggestions.

Student: Give me some suggestions.

---

[14]Because the parser cannot interpret "MC Hammer," it ignores it.

Great crested grebes have beaks. They have long beaks. Great crested grebes have beaks to help them to grip things.

This is a great video.

Would you like to see a video about that?

Student: Yes.

VIDEO: "GREBE DIVES FOR FISH"

Wait, that great crested grebe reminded me of a good video. This is a close-up video.

Squirrels also grip things. Only, instead of using their beaks to grip things, they use their short curved claws.

Is that something you would like to see?

Student: Yes.

VIDEO: "SQUIRREL OPENS NUT"

Great crested grebes are not the only animals that use their beaks in order to grip things.

For example, great blue herons have beaks to help them to grip things.

I have a cool video about that.

Do you want to see that?

Student: No.

So, your butterfly could have a beak to grip things.

You can commit to that now, or we can look at some other reasons animals have beaks and you can decide later.

   To grip things.

   Show me more reasons.

Student: To grip things.

Balanced Users

On average, balanced users took advantage of more of the aspects of Creanimate than users in the other groups. In this transcript, the user types in three different answers for the explanation question and sees several video clips.

Student: A butterfly that can dance.

Picture: Butterfly.

How do you want to change your butterfly so it can dance?

   Change its . . .

   Give it something new.

   Use its current . . .

   Give me some suggestions.

Student: Give it something new.

Ok, what should we give your butterfly to help it dance?

Give it . . .

Make it . . .

Give me some suggestions.

Student: Give it *wings.*

That's a good idea. Sage grouses use their feathered wings to help them dance.

Do you want to see that?

Student: Yes.

VIDEO: "GROUSE DANCES"

Sage grouses are not the only animals that dance by using their wings. For example, ostriches also use their wings to help them dance.

That is a funny video.

Would you like to see that?

Student: No.

So, your butterfly could use wings to help it dance. You can commit to that now, or we can look at some more ways animals dance and you can decide later.

What would you like to give it?

Wings.

Show me more ways.

Student: Show me more ways.

Can you think of another way to change your butterfly so it can dance?

Student: Give it something new.

Ok, what should we give your butterfly to help it dance?

Student: Give it *feathers.*

I don't know of any animals that have feathers so they can dance. But, I do know some other things that feathers are used for.

For example, night jar birds use their feathers to help them camouflage themselves.

Would you like to see a video about that?

Student: No.

That's the only thing that I know of that feathers are used for.

Those are all the reasons I know for having feathers. Are you sure you would like your butterfly to have feathers, or would you like to see some other ways that animals are able to dance?

Stick with feathers.

See ways that animals dance.

Student: See ways that animals dance.

Can you think of another way to change your butterfly so it can dance?

Student: Give it something new.

Ok, what should we give your butterfly to help it dance?

Student: Give it *legs.*

That's a good idea. Whooping cranes use their long legs to help them dance. Is that something you would like to see?

Student: Yes.

VIDEO: "CRANES DANCE"

Whooping cranes are not the only animals that dance by using their legs. For example, gulls also use their legs to help them dance.

I have a funny video about that.

Do you want to see that?

Student: No.

So, your butterfly could use legs to help it dance.

What would you like to give it?

Legs
Feathers
Wings
Show me more ways.

Student: Show me more ways.

Can you think of another way to change your butterfly so it can dance?

Student: Give me some suggestions.

3

Representation, Storage, and Retrieval of Tutorial Stories in a Social Simulation

Robin D. Burke
University of Chicago
Department of Computer Science

INTRODUCTION

Stories and Teaching

Case based reasoning is a model of human reasoning in which recollections of prior experience are key (Kolodner, 1993; Riesbeck & Schank, 1989). The reasoner stores previously solved problems; when a new problem comes along, he or she solves it by finding the most similar previous example and attempting to apply the same solution, adapting where necessary. The case based teaching architecture (Edelson, 1993; Schank, 1990a) is intended to mesh with a student's need to acquire relevant cases. Because new students in a domain will lack the experience needed to have a large case base, the goal of a case based teacher is to use students' involvement in a learning environment as a means of introducing important cases that they should know.

For case based teaching to work, a tutor must be able to pinpoint those moments in an interaction when a student can profit from a story, and it must know what kind of story to present. For such reasoning, a story-telling tutor must have three interrelated kinds of knowledge:

Relevance knowledge: Knowledge about what features of stories are important for making different kinds of points, and what features of a student's situation make these points good ones to make.

Indexing knowledge: An organized system of labels for stories, so that the tutor can find an appropriate example among the large number it possesses.

Recognition knowledge: An ability to monitor the learning environment, draw reasonable conclusions about what the student is doing, and relate its observations to the contents of the story base so that relevant stories can be retrieved.

SPIEL

Story Producer for InteractivE Learning (SPIEL) is a case based teaching system that finds relevant stories through the recognition of storytelling opportunities. It is part of the Guided Social Simulation (GuSS) architecture for teaching social skills using a learning-by-doing environment. GuSS incorporates several different forms of tutorial guidance of which SPIEL's storytelling is one. The GuSS architecture has been applied to create several applications that teach social skills.[1] This chapter includes examples from the most advanced of these, YELLO, which teaches account executives at Ameritech Publishing the fine points of selling Yellow Pages advertising. In all, SPIEL has 178 stories about performing this task, told by account executives with considerable experience and success in this job.

GuSS is a learning-by-doing architecture for social skills. In YELLO, the student is called on to develop and sell an advertising program through a series of sales calls. The student converses with the customer, attempts to gather information, and tries to make a convincing argument for a proposed advertising program. Stories are retrieved in response to the student's actions and the customer's reactions.

SPIEL's Stories. SPIEL's stories are everyday anecdotes—first-person narratives about actual experiences. It is useful to distinguish these stories from other kinds of cases that a tutor might use, such as design examples, reenactments, or invented cases. First-person stories have properties that make them particularly useful for instruction (Bruner, 1986; Hunter, 1991; Schank, 1990b; Witherell & Noddings, 1991), especially for complex social skills (Kass et al., 1993/1994):

Authenticity: the fact that such stories come directly from a person's real experience. It is one thing to hear an invented case that makes a

---

[1]In addition to YELLO, there are also GuSS applications for teaching novice consultants how to perform a business review (Blevis & Kass, 1991; Kass & Blevis, 1991), for teaching consultants how to sell consulting services (Kass, Burke, Blevis, & Williamson, 1992), and for teaching project managers how to conduct a performance review.

point (such as a fable), but quite another to hear someone describe a real situation in which that point was brought home. The authenticity of stories drawn directly from personal experience adds to their impact.

Detail: the tendency of such anecdotes to be vivid and detailed. Indeed, the value of detail in experientially based knowledge is one of the important claims of the case based reasoning model. Because it is difficult to anticipate all the ways that a case can be used, a case based reasoning system retains all the details of each case.

Cultural content: the way in which personal stories reflect a person's beliefs and values. Stories are cultural artifacts created by people to communicate their experiences to others (Polanyi, 1985). When experts tell their stories about selling Yellow Pages advertising, they teach something of their culture of practice (Lave & Wenger, 1991). Because stories include not just a recounting of events, but also a person's perspective on those events, students learn what happened as well as how events were thought about and perceived by participants. Lave and Wenger noted that learning the stories of a culture is an important way that a novice can begin to participate in it.

Although stories are crucial for learning, by themselves they are a poor curriculum. One could construct a documentary film about selling Yellow Pages ads by stringing together stories, but it would be difficult to make such a film interesting, even for a committed learner. It is hard to understand and make sense of the point of a story without having a context within which to place it.[2] For this reason, the case based teaching architecture requires that students be actively participating in an engaging task so that cases will be most effective.

An Example of SPIEL at Work. The task of students using the YELLO program is to try to sell Yellow Pages advertising. SPIEL watches their actions and the customer's reactions, and looks for opportunities to present relevant stories. Consider the following interaction:

Student: So, we're going to go ahead with the 1/4 page ad with color?
Customer: OK.
Student: Just sign right here.
Customer: [signs]

---

[2]One example of the successful use of a stories-only documentary can be found at the U.S. Holocaust Memorial Museum in Washington, DC. A continuous display of first-person stories is shown, but only at the end of the museum tour, when visitors have absorbed the context that the exhibits vividly provide.

Student:	I think the color is really going to attract people to your ad.
Customer:	I sure like the way it looks.
Student:	Ask your customers what they think. I'll bet you'll find it's an attention-getter. Thanks for your time.
Customer:	See you next year.
Student:	See you. [leaves]

This is a successful sales call, but SPIEL has a cautionary story to tell. Every moment that the student remains after the close of the sale gives the customer an opportunity to retract his buying decision. Although that did not happen in this case, it is a possibility that the student should be aware of.

SPIEL intervenes in the following way. First, it signals to the student that it has a story available:

| SPIEL: | A story showing the risks of your approach. |

Then, if the student expresses an interest in hearing the story (through a button press), an explanation for why the story has come up appears:

| SPIEL: | You kept talking to the client after the sale was closed. Nothing bad happened but here's a story in which doing that led to problems: |

Then the tutor shows a video, in which an experienced salesperson relates a personal experience.

| Video: | I was in the South Bend/Mishawaka area. This was my first or second year. I was calling on a swimming pool contractor. He had a quarter page in South Bend. I was proposing a quarter page in another directory. It was sitting at his kitchen table. And the guy was hesitating; he didn't know. . . . So, after a few more attempts, he says to me, "OK, I'll go with the other quarter page." He bought it. I pushed the order form in front of him. He signed it. It's done. As I'm putting my stuff together, I made this comment that cost me the quarter page. I said, as I'm packing up, "I'm sure that you're going to get a lot of phone calls from that new ad." He looked at me and he said, "You know, I don't need any more phone calls. I'll tell you what, let's not do that this year, maybe next." I talked myself out of a quarter page. I've never done it since. I walked out. There was nothing I could say. I had it and I lost it. All I had to say was, "Thank you very much Joe. See you |

next year." But I didn't. I had to tell him about the calls, which I'd already done twenty times.[3]

Finally, the storyteller sums up the story for the student:

SPIEL: Nothing bad happened to you because you kept talking to the client after the sale was closed, but sometimes the client changes his mind.

In this example, the storyteller augments the student's simulated experience in an important way. Without the "Talked myself out of a sale" story, the student, who was successful, might never realize the risks inherent in remaining after the sale. The story arrives just at the time when it is most relevant, after the risk is past and the student thinks all went well, and it is exactly on point as a counterexample: It shows a situation in which the same tactic had an opposite outcome. For SPIEL to intervene in this way, it needs the three kinds of knowledge discussed earlier. It has to recognize that a story about a failure to sell is relevant when the student has succeeded in selling using a similar tactic. It has to have a library of kinds of relevance that includes such notions as showing stories with opposite outcomes. To know that the "Talked myself out of a sale" story has relevance in this situation, SPIEL needs indexing knowledge. Its representation of what the story is about needs to include concepts such as the plan of continuing conversation after the sale is closed and the outcome of having the customer change his or her mind. Finally, to see that what the student is doing constitutes a storytelling opportunity, SPIEL has to have knowledge of recognition. It has to know that only after the student leaves has the danger passed that the customer will have a change of heart, and that the customer's signature constitutes the completion of the close of the sale, among many other things.

Relevance Knowledge

In asking the question "What makes a story relevant?", I am deliberately taking a different tack from that typically found in computer-based learning environments, such as intelligent tutoring systems (ITSs; Polson &

---

[3]"Talked myself out of a sale," story from interview with Denny Gant, video clip #150. This story and all the other examples used in this chapter are transcriptions made from videotaped interviews with experienced account executives at Ameritech Publishing in Troy, Michigan, on July 14 and 15, 1992. Interviews were conducted by Alex Kass, Michelle Saunders, Mary Williamson, and the author.

Richardson, 1988). Such systems are usually extensions of today's formal schooling. The designer of the system develops a set of instructional goals, puts together a computer environment where the knowledge relating to those goals can be transmitted and tested, and develops presentation material that helps students meet the instructional goals. This is a less appropriate design for a learning environment for teaching social skills. There are usually no hard-and-fast rules about the exercise of social skills, and often experts will have widely differing opinions about what exactly a student needs to learn. Many complex skills have the property that it is difficult to state exactly what is required for mastery (Funke, 1991).

A case based view of expertise contributes a different notion of curriculum. To be good case based reasoners, students need to learn a variety of cases so they will have background knowledge from which to reason when confronting new problems. Every one of SPIEL's stories is a real-world case that an expert found important enough to save and recall. What better source of a curriculum than the cases on which real expertise has been built?

Using stories as the primary pedagogical source also entails a different notion of tutorial intervention than found in ITSs (Anderson, 1988). The relevance of a story for a storytelling tutor is not based on a notion of the correct or incorrect way to perform a task. What characterizes a storytelling opportunity is the existence of a story that will catch a student's interest sufficiently well that the story will be understood and remembered. Rather than modeling what the student knows about the task and trying to ensure the student meets an expert standard, a case based teacher has the easier task of representing what the student is likely to be interested in (Edelson, 1993).

Stories can be intrinsically interesting for many different reasons—they can be funny, grotesque, dramatic, mysterious, etc.—but SPIEL is not interested in stories for their own sake; it does not strive to be a conversationalist. As a tutor, its role is to help the student, implementing what Papert (1980) called the "power principle"—the notion that a tutor should enable students to do something that they want to do. Therefore, SPIEL's stories must be interesting because they are relevant to the learning that students are already performing in GuSS's learning environment.

Failure-Driven Learning. Learning-by-doing is frequently driven by failures: unsuccessful results or unmet expectations. Failure-driven learning theory (Schank, 1982) holds that there is a central cycle in this type of learning. The learner makes predictions about the results of its own actions or the behavior of others, and tests these predictions by observing what happens. If all goes well, these expectations feed into decisions about the next action or prediction. However, if the expectations fail, the learner has made a mistake in understanding the world. The failure helps focus attention on exactly what may be wrong in the learner's model of the world or in its processing. To prevent future failures, the learner must explain how the failure occurred in sufficient detail to allow the problem to be fixed.

The failure-driven learning cycle makes it possible for a student to recover from errors independently of instruction, but doing so is dependent on the student's knowledge of the domain. In a domain where the student knows very little, failure-driven learning will degenerate into unproductive thrashing around because the student cannot perform any part of the learning cycle well. Unassisted failure-driven learning works best when the student knows enough about the domain to make the right kinds of observations and to construct reasonable explanations. When this is not the case, a tutor can assist by giving students the knowledge that they need to form good explanations. There are two sources of relevance for stories in a learning-by-doing environment: They can (a) point out errors that the student may be making when the environment does not provide sufficient feedback for the student to notice them, and (b) help the student explain expectation failures when the environment does not give all the information needed to construct an explanation.

SPIEL's Storytelling Strategies. To get its cases across, a case based teaching system needs an understanding of where the student's interests lie. In a learning-by-doing environment, interest will be governed by relationships between what the tutor presents and the issues of failure-driven learning: expectation failure and explanation. Building a system capable of recalling relevant stories entails explicitly representing these relevance relationships.

SPIEL's relevance knowledge comes in the form of storytelling strategies that represent the conditions under which a story with particular characteristics will be relevant to a student in the GuSS environment. SPIEL has 13 storytelling strategies. Each has a similar function: selecting stories of a particular type and characterizing situations in which they will be relevant. The strategies fall into four categories based on their relationship between the stories they present and the situations in which they present them. These categories cover the most important ways that stories can be relevant to students using GuSS. They concentrate especially on plans and outcomes, which is consonant with the emphasis in GuSS on learning-by-doing. Students are largely engaged in planning and acting in the social environment.

1. *Strategies that show the student alternatives. Demonstrate risks* falls in this category. Also in this category are the strategies *Demonstrate opportunities* and *Demonstrate alternative plan.*

2. *Strategies that critique the student's expectations.* There are six strategies in this category, three basic types, each of which has two subtypes. The basic types are *Warn about optimism*, *Warn about pessimism*, and *Warn about assumption.*

3. *Strategies that project possible results of actions the student is taking.* There are two strategies here: *Reinforce plan* and *Warn about plan.*

4. *Strategies that explain the perspectives of other people to the student.* In this category, there are two strategies: *Explain other's plan* and *Explain other's perspective.*

Indexing Knowledge

SPIEL uses its library of storytelling strategies to compare a story and a student's situation and determine if the story is relevant. For this comparison to be possible, SPIEL must know what its stories are about. Stories must be labeled so that the features crucial for comparison are readily available, and the system of labels must be organized so that the retriever can avoid having to look at every story. The problem of designing a representation to be used for labeling cases is known as "the indexing problem" (Domeshek, 1992; Schank, 1982). An index must include features that are good predictors of a case's usefulness (Hammond, 1989a; Hunter, 1989; Kolodner, 1989). One proposal for tutorial cases is to index them based on the situations in which they should be retrieved (Edelson, 1993). The problem with this approach is that it requires the creator of the index to consider all possible uses at the time that the case is indexed.[4] This means there will be a new index for every way that a case could be used.

SPIEL's alternative is to use an indexing representation that captures properties of the story, independent of possible tutoring function. The only consideration at index creation time is what the story means, not how it ultimately may be useful. With this indexing scheme, the index for a story need only be written once. The storytelling strategies examine each index to decide how and when to tell the story. Stories frequently

---

[4]Although research continues in automatic indexing of video material (see, e.g., Dimitrova & Golshani, 1994; Hampapur, Jain, & Weymouth, 1994), these techniques seek only to characterize the visual properties of the video signal, features that are media dependent. SPIEL needs to know what a story is about, not what it looks like. Such media-independent indexes cannot be extracted automatically, so SPIEL uses only manually created indexes.

encode interesting expectation failures or anomalies (Schank, 1982; Schank et al., 1990). Anomalies are what make a story memorable both to the teller and the hearer. Stories about anomalies and their explanations address issues important for students' active learning: experiences of expectation failures and attempts to explain them. The general form of an anomaly can be stated as follows: "Actor X had an expectation that Y would happen, but actually Z happened." A statement of the anomaly from the "Talked myself out of a sale" story is: "The salesperson expected the client would be reassured about his purchase, but actually the client decided not to buy."

Recognition Knowledge

Indexes represent what a story is about. Strategies represent how, in general, stories can be made relevant to a student. There is one final link that a storytelling tutor must make, which is the connection between students' actions and its notion of a relevant story. This involves a variety of considerations, including social knowledge (such as the scope of a conversation) and practical details (such as when a sale should be considered closed). This recognition knowledge has three different types: (a) task knowledge, both general and specific, (b) student stereotype knowledge, and (c) manifestation knowledge.

Of primary importance for a tutor is a general understanding of the task at hand. The tutor must know that the student is trying to sell, and that selling involves subgoals like gathering information, constructing presentations, making sales pitches, and answering objections. At a more concrete level, SPIEL must know particular details of how the selling task is achieved by the student in the YELLO application. It must know which kinds of answers from a customer constitute substantive information and which are evasions, what actions constitute the construction of a prospective ad, and so forth. The task of representing these details is of course greatly simplified by the fact that SPIEL is operating in a simulated environment with limited scope. It does not have to be concerned about every possible way a student can ask a question; it need only recognize those choices that GuSS actually permits.

SPIEL's knowledge of the student takes a much simpler form than the student models found in ITSs (Goldstein, 1982; vanLehn, 1988). Because SPIEL needs to represent students' states of interest, not their states of knowledge, it is sufficient for SPIEL to have a static notion of what will interest students because the things that they will find interesting do not change as fast as the things that they know. For example, to use the strategies that explain others' behavior, SPIEL must know what actions students will find unexpected. It has a static set of stereotypes that students are assumed to possess and tells stories when they show customers and others doing things that violate the stereotype.

SPIEL's expectation-directed strategies require that the system be able to tell stories that contrast with expectations the student is likely to have. Of course, SPIEL cannot read the student's mind. There will always be the possibility that the student has a certain assumption, but takes no action that clearly indicates it. There is little that any tutor can do about this, short of asking students directly what they are thinking. What SPIEL can do is identify situations in which there is a clear manifestation of a student's expectations. SPIEL's manifestation knowledge allows it to infer what symptoms it can observe that are likely consequences of a student having a particular expectation.

Retrieval Architecture

Even given all the appropriate knowledge, it is still no small matter to locate a relevant story out of a library of many. The way a retrieval problem is usually posed is in terms of cue formulation. There is one process that decides what type of information is needed and creates a retrieval cue, a description of what should be retrieved. A second process searches memory for a good match to this description.

But cue formulation is not the best way to think about tutorial storytelling. If there is no story to tell about the student's situation, the work invested in recognizing the need for a story and formulating a retrieval cue is wasted. A better approach is to use the stories as source material. SPIEL's stories are, in effect, a case based model of a social task. To critique a student's expectations, SPIEL need not develop a model of the student's thinking and pinpoint those expectations that may be suspect. Its stories tell it what expectations other salespeople incorrectly made. If a story talks about a failed assumption, SPIEL knows that at least one person had this assumption and had it violated. If it can identify that the student may have a similar assumption, the story will be relevant. Instead of diagnosing the student's failings, the system attempts to recognize storytelling opportunities, situations in which some story is relevant.

This is an inversion of the standard way that retrieval problems are conceived. Instead of asking, "What retrieval cue should the system build to represent a particular situation?", SPIEL asks, "What storytelling opportunity already characterized does this situation resemble?" This is analogous to the solution for natural language understanding found in the direct memory access parsing (DMAP) method (Martin, 1991; Martin & Riesbeck, 1986). DMAP changed the traditional natural language understanding question from "What knowledge structure should be built to represent this text?" to "What knowledge structure already in memory should be activated in response to this text?"

How SPIEL Works. SPIEL characterizes and recognizes storytelling opportunities in two phases. The first phase, called the *storage phase*, prepares the system for storytelling. The storyteller examines its stories in the light of its storytelling strategies and determines what kinds of storytelling opportunities it needs to look for. In the *retrieval phase*, the system tries to recognize those opportunities as the student is performing the task. A schematic picture of these phases of SPIEL is shown in Fig. 3.1.

The storage phase begins with the manual construction of indexes. An indexer watches the story on video and uses an indexing tool to construct one or more anomaly based representations of what it is about. Indexes are then processed using the storytelling strategies. SPIEL determines, for each combination of story and strategy, how and when it might tell the story using the strategy, thus characterizing the storytelling opportunities

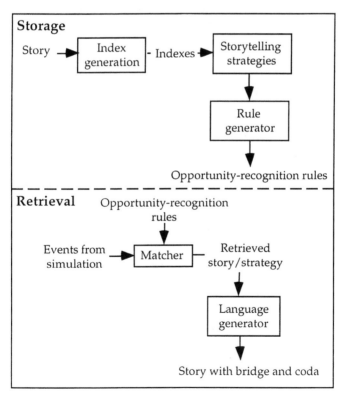

FIG. 3.1. How SPIEL works.

that the story affords. The rule generator converts descriptions of these opportunities into procedures for recognizing them, in the form of rules that are compatible with the GuSS simulation.

The retrieval phase of SPIEL is a teaching module in the GuSS architecture, implemented by a rule-based system. The rules created during the storage phase are matched against ongoing events in the simulated world, as the student takes actions and the simulated characters respond. Successful recognition of an opportunity causes a story and its associated strategy to be retrieved. To introduce and explain the system's remindings to the student, SPIEL creates natural language texts, called the *headline*, *bridge*, and *coda*, that tell the student why the story was retrieved and what connection it has to the current situation. These texts are presented to the student along with the story.

The Contributions of This Research

This work builds onto existing models of case retrieval a notion of case utility that is not strict similarity or association, but incorporates task considerations such as the pedagogical import of a story. Similar considerations enter into other communicative tasks, such as argumentation.[5]

SPIEL's indexing representation for stories evolved from the "universal indexing frame" proposal (Schank et al., 1990). The representation was pared to its essential elements: the notion of anomaly, based on expectation failure, and the notion of explanation underlying the failure. This representation is sufficient for a retriever to determine the applicability of a story for a wide range of pedagogical purposes.

Also significant is the way that SPIEL goes about its retrieval. Under the case based teaching architecture, the stories of practitioners are viewed as the curriculum for students to learn. Therefore, it is natural for a storytelling tutor to be implemented as an architecture that starts with stories and tries to figure out how best to tell them. Stories stored in memory do not passively await activation by other processes. They actively determine what features will be looked for in the learning environment. SPIEL has an opportunistic memory (Hammond, 1989b), seeking opportunities to tell its stories using its strategic knowledge of what kinds of situations make stories relevant.

Although SPIEL's storytelling strategies are specially tailored to the problem of teaching social tasks, the general principles they exemplify are more general. The two basic contributions of stories to learning-by-

---

[5]See Ashley (1990), Ashley and Rissland (1987) and Shafto, Bareiss, and Birnbaum (1992) for examples of case retrievers for argumentation.

doing are their value as explanations and their value as pointers to possible expectation failures. Every case based teaching system needs to implement these roles, although retrieval strategies will vary according to the type of expectations that are important in a given domain and the type of explanations that students are likely to need. SPIEL's retrieval architecture has three basic parts: (a) the indexing of cases based on their inherent features, (b) the a priori application of presentation strategies to characterize case presentation opportunities, and (c) the intervention of the tutor based on recognition of these opportunities. This framework applies to any case based teaching system, whatever its cases and presentation strategies.

SPIEL'S TEACHING ENVIRONMENT

GuSS and YELLO

This section briefly describes the operation of GuSS to give a feeling for the system as a whole and to explain the role of storytelling in it; the system is described in detail elsewhere (Burke, 1993; Kass, Burke, Blevis, & Williamson, 1992, 1993/1994). As emphasized in this research, a central objective of GuSS is to engage the student in the realistic practice of social skills in context. The central unit of instruction is the *scenario*, an extended interaction in which the student works on a realistic problem. In the course of a scenario, the student is confronted with a range of obstacles and opportunities typical of the real-world social task.

In the following discussion, the task confronting the user is to get to know the client's business, come to some understanding of its market and its advertising needs, construct a proposal geared to these needs and to the client's concerns, present that proposal in a convincing way, and get the customer to buy. This section illustrates that task using a scenario in which the student is selling to a roofing contractor, Swain Roofing. The cast of characters for Swain Roofing includes: (a) Ed Swain, the owner of the company; (b) Lucy Swain, the office manager, also Ed's wife; and (c) Dave Swain, the Swains' son, who is gradually taking over the business.

As is typical for small family-owned service contractors, the operation is run out of the Swains' home. Swain Roofing currently has a small ad in their local Yellow Pages directory. The underlying business situation, which the student may or may not uncover, is that the Swains' primary business—residential roofing—has been undercut by lower cost, lower quality competitors. The Swains are trying to get more business in the area of commercial roofing, where they feel their high-quality approach will be more valued. They are also interested in expanding their business into nearby areas they have not traditionally serviced. Ed and Lucy also want their son, Dave, to take over the business, and worry that it might not be strong enough for him to make a good living. Ed has given Dave responsibility for the firm's advertising, and Dave has started to look into cable TV ads as a way to get to potential customers.

A salesperson who asks good questions and discovers these concerns may be able to sell Swain Roofing a large ad campaign, including advertising in a "business-to-business" directory, a larger version of the current ad, small ads in headings other than "roofing," and display advertising in one or two directories in adjacent areas. A student who is less capable may have to settle for renewal of the existing ad.

The Swain Roofing scenario begins with the student receiving the account information for the company, with an appointment already set up to visit the Swains. The student goes to the Swains' house for the appointment, and greets Lucy at the front door.

Student: Hello. My name is Mike Johnson. I'm with Ameritech Pages Plus, the Bell Yellow Pages. I spoke with you on the phone about handling your account this year.

Lucy: Please come in, Mike. Ed knows you're coming and should be here shortly.

Figure 3.2 shows the appearance of the screen after this exchange. A picture of the scene, the Swains' kitchen, is at the right. Below this area is a picture of Lucy Swain. Above her is the text of what she has said most recently. Under her picture are emotion display meters that stand in for the multitude of cues to emotion given by people in social situations. Here the meters show that Lucy is being polite: Someone has just come to her house, so she is looking somewhat happy (the first scale indicates happy/angry), somewhat interested (the second scale is interested/bored), and somewhat calm (the third scale is calm/nervous).

The action constructor, through which the student acts in the simulation, appears on the left. Here the student makes choices from menus and submenus to create utterances and other types of actions. Mike's greeting was actually the result of four action constructor choices, appended to each other:

Under the "courtesy" menu, there is an entry for "greet." Choosing this gets the English phrase, "Hello."

Under the "tell about" menu, selecting the "self" submenu and the option "name" gets the next part of the utterance, "My name is Mike Johnson."

The description of Mike's job, "I'm with Ameritech Pages Plus, the Bell Yellow Pages," comes from the option "affiliation" under the "tell about self" submenu.

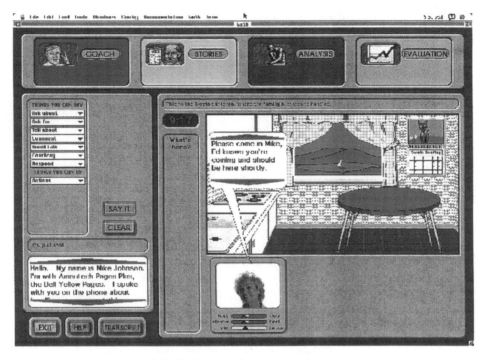

FIG. 3.2. Lucy Swain greets the student.

Finally, to refer to the appointment set up in the previous conversation, the student can look under the "tell about self" submenu and choose the option, "reminder of appointment." The sentence is, "I spoke with you on the phone about handling your account this year."

See Fig. 3.3 for a snapshot of the action constructor in use. Here the student is preparing to select "affiliation" from the "tell about self" submenu. The English language versions of the student's choices so far appear in the preview box at the bottom of the action constructor area. When the student finishes constructing an utterance, pushing the "Say it" button communicates it to the characters in the simulation.

Although Ed is the owner of the business, Lucy has an important role. An experienced salesperson would try to take advantage of Ed's absence to gather information about the business from her. However, a novice might not realize that Lucy could be an important source of information. In this scenario, the student engages Lucy only in small talk until Ed arrives. When Ed comes in, his picture appears in the scene, next to Lucy's.

Lucy: Well there's Ed now. Hi honey, this is Mike Johnson from the Yellow Pages.

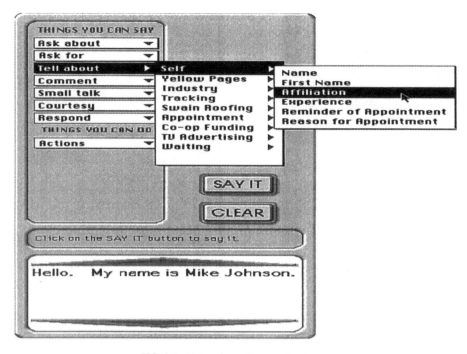

FIG. 3.3. Using the action constructor.

Because Lucy is deferential to Ed, the student has missed an opportunity to find out her thoughts about the business. From now on, he will be dealing with Ed. At this point, it is safe to conclude that the student does not expect Mrs. Swain to be useful in providing information about the business or, possibly, to have any role at all in the sale. Therefore, this is a good time to indicate to the student that the opportunity to hear Lucy's perspective has been missed.

SPIEL has a story that is relevant to this situation. When an opportunity to present a story appears, SPIEL signals the student by popping up and flashing its associated button, one of the four teaching module buttons across the top of the screen. The highlighted button contains a *headline*, a brief text indicating what kind of story is available. Here, SPIEL highlights the "Stories" button with the comment, "A warning about something you just did," as in Fig. 3.4. If the student presses the button, the Storyteller screen is shown as in Fig. 3.5. The first item on the screen is the *bridge*, a short explanation of why the story has come up. The student can use the buttons below the video frame to view a video of an Ameritech account executive telling a story from her own experience. Figure 3.4 shows a transcription of that story. Following the story, SPIEL sums it

Headline:

A warning about something you just did.

Bridge:

If you assume that Mrs. Swain will not have a role in the business, you may be surprised. Here is a story in which an account executive made a similar assumption that did not hold:

Story (from video):

"I went to this auto glass place one time where I had the biggest surprise. I walked in; it was a big, burly man; he talked about auto glass. So we were working on a display ad for him. It was kind of a rinky-dink shop and there was a TV playing and a lady there watching the TV. It was a soap opera in the afternoon. I talked to the man a lot but yet the woman seemed to be listening, she was asking a couple of questions. She talked about the soap opera a little bit and about the weather.

"It turns out that after he and I worked on the ad, he gave it to her to approve. It turns out that after I brought it back to approve, she approved the actual dollar amount. He was there to tell me about the business, but his wife was there to hand over the check. So if I had ignored her or had not given her the time of day or the respect that she was deserved [sic], I wouldn't have made that sale. It's important when you walk in, to really listen to everyone and to really pay attention to whatever is going on that you see."

Coda:

An assumption that a spouse will not have a role in the business may be unrealistic.

FIG. 3.4.   Telling "Wife Watching TV" story.[6]

all up for the student with a short coda that describes a lesson of the story as it applies to the student's situation.

This example illustrates the synergistic interaction between simulation and storytelling. Without the story to provide the impetus to examine the situation, the student might never realize that an opportunity had been missed. However, without active engagement in the simulation, the student might lack the motivation and context to understand and remember the story.

Figure 3.4 shows the *Warn about assumption* storytelling strategy at work. In the story, the salesperson is surprised because she did not expect the wife of the "big, burly man" to participate in the sale and she did. The student's behavior indicates there might be a similar assumption about Lucy Swain at work. The *Warn about assumption* strategy calls on SPIEL to use a story about an incorrect assumption to show that an analogous assumption of the student's may be wrong.

---

[6]Story from interview with Amber McLean, video clip #305.

FIG. 3.5. The storyteller screen.

After the student hears the story and closes the Storyteller window, the sales call can continue.

Ed: Hi Mike, nice to meet you, I'm Ed Swain—sorry if I kept you waiting. What can I do for you?

Student: Since I haven't handled your account before, Ed, I wanted to talk with you about what changes have taken place since last year. . . .

The student continues questioning Ed and finally wraps up the sales call:

Student: Is there anything I forgot to ask about the business?
Ed: You've covered it—why all the questions this year?

Student: It's important for me to know where you want your business to go in the upcoming year, Ed, so that we will have a better understanding of how to help you reach your goals. What are your long-term goals?

Ed: To make Dave work more so I can spend more time fishing!
Student: Thanks for your patience in answering all my questions.

Ed: OK. See you later.

The student has failed to seize an opportunity to probe into Ed's future plans for his business. Ed treats the question about long-term goals lightly, but his answer suggests many follow-up questions the salesperson should ask: What is Dave's future role? How close is Ed to retirement? This failure on the student's part is another opportunity for SPIEL. It brings up a story (shown in Fig. 3.6) about a salesperson who makes the most of a similar situation.

The "Long Term Goals" story illustrates an alternative approach to a similar situation. The salesperson in the story used the customer's long-term goals as leverage in selling a larger ad. This is distinctly different from what the student has done. This is an example of the *Demonstrate alternative plan* storytelling strategy. When a student has just handled a social situation unsuccessfully, SPIEL can tell a story about a similar situation that shows how another salesperson was successful.

Building a Social Simulation

Educational, technical, and practical constraints all entered into the design of GuSS. All simulations strive for accuracy, the property such that student actions have the same results as in real life. The differences in simulation design lie primarily in the degree of fidelity: the "feel" of using the simulation. A flight simulator is one extreme, where every effort is made to make using the simulator exactly like performing the task in real life. At the other extreme are "adventure"-style computer games, where the user is allowed to make multiple-choice decisions at predetermined choice points.

It might be assumed that maximum fidelity is the ultimate goal for every simulation, but there are good reasons to aim for less than total duplication of real life. In many domains, not every action performed in the course of doing a task is worth teaching. A simulation that leaves out unimportant aspects of an interaction or includes them only in schematic form will save the student from spending time doing things that have no educational significance. A simulation should aim for fidelity in those

You gathered information about long-term goals in a cursory manner without much success. Here is a story about a similar situation in which an account executive used a different method and was successful.

Recently, I made a call to an electric contractor in Springfield, Ohio. One of the greatest things that a Yellow Pages person ever hears is "Leave it like it is," that person is a very good customer. But it's also a guy who needs a little incentive of they should buy, or maybe even a little reinforcement as to why they're buying. This company is a small company owned by a father, his son and just one other partner, basically a three-person operation in a small town. They have a very large ad; they have a quarter page ad with four colors. At that classification it's probably the largest ad in the directory. As a matter of fact, I did a history of all the ads from the past three years in that classification and their ad and almost every other ad in that classification had remained the same.

So when I got in there he had already told me that he wanted to leave it like it is, but he gave me the sense that he wasn't really sure why he kept buying it. So what I did was ask him flat out, I could sense that something was bothering him, I asked him. I said, "John, what's bothering you?" He said to me he wasn't sure that the cost justified itself. He wasn't sure that the ad was actually paying for itself. He opened up to me for the first time, after that. It set him at ease and we started talking about how much value a customer is to him, each call, and how many calls he needs to make that a profitable ad.

We also got into ideas of goals of his in the next five years, with his son coming up in the business and he getting close to retirement. We started thinking about how much more business we would have to do so he could obtain those goals. My advice in this situation is if you can get a customer to open up about the business, he's going to tell you a lot more about it from a goals standpoint in the next five years. This customer ended up buying the next larger size ad up to increase his business in electric contracting so he could achieve the goal of having the business strong enough for his son to take over in the next five years. He also, by talking to him, realized that the value of the product was so significant, to have in the book. Just from a dollars standpoint, it didn't take that many calls be an actual cost-effective program for him.

You gathered information about long-term goals in a cursory manner. It didn't work well. In the future, you might consider probing deeply into the customer's long-term goals.

FIG. 3.6.   A story about a different approach you might try.

areas where the student's skills are most important, and where the student is likely to need to learn.

Although a technical apparatus, even a complex one like an aircraft cockpit, can be reproduced with great fidelity, this level of fidelity is not currently possible for social situations. Attempts at virtual reality notwithstanding, computers cannot easily provide the full range of signals and cues found in the social world, nor can they recognize and respond in a realistic manner to the student's tone of voice, body language, and so on. Radical simplifications of the environment must be made for a social simulation to be tractable. This is one reason that it is important to augment a social simulation with depictions of real-world situations such as stories, which can compensate for this loss of fidelity.

The major simplifications made in building GuSS fall into four categories:

1. *Physical action.* A student's physical activity is present in GuSS only in schematic form: The student does not have to drive to the Swains' house, poke through a file cabinet to get account information, or pick which chair to sit on in the Swains' kitchen. These kinds of actions, although part of the salesperson's life, are not what students need to learn about.

2. *Synchrony.* The simulation does not have real-time operation; it has to give students time to use the action constructor. Waiting for the student to act slows the simulation. In part, this also serves a pedagogical purpose; giving students time to think carefully before constructing their utterances in the simulated world should help them carry the habit of reflection to their real-time conversations. A negative consequence is that students do not feel pressure to think on their feet in the simulation as they would when confronted with a real person in conversation.

3. *Natural language.* Although conversation is the activity that the student does most in a GuSS simulation, the intent of GuSS was not to solve the natural language understanding and generation problem. As shown earlier, the GuSS interface uses a system of hierarchical menus for students to construct natural language utterances by composing natural language phrases. Although the menus encode a finite number of options, the sheer number of possibilities forces students to use the menu system to construct something to say, rather than choose a completed utterance. The set of options is also dynamic: The more the student finds out, the more issues can be raised. Preliminary experience with GuSS suggests that after a short period of acclimatization, during which students browse through the options in the action constructor, they begin to use it easily as a means to express themselves.

4. *Visual realism.* Because of the commitment in GuSS to an open-ended simulation, the program cannot carry on video conversations, complete with gestures, facial expressions, and body language. Every possible state must be recorded ahead of time in such a system.[7] Our compromise on this issue is the unrealistic, but useful, expression meters associated with each agent. Here the student can get a reading of the emotional expression of an agent. This is not the same as learning to read body language, but it does teach the student what features are worth learning to identify.

Because GuSS is founded on learning-by-doing, one aspect of the social world that is of crucial importance is open-endedness. For some domains,

---

[7]See Stevens (1989) for an interesting example of a social simulation that operates in this way.

a simulation with a small number of choices is acceptable, when in real life a practitioner has a fixed number of possible actions at any given time and the task is to pick the correct one. The range of possible actions in most social situations is large, and it may be difficult to generate a set of reasonable actions. Picking the right answer out of a small set of predefined choices is simply not an activity that has a counterpart in the social tasks where GuSS has been applied. This is the rationale behind the design of the action constructor and the design of GuSS' simulated characters.

The characters or social agents in the GuSS simulation operate in an autonomous, unscripted manner. They are, in effect, simple social planners. The agents observe events in the simulation and react to them based on internally represented goals and plans. In particular, when they converse with the user and with each other, they are enacting plans to say certain things—plans that are realized in particular utterances. Each agent is a self-contained production system, similar to those found in expert systems such as OPS5 (Brownston, Farrell, Kant, & Martin, 1985). At each point in the simulation, the agent looks for the productions, or decision rules, that match its current working memory, which is called the agent's *mental state* because it represents what the agent knows, believes, expects, and so on. The rule that matches best is fired, which causes the agent to perform some action.

With this design, agents are naturally extensible. If a new topic of discussion is needed, an agent can be given new decision rules to respond to that topic. Many of the decision rules that an agent needs are fairly generic: ones that any agent might have, or ones that can be strongly associated with a particular type of personality. Ed Swain expects that the salesperson will have some knowledge of terminology particular to his industry. He will get a little irritated if the student shows a lack of understanding of basic terms. This expectation would probably be common to many strong-minded business owners. In GuSS, those aspects of Mr. Swain's decision making that could be considered common to other such individuals are segregated into a personality stereotype: entrepreneurial spirit. Ed Swain, by virtue of having this personality, inherits mental states and decision rules associated with the stereotype.

Combining Instruction and Practice

The GuSS simulation is a complex mechanism for generating realistic social interaction that supports students' learning-by-doing. However, teaching modules such as SPIEL remain essential. Interaction with the simulator gives students experience with only one set of possibilities—those that have been put into a scenario. This is not enough for students to gain a broad understanding of the task they are learning. The social world has tremendous variation, and no amount of simulation would be enough for students to see all possible interactions or outcomes. This, of course, is true of learning-by-doing in all complex skills—the student cannot experience everything.

To become truly expert in a field, a student must learn the abstract principles at work and how those principles apply in practice. Simulated practice is useful, but students who have only faced the problems presented by a simulated environment may simply memorize the actions that work in the program, and thus be unable to adapt when faced with novel situations outside it. Formal schooling attempts to teach principles directly, but often fails to teach how they are applied. As a result, motivation is often low, and much of what is learned is quickly forgotten, or remains "unintegrated or inert" (Collins, Brown, & Newman, 1989).

GuSS combines instruction and practice, achieving a powerful synergism: Students can reflect on their experiences in the learning environment with the help of the instruction given by GuSS' teaching modules, of which SPIEL is one. The principles described by the teaching modules are motivated, operationalized, and made memorable by putting them to use (Schank & Jona, 1991; Williams, 1991). The job of a teaching module is to be an advisor: to look over the student's shoulder, watch the simulation, and give relevant advice. The guidance students receive in GuSS is provided by a library of teaching modules that observe the action in the simulation and intervene to present relevant material. In addition to SPIEL, the current implementation of GuSS has two other teaching modules: the Analyzer and the Coach, each presenting a different kind of material.

Although SPIEL holds the experiences reported by practitioners as a source of informal knowledge of a field, the Analyzer holds "textbook" knowledge. For YELLO, there are about 40 multi-media "textbook sections" relating to social practices, including information about personality types, communication tactics, and organizational behavior. The Analyzer in YELLO also has information about standard problems in selling, such as keeping a customer's attention or dealing with particular classes of objections. The Analyzer has the job of explicitly teaching principles and techniques, much as a standard textbook or lecture aims to do. Its multimedia capacity is obviously an improvement on these techniques, but the principal value of the Analyzer arises because of its association with GuSS. The Analyzer can present its material at the moment the student is likely to be interested, embedding its discussion of principles in contexts in which they are directly relevant.

The Coach teaches procedural principles of a social task. It has an abstract model of the goals a student should have and tracks those goals to see when they have been satisfied. In YELLO, the Coach uses a hierarchical decomposition of the steps in the process of selling Yellow Pages advertising and follows the student's accomplishments, letting the student see what important issues are outstanding.

For example, a student who is unsure about any part of the task can query the Coach by selecting elements of the task decomposition and using buttons, such as the "Why?" button. If the student asks "Why?" about a goal, the Coach explains how that goal fits into the overall task of selling. If the student asks "Why?" about the achievement or partial achievement of a goal, such as a piece of information the customer provides, the Coach will explain the relationship of the event to the goal. Students also have access to a "How?" button that calls on the Coach to give hints about general strategies for achieving goals, and a "Now what?" button that asks the Coach to give suggestions for what tactics to try next.

The Coach acts as a guide through what may be an unfamiliar process to many students. It lays out the general course of the selling process and makes explicit the relationships between its different steps. In negotiating this terrain, students can call on the Coach to remind them of why they are doing what they are doing, and to get hints about how to go about it. The Coach also records events that contribute to the success of various goals, so students can check to see how they are doing. In this way, the Coach acts as a *smart notebook* that automatically records important information.

Of all the teaching modules in GuSS, the Coach is probably the most similar to other types of tutoring systems, most of which have primarily procedural knowledge. It is perhaps closest in spirit to Elsom-Cook's "guided discovery tutoring" concept (Elsom-Cook, 1990) and the coached practice environment of SHERLOCK (Lesgold, Lajoie, Bunzo, & Eggan, 1992). What these systems have in common is their reliance on hinting and user control of the interaction with the tutor.

Teaching modules are combined with the simulation in the GuSS Shell, which is the basis for all GuSS applications. The Shell contains three major components: (a) the Interface Manager, which handles input from the student and displays information to the student; (b) the Simulation Engine, the general-purpose social simulation mechanism that manages the simulated world; and (c) the Teaching Modules, which monitor the state of the simulation looking for opportunities to present useful guidance.

Figure 3.7 is a schematic diagram of the Shell, showing the interconnections among these three components and their associated data. The student interacts with the Interface Manager, which passes the student's actions to the Simulation Engine. The engine computes the state of the simulated world, making use of the production system model of each

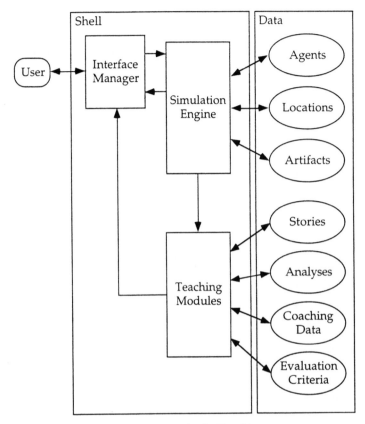

FIG. 3.7. The GuSS architecture.

agent, and using the location and artifact definitions that are specific to the particular scenario the student is in. The Simulation Engine sends messages back to the Interface Manager telling it to display changes in the simulated world. While this interaction is occurring, the Teaching Modules examine the state of the simulation, signaling the Interface Manager when they have something to present to the student.

Teaching Modules Versus Intelligent Tutoring Systems

GuSS may appear superficially similar to an intelligent tutoring system (ITS), the standard means of building computer-based tutors. ITS programs contain a tutoring component that, like a teaching module, monitors students' task performance and intervenes to provide guidance (Polson & Richardson, 1988; Sleeman & Brown, 1982). The significant

TABLE 3.1
Differences Between Social Skills and Those Typical to ITSs

Variable	ITS Domains	Social Skills
Existing student knowledge	Small	Very large
Complexity of task	Low	High
Solution procedure known	Yes	No
Agreement among experts	Yes	No

differences between GuSS' tutoring and that of ITS systems have to do with the kind of knowledge the tutor has and the way the tutor intervenes.

An ITS is composed of three modules: the expert module, the student model, and the tutor. The student model observes the student's behavior in the system and diagnoses the state of the student's knowledge. The expert module solves the same problem as the student using expert knowledge. The tutor compares the student's state of knowledge as represented in the student model against the expert standard and determines where the differences lie. These differences are what the student needs to learn. The tutor then decides how to intervene to correct the student. ITSs have been constructed to teach geometry (Anderson, Boyle, & Yost, 1985), introductory computer programming (Reiser, Anderson, & Farrell, 1985), and arithmetic (Burton, 1982). They have been notably less successful in teaching complex skills,[8] such as medical diagnosis (Clancey, 1982). Lesgold and Lajoie (1991) noted that even the technical skills involved in electronics troubleshooting turned out to be too complex for the standard ITS framework to be useful.

There are four sources of complexity in GuSS' domain, as shown in Table 3.1. These complexities have important consequences for applying the ITS model to the problem of tutoring for social skills. The large quantity of existing student knowledge that students bring to the learning of social skills makes the construction of a student model problematic for these tasks. In social arenas, the discourse is not new: Beginning account executives using YELLO will have encountered salespeople throughout their lives, and probably have experience in sales already. YELLO cannot teach as if its students were encountering the conceptual basis of selling for the first time. For students in YELLO, learning how to fit new concepts and new skills into their existing repertoire is at least as important as learning the new material. There is also the problem of exactly how expertise can and should be characterized. In domains of social expertise, the complexity of the task and the lack of a known solution procedure mean that there are often as many right answers as there are experts. This

---

[8]Complex in the sense of Funke (1991).

fact calls into question the whole pedagogical thrust behind the ITS approach.

Where SPIEL differs most from ITSs is the kind of material it presents and the kind of impact it aims to achieve. In the ITS paradigm, the comparison between the student's behavior and what is predicted by the expert model is intended to indicate defects in the student's understanding. The tutor intervenes when the student has diverged from what the expert model predicts, and its role is to get the student back on track. The intervention provided by ITSs is either procedurally based, intended to get the student to understand and follow the correct procedure for solving a problem, or fact based, intended to give students familiarity with a body of facts. Such teaching is less applicable in a social arena, where there often are no hard-and-fast rules and few useful universal facts.

The case based view of expertise implemented in SPIEL calls for the tutor to play a quite different role. Rather than tutoring knowledge that describes the correct solution procedure or some collection of facts, SPIEL has a set of stories—a range of experiences that bear on the problem at hand. Instead of saying the student is in error, the tutor can say, "Here's a situation in which what you're doing turned out to be a bad idea." Instead of saying the student should perform a certain action, it can point out a situation in which that action led to a good result.

The system can leave it to the student to judge whether such advice is relevant, and if so, how to apply it. The system does not have to guarantee that the student gets it right. If a student in the Swain Roofing scenario does not manage to make a sale to Ed Swain, the learning experience in YELLO is not greatly diminished. GuSS will be successful even if students do poorly in the simulation because they will come away having been exposed to some important cases and seen how they apply in particular contexts. Such students have begun to build the case base of experience on which their expertise will be founded.

Storytelling in GuSS

Storytelling is a type of tutoring that is well suited for advising students learning complex social tasks in a simulated environment. SPIEL presents stories told by people who are experts in the areas the student is studying—stories that are drawn from the expert's own experience. Such stories are particularly valuable in a simulated environment because students can see how the simulated situations they come across reflect the world of real practice.

The way SPIEL teaches is also important. It draws the student's attention to the associations it makes with others' experience, but it does not try to tell the student what to do. Because SPIEL is not required to present one "right" answer, it can show multiple perspectives on difficult issues. For example, it might bring up two stories: one about someone who was successful doing what the student is doing and another about a failure in the same situation. It is important for students to recognize that even experts can disagree about the best course of action.

One of the critical issues for any case based teaching system is the design of an indexing representation. What a retriever can do with cases will be largely determined by how it can access them. SPIEL's indexing representation captures intrinsic properties of stories, from which it derives possible tutorial uses for them. This kind of representation stands in contrast to other case based teaching systems, whose indexes directly incorporate an assessment of a case's pedagogical utility. SPIEL's modular approach allows experimentation with a range of pedagogical strategies because different strategies can be tried out on the same body of indexes. It also places less of a burden on the indexing step, which, in case based teaching systems, is performed manually. SPIEL's indexing representation is the subject of the next section.

LABELING STORIES

Introduction

For a storyteller to choose a story to tell, it must know what its stories are about. It must know that a story will convey a certain message to the student (e.g., that it will present an interesting alternative). Its knowledge of stories must be highly organized and efficiently used. In picking a story to tell, the storyteller should be like a librarian who can point out books worth reading without having memorized the text of every book in the library. There are two kinds of knowledge a librarian needs to do this: knowledge about what kinds of books are useful for what purposes and labels associated with the books to say what they are about. A storyteller needs similar knowledge. It must understand the tutorial functions its stories can serve, and it must know what stories can serve those functions. The first kind of knowledge is embodied in SPIEL's storytelling strategies. These are discussed in later sections. This section describes SPIEL's labels, or indexes,[9] descriptions that summarize stories for the purposes of tuto-

---

[9]*Index* is the term that has been traditionally used in CBR for the label given to an item stored in memory by which it can be retrieved. This has produced a certain amount of confusion with some of the other uses of the word, such as the "inverted index file" in information retrieval. I follow Owens' (1990) example and use the term *label* interchangeably with it.

rial retrieval, representing what stories are about well enough so a storyteller can decide which one to tell.

Labeling for Case Bases and Story Bases

The indexing of knowledge has become increasingly important in artificial intelligence. Researchers have moved from systems with knowledge in the form of small, easily described chunks, such as rules, to systems that reason with larger, more complex chunks of knowledge, such as the cases used by case based reasoning (CBR) programs.

The need for indexing is prominent in CBR systems because their knowledge sources—cases—are complex entities packaged as a single unit. Researchers in CBR realized early that a system cannot search every item in memory while deciding what to retrieve (Kolodner, 1984). It would be intolerably inefficient to examine the contents of each case to select good candidates. Cases must be labeled, and these labels must be organized so that search for an appropriate case is efficient.

The need for an organized vocabulary of labels for cases gives rise to what is known as "the indexing problem"—the problem of designing an indexing representation (Domeshek, 1992; Schank, 1982). The most important demand that an index must satisfy is utility: It must encode features that are predictively useful for the task. The second criterion is that an index must contain features that are computable: available at the time of retrieval. This criterion is often difficult to reconcile with the previous one. The demands of utility and computability frequently oppose each other because the most useful and predictive features are often those that are expensive to extract or ones that require solving the problem first. Creating an indexing representation for a particular CBR system requires making productive trade-offs between these two constraints.

SPIEL borrows from the CBR tradition, but the difference in task between case retrieval for problem solving and story retrieval for tutoring is significant, and has important consequences for SPIEL's index representation. The employment of stories in SPIEL is different from how cases are usually used in CBR. The standard problem-solving CBR system retrieves cases to re-use old solutions for new problems. It has one question to ask of a case: Can it solve my current problem? A storyteller is more like a CBR system for creative design (Kolodner & Wills, 1993); it has many possible uses for a given story and many storytelling strategies.

SPIEL also differs significantly from CBR systems, in that the contents of its case base are stories in video form, not representations. Video stories are opaque to SPIEL: it cannot reason with them. Some case based reasoners dip into the representation of a case when more detailed knowledge of it is sought. But SPIEL cannot do this; the retrieval of stories must be based entirely on the contents of the index. These differences require that SPIEL's indexes be richer than those typically found in CBR systems. They must contain all of the information needed for retrieval because there is no case representation to fall back on. SPIEL's information needs are greater because the system has multiple uses for its stories and needs a range of different details to satisfy the criteria of each different kind of utility.[10]

The index must contain everything a retriever needs to know about a story. For SPIEL, this means it must say enough about a story that its fitness for different storytelling strategies can be determined. One easy way to satisfy this criterion is to encode the events of a story literally in the story's index (Osgood & Bareiss, 1993), to have an event-level representation of the story's contents. Everything the story says can be encoded this way, therefore nothing will be left out. This is an appealing approach because it means that writing down the representation is straightforward: The index describes what the story says. Let us apply this approach to the following example of a reminding:

> Once while watching the demolition of a building in Chicago, I was struck by how ineffectively the work was being done. The wrecking ball hit one of the concrete supports near its center again and again with little result. It was frustrating to watch the lack of progress. This poorly-executed demolition reminded me of the time I saw a bull-fight in Spain. The matador kept dealing out blows to the bull with his sword with seemingly little effect. The failure to execute a "clean kill" made the whole affair grotesque. (Schank et al., 1990, pp. 7–8)

An event-level representation (adapting liberally from Osgood & Bareiss, 1993) of the "incompetent matador" story would look something like this: "The main event of the story was a matador stabbing the bull and being unsuccessful in killing it." Although this summarizes the story well, it does not go far in explaining the reminding. Consider a similar summary for a different story: "The main event of the story was a 2-year-old trying to tear a plastic bag and being unsuccessful at tearing it." Both stories describe failed destruction actions. The reason the matador story is a better analogy to the wrecking ball story has to do with the story's point of interest. What makes the story interesting is not the actions of the matador but the expectations of the person observing. The observer expects that professionals will be effective at their jobs, but both the

---

[10]There is a growing number of case based systems whose role is to advise a human user (Simoudis, 1992). These case based systems are similar to SPIEL in that they strictly retrieve, and often do not have knowledge of their cases beyond their indexes.

matador and the crane operator fail. The story about the 2-year-old is not as analogous because there is no such expectation for 2-year-olds.[11]

To understand why this should be so, we must look more closely at the phenomenon of reminding. As discussed in Schank (1986), explanation is one of the key processes for improving one's understanding of the world. Remindings help by bringing to mind past explanations that may contribute to understanding a new situation. In this interpretation, the matador story comes to mind because the teller is trying to understand why the crane operator is failing to do the job. The teller wants to know under what conditions he can count on professionals to do their jobs correctly. Because the matador story is an ineffective attempt at destruction carried out by a supposed professional, it provides another example to compare with failure of the crane operator.

In an educational context, the matador story would probably not be a great story to tell because it does not explain anything about the matador's action. However, suppose that the story was more explanatory: "This poorly-executed demolition reminded me of the time I saw a bull-fight in Spain. The matador kept dealing out blows to the bull with his sword with seemingly little effect. *It turned out that he had been wounded in a previous bull-fight and was afraid to get close enough to really finish the job.* The failure to execute a 'clean kill' made the whole affair grotesque." This version of the story does supply a possible explanation for the crane operator's failure. It raises certain explanation questions (Schank, 1986), such as, "Is the operator being unduly cautious, due to some previous accident?" or perhaps "Does the city have overly restrictive rules about crane operation due to fear of lawsuits?" A learner, in attempting to answer such questions, can come to a better understanding of the original situation.

An instructional storyteller is seeking this kind of explanation transfer. Students are presented with stories so that they will better understand and explain the problems they face (Schank, 1990a, 1990b). To be effective, the storyteller must know not just what is interesting about a story (the gruesome scene at the bullfight), but why it is interesting (the failed expectation about professionals). It is only through reference to the "why" that the storyteller will be able to determine what counts as a similar "what." The story about the 2-year-old has a similar failed destruction scene, but does not have any relation to the expectation, and does not help explain its failure as readily.

---

[11]It is always possible to argue that a reminding is useful. There will always be some way to "tweak" (Kass, Leake, & Owens, 1986) a recalled case into something useful. A rough notion of the relative goodness of cases can be estimated from how much tweaking is required to make each useful. Under this metric, the story about the 2-year-old is less useful than the matador story.

Event-level representations tend to leave out the "why" part of a story because it is also omitted by storytellers, who rely on their hearer's background knowledge to fill it in. The expectations "I thought a professional would be good at his job" and "I thought the bull would die quickly" do not appear anywhere in the events of the story, but readers easily infer them.

People are successful in understanding stories even when they are extremely oblique. Consider the following story from the film *Manhattan*: "She's seventeen. I'm forty-two, and she's seventeen" (cited in Schank, 1990b, p. 40). Schank argued that this is a story. The absence of normal story conventions, such as plot, has little effect on our ability to interpret it. In fact, the paucity of data is a cue that tells hearers to fill in what is missing with their own background knowledge.

This is obviously an extreme case, one where a direct translation of the story into an event-level representation would fail to capture anything about what makes the story interesting. In fact, no events are stated. It is the standards against which the story is judged that make the story interesting at all. In a culture where women marry early and age disparity is not considered important, there might be nothing anomalous or memorable about the *Manhattan* story. But in 20th-century America, it is a violation of cultural standards, and therefore arouses interest. Although this example is extreme, the point it makes often holds. People who tell stories do not mention those key features that make a story interesting because they can rely on the background knowledge that their hearers bring. Therefore, for educational purposes, an index must be more than a summary of a story. It must be an interpretation of a story whose creation, by necessity, entails the use of thematic knowledge, just as story understanding does (Schank & Abelson, 1977; Wilensky, 1983). The index must explain what is interesting in a story for a particular purpose, and why.

Experience with the Universal Indexing Frame

SPIEL's indexing framework had its starting point in the universal indexing frame (UIF; Schank et al., 1990). Approximately 160 of these stories were indexed for SPIEL using the UIF. The UIF was an attempt to create an indexing framework for stories; it was developed by observing story remindings in context and developing a framework within which remindings could be explained. Work on the UIF began with these insights:

- the importance of intentionality: the need to represent causality due to the actions of an intentional agent;
- the centrality of explanation: the role of explanatory coherence in reminding; and

- the anomaly: the representation of what is interesting in a story as a function of the violation of expectations.

The UIF was meant to be universal, in the sense that the widest possible range of stories could be indexed using its organization and vocabulary. Like any such universal scheme, it succeeded in some ways, but not in others. Where it succeeded best was in representing stories about social behavior that people find to be interesting. This is not surprising because the material we worked from in the development of the UIF was precisely this type of story. The UIF is given a thorough description in Schank et al. (1990). Those aspects of the representation that are a good starting point for understanding SPIEL's indexing system are recounted here.

The UIF has three main parts: the content grid, the context grid, and the global slots. The content grid shows four perspectives on the events in the story. Each perspective is distinguished by three values: the *viewer*, the person who holds the perspective; the *view*, the type of outlook held by that person; and the *agent*, the person whose actions are viewed. Three lessons informed the development of SPIEL's indexing system:

- Complex anomalies are rare. The anecdotes that salespeople told generally showed only one salient contrast between an expectation and reality.
- Explanations could be simpler. For stories about action in the business world, the belief, emotion, and analysis parts of the UIF were rarely important.
- The context grid was insufficient. Two-place relations between actors were not enough to capture all of the interesting relationships in stories.

These lessons were applied to the development of a considerably simplified version of the UIF that was used for YELLO. The most significant simplification was to reduce the complexity of the content grid. To capture the notion of expectation failure, it was enough to have one column that showed a perspective contrasted against one column that showed what actually happened. SPIEL's indexes could be limited to two columns, one of which would always be an actual column with the same agent as in the perspective column. This simplified content structure reduced the number of between-column differences to be recorded in the anomaly column—usually to just one. The anomaly column was therefore eliminated because it had no more information than could be found in the global anomaly slot. The columns were also simplified to better fit the stories. From the original 11 slots in the UIF, SPIEL's indexes use six: theme, goal, plan, result, positive side effect, and negative side effect.

These six are the core of the intentional chain in planning and acting (Schank & Abelson, 1977).

SPIEL is trying to draw analogies between stories and student situations. It must be able to compare what it knows about a story with what it can determine about the student. It is hard enough to detect that a student is using a particular plan, and much harder still to make a reliable determination as to why the student chose it. To compare the reasoning behind a choice made by a character in a story with the thinking behind a student's choice, SPIEL would have to understand the reasoning a student goes through in choosing a plan. Because students' social knowledge is likely to be large in extent and quite idiosyncratic, a complete understanding of it cannot be built simply by observing a brief interaction with the GuSS system. The difficulty in using a feature such as "goal→plan" at retrieval time argues against its inclusion in an index. The theme, goal, plan, result, and side effect aspects of the intentional chain are things that can be fairly readily observed or inferred without a substantial commitment to a detailed model of each student's reasoning.

It was also possible to simplify the structure of results and side effects. These slots all capture impacts on goals. The original UIF treated them all as more or less the same, the only difference being how central they were deemed to be. Whatever the creator of the index considered the most important effect would be the main result; the others would be side effects. In SPIEL's indexing frame, some of the ambiguity surrounding results and side effects has been removed. Because a plan in an index is enacted to achieve the goal found in the same column, its success in this regard is considered its primary result: The result slot is always an impact on the main goal.

Side effects also had a certain ambiguity in the UIF. They could be used to show the costs associated with a main result (e.g., that a plan was achieved only at tremendous cost). They also showed how the result achieved by one person impacted others. A side effect of a customer saving money by cutting back on expenses might be that a salesperson fails to make a sale. This second role of side effects turned out to be the most important one for SPIEL. So, in SPIEL'S indexing frame, side effects are always interpreted as effects on the goals of the *viewer*, rather than the agent. For example, a column in one of SPIEL's indexes shows a salesperson (viewer) who hoped that a customer (agent) would like an ad's design (result, impact on customer's goal), inclining him toward buying it (positive side effect for the salesperson's goal of getting a sale).

To allow relationships to be represented in more ways than the context grid allowed, it was replaced with a social setting slot. The slot contains a list of the social relationships relevant in the story, letting the system represent a notion like partnership, instead of as a two-place relation between business partners, as a larger relation, between all of the partners and the business that they jointly form. It also allows two people to have more than one relationship at the same time—a circumstance that could not be represented in the context grid.

SPIEL's Indexing Frame

The anomaly is the central organizing principle in SPIEL's indexes. Having simplified the UIF to fit SPIEL's stories more closely, I realized that the anomaly concept should be considered primary—the place where the creation of an index begins, rather than an emergent property of the contrasting intentional chains. The other parts of the index support and explain the anomaly. The general form of an anomaly represented in SPIEL can be stated as follows: "Actor X had an expectation that Y would happen, but actually Z happened." This interpretation meshes well with the original notion of an anomaly (Schank, 1982) as an expectation failure that demands explanation. A failure requires a contrast between an expectation and reality. In the prior "building demolition" story, the narrator wonders explicitly why the demolition was so ineffective. He expected a "clean kill," but it did not happen. SPIEL's representation would encode the anomaly as follows: "Observer assumed that the operator would knock the building down, but actually the operator failed to knock the building down."

The previous section showed an instance where the student was presented with the "Wife watching TV" story. It has the following as its central anomaly: "The salesperson assumed the wife would have the role of housewife, but actually she had the role of business partner." This corresponds to the point of the story that emerges when the story was told earlier. The student is reminded that his assumption about Mrs. Swain's role may be in error in the same way as in the story.

Assumptions are one kind of expectation that may fail, and hence one possible type of anomaly. SPIEL has five kinds of anomaly based on five different kinds of perspectives that someone might have:

1. *Assumed:* An assumption is an expectation that will generally always be present in the given task and is probably subconscious. (Called *Expected* in UIF terminology.)
   Example: The salesperson assumed the wife would have the role of housewife, but actually she had the role of business partner.
2. *Feared:* A negatively valenced expectation, or fear, will be present when someone acts to ward off a threat to a goal. Fears turn out to be misplaced when the threat is not realized.

Example: The salesperson fears that the client will object to the price of a proposed ad, but actually the client does not.

3. *Hoped:* When a character has unrealized hopes, it is usually a case of overoptimism, or a situation in which a plan is not well executed. (Called *Wanted* in UIF terminology.)
   Example: The salesperson hoped the customer would track how many calls the Yellow Pages ad was generating, but the customer would not do it.

4. *Standard:* Every field has its own set of standard beliefs and procedures. Novices learn these through instruction and then go out into the real world where they do not always apply. Instead of reading like "I expected X . . . ," a standard-violation anomaly reads more like, "You might expect that X. . . ." (Called *Ideal* in the UIF.)
   Example: You might expect that a salesperson would defend the merits of a proposal, but actually this salesperson agreed with the client's counterproposal.

5. *Perceived:* Stories sometimes highlight failures that result from misperception, such as reading something into a situation that is not there.
   Example: A salesperson perceived the client to be interested in a larger ad, but actually the client wanted to spend less money on advertising.

Anomalies are at the center of SPIEL's indexing representation. They summarize what is interesting in a story, bringing together five pieces of information: viewer, perspective, agent, perspective contrast, and actual contrast (see Fig. 3.8). The *viewer* is the person who had the expectation that was violated. Often this is the storyteller. The *agent* is the individual

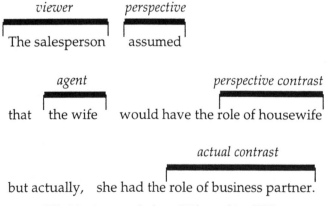

FIG. 3.8. An anomaly from "Wife watching TV."

toward whom the anomalous expectation was directed. This may be the same as the viewer, as in, "I thought I would fail, but I succeeded." For SPIEL's purposes, all expectations are about social actors, construed broadly to include social groups like companies. The *perspective* is one of the five types of anomaly discussed earlier: assumed, wanted, feared, standard, or perceived. The *perspective contrast* is the expectation that the viewer had about the agent. The anomaly places it in opposition to the *actual contrast*, which is what the story reports as actually occurring.

Anomalies are good summaries of what is interesting about a story, but they do not explain why the anomalous events occurred. To be able to tell its stories at times when they will help the student build explanations, SPIEL needs to have explanations for its stories. Consider the following situation. SPIEL is trying to advise a student who is having trouble with a gatekeeper, an intermediary who controls access to a decision-making client. There are many stories with a relevant anomaly: "The salesperson wants the gatekeeper to allow access to the decision maker, but the gatekeeper does not cooperate." One of the following stories might be relevant, but which one? Knowing no more than the anomalies, the storyteller could do no better than random guesswork.

Suppose we know that, in Story A, the gatekeeper is the office manager at a law firm; in Story B, the gatekeeper is the spouse of the owner of a small hardware store. If the student were selling to a law firm, we would probably want to prefer Story A because the difference in social context between the selling situations may make a significant difference for the way the task of selling is performed. Let us further imagine that, in Story A, the gatekeeper's goal is to protect the partners from interruption because their time is considered valuable; in Story B, the gatekeeper is interested in art and graphic design, and wants to be involved in the layout of the ad. Suppose that, in the student's situation, the gatekeeper is a closet artist who wants to have artistic input on the ad. Now Story B starts to look like the better choice because it shows an agent with intentions similar to those of the simulated character the student is facing.

Settings and intentions are important for remindings because they are important parts of explanations for social actions. What makes a story relevant to a student is the relationship between the causal structure of the situation the student is in and the causal structure of the situation described in the story. This relationship can take many forms, but an explanation of the story is always essential. It would be too inefficient to require a retriever to do explanation every time it considers a story. To explain the anomalies found in the stories in YELLO, SPIEL would have to have a deep understanding of social reasoning and social convention, as well as knowledge of the specialized social skills involved in selling. This is why it (and the UIF) uses explanations as part of the indexes. This is not a cognitively implausible stance because the explanations of events would have to be formed by an understander in the course of processing a story when it is told or experiencing first-hand the events from which it is made (Kolodner, 1993). Because they are clearly useful as labels, it makes sense that an understander would preserve explanations for indexing purposes.

Social actions always take place against a background or social setting. Every social setting has its own rules of behavior. This is true of common everyday settings, but it is also true of the specialized social settings in which the skills taught by GuSS are practiced. Selling a Yellow Pages ad to a tattoo artist is different than selling the same thing to a corporate law firm. The same kinds of techniques may be employed in these settings and many of the same principles apply, but the fine points of social performance are different.

The UIF incorporated the notion of setting, but paid it little attention. It is difficult to say anything general about settings because what background is important depends on the story. Again, the notion of explanation is important. Is the fact that a client is a lawyer an important piece of information in a story about setting Yellow Pages advertising? It is if the salesperson uses a strategy that is geared toward law firms, or if the client has needs specific to lawyers that the story addresses. In SPIEL, settings are treated as possible contributors to the explanations in the index. There are three types of information that typically figure in supporting explanations about selling Yellow Pages advertising. These are the stage in the sales process that the story describes, the type of business the client is engaged in, and the size of that business.

The stage of the sales process is often important because each stage establishes preconditions for the next. The information-gathering phrase (called the "pre-call") lets the salesperson gather the knowledge necessary to prepare a sales presentation. For example, a plan to ask about a client's competitors during the pre-call serves to persuade the customer by enabling arguments about competition that can be made later. The type and size of the client's business often figures in a salesperson's approach (see Fig. 3.9).

The relationships between agents, as represented in the UIF in the context grid, have a role similar to the social setting as possible contributors to the story's explanation. For example, the fact that someone is the

Scene:	pre-call
Business type:	service
Business size:	small

FIG. 3.9. Physical setting for "Wife watching TV."

Physical setting:	pre-call, service-business, small
Social setting:	business-partner, seller, married-couple
Viewer:	salesperson
Perspective:	expected
Agent:	wife
Anomaly Type:	theme

	Expected	Actual
Theme:	housewife	business-partner
Goal:	hospitality	contribute to buying decision
Plan:	small-talk	evaluate sales presentation
Result:		serve contribution
Side+:		sale for salesperson
Side–:		

FIG. 3.10. Index for "Wife watching TV."

spouse of a client may help explain why the salesperson had a certain expectation about that person. Because these two types of information are treated similarly, I have done away with the term *context grid* and introduced a notion of setting that has two parts: a social setting, the relationships between agents (formerly context grid); and a physical setting, the other aspects of the story's context (formerly global setting slot).

Instead of the grid of two-place relations in the UIF, the relationships between actors in a story are represented as a list of relations between individuals that can be of any order. In the index of "Wife watching TV," there is an instance of the seller/sales target relationship, a business partnership, and a marriage. SPIEL uses this information to align the actors in the story with the characters the student encounters in the simulated world. We are now ready to put all of the parts of an index together. Figure 3.10 is the entire "Wife watching TV" index described in this section, in a UIF-style format.

As Domeshek also found, it is important that the social setting represent relationships as structure. In SPIEL's indexes, each entry is a memory organization packet (MOP; Schank, 1982) that packages other pieces of representation. Figure 3.11 shows how the actors in "Wife watching TV" are packaged by the associated social context. Because each term found in the index is a MOP, there is also structure in the other parts of the index that is hidden in the UIF format. Figure 3.12 shows the same index,

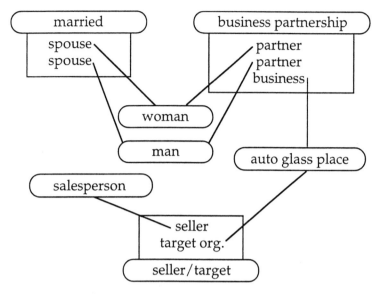

FIG. 3.11. Actors and social setting in "Wife watching TV."

including the structure of its MOPs. In the structured version, it is easy to see that any piece of the index can be extracted and used in reasoning without losing its connection to the rest. The instance of housewife theme has "woman" as the actor, the same person who has the marriage relationship to the auto glass man in the social setting, and so on. Although this representation is a truer picture of the index, the UIF-style format is used for simplicity.

SPIEL's Indexing Vocabulary

The UIF did more than show how indexes should be organized, although that is probably its most significant contribution. Along with the indexing frame, the UIF theory also established the classes of fillers for each part of the frame and some representation of these classes. It did not aim for a complete representational theory, intending to be suggestive, rather than exhaustive. The vocabulary proposed along with the UIF has many interesting facets. However, this section incorporates them into SPIEL's indexing language where they have been useful.

Like the index structure, the indexing vocabulary is also a function of the task served by retrieval. The UIF work and others on the indexing problem have considered cross-domain retrieval to be particularly important (i.e., the capacity for a system to get reminded of how to fix an airplane while working on a term paper; McDougal, Hammond, & Seifert, 1991). This is not SPIEL's mandate. SPIEL presents stories about a domain

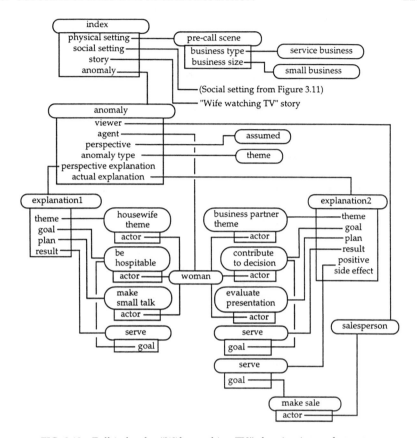

FIG. 3.12. Full index for "Wife watching TV" showing internal structure.

to students who are learning about the same domain. It uses domain-dependent criteria as much as it can.

SPIEL's indexing vocabulary has domain-independent and domain-dependent parts. The domain-dependent vocabulary, which is user-exten-
sible, includes concepts that are particular to the domain of YELLO, such
as the goal to sell an ad or the plan of presenting a keyed ad study as a
persuasive tool. Indexes are made up of these domain-dependent concepts
because they are what stories are about. Underlying the domain-dependent terms is the domain-independent vocabulary, the abstractions that
SPIEL uses in reasoning about indexes. It includes the basic components
of the intentional chain: theme, goal, plan, and result.

As in the UIF, an intentional explanation always starts with a *theme*, a
social role or other fairly long-lived predisposition toward certain behavior. A theme gives rise to goals that naturally co-occur. Themes are
distinguished by the threads, or areas of life, to which they relate. (Threads

are discussed in Domeshek, 1992; Schank et al., 1990.) SPIEL uses four major threads: economic, career, family, and personal.

Like themes, relationships are distinguished according to threads. SPIEL uses three major threads for relationships: career, those aspects of a person's life that have to do with vocation, such as an employer–employee relationship; economic, relationships that are strictly part of the sphere of commerce, such as the relationship between a buyer and a seller; and family relationships. Personal themes, by their nature, do not give rise to the kinds of relationships found in SPIEL's stories.

Themes give rise to goals. SPIEL recognizes two classes of goals: stative, goals to bring about particular states of the world; and policy, goals to hold certain things constant over long periods (known as A-GOALs and M-GOALs in Schank & Abelson, 1977). A typical stative goal is a salesperson's goal to sell a full-page ad to a particular client. An example of a policy goal is the desire to preserve close rapport with a client.

In the representation of goals, I have relied on the notion of resource similar to that in the UIF. A goal can be represented as an intention to affect a resource in a particular way. SPIEL represents five different kinds of impacts that an actor may wish to have on a resource. An actor may wish to obtain a resource or expend it. Other resource goals center on holding something true of a resource over time: maximizing the amount of resource one has, conserving a resource, or attempting to maintain a certain level of the resource. Goals can be evaluated by comparing their resource impacts. For example, a plan to obtain rapport with the customer is opposite from a plan to break off (expend) relations because they have an opposite impact on the resource.

Subcategories within these goal categories are distinguished by the type of resource under consideration. The actions that surround resources often depend on three important variables: maintainability, the amount of effort or other resources required to keep a resource usable; fluidity, the degree to which a resource can be converted into other resources; and creatability, the uniqueness or individuality of a resource. SPIEL uses a simple two-valued combination of these features to describe any given resource. For example, money has low maintenance requirements and high fluidity, and is creatable. Using permutations of these values for the three dimensions gives eight types of resources. The second domain-independent level of the goal hierarchy is therefore made up of all of the resource effects crossed with the eight types of resources, giving 40 categories of goals.

To bring about a goal, an actor executes a plan—a set of actions designed to achieve it. A typical plan for getting a customer to believe that a certain ad will bring increased revenue is the plan to show the customer a testimonial letter from a client who has experienced good results from a Yellow Pages ad. Usually the entire plan for accomplishing a high-level goal like sell an ad is long and complex, but there are useful subparts that act in service of the goal and can be extracted. The word *plan* is used to refer both to entire plans whose successful completion would achieve a goal, and subplans that are enacted in service of a goal.

Plans form the most complex of SPIEL's categories, containing about 60 domain-independent categories. Many plans belong to more than one category. Not all of them are covered here. The first breakdown of plans has to do with a similar distinction as was made for goals. Is the plan an implementation of a policy, a policy plan, or is it aimed toward achieving some state, an achievement plan? Policy plans are those designed to control resources. This can be control over how a resource is used, a deployment plan; control over which resource to employ, a selection plan; or control over upkeep of a resource, a maintenance plan. For example, a salesperson might have a plan to wait until the customer has been told the price of an ad before presenting a testimonial letter attesting to its value. This is a deployment plan in which the timing of the use of a resource is of primary importance.

Achievement plans aim to create a certain state of a resource. An agent can obtain a resource through a resource creation plan, or shed resources with a resource expenditure plan. Resources that are sharable, like information, can be hidden from others with a resource protection plan, or made available via a resource sharing plan. For example, a salesperson using a sharing plan might give customers marketing information.

Plans can be further distinguished by the class of resource they involve: physical, social, or mental, and by the resources used in achieving that aim. One important class of plans in YELLO are persuasion plans: creation plans for creating sales contracts. A persuasion plan that requires investment of time and effort (such as preparing and giving a presentation) is different from one in which a resource is given away in exchange (a bribe). Other persuasion plans may involve altering the contract, such as discounting a price, to make it more attractive.

Executing a plan leads to a result, an impact on a goal. SPIEL recognizes five kinds of impact: two positive, two negative, and one neutral. In the realm of positive impacts, there is achieve. The result of achievement holds if the goal is completely achieved through the use of a plan. Less definitive, but still positive, is a serve result. An action can contribute toward the achievement of a goal without completely achieving it, serving the goal. The negative outcomes are complementary. A block outcome means that the goal has been rendered unachievable by the original plan. Threaten means that its achievement has been hindered, but not stopped.

The neutral outcome is present when there is no impact on the goal. It is often found contrasting other results in an index. For example, a salesperson may hope that a sales pitch of a certain type will persuade the customer, but in fact it has no effect.

We have now seen the six concepts that are the primary elements in SPIEL's indexes: perspectives, themes, relationships, goals, plans, and results. To create an index, a user interprets a story in terms of expectation failure and encodes the expectation and its underlying explanation in this vocabulary. Table 3.2 summarizes these concepts and the major distinctions that SPIEL's indexing representation uses.

TABLE 3.2
Primary Elements in SPIEL's Indexes

Category	Discriminating Feature	Major Distinctions	Examples
Perspectives	Expectation type	Assumed	Assumption about someone's role
		Feared	Fear of customer's reaction
		Hoped	Hope of achieving a good result
		Standard	Standard of business conduct
		Perceived	Perception of customer reaction
Themes	Thread	Economic	Buyer, seller
		Career	Employee
		Family	Parent
		Personal	Independent living
Relationships	Thread	Economic	Sales target
		Career	Employer/employee
		Family	Marriage, father/son
Goals	Resource impact	Obtain	Get sales commission
		Expend	Waste time
		Maximize	Have the largest market share
		Conserve	Preserve personal status
		Maintain	Keep competitive advantage
Plans	Resource action	Resource deployment	Give testimonial after telling price
		Resource selection	Prefer radio ads over Yellow Pages
		Resource maintenance	Engage in small talk
		Resource creation	Buy a Yellow Pages ad
		Resource expenditure	Keep salesperson waiting
		Resource protection	Avoid giving business information
		Resource sharing	Give client marketing information
Results	Goal impact	Achieve	Making a sale
		Block	Failing to increase an ad program
		Serve	Getting the customer to agree to a point (when trying to make a sale)
		Threaten	Having the customer disagree about a point

The Story Indexing Tool

One important aspect of indexes yet to be discussed is their generation. In many case based problem-solving systems, new cases are added when the system has experiences. Indexes for these new cases are generated automatically in the course of problem solving. The nature of SPIEL's case and its task precludes the system from being able to acquire cases by interpreting stories. To understand videotaped stories, it would need natural language understanding, as well as voice and possibly gesture recognition. Indexes must be entered manually.

Tools for the efficient manual creation of indexes are crucial for the development of large story bases (Ferguson, Bareiss, Birnbaum, & Osgood, 1992). An indexing tool for SPIEL must do five things:

1. Allow the creation of stories so that they can be perused and labeled.
2. Enforce the structure of the index.
3. Render indexes intelligible and manipulatable.
4. Allow the maintenance of an indexing vocabulary.
5. Interface with the strategy application and rule generation components of SPIEL.

Development has concentrated mainly on Steps 2 and 3. The tool's interface to the other parts of SPIEL's processing, in particular, is not yet fully developed. Figure 3.13 shows the screen that the Story Indexing Tool (SIT) first presents to the user. This screen lists all of the stories that have been collected for a particular GuSS application and the formats in which they are available. The "Wife watching TV" story is selected; both a Quicktime™ and a text version of the story are available. A brief summary of the story can be seen at the bottom of the screen. The story and its associated indexes can be inspected in the indexing screen shown in Fig. 3.14. The top part of the screen holds information about the story: the teller, the original videotape source, a link to a Quicktime™ movie, a Laserdisc segment, or a text transcription. In the bottom half of the screen, the user begins constructing the index, starting with the physical and social settings, which are the same for all indexes for a given story. On this screen, the user has listed three actors from the story and established relationships between them, using a mechanism for browsing and instantiating SPIEL's MOPs. Figure 3.15 shows the MOP browser being used to instantiate the marriage relationship between the woman, the "Soap opera watcher," and her husband, the "Auto glass guy." (The names are solely for the user's benefit.)

The list near the bottom of the story screen shows what anomalies are associated with the story. Anomalies and their associated intentional

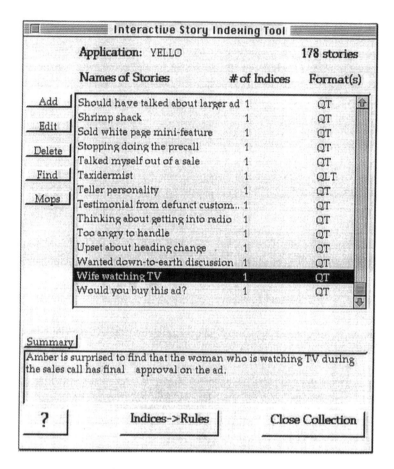

FIG. 3.13. Story Indexing Tool: listing of stories.

chains are created for a story in the anomaly-creation screen, shown in Fig. 3.16. Here the user first fills the viewer, perspective, and agent slots to begin the English-like anomaly description: "Amber assumed that 'Soap opera watcher' would be. . . ." Then the browser at the right (similar to that seen in Fig. 3.15) is used to select the perspective and actual contrasts, completing the description: "acting according to the theme of 'housewife-theme,' but instead 'Soap opera watcher' was acting according to the theme of 'business-partner-theme,' " as underlined in the figure. The rest of the intentional chains can be similarly instantiated to complete the index.

The Story Indexing Tool was used to index all 178 of the stories in YELLO's story base. Although a complex index has from 20 to 30 MOPs, an experienced user can create one in several minutes with the tool.

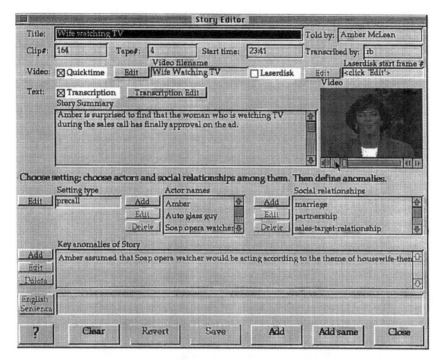

FIG. 3.14. Story Indexing Tool: story information.

TELLING RELEVANT STORIES

Implementing the Case Based Teaching Architecture

The combination of a storytelling tutor with a practice environment is known as the *case based teaching architecture* (Schank, 1990). The student works in a simulated environment, which the tutor monitors to present stories from its library when they are relevant to what the student is doing. For such a tutor, much hinges on the notion of relevance: What does it mean for a story to be relevant? This question is central to the case based teaching architecture, and its answer forms the basis for SPIEL's implementation. This section outlines SPIEL's solution to the question of relevance.

For SPIEL, a storytelling episode creates an analogy between the experiences of a practitioner reported in a story and the experiences of a student enacted in a GuSS application. This analogy contains a certain amount of overlap and a certain degree of difference. The analogy created by the story's telling must contain enough similarity so that a student will accept it as being a good analogy. A completely analogous story is not that instructive, however. Students engaged in learning-by-doing will

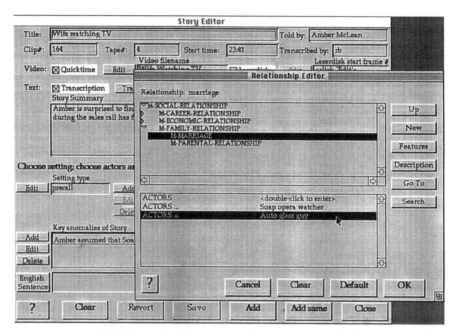

FIG. 3.15. Story Indexing Tool: instantiating a social relationship.

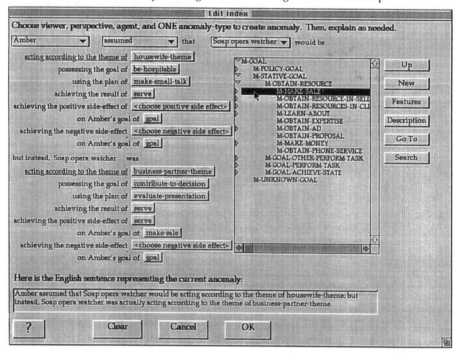

FIG. 3.16. Story Indexing Tool: creating anomaly and associated explanations.

learn best about the situation they are in by acting in it. A story that has no differences from their experience does not add to the experience.

However, a story that has some important difference challenges the student's understanding of the situation. Such stories raise explanation questions (Schank, 1986) that drive the student toward a deeper understanding of the subject matter. Without such challenges, students will tend to leave important assumptions untested (Klahr, Dunbar, & Fay, 1990) and tend to see only what confirms their hypotheses (Schauble, Glaser, Raghavan, & Reiner, 1991).

To assess the relevance of a story, a storyteller must be capable of recognizing both similarities and differences between stories and the situations in which they are told. To assess similarity and difference, there are three kinds of comparisons a tutor can make in the case based teaching architecture: (a) comparisons based on what the student does in the task environment, (b) comparisons based on what the student sees in the task environment, and (c) comparisons based on inferences about the student's reasoning about the task environment.

To find tutorial opportunities, a storyteller needs two kinds of knowledge: the knowledge of what a given story is about and the knowledge of how, in general, stories can make educational points. The first kind of knowledge comes from the indexes of stories (as discussed in the previous section). The second is an abstract body of knowledge about tutorial storytelling. Note that all of this knowledge is available to SPIEL before the student sits down to use the GuSS simulation. This fact suggests a particular kind of architecture for recognition—one where tutorial opportunities are characterized ahead of time and then searched for during the student's interaction with the system.

SPIEL's processing is divided into two phases: storage time and retrieval time. In the first phase, storage, new stories are entered into the system, and the system considers what tutorial opportunities it should look for in order to tell them. During retrieval, a student interacts with the GuSS system and SPIEL evaluates, in parallel, the features linked to tutorial opportunities, retrieving and presenting stories when their associated opportunities are recognized. This section concentrates on the storage-time aspects of SPIEL, and in particular on the role of storytelling strategies in the characterization of tutorial opportunities.

Figure 3.17 shows the steps that occur in each of these phases. At storage time:

1. Indexes are attached to stories manually using an indexing tool.
2. The storytelling strategies are applied to each index. For every index that a strategy finds compatible, it generates a recognition condition description (RCD). The RCD describes a tutorial opportunity af-

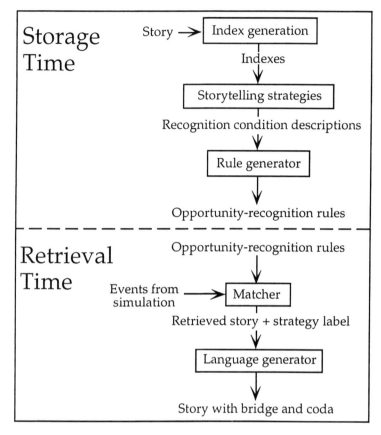

FIG. 3.17. Storage and retrieval phases of SPIEL.

forded by the story: a situation in which the story could be told using the strategy.

3. The rule generator then processes each RCD and generates a set of recognition rules for the tutorial opportunity described.

At retrieval time:

1. The student interacts with the GuSS simulation. The recognition rules are matched against the state of the simulation as the activity proceeds.

2. When a tutorial opportunity is recognized, the story associated with that opportunity is retrieved.

3. The retrieval conditions and the strategy are fed into a language generator to create explanations of the reminding for the student's

benefit. The generator recalls natural language templates for the headline, bridge, and coda associated with the strategy, and then fills them in.

The Recognition Condition Description

The RCD describes what situation the student would have to encounter for a story to be relevant. RCDs have three parts: (a) a context in which the student might encounter the circumstances that make the story worth telling, (b) conditions that indicate that the story is relevant in that context, and (c) the story and the manner in which it should be presented. The test for the establishment of the context is called the *trigger*. The recognition of the tutorial opportunity is performed by tests that gather *evidence*. The storytelling action that follows is the *presentation*. When the triggering conditions are met, SPIEL will try to find evidence that a tutorial opportunity is present. If it finds the evidence, it presents the story. These three parts can be thought of as filling roles in the following abstract rule form: "When *trigger*, look for *evidence*, then *presentation*."

The trigger describes the context in which it makes sense to look for a tutorial opportunity. A story whose triggering conditions are met will be under active consideration until there is evidence that it does not apply. Therefore, triggers are the first steps in SPIEL's incremental retrieval. They must be relatively stable so that the system can gather evidence while the trigger holds true.

SPIEL uses triggers derived from stories' social and physical settings. This is because the social activities SPIEL teaches are highly associated with particular social configurations. For example, selling requires the presence of a salesperson, something to sell, and a person to sell it to. Particular sales strategies are often predicated on the existence of certain social relationships, such as a partnership in a business. Settings remain stable during periods of social interaction.

After the triggering conditions have been satisfied, a tutorial opportunity is recognized through the evidence conditions of the RCD. Storytelling strategies differ most in how they create evidence conditions. A strategy that seeks to show a student a new way to do something will look for the student doing something very different from what someone did in the story, so that the story will appear to present an alternative. A strategy that seeks to project into the future possible consequences of a student's actions will look for the student doing something very similar to what someone does in the story, but without the consequences being apparent.

What the evidence conditions do not need to do is specify in detail how the tutorial opportunity might be recognized in the simulation. Ultimately, the RCD must be operationalized, turned into conditions that can be tested against the student's actions and the state of the simulated world. As described earlier, the operational component of SPIEL is a tutorial module that uses decision rules to operate within the GuSS simulation.

This level of operational detail is provided by the rule generator that translates the RCD into simulation-specific conditions. To create the description, SPIEL need not be concerned if the simulation requires the student to say one utterance or several, or take some other type of action. The rule generator must take concepts like "find out about future plans" and use its knowledge of the simulation to turn this into a rule that looks for specific actions with specific meanings. Because the RCD is independent of the implementation, the conditions it describes will be recognizable in any sufficiently rich simulation where the student can practice the target activity.

Applying Storytelling Strategies

Before a storytelling strategy can be applied to an index, SPIEL has to determine if the strategy and the story are compatible. Each strategy has a filter that can be applied to indexes to determine their compatibility. For example, *Warn about plan* is a strategy whose intent is to warn the student. It looks for stories that show someone in a position similar to the student's experiencing failure, so it can present the stories if the student looks to be heading in the same wrong direction. Stories that show success would probably not make convincing warnings.

The purpose of the filter is to select stories that are capable of making a certain kind of analogy. This analogy has a slightly different character in each strategy, and each filter looks for something slightly different. The filter almost always seeks to find someone in the story who is analogous to the student. This person is chosen through an examination of the roles given to the individuals mentioned in the index. The student in the simulation is playing a particular role: car mechanic, salesperson, and so on. The person in the story who is playing a role similar to the student's is an important figure for determining the kind of analogy the telling of a story will create. This person is called the *student analogue*.

The trigger is built from the social and physical contexts of the story as represented in the index. However, it is certainly too restrictive to demand that a story only be told when the student's context matches its physical and social settings exactly. So SPIEL must generalize the social and physical setting of a story. The identification of important aspects of features results from finding their role within an explanation in an explanation-based generalization (Carbonell, 1983). For SPIEL, this type of generalization is made somewhat easier because the index already contains explanations. It may have to elaborate slightly to see whether a feature of the setting is important to the point of the story that the index describes, but it does not have to construct a new explanation. Generalization is performed in SPIEL by dropping features of the setting that do not have a role in the explanations in the index.

It might be possible to do even better—to reason about how far to generalize those aspects of the setting that are found to be important. The amount of generalization of storytelling conditions that a system can perform is a function of how much it can explain about the events in its stories. Because SPIEL's indexes are already couched as explanations, it gets some explanation for free. Additional elaboration on top of what is contained in the index is quite difficult, however. Causal explanations require a causal theory for their construction. Explanations of phenomena in social interaction would require a broad causal theory of social cognition and interaction, the development of which is a long-term research project. SPIEL's storytelling strategies perform small bits of explanation where they must, but the system has no general explanation capacity.

The evidence part of the RCD is what describes the actual conditions of relevance. Creating the evidence conditions requires reasoning about evidence gathering, determining what should count as evidence for or against the recognition of the tutorial opportunity. Every storytelling strategy has its own method for reasoning from an index to a description of the evidence needed to recognize a storytelling opportunity involving the strategy and the story represented by the index.

Some of SPIEL's storytelling strategies involve a more complex relationship between story and RCD. The *Demonstrate risks* strategy calls on the storyteller to tell a story about a failure when the student has experienced success. The evidence conditions produced by this strategy look for the student to encounter a result opposite to the one represented in the index. To create such conditions, the strategy must be able to reason about opposites. All storytelling strategies have to reason about how concepts in the index, or those inferred from the index, may be manifested in observable actions in the simulation. In some cases, what is in the index is easily observed, such as whether a student makes a sale. In other cases, more inference is required.

In the evidence conditions, the same question of generalization arises as it did for the trigger. How specifically must a student's situation match the story? Similar issues arise for stories about an area of social expertise like selling. Suppose SPIEL has a story about getting the customer to buy an increased advertising program. If the student is trying to sell a renewal, should the story be considered similar or not? To a layperson, getting a renewal for an ad looks a lot like getting the customer to increase advertising. However, an analysis of cause and effect shows that these surface similarities hide a deeper difference. Arguing for a renewal is a different persuasion problem than arguing for more advertising. Different objections will arise and different counterarguments will be called for. Again, knowledge of the domain must enter into decisions to generalize.

Although the problem is the same as for the trigger condition, the solution is not. Evidence conditions cannot be generalized through reference to the explanations already existing in the index. The elements of the index involved in the evidence conditions, such as the goal, plan, and result, are already part of the explanations in the index. SPIEL will not be able to rule out any of them. The only other alternative is to construct more general versions of the evidence conditions while preserving the causal structure of the index. This would require additional explanation elaborating on the explanation in the index. A system with a good model of how cars operate and break could perform such reasoning in the domain of car repair, but such a model is not available for the areas that SPIEL teaches. In absence of this kind of causal knowledge, SPIEL cannot generalize the recognition conditions that gather evidence for the tutorial opportunity. It stays close to the level of specificity found in the index.

Another important issue in the generation of evidence conditions is the disparity of knowledge between the student and tutor. A tutor in a case based teaching system can inspect areas of the simulated world that are hidden from the student. If SPIEL infers that a student is hoping that a character in the GuSS simulation has certain intentions, it has the capacity to inspect the simulation data structures and find out whether that character has the desired intention. In fact, SPIEL cannot avoid using this capacity because, when characters make utterances, the student sees an English language string, which SPIEL does not have the capacity to understand. SPIEL can only look at the internal, hidden representation of the utterance.

So SPIEL does inspect the internals of the simulation; the question is how much it should use this capacity. There are two dangers here. If the storyteller intervenes based only on the external appearance of the simulation, it may miss some obvious hidden cue that would tell it the story is not appropriate. However, if the student gets only those stories that really apply in his or her current situation, the storyteller may end up giving away clues about the problem. If the student knows that the storyteller only intervenes when it has verified its analogy through reference to the hidden structure of the simulated scenario, the storyteller may inadvertently give away information about the scenario that the student would otherwise have to work to uncover.

This is a difficult dilemma, in which either alternative presents some problems: Use only visible evidence and risk giving bad advice, or use hidden evidence and risk creating an unrealistic practice environment. SPIEL's solution is to use visible evidence as much as possible, relying on hidden evidence only when the risk of bad advice is high. In most cases, the risk of bad advice is not high. Therefore, SPIEL does not look for hidden evidence to verify conditions that are suggested by external manifestations. This is not as hazardous as it may seem. Unlike a tutor that is giving directive advice, SPIEL is making analogies between students' situations and its stories. Students always have to interpret what the storyteller says. They must compare the actions described in the story against their own actions and determine if the story is a good analogy.

Sometimes, however, the danger of bad advice is high. Several of SPIEL's storytelling strategies concern themselves with the viewpoint of others in the simulation, unlike the majority that seek to explain the circumstances of a person in a role similar to the student's. In strategies that explain the situations of other characters, students cannot easily determine the quality of a story's intended analogy. This makes reliance on the external manifestations of internal states risky. Because the student cannot check the analogy, bad advice is more likely to be taken to heart. Therefore, it is important that SPIEL verify that the characters in the simulation are motivated in the way that a story suggests. It looks directly at the characters' internal states to gather evidence for this. This may result in some unwarranted hints to the student, but the danger of bad advice makes this risk worth taking.

Hidden evidence is also used to resolve conflicts between storytelling strategies. Suppose a student prepares to convince a customer about the benefits of geographic expansion, and hears a story reinforcing her approach—a story about someone who convinced a similar customer to buy ads to expand. The student puts this plan into action, but finds that the customer is not receptive and the sale is not successful. True independence between storytelling strategies would dictate that the same story should be told to show an opportunity that was missed: "You didn't succeed, but here's a story about someone who did. ..." This would probably be quite annoying. Because the student has already seen the story once, its re-presentation merely emphasizes the failure.

Pragmatic conversational considerations therefore require that the strategies that project possible outcomes try to avoid conflict with those that show alternative outcomes. This conflict can be detected if there is hidden evidence of a plan's failure before that failure has become evident to the student. In the geographic expansion example, the system might be able to detect that the customer is not actually interested in geographic expansion. It would then hold off telling the story until the failure became apparent.

Rule Generation

Creation of the trigger and evidence conditions completes the construction of an RCD. The RCD represents the recognition conditions for a tutorial opportunity describing a good time to tell a particular story using a particular strategy. The next part of the storage time processing of SPIEL is rule generation, the construction of GuSS decision rules capable of recognizing these tutorial opportunities. For an example, consider an RCD generated for the story "Long-term goals." This is a story about a salesperson who probes the customer for information about his long-term goals in business and then uses this knowledge to construct an effective sales presentation. The *Demonstrate alternative plan* strategy uses this story to demonstrate this tactic when the student has failed to gather any information about a customer's long-term goals; the RCD looks like this: "When the student is in the pre-call stage, and speaking to someone who is the decision maker, look for the student to perform cursory information gathering about the customer's long-term goals, and the student to fail to find out the customer's long-term goals. Then tell 'Long-term goal' as a 'Demonstrate alternative plan' story."

The first step in rule generation is to make the recognition conditions concrete, to reason about how these conditions might arise, and describe their occurrence in terms of actions the student might actually take. Sometimes a recognition condition is something that takes place over time. The example RCD contains the action of the student performing cursory information gathering about the customer's long-term goals. Several steps must take place before such an action can be recognized: The student must be in a conversation with the customer, and that conversation must end without the student having gathered much important information about long-term goals. Other actions may have more than one possible realization (e.g., the end of a conversation can occur when one of the participants leaves the room, or when the conversation is interrupted by someone else).

To perform this elaboration, SPIEL needs knowledge about observability in the simulated world. It must know what kinds of actions are and are not available to the student and the simulated agents. For abstractions that cannot be immediately recognized, it must be able to construct sets of observable features that would constitute that abstraction, if recognized in the appropriate context. The output of this step is an expanded RCD (eRCD) representing the same recognition conditions as the original RCD, but placing them in terms of their concrete, observable manifestations. Here is the eRCD for the prior RCD: "When the student is in the pre-call stage, and speaking to someone who is the decision maker, look for the student to leave without asking about the customer's long-term goals, or the student to ask about long-term goals, but not find out anything about them, and then leave. Then tell 'Long-term goal' as a 'Demonstrate alternative plan' story." Expansion has taken place in the evidence conditions. The test for cursory information gathering has been made more concrete, turned into two tests, each of which looks for a sequence of actions on the part of a student.

From the eRCD, the system designs a set of rules that will recognize the situation it describes. The initial stage of rule design is the construction of a *rule specification*, a directed graph indicating what production rules are needed and how they will relate to each other. An example is shown in Fig. 3.18. Each node in the graph is a rule the generator will have to produce. The connections in the graph represent rule sequencing: If Rule A enables Rule B, then there is a connection from A to B in the rule specification. Multiple outgoing paths indicate exclusive disjunction: If there is a connection from A to several nodes, B, C, and D, then only one of the rules can actually fire after A, whichever one's conditions are met first. Multiple incoming paths represent conjunction: If there is a connection from A and B to C, then both Rule A and Rule B must fire before C is enabled.

There are several different types of nodes in a rule specification, as Fig. 3.18 shows. The triggering rules recognize the context for storytelling. They are created from the trigger parts of the RCD. The event sequence rules, corresponding to the evidence conditions, form a branching se-

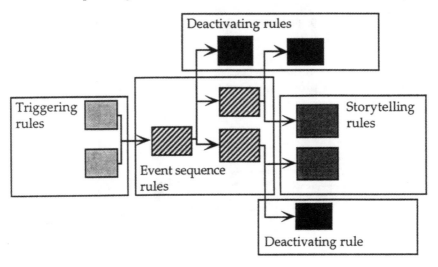

FIG. 3.18. Schematic of a rule specification.

quence of rules that fire in sequential order, each looking for the next temporally ordered step in the sequence of conditions leading to recognition. The last step in the recognition sequence is a storytelling rule that causes the simulation to retrieve the story and signal the student that it is available.

Deactivating rules hang from this recognition sequence. If the context established by the triggering rules is violated in some way, the opportunity cannot be recognized, and the recognition sequence must be aborted. For example, if an RCD depends on the fact that a salesperson is making a presentation to someone other than the decision maker, then the arrival of the decision maker will destroy the "absence of decision maker" context that makes the story relevant. At this point, SPIEL must stop looking for an opportunity to tell the story until the appropriate context reappears.

The initial creation of the rule specification is a straightforward transformation from the eRCD. However, once this initial rule specification is generated, two knowledge-based simplifications are performed. First, SPIEL eliminates conditions that can be assumed given the nature of the student's role. For example, in some contexts, the fact that the student is trying to make a sale can simply be assumed. Then SPIEL merges tests that can be performed in a single step, using some knowledge of how conditions become true in the simulation. If it needs to recognize the student's entrance at a location and the presence of a certain person at that location, it can merge these into one rule that, when the student enters a location, tests for the presence of the person.

A diagram of the rule specification for the "Long-term goals" example is shown in Fig. 3.19. The triggering conditions are implemented by two rules: one that looks for the individual who is the buyer, and one that looks for the student to begin the "pre-call" (information-gathering) step of the sales process. If the customer talks about his or her long-term goals in the course of the pre-call conversation, the story is not relevant because the student has succeeded rather than failed at finding out about the

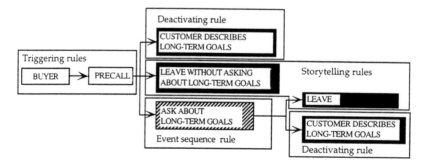

FIG. 3.19. Rule specification diagram for "Long-term goals" example.

customer's long-term goals. There is a deactivating rule that halts the recognition attempt if this happens. If the student leaves without asking the customer about long-term goals, this certainly counts as cursory information gathering on this topic, so the story gets told. A third possibility is that the student does ask about the customer's long-term goals. If there is a direct response, the story will not be told; but if the student never gets a straight answer, it will.

In the final rule specification graph, each node contains a condition or set of conditions that a rule will have to recognize. Rules are produced by walking through this graph translating from the descriptions into simulation states that rules can directly test for. For example, a "student entering a location" condition becomes a test for an entering event, with the actor and destination slots bound to certain values. A later section describes SPIEL's translation of its MOP-based representations into the vocabulary of GuSS simulation states.

Recall that the teaching modules in GuSS, like the simulated social agents, are implemented by production systems. The enabling relationship between rules, represented by the connectivity of the graph, is implemented through the working memory of SPIEL's production system (see Fig. 3.20). Each rule is linked to following rules by the placement of a *linking state* into working memory. Each linking state is unique and has no other function than to ensure proper rule sequencing. Connected rules, regardless of what other conditions they test for, must check for the presence of the linking state before being allowed to fire. This preserves

Rule specification

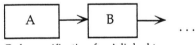

Rule specification for A linked to
rule specification for B.

Decision rules

Working memory

Rule for A fires, places linking state X into working memory.

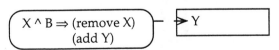

Rule for B tests for B and X and, on firing,
replaces linking state X with linking state Y.

FIG. 3.20. Implementing connectivity in GuSS.

the rule sequence. They must also remove the linking state when firing to preserve the property of exclusive disjunction.

Once the stories in the library have been through the processes of RCD creation and rule generation, SPIEL has a collection of rule sets. Each rule set is a collection of production rules designed to recognize a tutorial opportunity—a chance to tell a story using some strategy. The elaborate-and-index model used to derive these recognition rules treats each index separately, and therefore the rule sets are autonomous. They do not communicate with each other. This means that there is considerable re-dundancy between rule sets. There may be several stories that are relevant when a student is selling to a disgruntled customer, but the rule sets that look for opportunities to tell these stories would have their own tests for disgruntledness.

To eliminate this duplication of effort, SPIEL optimizes, trying to merge rules that perform the same tests into a single rule. Starting with the rules in each rule set that have no predecessors, it partitions the rules into equivalence classes containing rules with identical left-hand sides. When there is more than one rule in a partition, it creates a new rule that subsumes the entire partition. The process is then repeated for the rules that follow in sequence. In this way, independent rule sets can be made to share rules where possible.

Figure 3.21 shows a simple optimization example. For simplicity, the four initial rule sets, shown at the left, all have the same structure. The partitioning of the rule sets is shown in the center. Of the four rule sets,

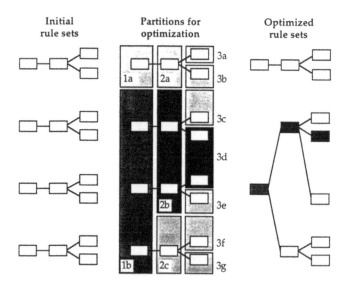

FIG. 3.21. Optimization example.

three of them have identical initial rules and are grouped in Partition 1b. These can be folded into a single rule, shown by the same-color node in the final optimized version of the rules shown at the right. There are three successors to this new rule; of these, two are identical, as seen in Partition 2b. They are combined to create the next merged rule. The next set of successors is then examined, yielding another case of overlap in Partition 3d, which produces the last optimized rule. In the final rule collection shown at the right, the top rule set is unchanged because none of its rules had anything in common with the others. The other rule sets have been optimized: Out of each partition containing more than one rule, only a single rule remains. The final collection has 12 rules, where the initial one had 16—a savings of 25%.

Natural Language Generation

Storytelling strategies determine when a story should be told. They also dictate how it should be told. Recall that each of the examples of tutorial storytelling contains three pieces of text that explain the system's reminding to the student:

1. *Headline:* The headline is the first notice to the student that a story is available. It gives just enough information for the student to tell what kind of story is coming: "A story about a different approach you might try."

2. *Bridge:* The bridge describes the connection SPIEL seeks to draw between the story the student is about to see and the situation the student was just in: "You gathered information about long-term goals in a cursory manner without much success. Here is a story about a similar situation in which an account executive used a different method and was successful."

3. *Coda:* The coda helps the student apply the message of the story to the situation that caused it to arise: "You gathered information about long-term goals in a cursory manner. It didn't work well. In the future, you might consider probing deeply into the customer's long-term goals."

These texts can be generated in a standardized way using templates associated with each storytelling strategy. For *Demonstrate alternative plan*, the three templates are:

1. *Headline:* "A story about a different approach you might try."

2. *Bridge:* "You <plan> without much success. Here is a story about a similar situation in which <gen-agent> used a different method and was successful."

3. *Coda:* "You <plan>. It didn't work well. In the future, you might
consider <story-plan>."

Items in angle brackets, such as <plan>, are used to instantiate a
template for a particular story. The headline is often sufficiently stereo-
typed that it does not need to be customized for each story. An exception
is the headline for *Explain other's plan.* It reads, "Do you understand what
<actor> is doing?" Filling in this template lets the student know whose
actions the story will attempt to explain.

The same mechanisms that SPIEL uses to determine what tutorial
opportunity it should try to recognize also can be used to instantiate the
templates. For example, when applying the *Demonstrate alternative plan*
strategy, SPIEL identifies the plan it will look for the student to have,
"cursory information gathering." It can translate that into an English
language phrase using a table of English equivalents for its MOPs and
fill in the template. In the case of the *Demonstrate alternative plan* strategy,
all of the fillers in the template can be computed at storage time:

<plan> is the "opposite" plan that the system seeks to recognize the
student using.

<story-plan> is the successful plan that the story describes, probing
the customer's long-term goals.

<gen-agent> is a generalization of the agent in the story. Mr. Beam is
the agent in the index, but he is generalized to become "account
executive."

Other fillers must be instantiated at the time the story is retrieved. In
the "Wife watching TV" story, the character that the student appears to
have the assumption about can only be identified at retrieval time. The
templates, in whatever stage of instantiation, are passed along through
the rule generation process, first as part of the recognition condition
description, until they are placed within the telling rules. Where I show
"Tell 'Long-term goals' as a 'Demonstrate alternative plan' story," for
simplicity, there is actually a more involved tell clause that incorporates
the explanatory texts. A more complete description of the telling action
in the RCD for the "Long-term goals" story would be as follows: "Tell
'Long-term goals' using Headline: 'A story about a different approach
you might try.' Bridge: 'You gathered information about long-term goals
in a cursory manner without much success. Here is a story about a similar
situation in which an account executive used a different method and was
successful.' Coda: 'You gathered information about long-term goals in a
cursory manner. It didn't work well. In the future, you might consider
probing deeply into the customer's long-term goals.' "

A story that addresses the student's expectations, such as "Wife watching TV," is a somewhat more difficult case for the natural language generator. What is important in telling this story is that the system has recognized that the student may have an assumption similar to the anomaly at work in the story. The bridge has to explain both parts of an anomaly. For anomalies, the generator must use some of the same reasoning that is applied in the *Warn about assumption* strategy. There are generation links associated with certain MOPs that highlight parts as important for description. In "theme," for example, the relationship to business decision making is considered important for describing a theme. Also important is whether a theme is one that is associated with an individual, like a personality trait, or one that is associated with a role, a role theme. In the case of "Wife watching TV," the important difference between themes can be summed up by the difference in business role. The housewife role is not associated with business decision making and the business partner role is. Hence, the translation for the assumption is "will not have a role in the business."

Storytelling Strategies

Storytelling strategies govern the elaboration of tutorial opportunities in SPIEL's elaborate-and-index model of opportunistic retrieval. They dictate how stories will be presented and at what times. In this capacity, they determine the conditions under which stories will be considered relevant to the student's situation. Each strategy aims for a different kind of relevance, drawing its own kind of analogy between story and storytelling situation. To reason about the relevance of stories, strategies need the ability to compare. SPIEL's storytelling strategies are, in part, a function of the types of comparisons that can be drawn between its representation of a story (the index) and its representation of the student's situation (the GuSS simulation). The next section describes SPIEL's 13 storytelling strategies.

STORYTELLING STRATEGIES

SPIEL's 13 storytelling strategies are explicit representations of how stories can be relevant to a student interacting with a learning-by-doing environment. Each has a similar function: selecting stories of a particular type and characterizing situations in which they will be relevant. The strategies fall into four categories based on their relationship between the stories they present and the situations in which they present them.

1. *Strategies that show the student alternatives.* These strategies present stories whose outcomes differ substantially from what the student has achieved in the simulated world. *Demonstrate risks* falls in this category. Confronting students with stories about alternative possibilities gets them to question their expectations about the simulated world. Also in this category are the strategies *Demonstrate opportunities* and *Demonstrate alternative plan.*

2. *Strategies that critique the student's expectations.* By showing examples of situations where people in a similar role had preconceptions that were incorrect, these strategies help students transfer expectations from their everyday social lives to the specialized social environment they are learning about. There are six strategies in this category, three basic types, each of which has two subtypes. The basic types are *Warn about optimism*, *Warn about pessimism*, and *Warn about assumption.*

3. *Strategies that project possible results of actions the student is taking.* Normally, students receive immediate feedback from the execution of their plans. If they do not get such feedback, projection strategies call for the storyteller to provide examples that show possible outcomes. There are two strategies here: *Reinforce plan* and *Warn about plan.*

4. *Strategies that explain the perspectives of other people to the student.* These strategies recall stories that explain why people acted as they did in real-world situations, making the unexpected actions of others in the simulation comprehensible. In this category, there are two strategies: *Explain other's plan* and *Explain other's perspective.*

Three Examples of Storytelling Strategies

In this section, three storytelling strategies are described as examples of the range of different relevance criteria that SPIEL can use. In the interests of space, an example from the "projection" category has been omitted because these strategies are similar in operation to those that show alternatives.

Whenever one confronts a complex problem, it is important to know the range of possible outcomes: What is the best and worst that could happen? What is reasonable to expect? Both in real life and in GuSS' simulator, the student gets to see only one outcome at a time. Stories that show a range of alternatives provide necessary balance, and delineate what might be expected based on other people's experiences. The alternative finding storytelling strategies are designed to bring stories to the student's attention when those stories differ in significant ways from the student's experience in the simulated world.

The idea behind *Demonstrate risks* is to tell a story about a failure when the student has experienced success. One reason this is important is that

- The student has successfully sold an ad and got the client's signature.
- The student keeps talking to the client for a little while before leaving.

A story showing the risks of your approach.

You kept talking to the client after the sale was closed. Nothing bad happened but here's a story in which doing that led to problems:

I was in the South Bend/Mishawaka area. This was my first or second year. I was calling on a swimming pool contractor. He had a quarter page in South Bend. I was proposing a quarter page in another directory. It was sitting at his kitchen table. And the guy was hesitating; he didn't know. . . . So, after a few more attempts, he says to me "OK, I'll go with the other quarter page." He bought it. I pushed the order form in front of him. He signed it. It's done.

As I'm putting my stuff together, I made this comment that cost me the quarter page. I said, as I'm packing up, "I'm sure that you're going to get a lot of phone calls from that new ad." He looked at me and he said, "You know, I don't need any more phone calls. I'll tell you what, let's not do that this year, maybe next." I talked myself out of a quarter page. I've never done it since. I walked out. There was nothing I could say. I had it and I lost it. All I had to say was, "Thank you very much Joe. See you next year." But I didn't. I had to tell him about the calls, which I'd already done twenty times.

Nothing bad happened to you because you kept talking to the client after the sale was closed, but sometimes the client changes his mind.

FIG. 3.22. Telling "Talked myself out of a sale" using the *Demonstrate risks* strategy.[12]

no simulation is perfect. If the simulation is not accurately reproducing the circumstances encountered in the story, the story points out possible differences between the simulation and the real world of practice. Another way that a *Demonstrate risks* story may arise is if the student successfully uses a risky strategy—one that fails 9 times out of 10. By showing how a situation similar to the one encountered in the simulation could have been a failure instead of a success, the storyteller demonstrates that a successful result in the simulation is not always repeatable in the real world.

Figure 3.22 shows *Demonstrate risks* in action in YELLO. Here, SPIEL observes the student continuing to converse with the client after closing a sale. This is a risky move: Every additional minute the salesperson hangs around is an opportunity for the customer to have a change of heart. When SPIEL tells a story about a customer who backed out of a deal in a similar situation, the student gets a chance to learn about this risk.

In general, the *Demonstrate risks* strategy needs to see that the student is in a situation similar to that in the story, but has achieved an outcome

---

[12]Story from interview with Denny Gant, video clip #150.

that is very different: The student has succeeded where the story shows a failure. The *Demonstrate risks* strategy calls on SPIEL to predict an outcome that would be "very different" from losing the sale—different enough that it makes sense to tell the story as an alternative. Such opposite finding inference occurs in each of the alternative finding strategies.

An opposite outcome is not something that contradicts the original in every respect. It does not make sense to say that the opposite of achieving X is failing to achieve Y, where X and Y are opposite goals. If anything, these would be similar outcomes. An opposite result is an opposite impact on the same goal. SPIEL has opposite links between impacts and their opposites, and generates opposite results by creating an instance of the opposite impact for the same goal. More complex cases of the opposite computation, such as that in the strategy *Demonstrate alternative plan,* where an opposite plan must be found, require more involved opposite finding inference. The details of the opposite finding algorithm and other inference mechanisms in SPIEL can be found in Burke (1993).

In areas of social expertise, newcomers may inappropriately carry over expectations from their social lives. For example, a new salesperson may think that a friendly talkative customer is more likely to buy than a "get down to business" type, when in many cases the opposite is true (Craig & Kelly, 1990). The anomalies in SPIEL's indexes represent contrasts between expectation and reality, so SPIEL is well poised to counter inappropriate expectations. There are three strategies that teach about expectations: *Warn about optimism, Warn about pessimism,* and *Warn about assumption.*

These perspective-oriented strategies are inherently more difficult to implement than the alternative finding strategies, such as *Demonstrate risks.* The system has to make decisions based on what the student's perspective is likely to be. In the alternative finding strategies shown so far, the problem of representing the student's thinking has not been severe because the stories that these strategies tell show alternatives to observable features of the simulation. Their relevance can be fairly certain. However, for perspective-oriented strategies, the important features are aspects of the student's mental state, such as hopes or fears. SPIEL must be able to recognize them. The problem of recognizing a student's state of knowledge is known as the problem of student modeling in intelligent tutoring systems (ITS) research.

This type of model is not easily extended to the kind of knowledge that SPIEL needs to capture. ITSs are designed to handle students who are complete novices. A model that captures all of what a student knows about an area is only possible when most of that knowledge comes from experience the student has with the tutor (vanLehn, 1988). A complex social skill, such as selling, is refined from the social expertise the student already has. Students have to learn which of their existing skills contribute to the new area and which detract. They learn new concepts and new skills, and fit both into their existing repertoire. Further, as a student becomes an expert, domain knowledge and experience are melded with existing abilities into a distinct personal style.

Adult students do not begin learning a social skill as complete novices. They bring to bear a great deal of prior knowledge and experience. The large quantity of existing student knowledge that students bring to the learning of social skills makes the construction of a student model problematic for these tasks. Some ITSs are able to handle students who bring with them a preexisting understanding of the concepts (Burton, 1982). They do so by building their student models from observation of students' performance in the task environment. In a social domain, the prior knowledge and experience that students have is so large that a tutor will not be able to discern the state of students' knowledge merely by observing a brief interaction with a simulated social world. It is unlikely that a model developed in this manner will successfully account for the individual idiosyncrasies in students' knowledge of and experiences in the social world.

It might be argued that students learning geometry, for example, have a lot of experience with lines and figures. However, there is an important distinction to be made here. A student learning geometry is trying to fit his or her intuitions about geometry into a new form of discourse involving the geometric proof. In social arenas, the discourse is not new: Beginning account executives using YELLO will have encountered salespeople throughout their lives, and probably have experience in sales already. YELLO cannot teach as if its students were encountering the conceptual basis of selling for the first time. For students in YELLO, learning how to fit new concepts and skills into their existing repertoire is at least as important as learning the new material.

SPIEL cannot have an operational model, one that represents the whole of a student's social reasoning. SPIEL does two things to confirm its guesses about the student's mental state using the perspective-oriented strategies. As part of its presentation, it prefaces the story with a question, saying essentially, "If you are expecting X, then I have a story for you . . ." and it tries to identify preparations that the student might make that characteristically indicate having a certain expectation.

Warn about assumption is used in the situation in Fig. 3.23. The student evidently assumes Mrs. Swain will not participate in the sale; otherwise, the time before Ed's arrival would have been used to better advantage. If the program has evidence that the student has a particular assump-

- Student arrives for a pre-call appointment with a roofing contractor.
- The contractor's wife greets her and they carry on small talk.
- The student turns immediately to the contractor when he arrives.

A warning about something you just did.

If you assume that Mrs. Swain will not have a role in the business, you may be surprised. Here is a story in which an account executive made a similar assumption that did not hold.

I went to this auto glass place one time where I had the biggest surprise. I walked in; it was a big, burly man; he talked about auto glass. So we were working on a display ad for him. It was kind of a rinky-dink shop and there was a TV playing and a lady there watching the TV. It was a soap opera in the afternoon. I talked to the man a lot but yet the woman seemed to be listening, she was asking a couple of questions. She talked about the soap opera a little bit and about the weather.

It turns out that after he and I worked on the ad, he gave it to her to approve. It turns out that after I brought it back to approve, she approved the actual dollar amount. He was there to tell me about the business, but his wife was there to hand over the check.

So if I had ignored her or had not given her the time of day or the respect that she deserved, I wouldn't have made that sale. It's important when you walk in, to really listen to everyone and to really pay attention to whatever is going on that you see.

An assumption that a spouse will not participate in the business may be unrealistic.

FIG. 3.23. Telling "Wife watching TV" using the strategy *Warn about assumption, other-focused.*[13]

tion about someone in the simulation, the *Warn about assumption* strategy calls for it to tell a story about a time when a similar assumption was wrong.

The assumption we are looking for is that the student assumes the spouse of the client will not have the role of business partner, which is a role critical for the formation of sales strategy, but instead to have the role of housewife, which is not important in sales strategy. How can this assumption be recognized? One possibility is that the student will specifically articulate an expected role for a person in the simulation. The student (if particularly sexist) might say something like: "Why don't we go into the next room, Mr. Swain, so Lucy can get on with fixing dinner?" This would be a pretty good indication that the student does not believe she has a role critical to the sales process.

When problems arise in social interactions, often what must be explained is the behavior of the other people involved; knowing what others are doing is just as important as knowing what to do oneself. Students need to hear stories about those with whom they are learning to interact. In selling, mistakes are often caused by a failure to understand the client's point of view. The bizarre and surprising expectations and actions of clients are an important part of the lore of salespeople.

[13]McLean, video clip #305.

SPIEL has to infer that the student may not understand some character's action in the simulation because the only reason to explain something is if the student is not likely to know about the phenomenon being explained. A student who is personally acquainted with many lawyers might not be surprised to hear a story about an attorney who was unfriendly toward salespeople, but someone with few dealings with the profession might need the explanation such a story provides. Other-directed stories only make sense if they are about things outside of normal experience, yet every student will have his or her own baseline of normal behavior. The answer is obviously not to model each student's experience, given the complexity of an individual's social experience and knowledge. As with perspective-oriented strategies, SPIEL uses a simple solution to this complex problem. It maintains a stereotype representing the average incoming student's stereotypes about those with whom they are interacting. It will only tell a story if it believes that the character's actions fall outside the normal range of what the student would likely expect. For example, a story about a customer who is concerned about the cost of advertising would not be exceptional, but one who wanted the salesperson to become a personal friend would be.

SPIEL has a static student knowledge stereotype that represents what students who are new to a domain of expertise can be expected to believe. These expectations are organized using a set of stereotypical roles in the domain being studied. In YELLO, these are the decision maker, gatekeeper, competing salesperson, and so on. For each role, there is a set of standard goals, a standard set of plans for achieving these goals within particular contexts, and a set of standard beliefs. This knowledge is used by the filters that choose which stories can be told using the other-directed strategies. A story in which someone violates the stereotype associated with their role is assumed to be of interest to a student.

In the other strategies discussed so far, the major portion of the effort of the strategy is directed toward looking for recognizable manifestations of the student's thinking. This problem does not arise in the same way for other-directed strategies because the characters' mental states can be directly inspected. Just looking at internal states, however, does not fulfill the mandate of the other-directed strategies to explain things that a student may not understand. A student has to see a character act on the basis of a plan or belief before there can be a failure to understand. SPIEL looks for visible manifestations of mental states as well as inspecting characters' representations.

The *Explain other's plan* strategy is used to tell stories that explain the unexpected actions of other people. A character may have a goal that the student did not anticipate. Imagine, for example, a student who is trying to get access to a decision maker and encounters a manager who demands to

- The student starts a pre-call with an attorney who is extremely rude and dismissive.

Do you understand what [the attorney] is doing?

Sometime an attorney will be rude to salespeople as a matter of policy. Here is a story about a time when that took place:

I cringe at the thought of this one attorney I did deal with. It was basically when I had first come into sales. It was my breaking in point there. I had talked to an attorney who had been in the business for 35 years. His ego was as big as. . . . He intimidated me very much. Being new, I didn't know how to handle it at first. He virtually tore me down to bits. I was ready to tell him "Good-bye" and that's it. Hang up on him.

After awhile talking to him, he explained to me that he does this to all his representatives. He felt that his 35 years in the business gave him the right to knock people down. I told him, I said "No, you don't have no right to do this to me. All I did was call. I wanted to improve your program for you, and be a friend." He was that bitter. It was his ego, basically. He was bitter about people and he wanted to let them know that he had earned the right to do this to people. At the end of it, he did apologize to me. He gets carried away, he told me. He told me he was sorry for what he did, but its in his nature to do this.

He sent me his book. He was a published author. We got to talking (this was on the second call.) Because after the first call, I just gave up on him for awhile. I called him back the second time. We did talk. He let me know more about himself, and what he had in mind for his Yellow Page advertising program. We put together a nice display ad for him. The following years I did have him back again. In fact, I had him for three years after that. We got to be real good friends. From that point we grew his advertising program and we did turn out to be good friends.

[The attorney] may be rude to salespeople as a matter of policy in order to gain an advantage. If you don't know, you should try to find out.

FIG. 3.24. Telling "Obnoxious attorney" using the *Explain other's plan* storytelling strategy.

be involved in the sales process. The most common explanation would be that the person is a "control freak" who wants to be in on everything. An alternative possibility that SPIEL can raise by telling a story is that the person is a frustrated artist who wants to have creative input on the design of the ad. This is a goal that a novice salesperson might never expect someone to have. It may also be that a character is using some unexpected means of achieving a well-known goal. This is what happens in Fig. 3.24. The client is being abusive because he thinks that doing so gives him an advantage over the salesperson and may result in a better deal.[14]

To determine whether a story can be told using this strategy, SPIEL uses the student knowledge stereotype. The agent in the index is the person who performed the actions that the story describes. SPIEL extracts the roles that the agent played in the sales process in the story, and looks at the stereotypes associated with these roles. The standard goals and plans that are associated with the agent's roles are compared against the

[14]From interview with Paul Cuglowski, video clip #243.

goal and plan in the "actual" part of the index. If a story contains someone using a typical plan to achieve a typical goal, it will not be considered worth telling because the student will probably be familiar with what the story shows. Only if the story contains goals, plans, or combinations of them that violate the stereotype is it useful for the *Explain other's plan* strategy. For example, the student knowledge stereotype contains the standard expectation that people will only use abusive language if they are angry and they want you to know it. In the story, the plan of abusing the salesperson is not serving a goal of expressing anger; the goal is to gain an advantage in the interaction. Therefore, the plan is not serving the goal that the stereotype associates with it, which is considered a violation of the stereotype and an indication that the story is worth telling using *Explain other's plan*.

Summary of Strategies

Table 3.3 summarizes SPIEL's storytelling strategies. One issue that has been conspicuously absent in this discussion is the question of strategy choice: When is it appropriate to employ what strategy? This omission is deliberate. The basic philosophy behind SPIEL's storytelling intervention is that any relevant story is worth telling, and therefore any storytelling opportunity should be capitalized on. Strategies are simply means of getting stories across.

SPIEL does not set itself up as an arbiter of right and wrong in selling. It attempts to connect the student's experience with that of others using the storytelling strategies. This architecture is a response to the nature of the tasks for which SPIEL has been employed. Expert social tasks such as selling are "weak-theory" domains (Porter, Bareiss, & Holte, 1990), where there is no complete causal model of the phenomena being studied. Worse yet, from the standpoint of a computer tutor, these skills are highly dependent on preexisting knowledge of social norms and practices, and have a significant cultural component. It is often impossible, even for a human expert, to say that a certain social action is definitely wrong because there are so many ways that social goals can be accomplished. For example, is it a good idea to continue conversing with customers after closing the sale? No, because they might change their minds. Yes, because sometimes customers need reassurance.

SPIEL's case based approach does mean that what the system teaches will be very dependent on its story base. Suppose SPIEL has a story about a salesperson who flirted with a customer and was successful in making a sale. If the student does a similar thing and gets into trouble, the *Demonstrate opportunities* strategy would call for system to tell the story as reassurance that flirting sometimes works. However, flirting with cus-

TABLE 3.3
SPIEL's Storytelling Strategies

Strategy Name	Tell a Story About:	When the Student:	What the Strategy Does
Demonstrate risks	the negative result of a particular course of action.	has executed a similar course of action with good result.	Shows alternatives.
Demonstrate opportunities	the positive result of a particular course of action.	has executed a similar course of action with poor result.	
Demonstrate alternate plan	a successful plan to achieve a particular goal.	has executed a very different plan and failed to achieve goal.	
Warn about optimism	a desire that someone had that was not realized.	appears to have the same hopes.	Critiques student's perspective.
Warn about pessimism	a fear that someone had that did not materialize.	appears to have the same fear.	
Warn about assumption	an assumption that someone made that did not hold.	appears to be making the same assumption.	
Warn about plan	an unsuccessful plan.	is executing a similar plan, but won't see the result soon.	Projects possible results.
Reinforce plan	a successful plan.	is executing a similar plan, but won't see the result soon.	
Explain other's plan	a plan that the student might not know about.	has just observed someone execute a similar plan.	Explains others' behavior.
Explain other's perspective	a belief that the student might not know about.	has just observed someone act on the basis of a similar belief.	

tomers is probably something that a salesperson should avoid, irrespective of a particular success story. Currently, the only way to avoid this problem would be to leave the flirting story out of the case base. Because the system is so uncritical of what it tells, only experienced and successful salespeople contributed stories to YELLO's story base.

It would be possible to build a storyteller that used storytelling strategies more discriminately. A system that had some heuristics about right and wrong could search for storytelling opportunities selectively. For example, if a student appears to be making serious mistakes, the storyteller might only look for opportunities to tell stories that make a negative point: opportunities to use the various "warning" strategies, not the positive strategies. In the case of the student who is flirting with a customer, a tutor could use such a heuristic to suppress this use of *Demonstrate opportunities* and prevent a flirting success story from being told.

Steps in this direction must be made with caution. If there were really good heuristics about how to sell, people would be able to teach it much better than they do (Craig & Kelly, 1990). The "rules of thumb" that experts give are frequently ignored under the appropriate circumstances. For example, salespeople often say that, in selling, one should always "aim for the sky"—try to sell as much as possible. If pressed, they will admit that, with certain customers and certain accounts, this is a bad idea. Blindly building in simple heuristics may cause useful reminders to be unnecessarily rejected.

RULE-BASED RECOGNITION OF STORYTELLING OPPORTUNITIES

An Overview of Rule Generation

As characterizations of storytelling opportunities, RCDs tell SPIEL what to look for. The system must go beyond these descriptions to recognize opportunities. Knowing what to look for is not the same as knowing how to look. Consider looking for an opportunity to help a friend. Opportunities can appear in many novel and subtle guises (Birnbaum, 1986).

Although SPIEL can characterize storytelling opportunities, it still must be able to recognize them. However, it does not have to deal with novelty. The environment in which it operates, the GuSS simulation, is a very constrained subset of the social environment. RCDs contain general descriptions of situations, such as "the student ignoring a person's input." The simulation limits the number and type of manifestations of a storytelling opportunity; only a few possibilities will be present within any GuSS application. SPIEL capitalizes on the constraints inherent in the environment to build simple rule-based recognition procedures for storytelling opportunities. This section describes how SPIEL performs the conversion of opportunity descriptions into recognition procedures, turning RCDs into GuSS rules, and how these rule-based recognition procedures are invoked to retrieve stories.

Rule generation in SPIEL can be thought of as an automated design process. The process begins with a general idea of what is desired, and this general design is refined in stages as additional constraints are added until it is completely specified. The constraints on the recognition procedure come in the form of more and more specific knowledge about the

TABLE 3.4
Processes and Knowledge Use in SPIEL

Process	Input	Output	Knowledge Type
Strategy application	Index	RCD	Storytelling strategies General manifestation knowledge Student stereotype
RCD elaboration	RCD	expanded RCD	Application-specific manifestation knowledge
Rule spec. creation	eRCD	Rule spec.	GuSS-specific rule application knowledge
Rule creation	Rule spec.	Rule set	Application-specific translation knowledge
Rule optimization	Rule sets	Optimized rules	Rule comparison and combination knowledge

form of the opportunity to be recognized and the structure of the environment in which it may appear.

Table 3.4 shows the steps in this design process and the knowledge that informs each. The strategy application process is included for completeness. Strategy application takes a description of a story in terms of its index and produces a description of an opportunity to tell that story. In doing so, it uses three kinds of knowledge: (a) knowledge about how a story can make an educational point, the storytelling strategies; (b) knowledge of how beliefs and intentions may appear in action, general manifestation knowledge; and (c) a set of default assumptions about the student, the student stereotype.

The second process is that of RCD elaboration. Here, the system takes into account the task the student will be performing and how that task is realized in the learning environment. These considerations further constrain how a tutorial opportunity may appear. For instance, if there are only a few actions that a student can take to argue for the value of an ad within the simulation, the system can focus on those particular actions if it needs to recognize the student's argument.

The eRCD is a more detailed description of a tutorial opportunity, but it does not yet take into account knowledge of the recognition process. The next stage of rule generation is the creation of the rule specification. Here the system develops the outline of a recognition procedure for the opportunity, using knowledge of how rules are applied in GuSS and how they interact. The output is a graph in which nodes correspond to rules and connections correspond to dependencies between rules. The recognition procedure is finally realized through the process of rule creation that produces a set of rules from the rule specification created in the previous step. At this point, the system must use knowledge of how the

MOP vocabulary used in SPIEL can be translated into rule clauses expressed in GuSS' vocabulary of internal simulation states. The result is a rule set that implements the recognition procedure. Of course, SPIEL is recognizing more than one storytelling opportunity at a time. After rule sets have been generated for many RCDs, they can be optimized and combined into a single large recognition procedure in which overlap between rule sets is eliminated. This is the process of rule optimization.

Expanding the Recognition Condition Description

The recognition conditions in the RCD are extremely general. It does not matter if the student is acting in a real-life role-playing game, the GuSS simulation, or some other environment where Yellow Pages ads are sold; an RCD would still describe an opportunity for storytelling. In this sense, the RCD is an environment-independent representation of a situation that constitutes a tutorial opportunity. It describes conditions that may be realized in different ways in different learning environments. The RCD for the "Wife watching TV" story is repeated here using the *Warn about assumptions* strategy: "When the student is in the pre-call phase, and the client has a business partner that is also a spouse, look for the student to exclude the spouse from the discussion, or the student to fail to gather information from the spouse. Then tell "Wife watching TV" as a "Warn about assumptions" story, other-focused." The eRCD is a less abstract version of this description, closer to the kinds of conditions that may arise in the GuSS simulation. The RCD is processed using elaboration rules that indicate how abstractions present in the RCD may appear in GuSS. These are similar to manifestation rules used by the storytelling strategies, except that they are specific to GuSS' learning environment.

Each part of the eRCD is something that can be directly recognized in the simulation, with the exception of one clause—the requirement that the student be in the pre-call phase. How is the system to know where the student is in the sales process? SPIEL could elaborate all of the necessary steps to recognize this fact, but almost every storytelling opportunity turns out to require the recognition of the student's progress through the sales call. This feature turned out to be so common that it became useful to create a special feature detector (Owens, 1990) for it. SPIEL has a small set of rules that track the student's position in the sales process, maintaining a record that reflects the student's current progress. Any recognition procedure can refer to this value, rather than having to gather its own evidence. Therefore, the rule set for "Wife watching TV" does not need to worry about all the possible ways that the student might end up in the "pre-call" part of the sale. It need only check that the "pre-call" recognition rule has matched.

In this tracking mechanism, SPIEL has what could be considered a dynamically updated student model. It tracks a certain aspect of the student's state using a model of the task and maintains a description of that state for the purposes of retrieval. Although I have argued elsewhere in this chapter that a complete dynamically updated student model is not feasible or appropriate as the basis for storytelling intervention, this is a case where it is possible and useful to do a small amount of modeling. It is possible to model the stages of the sales call because the model is a simple temporal succession, and because there is a simple set of rules for determining when the student is in each state. It is useful to do so because this feature turns out to be needed to recognize nearly every storytelling opportunity.

SPIEL has five sales call tracking rules that detect the student's progress through the selling task. The student always begins the scenario in the initial phase. The pre-call stage is recognized when customer contact begins. Pre-call ends when the student starts to prepare an ad campaign. At the point where the student contacts the customer to sell the prepared ad or ads, preparation ends and presentation begins. The system recognizes the close as the point in the presentation after the recommended ad program has been presented. These rules are part of SPIEL's rule set and continually update its representation of the student's position in the sales call process.

Designing the Recognition Procedure

The eventual output of the storage phase is a set of rules. With the eRCD, the system has a more concrete description of what it is looking for, but it does not yet have a recognition procedure. As a first step toward generating this procedure, SPIEL creates what is essentially a flowchart for recognition of the opportunity, showing what must be recognized and when. This flowchart, or rule specification, is a directed acyclic graph in which each node stands for a rule.

Figure 3.25 shows the rule specification for the "Wife watching TV" story. It is, for the most part, a simple transformation of the eRCD. Ignoring for a moment the "deactivate" rules, the specification has one node for each condition in the eRCD (lines in the English description), with the temporal and logical dependencies in the eRCD captured in the between-node connections. The deactivating conditions, which are not directly mapped from the eRCD, are present so that SPIEL can deactivate the recognition sequence if the context needed for recognition stops being true, or if events in the simulation render the retrieval conditions unachievable. These deactivation rules are necessary if the rule mechanism is to prevent spurious remindings (e.g., telling the "Wife watching TV" story if the student has succeeded in finding out business information from Mrs. Swain).

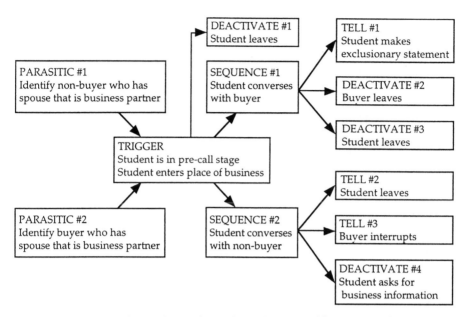

FIG. 3.25. Rule specification for "Wife watching TV" told using *Warn about assumptions* strategy.

In some cases, the deactivation conditions are explicit in the eRCD. In the prior example, the restriction "without having gathered business information ..." can easily be turned into deactivating Rule 4, which looks for the student to succeed in gathering information and halt recognition if that happens. In other cases, the deactivating conditions will have to be inferred from other aspects of the eRCD. Suppose the system is looking for the student to make a remark to Mr. Swain regarding Mrs. Swain (telling Rule 1), but the student never does. The system recognizes when the conversation ends that it should stop looking for such a statement. This is the role of Deactivating Conditions 2 and 3. If SPIEL did not have these rules, the telling rule would continue to try to find such a statement, even when the appropriate context for storytelling has passed by.

After deactivating conditions have been added, SPIEL makes a correction to eliminate redundancies between its branches: nodes where the same thing is recognized twice. This is more than an efficiency concern; it is a necessity. GuSS' rule mechanism fires only one rule at a time. If there are two rules under consideration at one time, both of which have the same left-hand side, only one will be permitted to fire. Because the situation in the simulation constantly changes, the more redundant rules there are, the more likely it is that the system will fail to recognize a storytelling opportunity because the relevant rule did not get a chance to function. Such duplicate rules can be eliminated by revising the design of the recognition procedure before rule creation occurs. For example, suppose an eRCD looks like this: "When A look for B followed by C followed by D, or B followed by C followed by E, or F followed by B followed by G." The rule specification graph would look like the left half of Fig. 3.26. Using a process similar to rule optimization, it is easy to determine that the tests for B and C in the first two sequences are redundant and can be merged. (The test for B in the third sequence cannot be shared because no other test for B has the precondition of F.) The right half of the figure shows the result of redundancy elimination.

A second kind of redundancy can occur between parts of a recognition sequence. Although the RCD is always expressed in terms of sequences of conditions, some pieces of a sequence do not require strict ordering. Suppose a rule specification contains a sequence of two conditions: (a) the student asking about the meaning of a term, followed by (b) the client having the expectation that the student would already know the meaning of the term. Because the client's expectation will be present at the same time as the student's action, it is possible to test for both of these conditions in a single rule. SPIEL uses persistence rules to check for these cases. Here is an example: "If A and B are adjacent rules, and A is a student action, and B is a character's mental disposition, and A has no other successor but B, then the merged rule A^B can replace the sequence A followed by B."

Rules for the GuSS Simulation Mechanism

GuSS models the simulated agents in its simulated world (including SPIEL and the other tutorial modules) using production systems similar to those found in expert systems (Brownston et al., 1985). At each point in the simulation, an agent looks for the production, or decision rule, that best matches its current mental state (what it knows, believes, expects, etc.) and fires it. For example, Lucy has a decision rule that causes her to respond to compliments about her house by saying: "Thank you, we like it." This rule fires when she observes the student's comment, "What a wonderful view of the lake you have." Other rules cause changes to her

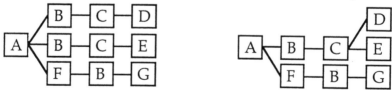

FIG. 3.26. A redundant rule specification and a simplified version.

mental state; she stops expecting Mike to arrive when she greets him, for example.

Each agent in GuSS is an independent planner, taking input from the simulation and responding in a manner designed to achieve its goals. Therefore, the internal states of such a planner represent intentions, such as goals and plans, and beliefs that support them. In the GuSS simulation, an agent's mental state is represented as a list of assertions of what the agent knows, feels, or intends. The list is ordered, reflecting a simple notion of priority: Those at the top of the list are more likely to influence processing. New states that arise are added to the top. Each agent's initial mental state is determined by the designer of the scenario when the initial conditions are established.

The production system-based agents interact with each other and the user in the GuSS simulation engine, a simple event-processing loop. Agents (and other objects in the simulation) respond to events, things that happen in the simulated world, as they are pulled from the *event queue*, a queue of the events that are scheduled to occur in the simulation. Agents may respond by generating new events, which are in turn placed back on the queue. For example, an agent who processes the event of hearing a phone ring may make a decision to answer it, generating a new event of picking up the phone. The agent on the other end of the line will notice this event and respond appropriately. When the student performs actions using the action constructor, each action becomes an event that is placed on the event queue.

Like production rules, GuSS' decision rules are condition/action pairs. However, the condition part of each rule is divided into three parts: retrieval, filtering, and discrimination. Retrieval conditions are used to access each agent's table of decision rules. An agent makes a decision by first using its mental state to key into the table. It retrieves a set of candidate rules, each of which has retrieval conditions compatible with the agent's current mental state. Because an agent's entire mental state can be quite large, on the order of several hundred SOMs, GuSS only permits a subset of the mental state to be used for retrieval conditions: only goals, plan steps, observation, and members of a special class of belief called *awares:* For example, suppose Ed Swain observes someone enter his office. He may have several rules whose retrieval conditions are compatible with this situation. The rules in Fig. 3.27 would all be retrieved as possible candidates.

The filtering conditions are employed to filter the candidate decision rules chosen by the retrieval conditions. There are "only when" conditions that must match for the rule to be executed, and there are "not when" conditions that, if matched, cause the rule to be rejected. If Ed is meeting with someone, he will reject Rules 1 and 2 and use Rule 3. The discrimi-

Rule #1:
If
(retrieval conditions)	I observe someone enter my office, and
(filtering conditions)	I am by myself, and
(discrimination conditions)	I'm expecting that person to come at a certain time, and it's the right time, then
(actions)	I will say "Hello," stop expecting the person to arrive, and start believing that the person has arrived on time.

Rule #2:
If
(retrieval conditions)	I observe someone enter my office, and
(filtering conditions)	I am by myself, and
(discrimination conditions)	I'm engaged in an activity, and I expect that people will not interrupt me, then
(actions)	I will say "What?," become somewhat angry, and start to believe that the person is rude.

Rule #3:
If
(retrieval conditions)	I observe person A enter my office, and
(filtering conditions)	I am conversing with person B, and
(discrimination conditions)	I'm expecting person A to come at a certain time, and it's the right time, then
(actions)	I will say "Hello," stop expecting the person to arrive, and start believing that the person has arrived on time, and come to have the goal of ensuring that person A is acquainted with person B.

FIG. 3.27.

nation conditions are used to rank candidates if there are several that pass the other tests. They are matched against the agent's state of mind using a match algorithm that returns a numerical score. The highest scoring decision rule is executed. If Ed Swain were alone and expecting a visitor, Rule 1 would match better than 2, and thus would be executed.

There are a few major differences between GuSS' agents and common production system models, such as OPS5 (Brownston et al., 1985). Most important, GuSS uses retrieval conditions to perform retrieval prior to the matching step. Therefore, the matching step occurs only on a small set of rules—the ones that are retrieved because they are likely to be relevant to the agent's current situation. This means that working memory and the set of productions can be larger without incurring much additional pattern matching. Giving Ed Swain new topics to discuss will not slow down his existing responses greatly because the rules that implement his conversation about one topic will not be retrieved when the conversation is about another topic. Another advantage to the two-level matching scheme is that generic rules can easily be overridden by agent-specific ones and still be available as fallback options.

Another important aspect of GuSS' decision rule mechanism is its conflict resolution. Discrimination among decision rules occurs on the basis of the qualitative measure returned by the pattern matcher. GuSS uses a hierarchy of concepts when performing its matching, giving greater weight to matches that are specific. A rule containing an abstraction will match a mental state that contains a more specific concept, but not as strongly as a rule that matches exactly. The matcher also prefers matches that do not involve unbound variables. Using the example rules given earlier, if Ed is both expecting an appointment and engaged in an activity, Rule 1 would match better because the expectation of the appointment, containing a reference to a particular person, is more specific than the discrimination conditions in Rule 2. This notion of specificity is different from the measure of rule specificity in OPS5, which counts the number of conditions in a rule's left-hand side as the measure of how specific it is.

Because SPIEL's retrieval time component is implemented as an agent in the GuSS simulation, it participates in the central cycle of observation and action, just like the characters with whom the student is interacting. However, the SPIEL agent has special properties. It must occasionally inspect the mental state of other agents—something that no character is permitted to do. Also, as described later, SPIEL attaches decision rules to other agents in the simulation, so-called *parasitic rules*, to perform certain computations. The SPIEL agent also requires additions to the GuSS vocabulary to create the unique linking states that tie a rule set together.

Rule Creation

In the rule specification, each node represents some state or conjunction of states that must be recognized at a particular point in the recognition sequence. The task of the rule creation step is to create production rules that will recognize these states within the GuSS simulation. There are two primary problems associated with this task. The most obvious problem is that of vocabulary. The states expressed in the rule specification are essentially in the same vocabulary as the index (i.e., MOP structures). The states against which rules must match in the GuSS simulation are in a different vocabulary. SPIEL must convert its recognition procedures into GuSS' language. The second problem is communication between rules, to preserve the structure of the recognition procedure and maintain consistency.

GuSS' representation of states and actions is quite different from that used in SPIEL. MOPs are essentially frame-based representations in which packaging relationships are very significant; in GuSS, each agent's working memory is represented by a list of assertions, states of mind (SOMs).

An SOM cannot package or point to others. They are always of the following form:

```
(predicate (agent act aspect object)).
```

For example, an observation of the student asking about plans for the expansion of Swain Roofing would be as follows:

```
(observe (student ask-about (plans-for expansion-of) swain-
roofing)).
```

The predicate part indicates what kind of mental state the SOM represents. There are eight types: observations, goals, plan steps, expectations, beliefs, awares, attitudes, and emotions. The agent is the person that the mental state is about. The act is the action that the SOM asserts. Aspects are modifiers that operate on the object of the SOM. Acts are the verbs of the SOM language, aspects are its adjectives, and objects and agents its nouns. In the example, the object is "Swain Roofing," the business owned by Mr. Swain. Multiple aspects in an SOM are composed to yield its meaning, as in the example.

Acts, as well as other terms in GuSS's vocabulary, are drawn from a large representational hierarchy. They are related to each other using "isa" relationships. For example, "Ask about" is a type of "speech act," which is a type of "act." Figure 3.28 shows a fragment of the term hierarchy for acts in GuSS. A single SOM is obviously limited in its ability to express structured concepts because acts and objects are simple terms, and the only type of embedding permitted in aspects is simple conjunction. For example, it is not possible to represent an assertion that contains a disjunction such as, "John believes that either Sue or Mary wrote the letter." Complex mental states must be broken into smaller assertions to be represented.

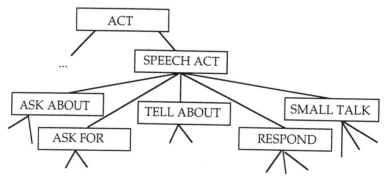

FIG. 3.28.   A fragment of GuSS term hierarchy.

Consider the recognition that the student has engaged the owner's spouse in conversation. The rule has to recognize the student speaking, the spouse being present, and the owner being absent. (In GuSS' world, everyone who is at a given location is automatically part of the conversation, so the only way the student could talk just to the spouse would be if the owner were absent.) SPIEL has a table of translation rules that enables it to convert MOPs into SOM equivalents in decision rules. Here is the translation rule for a conversation involving someone who is not the buyer: "To recognize a conversation between the student and someone other than the buyer, a rule needs retrieval conditions: the student says something; only when: the person who is not the buyer is present; not when: the buyer is present." The retrieval conditions look for the student to make some speech act. The "only when" verifies that the nonbuyer person is present in the room, and the "not when" condition prevents the rule from firing if the buyer is present.

One unusual feature of GuSS' rule matcher is that it lacks the capacity to backtrack. This creates problems for SPIEL in searching for characters with certain characteristics. In evaluating the retrieval, filtering, and discrimination conditions of a rule, GuSS' matcher operates on one condition, one SOM, at a time. It searches the agent's mental state for any matching SOMs. If the rule contains a variable, that variable will be bound for the rest of the evaluation of that rule to the corresponding value in the first matching SOM in the agent's mental state.[15] If the matcher fails when attempting other matches using that variable binding, it does not go back and try other possible bindings.

This limitation of the pattern matcher means that a rule containing a variable cannot be guaranteed to operate correctly unless (a) there is only a single possible match in the agent's mental state, or (b) the rule does not involve conjunctions of conditions using the same variable. GuSS' simulation rules are usually written this way. In contrast, SPIEL must frequently select a character with a conjunction of characteristics out of several that may be present in a scenario. SPIEL needs to be sure that, if there is a character with the desired characteristics, it can latch onto it.

To see how SPIEL gets the desired behavior out of GuSS' rule application mechanism, it is useful to recognize that backtracking is merely the most common implementation of nondeterministic choice. If a matching algorithm needs to make a choice between possible variable bindings, it can be guaranteed to find the right one if it makes a choice while remembering the bindings it did not choose, so they can be tried if the selected ones fail. Another implementation of nondeterministic choice is to pursue all choices

---

[15]In GuSS, variables will only appear in rules. They are not permitted in an agent's mental state.

in parallel: If there is a correct binding, then one of the parallel matches will succeed. Because agents are the objects between which SPIEL must choose when making bindings, and because agents are allocated their own processing time (essentially in parallel) to process events, SPIEL can piggyback on each agent, getting them to evaluate their own characteristics.

Whenever SPIEL needs to identify a character with certain properties, such as a business owner, it creates a parasitic decision rule.[16] These rules, while created by SPIEL and serving to help the story retrieval process, actually exist in the decision rule tables of the characters in the simulation. As their name suggests, parasitic rules steal a small amount of processing from each agent, usually only once at the beginning of the scenario. The rules inspect the agent to which they are attached, determining if the agent meets the necessary criteria. They signal the teaching module if their character meets the desired conditions. In this way, SPIEL can determine which characters have the desired characteristics.

Figure 3.29 shows an example of a parasitic decision rule used for the "Wife watching TV" story. To explain this rule, a few more details of GuSS' rule application mechanism need to be discussed. The retrieval conditions are called (somewhat confusingly) *indexes*. The term *retrieval conditions* is used to avoid confusion with SPIEL's indexes for its stories. In this rule, the retrieval conditions correspond to the agent's ongoing awareness of time—something that is always present from the beginning of the simulation. This rule will therefore be retrieved as soon as the simulation starts up.

This rule, like all parasitic rules, belongs to all agents. All characters in the simulation decide whether they meet the criteria of the rule and pass that information to SPIEL. Because its retrieval conditions are so general, this rule will always be retrieved. The rest of the conditions are filtering conditions that determine whether, for a given agent, this rule will be fired. First are the "only when" conditions, all of which must be true for the rule to fire. For this rule, the agent must believe that it has a spouse, and that the same person is also a business partner. It also must expect to be in control of a business—a state that marks a character as a business owner in YELLO. These are conditions that would hold true of Mr. Swain. The rule will also be retrieved for Mrs. Swain and Dave Swain, but Mrs. Swain fails the "ownership" test and Dave fails the "spouse" test.

For Mr. Swain, then, this rule will be retrieved and the "only when" conditions will be met. A successful match means that the action part of the rule is performed—in this case, the "poke" action. It places two linking states in the SPIEL agent's state of mind as a record that this match has

---

[16]I am indebted to Tom Murray for the term *parasitic* and the realization that parasitic decision rules could be viewed as a solution, rather than a problem.

```
;; PARASITIC D-Rule <SPIEL-PARA-DRULE-1952> for story: "Wife watching TV"
;; For AGENT
;; Vars: ((*SELF #<agent>)
;;         (*AGENT1935 #<agent>)
;;         (*AGENT1936 #<agent>))
;; Indices:       ((AWARE (*SELF #<know about> #<anything> #<time>)))
;; Only-when:     ((BELIEVE (*SELF #<is spouse> #<anything> *AGENT 1936))
;;                 (BELIEVE (*SELF #<is business partner> #<anything> *AGENT
;;                     1936))
;;                 (EXPECT (*SELF #<possess> #<control of> #<business>)))
;; Not-when:      <none>
;; Peek:          <none>
;; Not-peek:      ((AWARE (SPIEL-AGENT #<linking som 1939> #<anything>
;;                     *AGENT1936))
;;                 (AWARE (SPIEL-AGENT #<linking som 1938> #<anything> *SELF)))
;; Agent peeked: SPIEL-AGENT
;; Poke:          ((AWARE (SPIEL-AGENT #<linking som 1939> #<anything>
;;                     *AGENT1936))
;;                 (AWARE (SPIEL-AGENT #<linking som 1938> #<anything>
;;                     *SELF)))
;; Agent poked:  SPIEL-AGENT
;; Action:        <none>
;; Forget:        <none>
;; Learn:         <none>
```

FIG. 3.29. Parasitic decision rule for "Wife watching TV" story.

been successfully performed. Because he will retain his ownership of
Swain Roofing and his marriage throughout the scenario, there is nothing
in the conditions seen so far to prevent Ed from firing this rule at every
time step, filling the SPIEL agent's mental state with new copies of the
same information. To prevent such an inefficiency, the rule must actively
prevent itself from firing again after it has fired once. This is the reason
for the "not peek" conditions in the rule, which are analogous to the "not
when" conditions, except that they reference the mental state of another
agent—in this case, the SPIEL agent. The rule tests to see that the linking
states that it gives the SPIEL agent are not already present. If they are,
the rule has already fired and it can be ignored.

As described earlier, SPIEL's rules communicate with each other
through the use of linking states. Rules need to coordinate when they are
connected in a temporal relation to each other. The predecessor rule needs
to tell its successors, "I've fired," so that the successors can begin trying
to recognize their piece of the recognition sequence. The "I've fired"
message comes in the form of a unique SOM that the predecessor rule
adds to the SPIEL agent's mental state. Rules that follow use the presence

of this state as a filter. They are inhibited from firing until the predecessor fires and inserts the linking state. A successor rule will remove the linking state upon firing so that only one recognition path is followed.

Linking states are the synchronization mechanism for predecessor and successor rules, but they also serve two other purposes that are apparent in the parasitic rule example: (a) they block the repeated firing of the rule that created them, and (b) they record important variable bindings. For parasitic rules, in particular, this last function is important. The only reason for having these rules is to obtain correct variable bindings because the rule matcher cannot be guaranteed to do so. These bindings are communicated to the rest of the recognition procedure using the linking states. In fact, rules of all types frequently must communicate values to each other in this way. If a context depends on Ed Swain not being in a certain location, that location must be bound and passed along so that future rules will be able to detect if Ed has entered that location.

The communication of variable bindings can be seen in the two linking states created by the parasitic rule shown previously: one containing the person whom the rule matches and one containing the spouse of that person. If a later rule needs to know who the owner's spouse is, it needs to have a condition of the following form:

```
(AWARE (SPIEL-AGENT {UNIQUE LINKING ACT} #<anything> *VARIABLE))
```

The "act" part of the SOM is unique to the particular rule that created the linking state. This condition will only match the SOM created by that rule in which the correct binding can be found. Therefore, *variable* will be bound to the owner's spouse.

The parasitic rules recognize characteristics of people that do not change over the course of the scenario. Ed and Lucy will not divorce while the sales call is happening. The rules need only detect their properties once. These linking states are therefore permanent, not removed by other rules. Any rule with a question about an agent's characteristics can consult the linking states created by the parasitic rules. However, most linking states communicate information of transitory value, such as "the student has just walked into the Swains' kitchen." Each of these linking states is a trigger for some following rule, which removes the state from SPIEL's mental state on firing. The binding in such states cannot be universally relied on.

Therefore, it may happen that a rule binds a variable and passes it to the next rule—a rule that binds a different value and communicates it. A later part of the recognition procedure may need to refer back to the earlier value, but it is now forgotten. For example, suppose we have the following simple rule set:

FIG. 3.30. Communication of values within a rule set.

Rule A looks for the student to create an ad with certain properties;

Rule B looks for the student to go to the client's place of business;

Rule C matches against the student's action of presenting the ad to the client; and

Rule D deactivates the recognition if the student leaves without presenting the ad.

Suppose the first two rules match successfully, as shown in Fig. 3.30. What value should Rule B pass along in its linking state? Rule C wants to know the identity of the ad to look for the presentation of it. It cannot refer back to the linking state produced by Rule A because that state was removed by Rule B. Rule D needs to have the value of the location so it can look for the student leaving that location. To satisfy the needs of both of its successor rules, Rule B must produce two linking states to pass along both values. The rule creation algorithm takes note of the values that each rule needs to test its conditions, and checks to see whether these values have been previously bound in the recognition procedure. If they have, the rule generator adds linking states to all of the rules between the original binding and the place where the value is needed to create a bucket brigade that passes the value along.[17]

Rule Optimization

For every recognition condition description, the rule-generation process creates a rule set that implements a recognition procedure for the RCD's tutorial opportunity. The rules, as shown, are tightly coupled with each other through linking states and variable bindings. However, there are

---

[17]In the current implementation of rule generation, linking states have only been called on to pass the values of objects between rules, never aspects or acts. Other types of values could easily be communicated in a similar way.

many redundancies between rule sets. This occurs most frequently in the case of triggering conditions. Many stories require that the system identify who "the buyer" is and watch how the student interacts with that person. Many stories can only be told in a particular phase of the sales call, such as the sales presentation.

As was the case for rules within a recognition procedure, it is desirable wherever possible to merge redundant rules—ones that have the same predecessors and the same retrieval, filtering, and discrimination conditions. Optimization proceeds by moving forward through all of the rule sets simultaneously. It looks first at rules that do not depend on others, ones that initiate recognition sequences. This will usually be the parasitic rules. It partitions the group of rules based on redundancies. All rules in the same partition are replaced with a single rule that performs the same test. The process then moves along to the rules that follow those just optimized, until there are no more rules left.

SPIEL optimizes by walking through the recognition procedures from left to right, preserving their linear, sequential structure, but consolidating across procedures where possible. Its criteria for redundancy are fairly strict: The left-hand sides must be identical (except for linking state information) and the predecessors must be the same. A rule that is three steps along in the recognition chain can only be merged with another one that is three steps into the same chain. For the optimizer to realize that the rules are in fact steps along the same chain, it must have already optimized their predecessors.

So far throughout the rule-generation process, each tutorial opportunity has kept its distinct identity: Each RCD has an eRCD, a rule specification, and a rule set. However, once the final stage of optimization is complete, the rule sets are no longer distinguishable. The whole collection of rules has been merged to create an opportunity recognition machine for all of the storytelling opportunities. Optimization operates on the whole collection of rule sets, which may contain as many as several thousand rules. For illustration, a miniature example using two rule sets is shown. Consider the two rule specification graphs shown in Figures 3.31 and 3.32. They are for the rule sets that recognize opportunities to tell the "Taxidermist" story using the *Warn about pessimism* strategy, other focused, and "Obnoxious attorney" using the *Explain other's plan* strategy. (In the "Taxidermist" story, the salesperson is afraid that her ignorance will be a turn-off to the professional taxidermist, but he ends up buying anyway. The strategy calls on SPIEL to look for evidence of a similar fear on the part of the student, and to tell the story to point out that the fear may be unrealistic.) Although optimization occurs on the rules themselves, it is easier to see the optimization process with the graphical representation— the rule specification.

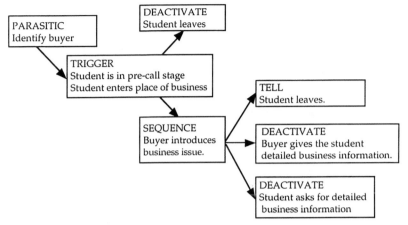

FIG. 3.31. Rule specification for telling "Taxidermist" using the *Warn about pessimism* strategy, other focused.

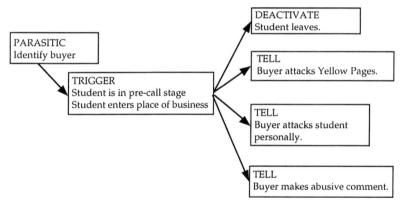

FIG. 3.32. Rule specification for "Obnoxious attorney" using the *Explain other's plan* strategy.

Because both parasitic rules recognize the same thing, the presence of the buyer, they can be optimized in the first optimization step. A new rule is created with the same retrieval and discrimination conditions, a test for buyerhood, and a new action passing along a new linking state. The rules that come after these parasitic rules in their respective rule sets are then adjusted to look for the linking state created by the new rule, effectively drawing the new rule into the recognition sequence. The rule sets are shown in Fig. 3.33 after the first optimization step. The darker box surrounding the parasitic rule shows that it has been optimized. Now the two triggering rules are inspected. They perform the same recognition

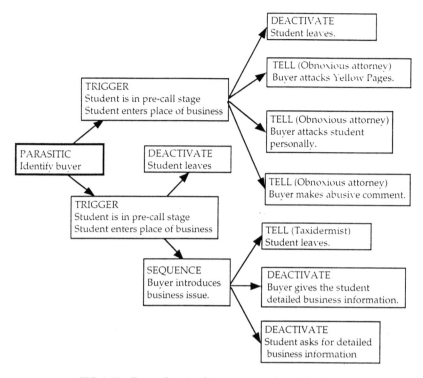

FIG. 3.33. Two rule sets after one stage of optimization.

function and have the same predecessor, and are therefore merged in the second step.

Following the triggering rules, each rule set has a deactivating rule that looks for the student to leave. They are consolidated in the third step of the optimization. At this point, the recognition procedures diverge and no more optimization is possible. The final rule set is shown in Fig. 3.34. Three rules have been eliminated, but the recognition sequences for both tutorial opportunities have been preserved.

Rule Application

The storage time processes in SPIEL build rule-based recognition procedures. At retrieval time, a student interacts with a GuSS scenario and the SPIEL agent attempts to use its recognition machinery to retrieve stories. This section shows a trace of how the "Wife watching TV" story is retrieved. Again, simplification has been necessary. Recognition actually takes place using the optimized rule collection, in which no single storytelling opportunity has a distinct recognition procedure. Rules do not "belong" to a particular story at this point. However, for the purposes of exposition, the

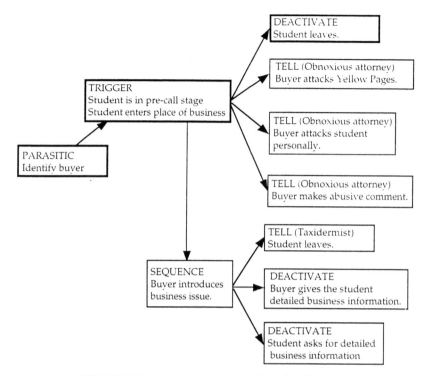

FIG. 3.34. Two rule sets after completion of optimization.

"Wife watching TV" recognition procedure is treated as if it were operating on its own. Figure 3.35 shows the rule specification for this story.

This is a fairly complex rule set. There are two parasitic rules: one that looks for the spouse who is the owner, and another that looks for the one who is not. After these characters have been identified and the pre-call stage has begun, there are two possible recognition paths, corresponding to the disjunction in the original RCD. The student will either engage in conversation with the owner or the spouse. (If the student does not talk to either and leaves the pre-call phase, then the recognition process halts.) If the student talks with the owner, the story gets told if the student explicitly excludes the other spouse from the conversation. The second possibility is that the student will talk to the nonowner spouse. Then the story gets told if the conversation ends with the student having failed to take advantage of the information-gathering opportunity.

The first parasitic rule was examined in detail in the rule-generation section. The function of the rest of the rules are described here without going into their implementation. The full implementation of this rule set can be found in Burke, 1993. The second parasitic rule matches Mrs. Swain because she is not a business owner. Figure 3.36 describes the mental

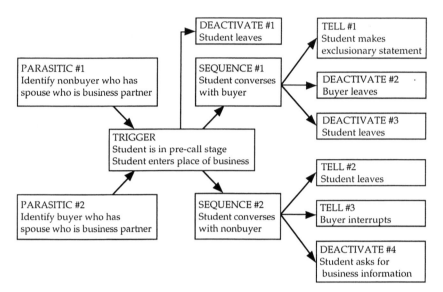

FIG. 3.35. Rule specification for "Wife watching TV" told using *Warn about assumptions* strategy.

state of the SPIEL agent after the simulation has started, and the two parasitic rules have had a chance to put linking states into the SPIEL agent's mental state. These four linking states serve to communicate the structure of the relationship between Mr. and Mrs. Swain.

A triggering rule comes next. It verifies that Mrs. Swain is both business partner and spouse to the same person that has her as a business partner and spouse: Both directions of the relationship are confirmed. The triggering rule does not remove the linking states that are due to the parasitic rules because they will remain true throughout the course of the simulation, and may be referred to by other rules. It does add its own linking state for its successors to refer to. Because rules in this sequence depend on knowing the location where the pre-call is taking place, this linking state records the location that the student is in. Figure 3.37 shows the

Parasitic rule #1 matched against "Lucy Swain."
Parasitic rule #1 matched against spouse & bus. partner "Ed Swain."
Parasitic rule #2 matched against "Ed Swain."
Parasitic rule #2 matched against spouse & bus. partner "Lucy Swain."
Student is in the initial stage of the sales call.

FIG. 3.36. SPIEL agent's mental state after firing the parasitic rules.

Triggering rule matched with location "Swain's kitchen."
Student is in the pre-call stage of the sales call.
Parasitic rule #1 matched against "Lucy Swain."
Parasitic rule #1 matched against spouse & bus. partner "Ed Swain."
Parasitic rule #2 matched against "Ed Swain."
Parasitic rule #2 matched against spouse & bus. partner "Lucy Swain."

FIG. 3.37. SPIEL agent's mental state after firing triggering rule.

SPIEL agent's state following this rule firing. Note that the rules responsible for maintaining the record of the student's progress through the sales call have recorded the fact that the student is now in the pre-call stage. SPIEL is primed to look for the storytelling opportunity.

The next important event in the simulation is that the student begins talking to Mrs. Swain. This signals the information-gathering opportunity to which the recognition conditions refer. This fact is recognized by sequence Rule 2. It picks the binding for the two spouses from the linking SOM, and checks for the presence of the nonowner spouse and the absence of the owner (if Ed were there, it would count as a conversation with him, not with Lucy).

Having recognized the initiation of the conversation, the sequence rule removes the linking state contributed by the triggering rule and replaces it with one of its own. This prevents the firing of either of the other two rules that are successors to the triggering rule, deactivation rule 1 or sequence rule 1 (see Fig. 3.38 to see what the SPIEL agent knows at this point). Although the sequence rule does not actually use the location value passed to it, it continues to transmit it to the rules that follow because they look for the student's location.

Now the question is, Will the student find out what Lucy knows? The story will only be told if the student fails in information gathering. What happens is that Ed arrives and the student is still talking about fishing. The information-gathering opportunity has been missed. The telling rule (3) that notices this is quite simple: It looks for the owner arriving, removes the last linking state, and signals the interface to recall and present the story.

Sequence condition #2 matched, passes location "Swain's kitchen."
Student is in the pre-call stage of the sales call.
Parasitic rule #1 matched against "Lucy Swain."
Parasitic rule #1 matched against spouse & bus. partner "Ed Swain."
Parasitic rule #2 matched against "Ed Swain."
Parasitic rule #2 matched against spouse & bus. partner "Lucy Swain."

FIG. 3.38. SPIEL agent after recognizing the conversation.

The reason the telling rule can be so simple is that there is a deactivating rule (4) that looks for the student gathering business information from Lucy. If that rule had fired, the linking state from the sequence rule would have been removed, and the telling rule would never have been retrieved. Therefore, having made it this far with the linking state still present, the system knows that the student did not take advantage of the opportunity, and therefore the "Wife watching TV" story is relevant.

Retrieval in SPIEL

This section offered a tour through the innermost details of SPIEL's rule-based retrieval mechanism. This discussion completes our examination of SPIEL's story retrieval process. SPIEL starts with a library of stories and computes the set of recognition conditions for opportunities to tell them. It is the job of the retrieval mechanism described here to find these opportunities in the midst of the student's interaction.

SPIEL's rule-based recognition method is an implementation of the general idea of retrieval as opportunity recognition, which is an alternative to the standard cue-based retrieval paradigm. There is nothing in SPIEL's retrieval that corresponds to either the cue formulation step or the memory search step found in cue-based retrieval. SPIEL has more in common with systems for opportunistic planning and acting (such as RUNNER; Hammond, 1989b) than with information retrieval systems or most case retrievers. This section addressed some of the important issues found in any opportunistic system. Most important is the issue of matching: how an abstractly characterized opportunity can be compared against a specific situation to determine if an opportunity exists. In SPIEL, this is accomplished, for the most part, at storage time by using elaboration knowledge to create concrete descriptions of each opportunity that can be directly matched against the simulation. An opportunistic system must also be capable of looking for many opportunities at once. SPIEL's rule-generation and optimization mechanisms create a network of rules in which multiple storytelling opportunities share in the accumulation of evidence.

CONCLUSION

SPIEL's first-person stories attempt to give students a second-hand version of actual experiences in the social world. Not only do students hear about events from a participant's perspective, but the personal values and beliefs of experts, and by extension, the community of expertise inevitably shows up in stories (Orr, 1986). Stories that are first-hand reports of actual events communicate experience in a case based form, but allow it to be filtered and distilled by the expert's perspective.

The goal of every case based teacher is to capitalize on students' natural case based learning. This can be done by giving students rich experiences they will remember. Or it can be done by describing, in a rich manner, the experiences of others. It is important to guard against the use of "cases" that are really descriptions of general principles or methods, unless such descriptions can be supported by detailed examples, as GuSS' analyzer does using reenactments. Impoverished examples lead to impoverished indexing and diminished chances for learning.

Because case based teaching systems attempt to help students acquire the case library they need as the basis for case based reasoning, such systems should be a good test of the case based reasoning model. If teaching students cases helps them build up their expertise in a domain, then both the teaching method and the reasoning model can be confirmed. The experience with YELLO has shown that students certainly respond to SPIEL's first-person stories and consider them a valuable part of the interaction.

However, there are pitfalls in trying to assess today's case based teaching systems, SPIEL included. The most important feature of a case based teacher is not merely that it presents cases, but that those cases are integrated with a compelling instructional environment and presented at just the right times. It is also important that a tutor's presentation strategies correctly estimate students' interest, so that the cases it presents are perceived as relevant. Finally, the tutor must help the students understand the relevance of retrieved cases through appropriate bridging comments. It is difficult to evaluate the value of a case based teaching system without a greater understanding of the issues of learning environments, relevance assessment, and case explanation. These are the major topics along which research in case based teaching must continue.

APPENDIX A: REPRESENTING STORYTELLING STRATEGIES

SPIEL's storytelling strategies are defined in a simple declarative language. This appendix describes the general form of a strategy definition and the set of operations allowed in the language. It also shows the representation of SPIEL's 13 strategies.

The Strategy Definition

The basic structure of a storytelling strategy is as follows:

```
(defStrat name description
      :filter filter_conditions
      :recognition recognition_condition_constructors
      :headline headline_template
```

```
:bridge bridge_template
:coda coda_template
:vars template_variable_bindings)
```

Here is the *Demonstrate risks* storytelling strategy expressed in this form:

```
(defStrat DRK
    "Tell a story about a negative result of a particular
course of action when the student has just executed a similar
course of action but had success."
    :filter
    (and (:actual-result m-negative-result)
         (:agent m-student-role))
    :recognition
    ((:soc-setting :gen)
     (:phys-setting :gen)
     (:actual-theme :manif)
     (:actual-goal :manif)
     (:actual-plan :manif)
     (:actual-result :result-opp :manif))
    :headline "A story showing the risks of your approach."
    :bridge "You <plan>. Nothing bad happened but here is a
story in which doing that led to problems:"
    :coda "Nothing bad happened to you as a result of <plan>,
but sometimes <bad-result>."
    :vars ((plan :store :actual-plan)
           (bad-result :store :actual-result)))
```

The mechanism of the strategy lies in the first two parts after the description: the filter conditions, instructions for how to test an index to see if it is compatible with the strategy; and the recognition condition constructors, instructions for how to manipulate an index to arrive at a recognition condition description.

The basic operation in the filter conditions is comparison. To represent comparison, the name of a slot is paired with the name of an MOP. The condition is considered met if the filler of the slot in the index satisfies the condition of the MOP. For example, (:actual-result m-negative-result) would be satisfied by any index in which the actual column contained a result that was some kind of negative result.[18] These tests can be combined using the logical operators *and, or,* and *not.*

One special filtering predicate is required by the strategies that explain the behavior of others. The *in-student-stereotype?* predicate is used to test whether MOPs correspond to the static student stereotype. Only stories

---

[18]For the definition for the satisfied predicate, see Riesbeck and Schank (1989).

that deviate from what the student is expected to know are told using these strategies. For example, in the *Explain other's plan* strategy, the following test is performed: *(in-student-stereotype? :agent :actual-goal :actual-plan)*. The predicate tests whether the stereotype students are likely to associate with characters of type *agent* includes the actual goal and actual plan from the index. The recognition condition constructors are associations between slots and operations. To generate recognition conditions for an index, the strategy extracts the value from each slot and performs the associated operations. An example is the recognition section from the *Warn about optimism* strategy:

```
((:soc-setting :gen)
 (:phys-setting :gen :prep)
 (:anomaly :search :belief :anomaly-manif))).
```

This declaration calls on SPIEL to take three steps to create the recognition conditions: (a) It extracts the values from the social setting slot and performs generalization, eliminating elements without an explanatory connection to the index. (b) For the physical setting slot, a similar generalization is performed, followed by inference to find the setting in which the student might prepare for action such as that found in the story. (c) Then the anomaly is examined, and anomaly derivation search is performed to find the most salient anomaly to be recognized. Once the salient anomaly is located, it is converted into a belief to be recognized: The student hopes for one thing as opposed to another. Then manifestation knowledge is applied to find observable indicators of that belief.

Inference Types

There are six types of inference performed in the service of creating RCDs. They are shown in Table 3.5. Opposite finding and manifestation inference each contain several subtypes. Opposite finding computation is different for results and plans discussed earlier. The computation of an opposite result is a simple application of opposite links from one type of goal impact to another, but finding the aspect of the outcome where the difference between columns lies may involve some search. This distinguishes this operation from the computation of opposite plans.

Under manifestation, there are four subtypes. Finding manifestations of anomalous beliefs requires identifying evidence for the anomalous belief and finding evidence against the actual contrasting belief (restrictions), so anomalies use a special version of the manifestation inference. For *Reinforce plan*, the creation of recognition conditions must include the stipulation that a plan has not already failed, to prevent the strategy from stealing storytelling opportunities from the *Demonstrate opportunities*

TABLE 3.5
Inference Types and Labels in Storytelling Strategy Definitions

Inference Type	Label	Description
Generalization	:gen	Generalization of setting.
Manifestation	:manif	Identification of observable manifestations
	:anomaly-manif	Identifying manifestations of an anomalous belief.
	:reinforce-manif	Finding the manifestations of a plan for the purposes of reinforcement.
	:warn-manif	Find the manifestations of a plan for the purposes of warning.
Opposite	:result-opp	Computing an opposite result.
	:plan-opp	Computing an opposite plan.
Anomaly search	:search	Searches for a salient anomaly.
Preparatory setting	:prep	Finding the setting in which preparation occurs.
Belief conversion	:belief	Turning an anomaly into a corresponding belief.
Remote indication	:remote	Finding indicators that show an outcome that would normally occur in one context will actually occur in some other context.

strategy. Therefore, the manifestation of a plan for the purposes of reinforcing its use includes the test for the plan's failure conditions, something that does not appear in ordinary reasoning about manifestations. A similar issue arises for the *Warn about plan* strategy, so there is also a special type of manifestation computation for the purposes of warning.

Natural Language Templates

Also associated with each strategy is a set of natural language templates for the headline, bridge, and coda, the three texts that explain each reminding to the student. The templates are English language texts with embedded variables that are replaced by short phrases to build complete explanations. The last piece of the strategy definition is a set of variable assignments that specify what values to use to create the texts to replace the variables in the templates.

Some variables will have their values known at storage time (such as the plan that the recognition conditions attempt to identify the student using). Others will only be known at retrieval time when the student takes action (such as the person to whom the student asks a certain question). In the variable assignments, each variable is associated with a descriptor indicating when that piece of the template can be filled (storage or retrieval time) and where in the index the corresponding MOP can be found. For retrieval time values, the MOP in the index is used to match against variables that are created at rule-generation time, to determine which variable has the correct value.

In *Demonstrate alternative plan*, the variable assignment also makes use of the opposite finding inference mechanism. The reason is that the bridge must refer to the plan that SPIEL tries to recognize the student following, such as the "cursory information-gathering" plan in the "Long-term goals" example shown earlier. This plan is the result of applying the opposite finding algorithm to the actual plan in the index, so the bridge must perform the same inference to incorporate it. The variable assignment uses a syntax similar to what is used in the recognition condition constructor: *(plan :store :actual-plan :opp)*. It calls on SPIEL to extract the actual plan at storage time, and also perform the opposite inference before creating natural language text to explain the storytelling opportunity.

Alternative-Finding Strategies

Demonstrate risks

```
(defStrat DRK
     "Tell a story about a negative result of a particular course
of action when the student has just executed a similar course of
action but had success."
     :filter
     (and (:actual-result m-negative-result)
     (:agent m-student-role))
     :recognition
     ((:soc-setting :gen)
     (:phys-setting :gen)
     (:actual-theme :manif)
     (:actual-goal :manif)
     (:actual-plan :manif)
     (:actual-result :result-opp :manif))
     :headline "A story showing the risks of your approach."
     :bridge "You <plan>. Nothing bad happened but here is a story
in which doing that led to problems:"
     :coda "Nothing bad happened to you as a result of <plan>,
but sometimes <bad-result>."
     :vars ((plan :store :actual-plan)
          (bad-result :store :actual-result))))
```

Demonstrate opportunities

```
(defStrat DOP
     "Tell a story about a positive result of a particular course
```

of action when the student has just executed a similar course of action but had a poor result."
```
    :filter
    (and (:actual-result m-positive-result)
         (:agent m-student-role))
    :recognition
    (((:soc-setting :gen)
     (:phys-setting :gen)
     (:actual-theme :manif)
     (:actual-goal :manif)
     (:actual-plan :manif)
     (:actual-result :result-opp :manif))
```
:headline "A story that shows an opportunity that didn't arise here."
:bridge "You <plan>. It didn't work well, but here is a story in which that strategy worked:"
:coda "You didn't have a good result from <plan>, but sometimes <good-result>."
```
    :vars ((plan :store :actual-plan)
           (good-result :store :actual-result)))
```

Demonstrate alternative plan

```
(defStrat DAP
```
"Tell a story about a successful plan to achieve a particular goal when the student has executed a different plan and failed to achieve the goal."
```
    :filter
    (and (:actual-result m-positive-result)
         (:agent m-student-role))
    :recognition
    (((:soc-setting :gen)
     (:phys-setting :gen)
     (:actual-theme :manif)
     (:actual-goal :manif)
     (:actual-plan :plan-opp :manif)
     (:actual-result :result-opp :manif))
```
:headline "A story about a different approach you might try"
:bridge "You <plan> without much success. Here is a story about a similar situation in which <gen-actor> used a different method and was successful."
:coda "You <plan>. It didn't work well. In the future, you might consider <story-plan>."
```
    :vars ((plan :store :actual-plan :opp)
           (story-plan :store :actual-plan)
           (gen-actor :store :agent)))
```

Critiquing Strategies

Warn about optimism, student focused

```
(defStrat WOP1
    "Tell a story about a desire that a salesperson had about
their own actions which was not realized when the student ap-
pears have a similar desire."
    :filter
    (and (:view-result m-positive-result)
         (not (:actual-result m-positive-result))
         (:agent m-student-role)
         (:viewer m-student-role)
         (:perspective m-wanted)
    :recognition
    ((:soc-setting :gen)
     (:phys-setting :gen :prep)
     (:anomaly :search :belief :anomaly-manif))
    :headline "A warning about something you just did"
    :bridge "If you are hoping that you <desired>, you may be
disappointed. Here is a story in which <actor> had a similar hope
that was not realized:"
    :coda "The hope that you <desired> may be unrealistic."
    :vars ((actor :store :agent)
           (desired :store :anomaly))))
```

Warn about optimism, other focused

```
(defStrat WOP2
    "Tell a story about a desire that a salesperson had about
someone else which was not realized when the student appears have
a similar desire."
    :filter
    (and (:view-side+ m-positive-result)
         (not (:actual-side+ m-negative-result))
         (:viewer m-student-role)
         (not (:agent m-student-role))
         (:perspective m-wanted))
    :recognition
    ((:soc-setting :gen)
     (:phys-setting :gen :prep)
     (:anomaly :search :belief :anomaly-manif))
    :headline "A warning about something you just did"
    :bridge "If you are hoping that <actor> <desired>, you may
be disappointed. Here is a story in which <viewer> had a similar
hope that was not realized:"
    :coda "The hope that <gen-actor> <desired> may be unrealis-
tic."
```

```
    :vars ((actor :retrieve :agent)
       (gen-actor :store :agent)
       (viewer :store :viewer)
       (desired :store :anomaly)))
```

Warn about pessimism, student focused

```
(defStrat WPS1
    "Tell a story about a fear that was not realized when the
student appears to have the same fear about themselves."
    :filter
    (and (:view-result m-positive-result)
         (not (:actual-result m-negative-result))
         (:agent m-student-role)
         (:viewer m-student-role)
         (:perspective m-feared))
    :recognition
    ((:soc-setting :gen)
     (:phys-setting :gen :prep)
     (:anomaly :search :belief :anomaly-manif))
    :headline "A hint about something you just did"
  :bridge "If you fear that you <fear>, you may be surprised.
Here is a story in which <actor> had similar fears that were not
realized:"
    :coda "A fear that you <fear> may be unrealistic."
    :vars ((actor :store :agent)
       (fear :store :anomaly)))
```

Warn about pessimism, other focused

```
(defStrat WPS2
    "Tell a story about a fear that was not realized when the
student appears to have the same fear about someone else."
    :filter
    (and (:view-side- m-negative-result)
         (not (:actual-side- m-negative-result))
         (:viewer m-student-role)
         (not (:agent m-student-role))
         (:perspective m-feared))
    :recognition
    ((:soc-setting :gen)
     (:phys-setting :gen :prep)
     (:anomaly :search :belief :anomaly-manif))
    :headline "A hint about something you just did"
    :bridge "If you fear that <actor> <fear>, you may be sur-
prised. Here is a story in which <viewer> had similar fears that
were not realized:"
```

```
:coda "A fear that <gen-actor> <fear> may be unrealistic."
:vars ((actor :retrieve :agent)
       (gen-actor :store :agent)
       (viewer :store :viewer)
       (fear :store :anomaly)))
```

Warn about assumption, student focused

```
(defStrat WAS1
    "Tell a story about an assumption that someone made which
did not hold when the student appears to have a similar assump-
tion about themselves."
    :filter
    (and (:agent m-student-role)
         (:viewer m-student-role)
         (or (:perspective m-assumed)
             (:perspective m-standard)))
    :recognition
    (((:soc-setting :gen)
      (:phys-setting :gen :prep)
      (:anomaly :search :belief :anomaly-manif))
    :headline "A warning about something you just did"
    :bridge "If you assume that you <assumption>, you may be
surprised. Here is a story in which <actor> had a similar as-
sumption that did not hold:"
    :coda "An assumption that you <assumption> may be unrealis-
tic."
    :vars (actor :store :agent)
          (assumption :store :anomaly)))
```

Warn about assumption, other focused

```
(defStrat WAS2
    "Tell a story about an assumption that someone made which
did not hold when the student appears to have a similar assump-
tion about someone else."
    :filter
    (and (:viewer m-student-role)
         (not (:agent m-student-role))
         (or (:perspective m-assumed)
             (:perspective m-standard)))
    :recognition
    (((:soc-setting :gen)
      (:phys-setting :gen :prep)
      (:anomaly :search :belief :anomaly-manif))
    :headline "A warning about something you just did"
```

```
     :bridge "If you assume that <actor> <assumption>, you may
be surprised. Here is a story in which <viewer> had a similar
assumption that did not hold:"
     :coda "An assumption that <gen-actor> <assumption> may be
unrealistic."
     :vars ((actor :retrieve :agent)
            (gen-actor :store :agent)
            (viewer :store :viewer)
            (assumption :store :anomaly)))
```

Projection Strategies

Reinforce plan

```
(defStrat RIP
     "Tell a story about a successful plan to achieve a particu-
lar goal when the student has just started to execute a similar
plan."
     :filter
     (and (:actual-result m-positive-result)
          (:agent m-student-role))
     :recognition
     ((:soc-setting :gen)
      (:phys-setting :gen)
      (:actual-theme :manif)
      (:actual-goal :manif)
      (:actual-plan :reinforce-manif)
      (:actual-result :remote))
     :headline "A success story about a situation like yours."
     :bridge "<plan> is sometimes important for <goal>. Here is
a story about how a <actor> succeeded using a similar approach."
     :coda "Sometimes <plan> is the right thing to do. Keep
working at it."
     :vars ((actor :store :agent)
            (plan :store :actual-plan)
            (goal :store :actual-goal)))
```

Warn about plan

```
(defStrat WAP
     "Tell a story about an unsuccessful plan when the student
has begun executing a similar plan."
     :filter
     (and (:actual-result m-negative-result)
          (:agent m-student-role))
     :recognition
```

```
((:soc-setting :gen)
 (:phys-setting :gen)
 (:actual-theme :manif)
 (:actual-goal :manif)
 (:actual-plan :warn-manif)
 (:actual-result :remote))
:headline "A story about a failure in a situation similar
to yours."
:bridge "You <plan>. Here is a story in which doing that
led to problems."
:coda "You <plan>. That might not be a good idea."
:vars ((plan :store :actual-plan)))
```

Other-Directed Strategies

Explain other's plan

```
(defStrat XOP
     "Tell a story about a plan that the student might not know
about when the student has just observed some agent execute a
similar plan."
     :filter
     (and (not (:agent m-student-role))
               (not
               (in-student-stereotype? :agent :actual-goal :ac-
tual-plan)))
     :recognition
     ((:soc-setting :gen)
      (:phys-setting :gen)
      (:actual-theme :manif)
      (:actual-goal :manif)
      (:actual-plan :w-manif))
     :headline "Do you understand what <actor> is doing?"
     :bridge "Sometimes <gen-actor> will <plan>. Here is a story
about a time when that took place."
     :coda "<actor> may be trying <goal> by <plan>. If you don't
know, you should try to find out."
     :vars ((actor :retrieve :agent)
              (gen-actor :store :agent)
              (plan :store :actual-plan)
              (goal :store :actual-goal)))
```

Explain other's perspective

```
(defStrat XOV
     "Tell a story about an expectation that the student might
not understand when the student has just observed some agent act
```

on the basis of a similar expectation."
```
    :filter
    (and (not (:agent m-student-role))
          (not (in-student-stereotype? :agent :anomaly)))
    :recognition
    ((:soc-setting :gen)
     (:phys-setting :gen)
     (:anomaly :search :belief :anomaly-manif))
    :headline "Do you understand <viewer>'s perspective in
```
this situation?"
```
    :bridge "Sometimes <gen-viewer> will <persp> that <actor>
```
<expectation>. Here is a story about a time when that took place."
```
    :coda "<viewer> may <persp> that <actor> <expectation>. If
```
you don't know, you should try to find out."
```
    :vars ((viewer :retrieve :viewer)
            (gen-viewer :store :viewer)
            (actor :retrieval :actor)
            (expectation :store :anomaly)))
```

REFERENCES

Anderson, J. R. (1988). The expert module. In M. C. Polson & J. J. Richardson (Eds.), *Foundations of intelligent tutoring systems* (pp. 21–53). Hillsdale, NJ: Lawrence Erlbaum Associates.

Anderson, J. R., Boyle, C. F., & Yost, G. (1985). The geometry tutor. In *Proceedings of the ninth international joint conference on Artificial Intelligence* (pp. 1–7). Los Altos, CA: Kaufmann.

Ashley, K. D. (1990). *Modeling legal argument: Reasoning with cases and hypotheticals.* Cambridge, MA: MIT Press.

Ashley, K., & Rissland, E. (1987). Compare and contrast, A test of expertise. In *Proceedings of sixth national conference on Artificial Intelligence* (pp. 273–278). Menlo Park, CA: AAAI Press.

Birnbaum, L. A. (1986). *Integrated processing in planning and understanding.* Unpublished doctoral dissertation, Yale University. Technical Report 489.

Blevis, E., & Kass, A. M. (1991). Teaching by means of social simulation. In L. Birnbaum (Ed.), *International conference on the learning sciences: Proceedings of the 1991 conference* (pp. 45–51). Charlottesville, VA: AACE.

Brownston, L., Farrell, R., Kant, E., & Martin, N. (1985). *Programming expert systems in OPS5.* Reading, MA: Addison-Wesley.

Bruner, J. (1986). *Actual minds, possible worlds.* Cambridge, MA: Harvard University Press.

Burke, R. (1993). *Representation, storage and retrieval of tutorial stories in a social simulation.* Unpublished doctoral dissertation, Northwestern University. Issued as Technical Report #50, Institute for the Learning Sciences.

Burton, R. R. (1982). Diagnosing bugs in a simple procedural skill. In D. Sleeman & J. S. Brown (Eds.), *Intelligent tutoring systems* (pp. 157–183). New York: Academic Press.

Carbonell, J. G. (1983). Learning by analogy: Formulating and generalizing plans from past experience. In R. S. Michalski, J. G. Carbonell, & T. M. Mitchell (Eds.), *Machine learning: An artificial intelligence approach* (pp. 331–363). Los Altos, CA: Kaufmann.

Clancey, W. J. (1982). Tutoring rules for guiding a case method dialogue. In D. Sleeman & J. S. Brown (Eds.), *Intelligent tutoring systems* (pp. 201–225). New York: Academic Press.

Collins, A., Brown, J. S., & Newman, S. E. (1989). Cognitive apprenticeship: Teaching the crafts of reading, writing, and mathematics. In L. B. Resnick (Ed.), *Knowing, learning, and instruction: Essays in honor of Robert Glaser* (pp. 353–394). Hillsdale, NJ: Lawrence Erlbaum Associates.

Craig, R. L., & Kelly, L. (Ed.). (1990). *Sales training handbook: A guide to developing sales performance.* Englewood Cliffs, NJ: Prentice-Hall.

Dimitrova, N., & Golshani, F. (1994). Rx for semantic video database retrieval. In *ACM Multimedia* (pp. 219–226). San Francisco: ACM Press.

Domeshek, E. A. (1992). *Do the right thing: A component theory for indexing stories as social advice.* Unpublished doctoral dissertation, Yale University. Issued as Technical Report #26, Institute for the Learning Sciences, Northwestern University.

Edelson, D. C. (1993). *Learning from stories: Indexing, reminding and questioning in a case-based teaching system.* Unpublished doctoral dissertation, Northwestern University. Issued as Technical Report #43, Institute for the Learning Sciences, Northwestern University.

Elsom-Cook, M. (Ed.). (1990). *Guided discovery tutoring.* London: Chapman.

Ferguson, W., Bareiss, R., Birnbaum, L., & Osgood, R. (1992). *ASK systems: An approach to the realization of story-based teachers* (Tech. Rep. No. 22). Evanston, IL: Institute for Learning Sciences, Northwestern University Press.

Funke, J. (1991). Solving complex problems: Exploration and control of complex systems. In R. J. Sternberg & P. A. Frensch (Eds.), *Complex problem solving: Principles and mechanisms* (pp. 185–222). Hillsdale, NJ: Lawrence Erlbaum Associates.

Goldstein, I. P. (1982). The genetic graph: A representation for the evolution of procedural knowledge. In D. Sleeman & J. S. Brown (Eds.), *Intelligent tutoring systems* (pp. 51–77). New York: Academic Press.

Hammond, K. J. (1989a). *Case-based planning: Viewing planning as a memory task.* New York: Academic Press.

Hammond, K. J. (1989b). Opportunistic memory. In *Proceedings of the eleventh international joint conference on Artificial Intelligence* (pp. 504–510). Menlo Park, CA: AAAI Press.

Hampapur, A., Jain, R., & Weymouth, T. (1994). Digital video segmentation. In *ACM Multimedia* (pp. 357–364). San Francisco: ACM Press.

Hunter, K. M. (1991). *Doctors' stories: The narrative structure of medical knowledge.* Princeton, NJ: Princeton University Press.

Hunter, L. (1989). *Knowledge acquisition planning: Gaining expertise through experience.* Unpublished doctoral dissertation, Yale University. Technical Report 678.

Kass, A. M., & Blevis, E. (1991, May). *Learning through experience: An intelligent learning-by-doing environment for business consultants.* Paper presented at the Intelligent Computer-Aided Training Conference, Houston, TX.

Kass, A. M., Burke, R., Blevis, E., & Williamson, M. (1992). *The GuSS project: Integrating instruction and practice through guided social simulation* (Tech. Rep. No. 34). Evanston, IL: Institute for Learning Sciences, Northwestern University Press.

Kass, A. M., Burke, R., Blevis, E., & Williamson, M. (1993/1994). Constructing learning environments for complex social skills. *Journal of the Learning Sciences, 3*(4), 387–427.

Kass, A. M., Leake, D. B., & Owens, C. C. (1986). SWALE: A program that explains. In Roger C. Schank (Ed.), *Explanation patterns: Understanding mechanically and creatively* (pp. 232–254). Hillsdale, NJ: Lawrence Erlbaum Associates.

Klahr, D., Dunbar, K., & Fay, A. L. (1990). Designing good experiments to test bad hypotheses. In J. Shrager & P. Langley (Eds.), *Computational models of scientific discovery* (pp. 355–402). Palo Alto, CA: Kaufmann.

Kolodner, J. L. (1984). *Retrieval and organizational strategies in conceptual memory*. Hillsdale, NJ: Lawrence Erlbaum Associates.

Kolodner, J. L. (1989). Judging which is the "best" case for a case-based reasoner. In *Proceedings: Case-based reasoning workshop (DARPA)* (pp. 77–81). San Mateo, CA: Kaufmann.

Kolodner, J. L. (1993). *Case-based reasoning*. San Mateo, CA: Kaufmann.

Kolodner, J. L., & Wills, L. M. (1993). Paying attention to the right thing: Issues of focus in case-based creative design. In D. Leake (Ed.), *AAAI workshop on case-based reasoning* (pp. 19–25). Menlo Park, CA: AAAI Press.

Lave, J., & Wenger, E. (1991). *Situated learning: Legitimate peripheral participation*. New York: Cambridge University Press.

Lesgold, A., & Lajoie, S. (1991). Complex problem solving in electronics. In R. J. Sternberg & P. A. Frensch (Eds.), *Complex problem solving: Principles and mechanisms* (pp. 287–316). Hillsdale, NJ: Lawrence Erlbaum Associates.

Lesgold, A., Lajoie, S., Bunzo, M., & Eggan, G. (1992). SHERLOCK: A coached practice environment for an electronics troubleshooting job. In J. H. Larkin & R. W. Chabay (Eds.), *Computer-assisted instruction and intelligent tutoring systems* (pp. 201–238). Hillsdale, NJ: Lawrence Erlbaum Associates.

Martin, C. E. (1991). *Direct memory access parsing*. Unpublished doctoral dissertation, Yale University.

Martin, C. E., & Riesbeck, C. K. (1986). Uniform parsing and inferencing for learning. In *Proceedings of the fifth national conference on Artificial Intelligence* (pp. 257–261). Menlo Park, CA: AAAI Press.

McDougal, T., Hammond, K., & Seifert, C. (1991). A functional perspective on reminding. In *Proceedings of the thirteenth annual conference of the Cognitive Science Society* (pp. 510–515). Hillsdale, NJ: Lawrence Erlbaum Associates.

Orr, J. (1986). Narratives at work: Story telling as cooperative diagnostic activity. In *Proceedings of the conference on computer-supported cooperative work* (pp. 62–72). New York: ACM Press.

Osgood, R., & Bareiss, R. (1993). Index generation in the construction of large-scale conversation hypermedia systems. In *AAAI symposium on case-based reasoning and information retrieval* (pp. 78–89). Stanford, CA: AAAI Press.

Owens, C. C. (1990). *Indexing and retrieving abstract planning knowledge*. Unpublished doctoral dissertation, Yale University.

Papert, S. (1980). *Mindstorms: Children, computers and powerful ideas*. New York: Basic Books.

Polanyi, L. (1985). *Telling the American story: A structural and cultural analysis of conversational storytelling*. New York: Ablex.

Polson, M. C., & Richardson, J. J. (Eds.). (1988). *Foundations of intelligent tutoring systems*. Hillsdale, NJ: Lawrence Erlbaum Associates.

Porter, B. C., Bareiss, R., & Holte, R. C. (1990). Concept learning and heuristic classification in weak-theory domains. *Artificial Intelligence, 45*, 229–263.

Reiser, B. V., Anderson, J. R., & Farrell, R. G. (1985). Dynamic student modeling in an intelligent tutor for lisp programming. In *Proceedings of the ninth international joint conference on Artificial Intelligence* (pp. 8–14). Los Altos, CA: Kaufmann.

Riesbeck, C. K., & Schank, R. C. (1989). *Inside case-based reasoning*. Hillsdale, NJ: Lawrence Erlbaum Associates.

Schank, R. C. (1982). *Dynamic memory: A theory of learning in computers and people*. New York: Cambridge University Press.

Schank, R. C. (1986). *Explanation patterns: Understanding mechanically and creatively*. Hillsdale, NJ: Lawrence Erlbaum Associates.

Schank, R. C. (1990a). *Teaching architectures* (Tech. Rep. No. 3). Evanston, IL: Northwestern University Press.

Schank, R. C. (1990b). *Tell me a story: A new look at real and artificial memory*. New York: Scribner's.

Schank, R. C., & Abelson, R. (1977). *Scripts, plans, goals and understanding*. Hillsdale, NJ: Lawrence Erlbaum Associates.

Schank, R. C., & Jona, M. Y. (1991). Empowering the student: New perspectives on the design of teaching systems. *Journal of the Learning Sciences, 1*(1), 7–35.

Schank, R. C., Osgood, R., Brand, M., Burke, R., Domeshek, E., Edelson, D., Ferguson, W., Freed, M., Jona, M., Krulwich, B., Ohmaye, E., & Pryor, L. (1990). *A content theory of memory indexing* (Tech. Rep. No. 2). Evanston, IL: Institute for Learning Sciences, Northwestern University Press.

Schauble, L., Glaser, R., Raghavan, K., & Reiner, M. (1991). Causal models and experimentation strategies in scientific reasoning. *Journal of the Learning Sciences, 1*(2), 201–238.

Shafto, E., Bareiss, R., & Birnbaum, L. (1992). A memory architecture for case-based argumentation. In *Fourteenth annual conference of the Cognitive Science Society* (pp. 307–312). Hillsdale, NJ: Lawrence Erlbaum Associates.

Simoudis, E. (1992). Using case-based retrieval for customer technical support. *IEEE Expert, 7*(5), 7–13.

Sleeman, D., & Brown, J. S. (Eds.). (1982). *Intelligent tutoring systems*. New York: Academic Press.

Stevens, S. M. (1989). Intelligent interactive video simulation of a code inspection. *Communications of the ACM, 32*(7), 832–843.

vanLehn, K. (1988). Student modeling. In M. C. Polson & J. J. Richardson (Eds.), *Foundations of intelligent tutoring systems* (pp. 55–78). Hillsdale, NJ: Lawrence Erlbaum Associates.

Wilensky, R. (1983). *Planning and understanding*. Reading, MA: Addison-Wesley.

Williams, S. M. (1991). Putting case-based instruction into context: Examples from legal, business, and medical education. *Journal of the Learning Sciences, 2*(4), 367–427.

Witherell, C., & Noddings, N. (Eds.). (1991). *Stories lives tell: Narrative and dialogue in education*. New York: Teachers College Press.

4

Representing and Applying Teaching Strategies in Computer-Based Learning-by-Doing Tutors

Menachem Y. Jona
The Institute for the Learning Sciences
Northwestern University

INTRODUCTION

A Practical Problem

A serious problem exists in the current methodology of developing educational software. Each application is developed independently, and teaching knowledge is hard-coded into individual applications. There is little re-use of teaching code or teaching knowledge between applications because we lack a standard language for representing the knowledge, a standard interface to allow applications to access the knowledge, and a set of tools to allow designers to manipulate the knowledge.

Hard-coding teaching knowledge into educational applications complicates the re-use of that knowledge in subsequent systems. When tutoring systems are not designed in a way that makes it easy to change the control structure that implements teaching decisions, changing the style of teaching involves digging into the code of the system, a difficult undertaking even for skilled programmers (Clancey, 1982; Clancey & Joerger, 1988). Doing things this way also excludes professional teachers and other subject matter experts from the development of educational software. In describing the state of building intelligent tutoring systems (ITSs), Clancey and Joerger (1988) lamented that, ". . . the reality today is that the endeavor is one that only experienced programmers (or experts trained to be programmers) can accomplish. Indeed, research of the past decade has only further increased our standards of knowledge representation desirable for teaching, while the tools for constructing such programs lag far behind or are not generally available."

To solve these problems, we must look more closely at what one needs to know to be a good teacher. Teachers need to know about the subject matter to be taught, but they also need to know a lot about teaching: What techniques work well in which situations? What tell-tale signs of student misunderstandings should be watched for? What different types of students are there, and how should each type of student be helped when misunderstandings and misconceptions arise? Some of this teaching knowledge is specific to a particular subject matter, although much of it is fairly general and can be used independently of the subject matter being taught (Berliner, 1987; Calderhead, 1988; Collins & Stevens, 1982, 1983; Rosenshine & Stevens, 1986; Wilson, Shulman, & Richert, 1987). Teaching also requires both domain knowledge—knowledge about the material being taught—and teaching knowledge—strategies and techniques for helping students learn (Clark & Peterson, 1986; Wilson et al., 1987).

By identifying and codifying general teaching strategies, we may be able to address the methodological problems that prevent re-use of teaching knowledge in building educational software. Specifically, by creating a software tool that serves as a repository of teaching strategies and provides a means for incorporating these teaching strategies into educational applications, teaching strategies used in earlier programs can be re-used when building new programs that require similar teaching interventions. Thus, instead of having to encode both the domain and teaching knowledge for each new program, previously created teaching strategies could be obtained from the repository, and only the domain knowledge would have to be represented and incorporated into the system.

Learning-by-Doing Tutors

This chapter focuses on a broad class of teaching called *learning-by-doing tutors* (LBD tutors). LBD tutors help a student learn a new skill by looking over the student's shoulder while he or she practices that skill, monitoring the student's progress, and offering guidance and advice when needed. To allow the student to go about practicing the skill to be learned, an environment must first be created that allows the student to actively engage in that skill in an authentic context. Finding a way to allow a student to practice the skill to be learned can be difficult. Sometimes the skill is too expensive or dangerous to actually let a student practice it (e.g., flying a 747); other times it is simply impractical (e.g., running a Fortune 500 company). Computer simulations can provide a way around these difficulties by creating a realistic environment for a student to practice almost any skill, regardless of its real-world danger or expense. These qualities make the computer a particularly effective tool for creating LBD environments (Ohlsson, 1988).

Creating a realistic computer-based environment that allows the student to practice a skill, although beneficial, does not make an optimum learning environment. To maximize the educational value of an LBD system, a tutor must be provided that can monitor the student's progress and intervene when necessary to provide advice and guidance (Bloom, 1984; Collins, Brown, & Newman, 1989; Merrill, Reiser, Merrill, & Landes, 1993; Merrill, Reiser, Ranney, & Trafton, 1992). This was accomplished here with the development of the "Teaching Executive," used to create the tutoring component in LBD tutors.

Consider the following examples of two LBD tutors created with the Teaching Executive. The first system, BC Cashier, is designed to teach employees of a fast food restaurant how to operate the cash register.[1] In this system, the student plays the role of a cashier, and is presented with various customers' orders to ring up. The computer screen displays a realistic simulation of the actual cash register used in the store, and the student uses the mouse pointer to press the cash register buttons. In addition, there are various buttons on the screen that allow the student to talk to the customer and ask the tutor for help (e.g., "Why?", "Now what?"). As the student rings up a customer's order, the tutor monitors the student's actions. One common mistake that novice students make is that they do not recognize a particular item and, as a result, they ring up that item incorrectly. For example, the following interaction shows a student ringing up a large drink as a small one because he does not recognize the difference between the two sizes.

Student: Presses $1.19 DRINK key
Tutor [intervenes]: You don't need to ring up the large drink.
Student: Presses "Why?" button
Tutor: You don't need to ring up the large drink because it's not the right size.
Student: Presses "Now what?" button
Tutor: You need to void out the last item.
Student: Presses "How do I do that?" button
Tutor: To void out the last item, you need to press the VOID key twice. It is the key you see flashing on the register now.
[key flashes on screen]

This short interaction shows four different teaching strategies at work:

---

[1]Both the BC Cashier and BC Server systems were developed by Guralnick (1996).

- The *Point out that step taken is not part of task* strategy is activated in response to the student ringing up the wrong size drink.
- The *Explain why step not needed* strategy is used to provide the student with an explanation about why ringing up the large drink is not correct.
- A *Tell about next step* strategy is used to answer the student's "Now what?" question, and to describe the next step the student must perform.
- An *Explain actions required to perform step* strategy is triggered in response to the student asking how to go about voiding out the last item.

BC Server is a system designed to teach employees of the same fast food restaurant how to properly gather and package a customer's order. In this system, the student plays the role of the server, and is presented with a series of video clips depicting various customers coming up to the counter and placing orders. The computer screen displays a mock-up of the food items and containers available; the student uses the mouse to put the food items ordered by the customer in the proper containers. The task is tricky because of the wide range of food items on the menu, and because some items implicitly include other items as part of the order. As in the BC Cashier system, there are various buttons on the screen that allow the student to talk to the customer and ask the tutor for help.

In the following sample interaction, the student takes a customer's order, which includes a serving of chicken salad. Instead of the chicken salad, however, the student begins to fill a container with a pasta salad that looks similar to the chicken salad.

Student: [moves chicken and pasta salad to a container]
Tutor [intervenes]: You don't need to put chicken and pasta salad in the individual container now.
Student: Presses "Why?" button
Tutor: You don't need to put chicken and pasta salad in the individual container because the customer ordered chunky chicken salad, not chicken and pasta salad.
Student: Presses "Now what?" button
Tutor: You need to put the individual container in the trash.
Student: Presses "Why?" button
Tutor: You need to put the individual container in the trash because you put the wrong item in it.
Student: [moves individual container to trash]

Although this interaction deals with a different skill, it is quite similar to the previous one in terms of the kinds of teaching strategies being used:

- The *Point out that step taken is not part of task* strategy is activated in response to the student putting the wrong item in the container.
- The *Explain why step not needed* strategy is used to provide the student with an explanation about why packaging the chicken and pasta salad is not correct.
- A *Tell about next step* strategy is used to answer the student's "Now what?" question, and to describe the next step the student must perform.
- The *Explain why step needed* strategy is used to provide the student with an explanation about why throwing the container out is required.

As the prior descriptions indicate, the tutor in both systems employs teaching strategies that tell it how to recognize when the student makes a mistake in performing the appropriate procedure, and whether and how to intervene when that happens. In addition, the tutor has teaching strategies for responding to student questions like "Now what?", "How do I do that?", and "Why?" The two previous interactions illustrate an important point: The teaching strategies used in BC Server are nearly identical to those used in BC Cashier. This similarity suggests that many of the teaching strategies employed in one LBD tutor can be re-used in other similar LBD tutors and need not be created from scratch each time.

Challenges in Building a Computer-Based Tutor That Re-Uses Teaching Strategies

To take advantage of the re-usability of teaching strategies in building LBD tutors, three main challenges must be met. First, a standard language for representing teaching strategies is needed. If each LBD tutor used a different language for representing teaching strategies, sharing strategies would be prohibitively complicated. Second, once teaching strategies are codified and stored in a repository, a standard architecture must be created to allow LBD tutoring systems to access the teaching strategies in the repository and use them to implement tutoring interventions. Third, a set of authoring tools is needed that allows system designers to enter teaching strategies into the repository using the standard representation language. The Teaching Executive attempts to address each of these three challenges.

To create a standard language for representing teaching strategies, the Teaching Executive uses a data structure called a *pedagogical knowledge bundle* (PKB). A PKB bundles together the knowledge a tutor needs to recognize an opportunity to apply a particular teaching strategy, decide whether and how to intervene, and deliver the appropriate tutorial response. The PKB framework provides a consistent means to encode and store teaching strategies. In addition, the PKB structure allows teaching strategies to be efficiently retrieved and applied to create tutorial interventions. As part of the effort to create a standardized architecture to allow new tutoring systems to access the teaching strategies in a teaching strategy library and use them to implement tutoring interventions, the Teaching Executive was integrated with the MOPed authoring tool, a graphical authoring tool for creating task environments that allow a student to learn by doing. The Teaching Executive extends MOPed by facilitating the creation of a computer-based tutor that will look over the student's shoulder as he or she uses the task environment and offer guidance and assistance when required.

In building LBD tutors, the task environment and the tutoring are developed separately. The system designer uses MOPed to build the task environment, but does not include any teaching decisions. The designer then uses the "TE toolbox," a suite of graphical software tools provided by the Teaching Executive, to author teaching strategies that are appropriate for the subject matter being taught. Ideally, many or most of the required teaching strategies will already exist, having been previously created for use in other systems. These teaching strategies are stored in a separate teaching strategy library.

At run time—when the student sits down to use the LBD tutor—tutorial interventions are made by the Teaching Executive, as directed by the teaching strategies contained in the library. As the student uses the system, the Teaching Executive monitors the student's actions in the task environment, trying to detect opportunities for tutoring. It does this by attempting to retrieve a teaching strategy from its library that is relevant to the student's current situation. If a relevant teaching strategy is found, the teaching decisions encoded by that strategy are executed, and a tutorial intervention is generated. Figure 4.1 provides an overview of how the Teaching Executive and TE toolbox are used both at design time and run time.

An Architecture for LBD Tutors That Facilitates Re-Use

To create effective tutoring in a learning-by-doing environment, one first needs to analyze the kind of task the student is to perform so that the appropriate guidance and support can be provided by the tutor. The emphasis on the student's performance of a concrete skill or task in LBD tutors has implications for the kinds of tutoring required, as well as how LBD tutors are constructed. A computer-based LBD tutor consists of these basic layers: interface, task environment, and tutoring. The task environment layer consists of a simulation or other mechanisms that allow the student to actually engage in a task. The tutoring layer implements any

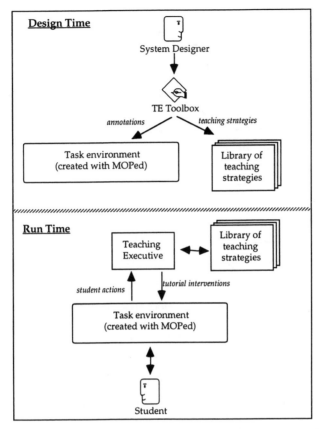

FIG. 4.1. Role of the Teaching Executive and TE toolbox in creating LBD tutors at design time and run time.

guidance the student is to receive while interacting with the task environment. The interface layer presents a graphical user interface of the task environment and means for displaying any tutorial guidance to the student. Figure 4.2 shows a schematic of the three layers of an LBD tutor and the communication pathways among the layers. As the student performs a task in the task environment (via the user interface), the tutoring layer monitors his or her actions and decides if any intervention is required.

The tutoring layer is composed of two components: a set of teaching strategies and a task model. The teaching strategies represent the tutor's pedagogical expertise. They describe the kinds of mistakes and misconceptions the tutor should look for, and the tutorial response that is appropriate in each case. The task model provides the tutor with a description of the student's task necessary for interpreting the student's actions correctly. The task model allows the tutor to determine which of its teaching strategies are relevant to the student's current situation.

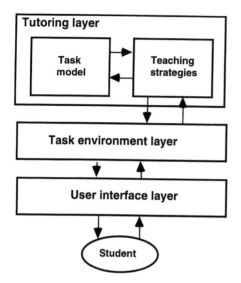

FIG. 4.2. Architecture of an LBD tutor.

Teaching strategies that are crafted specifically for a particular LBD tutor will usually be expressed in a language unique to that LBD tutor. This has the advantage of making it very straightforward for the tutor to recognize from the student's actions when a strategy should be applied and what response the tutor should give. However, because of the specificity with which they were written, these teaching strategies will be difficult to re-use in other LBD tutors without extensive translation or rewriting.

Another approach to writing teaching strategies is to express them at a generic level. This creates a set of teaching strategies that are useful across a wide range of LBD tutors, making the investment of creating the strategies pay off by being able to use the same strategies in numerous LBD tutors. Unfortunately, although this goal seems admirable in the abstract, it suffers from at least two serious problems. First, and most troubling, is the realization that different LBD tutors require the student to perform different types of tasks, and many of the tasks employed in LBD tutors have idiosyncrasies not shared with other tasks. Writing general teaching strategies that could recognize and respond to all the idiosyncratic mistakes a student could make across a wide range of tasks would be an extremely time-consuming and difficult endeavor. A tutor without the ability to recognize and respond to the entire range of mistakes or misconceptions a student could have does not promise to be a very effective tutor.

Even assuming that some set of teaching strategies could be written at a general level, another serious problem must still be faced in actually applying those strategies. Specifically, the tutor must be able to connect specific student actions (i.e., pressing buttons, using menus) to the more general descriptions of student mistakes contained in the teaching strategies. In essence, then, what these problems reveal is a three-way trade-off among the re-usability of teaching strategies across a number of LBD tutors, the ability to describe the range of possible student mistakes, and how difficult the strategies are for a tutor to apply in practice. The more general the language used to create teaching strategies, the greater the potential for being able to use them in a wide range of systems, but the harder it is to describe the entire range of student errors in that language and to apply the strategies at run time. Writing teaching strategies using specific language makes it easier to encode all of the student's potential mistakes, and makes applying the strategies much simpler. The downside is that adapting these specific strategies for use in other systems may require as much work as creating new teaching strategies from scratch.

How can we create teaching strategies that are re-usable across a range of systems and, at the same time, expressive enough to capture the kinds of errors a student is likely to make in a given task, and easy enough for a tutor to apply at run time? The solution lies in selecting the appropriate level of description at which to create the teaching strategies. Because LBD tutors are primarily concerned with the performance of a task by the student, teaching strategies should be written not at a level to handle individual tasks, nor at a level to handle all possible tasks, but at a level to handle a class of tasks with common characteristics.

The approach of creating different teaching strategies for different types of tasks is based on the recognition that tasks of the same type will, because of their structure, share similar kinds of mistakes and misconceptions; as such, they will require similar kinds of tutorial interventions. This means that it should be both possible and practical to enumerate the range of mistakes a student is likely to make while performing a given type of task, and craft teaching strategies to respond to those mistakes. It also means that teaching strategies created for one task will be re-usable in other tasks of the same type with little or no modification.

But just creating a set of teaching strategies for tasks of a given type is not enough to build the tutoring layer of an LBD tutor. For the tutor to interpret the student's actions as he or she performs a task, and for the tutor to have any hope of applying its teaching strategies, the tutor must have some knowledge of the task the student is trying to perform. This knowledge is usually encoded in the form of a task model (i.e., a computer representation of the task the student is to perform).

Creating a model of the task the student is to perform in an LBD tutor serves several important purposes. First, it allows a tutor to recognize the actions taken by the student, and to interpret those actions in the context of the overall task. This gives the tutor a better chance to determine what the student is doing, and, consequently, to apply the appropriate teaching strategies. Second, a task model provides a language for describing the student's task at a level that is abstracted away from interface-level descriptions (e.g., mouse clicks, menu choices). By using a task-level language to describe the conditions that warrant tutorial intervention, it becomes possible to create teaching strategies that can be used for any task that shares the same task model. However, teaching strategies that use interface-level descriptions of student actions will have to be rewritten each time the interface changes or a new system is built, even if the task remains essentially the same. Third, creating a task model explicitly defines which student actions are pedagogically relevant and which actions can be safely ignored by the tutor. This information is useful because it delimits the kinds of communication needed between the task environment layer and the tutoring layer of an LBD tutor. Establishing adequate communication channels between these two layers is critical in allowing the tutor to monitor the student's actions so that appropriate guidance can be given when necessary. In particular, defining the set of pedagogically relevant task environment events can be used to help a system designer create the necessary communicative links between the task environment and tutoring layers. This issue is examined in greater depth later. Fourth, a task model allows a tutor to deliver concrete, task-specific guidance relevant to the student's current situation. Without being able to refer to a detailed model of the student's task, a tutor would know very little about the specifics of what the student was doing, and would thus be limited to providing only general advice about how to proceed.

Analyzing Learning-by-Doing Tasks

Now that we have seen the importance of creating task models and teaching strategies for similar types of tasks, the next logical question to consider is: What types of tasks are used in LBD tutors? Answering this question is important because it will give an idea of the different sets of teaching strategies and accompanying task models that need to be created. Because the focus in LBD tutors is on the student's performance of task, the kind of tutoring that is needed is determined largely by what the student's task is like. To create effective tutoring in a learning-by-doing environment, one first needs to analyze the kind of task the student is to perform so that appropriate guidance and support can be provided by the tutor. Two factors are important to consider when analyzing the student's task: (a) the pedagogical goal that is achieved by having the student engage in the task, and (b) the structure of the task to be performed.

Defining a system's pedagogical goals is essential. Doing so defines the knowledge the tutor needs to have, and the kinds of strategies that will be appropriate in that LBD tutor. The goal is to have the student practice a task to actually learn how to perform that task, or to use the task as a way to get the student to learn about some other subject matter. A third possibility is that learning both the task and the subject matter are desired.

In a situation where it is important for the student to learn a task, but where there is little or no background knowledge needed to perform it successfully, we are dealing with *procedural tasks*—tasks where the goal is to have the student learn to perform a procedure, or set of related procedures, by practicing until the procedure is mastered. The focus is on learning the task, rather than on learning some background knowledge. The tutoring needs to be oriented toward helping the student learn the steps that comprise the procedure, the ordering constraints on those steps, and how to notice and recover from errors.

An LBD tutor is also effective when the task at hand is being used to help get the student to learn some other subject matter. In this case, the primary goal is not to have the student learn the task, but rather to learn some set of background knowledge, often called the *target domain*. Using the performance of a task in this way is referred to as an *incidental learning task* (Schank & Jona, 1991). An example of an incidental learning task is using the task of being an evening newscast producer to teach current events (Kass, Dooley, & Luksa, 1993). Another example is using the task of planning and executing a road trip as a way to teach geography (Kass & McGee, 1993).

In LBD tutors of this type, tutoring tends to be focused on helping the student learn the concepts of the target domain. These tasks differ from procedural tasks; although the tutor must still have some knowledge of the task the student is to perform, it must also possess knowledge of the target domain the student is to learn about in the course of performing the task. In particular, the ordering and appropriateness of the steps in an incidental learning task depend on the specifics of the target domain and cannot be well specified ahead of time. This feature, among others, distinguishes incidental learning tasks from procedural tasks.

Finally, in some cases, it is desirable for the student to learn both the task and the background knowledge on which successful performance of the task depends. This situation gives rise to a third category of tasks used in LBD tutors: *complex domain-dependent tasks*. Diagnosing a disease and designing a new kind of bridge are two examples of complex domain-dependent tasks: Successfully performing either task relies on mastering a set of background knowledge. This category of task shares elements of both the procedural and incidental learning task categories described earlier. In a complex domain-dependent task, the tutoring is geared toward helping the student perform the task, as well as helping the student understand the concepts of the target domain. However, as is the case with incidental learning tasks, because the structure of the task depends on the specifics of the target domain, complex domain-dependent tasks differ significantly from procedural tasks. A later section discusses how complex domain-dependent tasks can be modeled, and the kinds of teaching strategies needed for them.

A second important criterion for analyzing the tasks used in LBD tutors is determining the structure of that task. For a tutor to be effective, it must be able to track the student's performance of the task. How much and what kind of knowledge a tutor needs depends on whether the task to be learned is a procedural task or an incidental learning or complex domain-dependent task. As discussed earlier, in the case of procedural tasks, much more emphasis is placed on the student learning the structure of the task. This means the tutor must have a thorough knowledge of the details of the structure and organization of the task. In contrast, incidental learning and complex domain-dependent tasks are structured so that the task requires specific subject matter knowledge to be performed correctly. This requires the tutor to have a representation of that subject matter knowledge so it can be in a position to monitor and guide the student. Nonetheless, the structure of the task is still critical because it determines how this subject matter knowledge should be represented in the computer.

Procedural and Diagnostic Tasks

Procedural tasks require the student to learn a scripted procedure—one in which there are often few, if any, interesting reasons behind the ordering of the steps. The main pedagogical goal is simply to have the student master the procedure. This type of task is common in business training situations, where an employee is learning to operate a piece of equipment or perform other routinized procedures. The primary goal for a tutor is to help the student learn how to perform the procedure. This usually translates into helping the student learn the structure of the task—that is, what steps comprise the procedure—and the applicable constraints on how those steps must be performed.

Unlike procedural tasks, incidental learning and complex domain-dependent tasks are structured so that successful performance depends on knowledge of the target domain or subject matter. Although this means that a greater emphasis is placed on giving the tutor access to an internal representation of this knowledge, it does not mean that the structure of the task is unimportant. On the contrary, analyzing the structure of the task used to get a student to learn about the target domain is critical in building a tutor for that learning environment.

The work reported here focuses on one kind of complex domain-dependent task. Specifically, it analyzes in detail the kind of task model and teaching strategies needed to teach diagnosis tasks. In this type of task, the student is asked to collect evidence about a problem and then diagnose the problem. In addition, the student will often be asked to select the appropriate actions required to remedy the problem. In general, diagnosis tasks are useful whenever the goal is to have the student learn and exercise a causal model of a particular domain.

TEACHING KNOWLEDGE AND TUTORING SYSTEMS

Introduction

The Teaching Executive system and the sets of teaching strategies identified in the following sections are part of a larger body of research on both teaching strategies and computer-based tutoring systems. This section places the Teaching Executive in the context of other work in the field by identifying four key ideas embodied in the Teaching Executive system that help crystallize both the commonalities and differences between it and other related work. In particular, it describes other efforts at:

- identifying teaching strategies or teaching knowledge,
- building computer-based tutors that employ explicit teaching strategies,
- using teaching strategies in tutoring systems that teach significantly different subject matters, and
- creating authoring tools that enable teachers and other nonprogrammers to participate directly in the process of building tutoring systems through the creation and modification of teaching strategies.

The Study of Teaching Knowledge

The first key idea that forms the foundation for building the Teaching Executive is that teaching knowledge or teaching strategies can be identified and studied. A critical element of the work reported here concerns the identification of teaching strategies useful in teaching procedural and diagnosis tasks. A number of other researchers have sought to investigate teaching knowledge, primarily by studying classroom teachers. This work lends support for the general approach of explicitly identifying teaching knowledge or teaching strategies.

The first set of evidence for the existence of teaching knowledge comes from researchers who study the activities of human teachers in the classroom. Interestingly, the history of research on the kinds of knowledge and decisions teachers make while teaching is surprisingly brief. In fact, as recently as 1986, a leading researcher, in a review of the research-on-teaching field, remarked: "There have been no studies of teachers' knowledge, of the schemata or frames they employ to apprehend student understandings or misconceptions" (Shulman, 1986, p. 25). Nevertheless, there are some research findings that provide some indirect evidence.

In reviewing research on teachers' thought processes, Clark and Peterson (1986) characterized three main areas of study: teacher planning (before and after teaching), teachers' interactive decision making, and teachers' theories and beliefs. Of these, the most relevant for our purposes is the research on teachers' interactive decision making. Among other things, Clark and Peterson found that the content of teachers' interactive thoughts are mostly concerned with the state of the students' understanding; teachers make approximately one interactive decision every 2 minutes; alternative teaching strategies (or courses of action) are considered about 20%–30% of the time; and although usually only one alternative teaching strategy is considered, sometimes as many as three or four alternatives are considered.

Although this evidence seems to point to the use of decision-making knowledge by teachers, the content of such research on teaching has been less than useful in building educational software. The research has typically been too coarse-grained, and too often it is concerned with the classroom teacher, who must perform many different tasks in addition to teaching (e.g., discipline and classroom management; Goodyear, 1991). Specifically, most of the theoretical findings from research on teaching are not operationalized to a level that is useful in designing and building educational software (Murray & Woolf, 1990).

Another line of evidence that more strongly supports the existence of teaching knowledge comes from the cognitive science tradition of comparing expert and novice performance (e.g., Chi, Feltovich, & Glaser, 1981; Chi, Glaser, & Rees, 1982). The essence of this approach is to analyze the knowledge that experts must have—and that novices lack—to account for the differences in their performance. Leinhardt and Greeno (1986) took the view that teaching is a complex cognitive skill, and considered successful teachers as being similar to other kinds of expert practitioners. Leinhardt argued that skilled teachers have large repertoires of activities—called *routines*—that have become automatic through repeated practice (Leinhardt & Greeno, 1986; Leinhardt, Weidman, & Hammond, 1987). Leinhardt considered these automatic routines a type of situated knowledge (i.e., knowledge that is used to guide a teacher's actions in a specific context; Leinhardt, 1988).

In a study comparing expert and novice teachers, Leinhardt and Greeno (1986) found that a major difference between the groups was that expert teachers needed to make much heavier use of these routines than the novice teachers. In addition, Leinhardt and Greeno argued that expert teachers possess knowledge schemes that allow them to efficiently structure and retain more information, enabling them to reduce the cognitive complexity of the teaching task and stay in control of their teaching agenda. These differences between expert and novice teachers would seem to indicate that the expert teachers in the study had, through experience, acquired teaching knowledge (in the form of routines or schemes) that the novice teachers lacked.

The research outlined here points to the existence of teaching knowledge in human teachers, and therefore raises the possibility of identifying and encoding explicit teaching rules or strategies for use in computer-based tutoring systems. Because the teaching strategies described here are designed for use in a computer-based tutoring system, they are of necessity operationalized to a much more detailed level than those identified in the studies of classroom teachers.

Tutoring Systems That Use Explicit Teaching Strategies

The goal of the research reported here is not just to identify useful teaching strategies, but to represent and use these strategies explicitly in a computer-based tutoring system. This permits the teaching behavior of a tutoring system to be more easily modified. Furthermore, it raises the possibility that these strategies might be re-used in building subsequent tutors. There are several researchers who, in a similar vein to the work reported here, have sought to identify teaching knowledge so that it may be codified and used in building computer-based tutoring systems.

Collins (1977) and Stevens and Collins (1977) were among the first to attempt to articulate a computationally feasible process theory of the strategies used by human tutors. By examining transcripts of teachers skilled at inquiry teaching (also known as the Socratic or case method), they initially identified 24 teaching strategies that were being used consistently. These teaching strategies were incorporated into the WHY system, a Socratic-style computer-based tutor that teaches students how to reason about the factors affecting rainfall in different regions of the world (Stevens & Collins, 1977). After analyzing additional examples of inquiry teaching, the theory was extended to include nearly 60 teaching strategies (Collins & Stevens, 1982).

Another early ITS to represent tutoring rules explicitly was the GUIDON system (Clancey, 1982). GUIDON represented teaching strategies as production rules (i.e., IF condition THEN action) called T-RULES (short for tutoring rules). These T-RULES would tell the tutor, among other things, what topics to discuss with the student next, and what "discourse procedure" should be used to discuss them. GUIDON contained about 200 tutoring rules; these were grouped into sets to handle about 40 different situations (Clancey, 1986).

Two other ITSs from the same era as GUIDON also employed teaching strategies. The first was WEST, a system that coached a student in a mathematics board game (Burton & Brown, 1982). The 12 teaching strategies in WEST were quite sophisticated, and served as a model for many coaching systems that followed. However, the teaching strategies were compiled into the code of the system, and not represented declaratively, hindering the ease in which they might be re-used later. The second system was the Quadratic Tutor, which taught quadratic equations using the discovery method (O'Shea, 1982). Like GUIDON, this system represented teaching strategies using production rules. A unique feature of the Quadratic Tutor was that it was self-improving; it attempted to learn new tutoring rules based on the success rate of the student.

Anderson and his colleagues (Anderson, Boyle, Corbett, & Lewis, 1990) also used production rules to represent teaching strategies in their LISP, algebra, and geometry tutors. Because all knowledge in these systems is represented as production rules, it is not clear whether this was a direct attempt to explicitly codify teaching strategies, or merely a side effect of the production system paradigm in which the tutors were built. In any case, these systems do separate domain knowledge from pedagogical knowledge. Although the tutoring strategies used in all the tutors are similar, it does not appear that the rules are actually shared or re-used among the various tutors. In fact, Anderson acknowledged that separate tutoring components have been built for each system (Anderson et al., 1990).

Elsom-Cook (1991) constructed several tutoring systems that used explicit teaching rules. The IMPART system tutored students in Lisp programming. IMPART contains 20 teaching rules that are used primarily to control the flow of the dialogue with the student, and to select and order the topics to be discussed. The DOMINIE system (Elsom-Cook, 1991; Elsom-Cook & Spensley, 1987) teaches students to use a computer application. DOMINIE is interesting because it can use eight different teaching styles or strategies. These teaching styles are embodied in a number of rules that tell the tutor what to teach and how to teach it using that particular style. DOMINIE also has rules that allow it to dynamically select a different teaching style as conditions warrant.

Tutoring Systems That Support the Re-Use
of Teaching Strategies Across Multiple Domains

To effectively facilitate the creation of tutoring systems, the teaching strategies developed for one system should be re-used in building subsequent systems. There are several researchers who, after identifying teaching strategies useful in one domain, investigated whether these teaching strategies could be successfully applied to other domains as well. Some efforts have also been made at creating generalized tutoring architectures or shells to facilitate building tutors for multiple domains, although not many of these focus on the re-use of teaching strategies.

After developing Socratic-style teaching strategies for the WHY system, Collins and Stevens (1983) examined how these same teaching strategies could be applied in other domains as well. In particular, they showed how the teaching strategies could describe examples of inquiry teaching in the domains of arithmetic, moral education, and geography. Although each of the domains emphasized the use of different subsets of the teaching strategies, Collins and Stevens (1982) noted that, "the unity between the various domains is perhaps more surprising than the differences" (p. 95). Although this work demonstrated the theoretical generality of the Socratic teaching strategies, the strategies were apparently not used in an actual tutoring system for these other domains.

In building the GUIDON system, Clancey made an explicit attempt to separate teaching expertise from domain knowledge, and in so doing recognized the potential for creating a "multiple-domain tutorial program" (Clancey, 1982). As Clancey (1982) noted, "one advantage of this system is that a fixed set of teaching strategies can be tried in different domains, affording an important perspective on their generality" (p. 203). A significant feature of GUIDON was that the same tutoring rules developed for it were later used to build a system for teaching a student how to select the appropriate structural analysis software packages to run to analyze a particular structure (Clancey, 1986). Based on this earlier work, "Training Express" (Clancey & Joerger, 1988) was an effort to build a practical tool for creating simple versions of these types of ITSs. However, because these systems are based on the production system framework, their use is limited to building tutoring systems for procedural tasks or other domains that can be effectively captured by the production rule formalism.

The system that is closest in spirit to the ideas embodied in the Teaching Executive is KAFITS (Murray, 1992). KAFITS (knowledge acquisition for intelligent tutoring) uses parameterized action networks (PANs), a derivative of augmented transition networks (Woods, 1970), to explicitly represent multiple related teaching/discourse strategies in a single structure. The KAFITS system was used to create a tutor for teaching high school physics. Although Murray claimed that the KAFITS architecture and the teaching strategies could be applied to other domains, this was not actually attempted, leaving open the question of how general the teaching strategies truly are.

It is important to differentiate a tutoring system that re-uses teaching strategies originally created to teach another domain from the creation of "generic tutoring shells." The point of systems like the Teaching Executive is not only to create a software architecture for developing tutoring systems, but specifically to accelerate that development process by making it possible to re-use previously authored teaching strategies. Although several generic tutoring shells have been built, most have not focused on the re-use of explicit teaching strategies. Instead, the focus has been on helping the system designer create the domain knowledge base or interface components of the tutoring system.

Some of the more well-documented examples of domain-independent tutoring shells whose focus is not specifically on the re-use of teaching strategies include:

- PIXIE (Sleeman, 1987)
- ITS Challenger (Augusteijn, Broome, Kolbe, & Ewell, 1992)
- Bite sized tutor (Bonar, Cunningham, & Schultz, 1986)
- IDE interpreter (Russell, 1988; Russell, Moran, & Jordan, 1988)
- PTA - Pups tutoring architecture (Anderson & Skwarecki, 1986)

Authoring Tools for Manipulating Teaching Strategies in Tutoring Systems

The Teaching Executive is more than another tutoring system that uses explicit teaching strategies and supports their re-use in multiple domains. Another key aspect distinguishing the Teaching Executive from other work is that it provides—via the TE toolbox—an authoring tool that permits teachers and other content experts who are nonprogrammers to participate directly in building educational software.

As mentioned previously, the system closest to the ideas embodied in the Teaching Executive is the KAFITS system (Murray, 1992). KAFITS takes seriously both the explicit representation of teaching strategies and the usability of its authoring interface by teachers who are not programmers. KAFITS provides a graphical interface that allows a system designer to encode domain knowledge (in this case, about high school level physics). It also provides a graphical editor for the PANs that are used to represent teaching strategies. Murray tested the authoring tool component of the KAFITS system with a high school physics teacher who acted as the subject matter expert, thereby lending some credence to his assertion that the system was usable by nonprogrammers.

Overall, KAFITS shares many of the same design goals as the Teaching Executive—both represent teaching strategies explicitly, and both have authoring interfaces designed to be used by nonprogrammers. The one element missing from KAFITS is application to more than one domain. Without this crucial test, we cannot know how truly general the KAFITS architecture is, nor whether the teaching strategies are usable in domains other than the high school physics lessons for which they were developed.

Other Approaches to Building Computer Tutors

This section briefly describes some alternative approaches to building computer tutors and how they compare to the approach embodied by the Teaching Executive system. The default method for building tutoring systems to date has been to simply hard-wire the tutoring responses as part of the computer code used to implement the system.[2] This approach works by linking specific student actions in the user interface with specific elements of text, graphics, or video that constitute the tutor's response. This linkage is typically done by the system programmer in whatever programming language is being used. Because the tutor's responses are determined solely by the program code, no task model is needed.

Although this approach has the benefit of simplicity, especially for small tutoring systems, there are many disadvantages. First, when the size and complexity of the tutoring system increases, the combinatorics of linking the tens or hundreds of student actions to appropriate tutoring interventions quickly become untenable (Goodyear, 1991). Second, changing any of the system's tutoring behavior (e.g., adding a new intervention, changing the wording of a particular tutorial response), requires the programmer to go back through the system code, make the requisite changes, and recompile the code again. This can be an extremely labor-intensive process. Third, because the tutoring decisions are mixed in with the rest of the system code, re-using those tutoring decisions in a new system can be much more complicated. This typically means that all of the tutoring decisions must be reimplemented when a new tutoring system is built, even if the two systems teach similar topics and need the same sorts of tutoring. Fourth, implementing the tutoring in the system code effectively precludes a nonprogrammer from being directly involved in implementing the tutoring behavior of the system. This means teachers and other subject matter experts cannot be directly involved in the creation of the tutoring component of a computer-based tutoring system.

Another similar approach to building a tutor is to provide the system designer with prespecified code segments that can be mixed or matched to create tutoring decisions. In this approach, exemplified by the Financial Report Analyst (FRA) system (Foster, 1996), the code to test for various interface actions by the student is packaged into modular units called "condition testing functions." These testing functions allow the system designer to create tutorial interventions based on conditions like the number of times a button has been pressed, the number of minutes since

---

[2]The GUIDON system (Clancey, 1982) employed a version of this approach. In that system, tutoring rules were encoded as LISP procedures. Clancey did not discuss the implications of this approach for allowing nonprogrammers to modify or extend the tutoring rules.

the student took a particular action, or the number of times a particular video has been watched.

Under this approach, there is no need for a task model because the language of teaching decisions is expressed in terms of interface-level actions. Although the condition testing functions do make it easier for a system designer to create tutoring decisions than in the hard-wiring approach, there are still several important disadvantages. Because the condition testing functions provided to the system designer are primarily concerned with interface-level actions by the student, to use the provided functions, the system designer must translate tutoring decisions from more conceptual, task-level descriptions into equivalent interface actions.

Another disadvantage of creating tutoring decisions from prespecified code segments is that a nonprogrammer, although perhaps able to use the provided code segments, may be unable to modify or extend the decision-making vocabulary in any way. In addition, because the code segments test for interface-related actions by the student, any time there is a significant change in the interface, new code segments will have to be written and existing ones changed. Finally, the chance of re-using tutoring decisions in new systems, even those that teach a similar task, is very slim. Because the prespecified code segments used in creating tutoring decisions are tied to the system interface, it is unlikely that they will transfer easily to a new system that has a different interface.

The approach of creating teaching strategies that rely on a model of the student's task differs from that of more traditional ITS work (e.g., Polson & Richardson, 1988; Sleeman & Brown, 1982). Many traditional ITSs base their tutoring decisions on a model of the student's cognitive state—a difficult and error-prone undertaking, especially when the student's task is complex (Clancey, 1982; Lesgold & Lajoie, 1991; Self, 1988; VanLehn, 1988). In the approach taken by the Teaching Executive, the task to be performed is carefully modeled, and the tutoring interventions are based on this task model. LBD tutors permit this change in focus by emphasizing the performance of a concrete task by the student. This has several advantages over the student modeling approach used in traditional ITSs.

First, by carefully constructing the task environment to permit the student to perform the actions necessary to accomplish a task, much of the burden of interpreting the student's actions is done by the system designer during the authoring process. To create a task environment that permits the necessary range of student actions, the system designer must consider up front the structure of the task, the set of actions a student can take, and the repercussions of those actions. This task analysis can then be incorporated into a task model by the system designer as the task environment is being constructed. The tutor can then use the task model to help it interpret the student's actions as the student uses the system.

In traditional ITSs, tutoring decisions are based on a student model (i.e., a representation of the student's knowledge of the subject matter to be learned). The student model must be continually updated as the student uses the system to reflect the tutor's beliefs about the student's current knowledge state. To decide whether intervention is needed, the tutor must analyze the student's knowledge level, as represented in the student model, and look for missing or faulty knowledge. There are two critical differences between this approach to implementing tutoring and the LBD tutor approach described earlier. First, it is the ITS, as opposed to the system designer, that must do most of the analysis on which tutoring decisions are made. Second, this analysis is done by the ITS on the fly as the student uses the system, instead of ahead of time in LBD tutors.

As an example of how tutors based on traditional student models differ from the LBD tutor approach, consider the Lisp, geometry, and algebra tutors built by Anderson and his colleagues (Anderson et al., 1990). These tutors are based on a model of the knowledge of an ideal student represented as a production system (i.e., a set of if–then rules). The system keeps track of what the student knows by associating with each production rule a probability estimate of how likely it is that the student knows that rule. To determine whether and where a student has made an error, "the tutor tries to simulate the student's problem solving in real time as it is taking place" by finding a set of production rules that match the student's behavior—a process called *model tracing* (Anderson & Corbett, 1993, p. 240). If the tutor cannot find a set of rules that duplicate the student's performance, the assumption is that the student is missing (i.e., doesn't know) one or more production rules. The tutor then searches for the rule that would have allowed the student to achieve the correct response, and tutorial remediation is based on imparting this missing rule.

Needless to say, having the system designer analyze the structure of the task in detail before the student shows up is much easier than having the computer try to elucidate the state of a student's knowledge dynamically while he or she is engaged in using a traditional ITS. The structure of the student's task can be well understood, whereas the structure of a student's thought processes and cognitive states is not well understood at all (Self, 1988; VanLehn, 1988). This makes the job of modeling the student's knowledge state much more difficult than modeling the student's task. For example, one criticism of the model-tracing tutors described earlier is the real possibility that the set of rules used to model the student's knowledge is incomplete or incorrect. When this happens,

TABLE 4.1
Differences in Modeling Between LBD Tutors and Traditional ITSs

Factor	LBD Tutors	Traditional ITSs
Focus of modeling	Task	Student
Structure being modeled	Task structure	Student knowledge structures
Difficulty of modeling	Relatively easier	Relatively harder
Nature of model	Relatively static	Relatively dynamic
Time of main analysis	Design time	Run time
Modeling performed by	Designer	Tutoring system
Availability of student performance cues	Easy to obtain, provided by task performance	Subtle, difficult to obtain, tutor must actively seek out
Primary focus of tutorial interventions	Guidance on task performance	Knowledge structures (i.e., conceptual bugs, rule acquisition)

the tutor may not be able to identify which rule the student is missing, or will decide that the student is missing a rule that in reality he or she is not. As a result, the tutor will not know how to help the student, or may mistakenly tutor the student on a rule he or she already understands.

A second advantage inherent in the use of task models in LBD tutors is that the cues a tutor needs to notice when tutoring is called for are much more readily available (Self, 1988). Because the student is focused on performing a task, any misconceptions he or she may have are manifested by problems in performing the task correctly. By relying on a task model, the tutor can quickly notice when the student is having trouble by detecting errors in the student's performance of the task. In a traditional ITS, because the tutor relies on a model of the student's knowledge structures, such cues are not as readily available. To detect misconceptions, the tutor may sometimes have to actively seek out information about the state of the student's knowledge by asking the student questions. Table 4.1 summarizes some of the main differences between the modeling done in LBD tutors and traditional ITSs.

LEARNING-BY-DOING TUTORS FOR TEACHING PROCEDURAL TASKS

Introduction

In LBD tutors, the student practices a skill while the tutor looks over the student's shoulder to offer advice and guidance. Because the focus in LBD tutors is on the student's performance of task, the kind of tutoring that is needed is determined largely by what the student's task is like. To create effective tutoring in an LBD environment, one needs to first analyze the kind of task the student is to perform so that the appropriate guidance and support can be provided by the tutor.

Two LBD Tutors for Teaching Procedural Tasks

To illustrate what an LBD tutor that teaches a procedural task is like, two LBD tutors for procedural tasks that have been built with the Teaching Executive are considered. This section looks at sample interactions a student might have with these systems to get a feel for the kind of procedural tasks they teach, and the kind of tutorial assistance a student might need while engaged in learning such a task. A more in-depth discussion of these systems can be found in Guralnick (1996).

BC Cashier was designed to teach employees of a fast food restaurant how to operate the special cash register used in the store. The student plays the role of a cashier, and is presented with various customers' orders to ring up. The computer screen displays a realistic simulation of the actual cash register used in the store; the student uses the mouse pointer to "press" the cash register buttons. Performance meters give the student feedback on his or her overall speed and accuracy. In addition, there are various buttons on the screen that allow the student to talk to the customer and ask the tutor for help (e.g., "Why?", "Now what?"). Figure 4.3 shows the screen interfaces as seen by the trainee.

There are several skills being taught by the BC Cashier system. The first is familiarity with the cash register keyboard. A skilled cashier is expected to be able to ring up a customer's order quickly without having to hunt for the correct key on the register. Because there are nearly 100 different keys, this is not as easy as it might seem. The second skill is familiarity with the restaurant's menu. Most meals include one or more side dishes at no additional charge. This means a cashier must recognize these groups of items and ring them up using the designated key, instead of ringing up each item individually and charging the customer too much.

The following transcript is typical of an interaction a first-time student might have with the system. It shows how the tutor can help even a complete novice get through the steps needed to successfully ring up a customer's order.

[In a video, the "server" (the employee whose job is to package the customer's order) tells the student that the customer has ordered a half chicken with sides, a cornbread, and a small drink (drinks come in 79-cent and $1.19 sizes)]

Student: Now What?

Tutor: You still need to ring up the 1/2 chicken with sides, ring up the drink, and ring up the cornbread.

Student: How Do I Do That?

Tutor: To ring up the 1/2 chicken with sides, you need to press the "1/2 WITH SIDES" key. It is the key you see flashing on the register now.

[key flashes on screen]

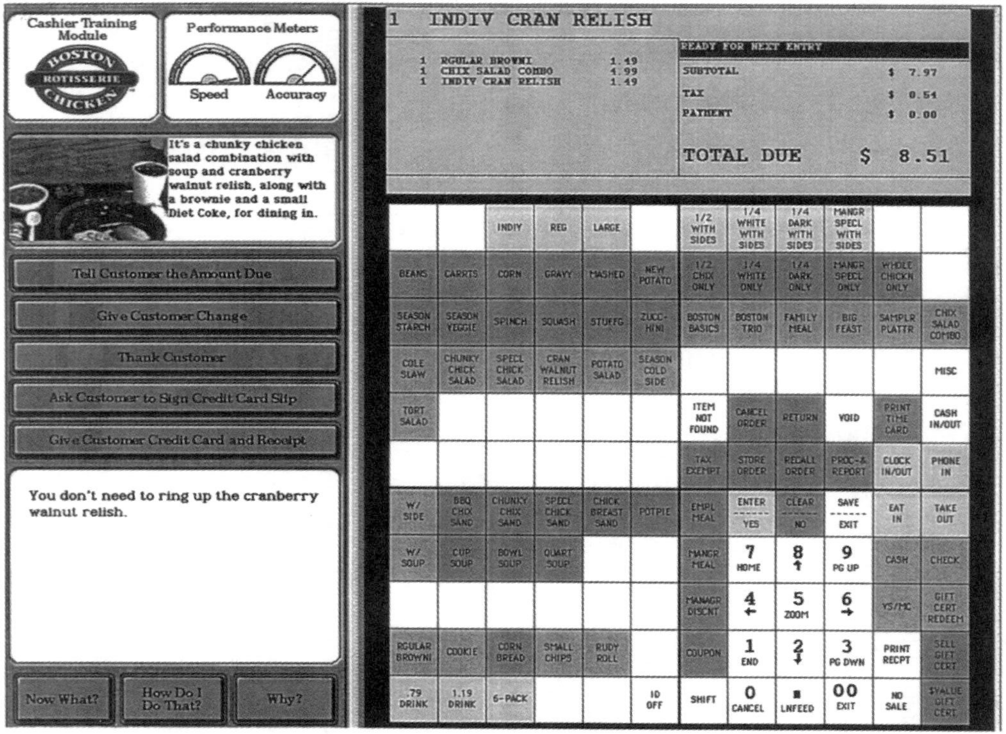

FIG. 4.3. The BC Cashier interface.

Student: 1/2 WITH SIDES

Student: 1.19 DRINK

Tutor [intervenes]:   You don't need to ring up the drink.

Student: Why?

Tutor: You don't need to ring up the drink because it's not the right size.

Student: Now What?

Tutor: You need to void out the last item.

Student: How Do I Do That?

Tutor: To void out the last item, you need to press the VOID key twice.
              It is the key you see flashing on the register now.

[key flashes on screen]

Student: VOID

Student: VOID

Student: Now What?

Tutor: You still need to ring up the drink and ring up the cornbread.

Student: How Do I Do That?

Tutor: To ring up the drink, you need to press the ".79 DRINK" key. It
              is the key you see flashing on the register now.

[key flashes on screen]

Student: .79 DRINK

Student: CORN BREAD

Student: Now What?

Tutor: You need to ring up that this is a dine-in order.

Student: How Do I Do That?

Tutor: To ring up that this is a dine-in order, you need to press the EAT
              IN key. It is the key you see flashing on the register now.

[key flashes on screen]

Student: EAT IN

Student: Now What?

Tutor: You need to get the customer to pay you.

Student: How Do I Do That?

Tutor: To get the customer to pay you, you need to press the "Tell
              Customer Amount Due" button above, then enter the amount
              owed.

Student: Why?

Tutor: You need to get the customer to pay you because you've already
              rung up all the items in this order.

Student: TELL-DUE

Student: That will be $7.66, please.

[customer pays $7.66]

Student: Now What?

Tutor: You need to enter the amount of money the customer gave you into the register.

Student: How Do I Do That?

Tutor: To enter the amount of money the customer gave you into the register, you need to use the numbered keys and decimal point key.

Student: 7.66

Student: Now What?

Tutor: You need to enter that the customer is paying in cash.

Student: How Do I Do That?

Tutor: To enter that the customer is paying in cash, you need to press the CASH key. It is the key you see flashing on the register now.

[key flashes on screen]

Student: CASH

Student: Now What?

Tutor: You need to thank the customer for coming to Boston Chicken now.

Student: TELL-THANKS

Tutor: Congratulations! You've completed the order. Speed rating 40 out of 100. Accuracy ratio 90 out of 100. Overall speed rating 34 out of 100. Overall accuracy rating 80 out of 100.

BC Server was designed to teach employees of the same fast food restaurant how to properly gather and package a customer's order. In this system, the student plays the role of the server, and is presented with a series of video clips depicting various customers coming up to the counter and placing orders. The computer screen displays a mock-up of the food items and containers available, and the student uses the mouse to put the food items ordered by the customer in the proper containers. The task is tricky because of the wide range of food items on the menu, the variety of ways in which the items should be packaged, and because some items implicitly include other items as part of the order. As in the BC Cashier system, there are various buttons on the screen that allow the student to talk to the customer and ask the tutor for help. Figure 4.4 shows the interface screen for the BC Server system. The following transcript shows the kind of interaction a novice student might have with the system.

Student: Click Here to Start

Tutor: A customer walks up to the counter.

Student: Now What?

Tutor: You need to greet the customer and put a tray on the counter.

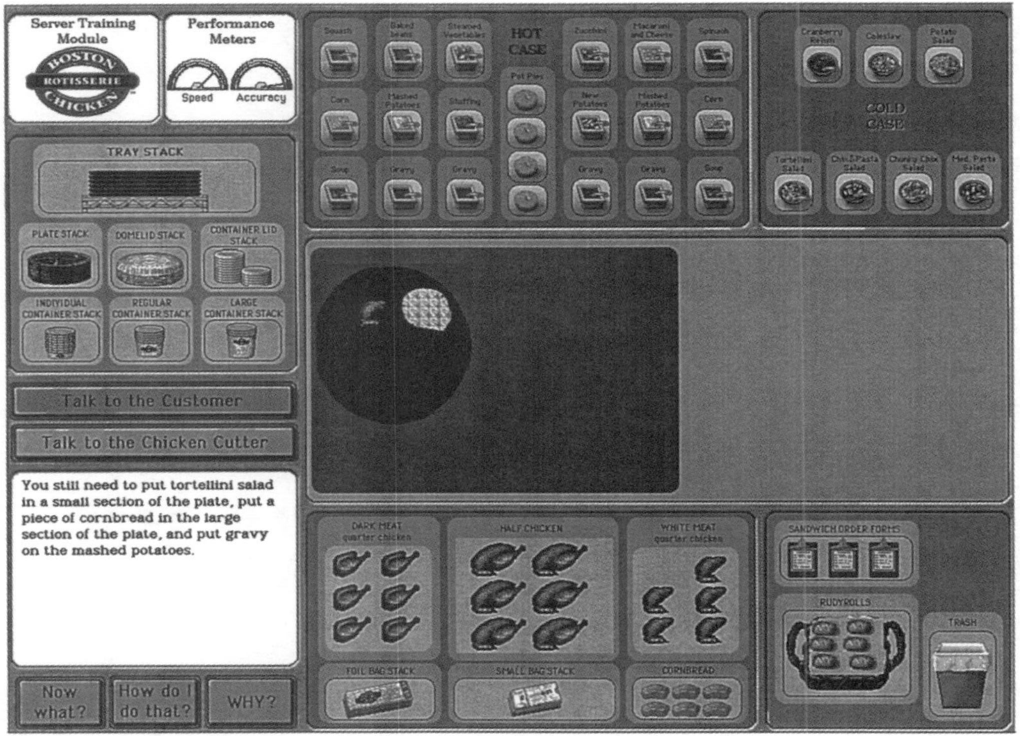

FIG. 4.4. The BC Server interface.

Student:	How Do I Do That?
Tutor:	To greet the customer, you need to click the "Talk to the Customer" button, then click on the "Welcome to Boston Chicken" button.
Student:	Talk to the Customer
Student:	"Welcome to Boston Chicken. What would you like today?"
Tutor:	The customer orders an individual chunky chicken salad, to take home.
Student:	Now What?
Tutor:	You still need to put a tray on the counter.
Student:	How Do I Do That?
Tutor:	To put a tray on the counter, you need to select a tray from the stack of trays and move it to the counter.
Student:	Moves tray to countertop
Student:	Now What?
Tutor:	You need to package the chunky chicken salad.
Student:	How Do I Do That?
Tutor:	To package the chunky chicken salad, you need to put an individual container on the tray, fill it with chunky chicken salad, and put a lid on it.
Student:	How Do I Do That?
Tutor:	To put an individual container on the tray, you need to select the stack of individual containers and drag it to the tray.
Student:	Moves individual container to tray
Student:	Moves lid to individual container
Tutor:	You don't need to put a lid on the individual container now.
Student:	Why?
Tutor:	You don't need to put a lid on the individual container because you haven't put the chunky chicken salad in the container yet.
Student:	Now What?
Tutor:	You need to put the lid back on the stack of lids.
Student:	How Do I Do That?
Tutor:	To put the lid back on the stack of lids, you need to select the lid and move it to the stack of lids.
Student:	Moves lid to stack of lids
Student:	Now What?
Tutor:	You still need to finish packaging the chunky chicken salad.
Student:	How Do I Do That?
Tutor:	To finish packaging the chunky chicken salad, you need to put chunky chicken salad in the individual container and put a lid on the individual container, in that order.

Student:	Moves chicken & pasta salad to container
Tutor:	You don't need to put chicken & pasta salad in the individual container now.
Student:	Why?
Tutor:	You don't need to put chicken & pasta salad in the individual container because the customer ordered chunky chicken salad, not chicken & pasta salad.
Student:	Now What?
Tutor:	You need to put the individual container in the trash.
Student:	Why?
Tutor:	You need to put the individual container in the trash because you put the wrong item in it.
Student:	Moves individual container to trash
Student:	Now What?
Tutor:	You need to package the chunky chicken salad.
Student:	How Do I Do That?
Tutor:	To package the chunky chicken salad, you need to put an individual container on the tray, fill it with chunky chicken salad, and put a lid on it.
Student:	Moves individual container to tray
Student:	Moves chunky chicken salad to container
Student:	Moves lid to individual container
Student:	Now What?
Tutor:	You need to ask the customer to step over to the cash register.
Student:	How Do I Do That?
Tutor:	To ask the customer to step over to the cash register, you need to click the "Talk to Customer" button, then click on the "Please step over to the register" button
Student:	Talk to the Customer
Student:	"Please step over to the register and a cashier will ring up your meal."
Tutor:	Congratulations! You've completed the order.

A Closer Look at Procedural Tasks

Both the BC Cashier and BC Server systems are examples of LBD tutors that teach procedural tasks. As the two transcripts illustrate, the two systems share many of the same tutorial interventions. Because variations in a task can entail variations in the kinds of teaching strategies needed to help a student learn that task, it is important to carefully define the characteristics of the task. This raises several questions:

- What specifically do the two tasks have in common that make them both procedural tasks?
- How can other similar procedural tasks be identified?
- What kinds of knowledge does a tutor need to provide the kinds of tutoring shown in the prior transcripts?

Before attempting to answer these questions, it is important to explain what is meant by the term *procedural task,* and to define the characteristics that such tasks have. This will clarify which types of procedural tasks can and cannot be handled by the solutions described here. Four factors define the type of procedural tasks described in this section and the next: (a) pedagogical goals of the LBD system, (b) constraints on the ordering of steps, (c), conditional branching, and (d) static versus dynamic explanations.

There are two basic pedagogical goals one could have in mind when selecting a task around which to build a LBD tutor. The goal is either to have the student practice a task to actually learn how to perform it (procedural task), or to use the task as a way to get the student to learn about some other subject matter. A third possibility results from a combination of these two goals—namely, that both learning the task and learning the subject matter are desired.

Procedural tasks are composed of a number of steps. To learn the procedure, the student must learn what steps comprise it, how to perform those steps, and in what order. A second factor that affects the complexity of a procedural task, and that defines the range of procedural tasks being considered here, are the constraints that exist on the order in which the steps may be performed. The ordering of the steps in a procedural task may be totally constrained, meaning there is only one correct sequence of steps, or it may be only partially constrained with steps that can be performed in a variety of sequences.

In the BC Cashier and BC Server systems, there are two ways that the steps in a given procedure can be constrained: either the steps are totally ordered, in that they must be performed in a specific sequence, or they are unordered and can be performed in any order so long as each step is performed only once. Other possibilities for how steps in a procedure may be constrained are:

Exclusive OR steps. A set of two or more steps that are equivalent, such that performing any one step is acceptable, but performing more than one is not.

Simultaneous steps. A set of two or more steps that must be performed simultaneously to be correct; performing only some of the steps simultaneously, or performing the steps in sequence, is considered incorrect.

The task model and teaching strategies discussed next and in the following section are only concerned with procedural tasks whose steps are constrained to be totally ordered or unordered because the development of BC Server and BC Cashier required only these two constraints on the ordering of steps. Other types of constraints could be accommodated by extending the task model in fairly straightforward ways. Guralnick (1996) extended the model to handle additional varieties of step ordering constraints.

A third factor that contributes to the complexity of procedural tasks is whether there is any conditional branching in the sequence of steps that comprise the task. A conditional branch is a point in the task where a different sequence of steps must be performed, depending on the context in which the task is being performed or on the steps taken up to that point.

Conditional branching adds to the complexity of a procedural task because a tutor must keep track of the conditions that affect the various branches so a determination can be made about whether the student has followed the correct branch in the procedure. The procedural tasks in the BC Server and BC Cashier systems include almost no conditional branching. The single exception to this is conditional branching, which is done when the student makes a mistake. When this occurs, the student must perform an error-recovery subtask (i.e., the main task is suspended while the student takes the necessary steps to undo the mistake). For example, in BC Cashier, when an incorrect item is rung up, the student must void that item to remove it from the total. This requires a special sequence of steps that would not otherwise have been necessary.

The procedural tasks focused on here, like the ones in BC Server and BC Cashier, are ones that have little conditional branching. Any conditional branches that are present are triggered solely by the step just taken by the student. Procedural tasks that contain many complex conditions that determine which sequence of steps the student must take require that the student understand these conditions and when they apply. Furthermore, branches in a procedure that are dependent on nonlocal conditions (i.e., by the entire history of student actions and not just the last step) can be difficult for the tutor to keep track of, and may require specialized data structures. Once this level of task complexity is reached, the task is better characterized as a complex domain-dependent task because the student is clearly expected to master some background knowledge to successfully perform the task. Moreover, in such tasks, the tutor must have a much more elaborate model of the task to provide appropriate guidance to the student.

A fourth factor that has an impact on the complexity of tasks used in LBD tutors and the tutoring associated with them is the nature of the explanations for why a given step is or is not part of a task. Students learning a new task frequently want to know why a particular step is required, or why a step just taken is incorrect (Jona, Bell, & Birnbaum, 1991). Consequently, a tutor must be prepared to provide the student with these types of explanations when needed. What types of explanations are required for a particular task, and the method by which those explanations are generated, can affect the complexity of implementing appropriate tutoring in an LBD system.

The class of procedural tasks focused on requires only a small, well-defined set of explanations to assist the student in learning the task. Specifically, for the type of procedural task discussed here, the explanation for why a given step is or is not necessary changes little or not at all over the course of the procedure. In other words, the explanations associated with a particular step are *static* throughout the task. The primary reason for this is that procedural tasks, as defined here, require the student to learn little or no background knowledge to perform the task. Thus, there is no complex set of concepts that must be referenced in explaining the task to the student. This fact greatly simplifies the explanation generation mechanisms an LBD tutor must have to provide relevant explanations to a student learning a procedural task.

Other types of tasks that depend on learning a set of background knowledge do not share this characteristic. In incidental learning tasks and complex domain-dependent tasks, for example, the explanations for why a step is needed or not depend on the nature of the target domain. This has two consequences. First, the set of explanations a tutor might be required to give may not be as limited or well defined. Second, the explanation for why a particular step is required or not required at a given point in the task may change depending on when that step is performed and in what context. These types of tasks can be characterized as requiring dynamic explanations (i.e., the explanations can change radically as the student progresses through the task). Because of the dynamic nature of explanations in these sorts of tasks, a tutor must be able to generate relevant explanations on the fly, depending on the context in which the student asks for one. This capability requires a much more sophisticated explanation-generation mechanism than in tasks with static explanations.

For these reasons, the nature of the explanations required in providing tutoring for a task is an important factor in defining the type of task focused on here. The task model and teaching strategies discussed next rely on the static nature of explanations required for procedural tasks. Other types of tasks, and even other types of procedural tasks, that require dynamic explanation generation cannot be handled directly by the solutions proposed here. It would of course be possible to extend both the task model and teaching strategies to accommodate a dynamic explanation mechanism, but that possibility is not explored in this work.

Modeling Procedural Tasks

This section describes a mechanism for modeling procedural tasks that provides a tutor with the information needed to track the student's performance of the task, and provides a framework for answering the student's questions while he or she is engaged in the task. The model described here can provide the information required by the teaching strategies described later in this section. Other procedural task models could also be used, so long as they too provided the same kinds of information.

The simplest way to model a procedural task is as a set of steps that must be performed to accomplish that task. This is similar to the idea of a script that prescribes what steps must be taken and in what order (Schank & Abelson, 1977). This model works well in describing simple procedural tasks where there is no internal grouping to the steps (e.g., dialing a local phone number). The phone dialing task is composed of seven steps, dialing each of the seven digits of the phone number, and there is no meaningful internal grouping of these steps. Most interesting tasks are not this simple, however. In particular, the steps that make up a task rarely have a completely flat structure, as described earlier; instead, the steps are often grouped into conceptual units or subtasks. To handle these more complex procedural tasks, a more elaborate model must be used. In the general model, a procedural task is a hierarchical, treelike structure made up of subtasks and individual steps. Organizing tasks and subtasks in a hierarchical fashion provides the capability of modeling tasks with a more complex structure.

In addition to representing the structure of procedural tasks in a hierarchical way, a general task model must also support variations in the order in which the steps must be performed. As discussed earlier, there are two basic orderings of steps in procedural tasks we will be concerned with modeling. Some tasks, like phone dialing, have steps that must be performed in a specified sequence. These tasks, called *ordered procedures*, are not completed correctly if any of the steps are performed out of sequence. Other procedural tasks have steps that can be performed in any order, usually with the stipulation that none of the steps be performed more than once. These are *unordered procedures*. Writing a personal check is an example of an unordered procedure: The steps of filling out the name of the payee, the date, the amount, and the signature can be done in any order, so long as each step is done only once.

Although most tasks are easily modeled as either ordered or unordered procedures, there are tasks that share characteristics of both. In particular, some ordered procedures also have one or more steps that can be performed at any point, as one might find in an unordered procedure. These are called *floating steps* to indicate that their position in the task can float relative to the other steps that must be performed in sequence. Consider the following example of an ordered procedure with floating steps. An attendant at a full-service gas station must fill up the customer's tank with gas, check the oil, and take the customer's payment. In this procedure, checking the oil is a floating step (actually a set of steps), in that it is permissible to do it at any point during the task of filling up the tank or taking the customer's payment (and perhaps even after taking the payment).

When a hierarchically structured task—one that is composed of several subtasks—has floating steps associated with it, can those floating steps be performed at any point in any of the subtasks? In other words, are floating steps "inherited" from a containing task? Tasks that do not inherit floating steps are called *isolated tasks*, whereas tasks that do are called *nonisolated tasks*. Each task and subtask in the model is labeled as either one or the other. This is an important piece of information that the tutor refers to almost constantly. For the tutor to evaluate the student's current step, it must be able to determine whether that step is part of the current task. Even if the step is not part of the task, it is not necessarily incorrect. Whether the current task is isolated or nonisolated will determine whether the tutor makes an additional check to see if the step just taken is an inherited floating step.

Isolated tasks are particularly useful for representing error-recovery procedures. When the student takes an incorrect step, an error-recovery subtask is usually entered. This subtask captures the sequence of steps necessary to undo the mistake and continue the task. For example, if the student rings up an incorrect item in the BC Cashier system, he or she must void out that incorrect item by pressing a sequence of keys on the cash register. This special void key sequence is represented as an isolated subtask because the student should not be performing any other floating steps while in the middle of recovering from an error.

Annotating the Model With Explanations

As discussed in the following section, students learning a new procedural task will undoubtedly want to know why the task is structured as it is. In particular, students will want to know why particular steps are required, or why other steps are incorrect. Thus, in addition to capturing the structure and organization of a procedural task, a task model must contain the information needed so that these types of explanations can be provided to the student.

Providing the information needed for explanations is not as straight-forward as it might at first seem. For any given task, there can be many idiosyncratic reasons why particular steps are required and why others are not required in certain contexts. There are two basic approaches for providing a tutor with an ability to generate these sorts of explanations for the student. The first approach is to provide the tutor with a detailed representation of the task that would allow it to reason about the task and generate explanations for why steps were needed or unneeded on the fly. However, because the procedural tasks being taught here are of the sort that have little or no underlying theory that organizes their structure, this knowledge-intensive approach is not appropriate. This is true for at least two reasons. First, the explanatory theory behind the structure of these types of procedural tasks is so thin that there would be little to represent. Second, even if a representation could be constructed that would allow a tutor to generate explanations, it would likely be so idiosyncratic to a particular task that the same representation would be useless in generating explanations for other procedural tasks. This means a new representation would have to be constructed each time an LBD tutor for a new procedural task was built—an extremely difficult and time-consuming endeavor.

A second approach to providing the student with explanations is to have the designer generate the explanations and then store them in the task model so they can be retrieved by the tutor when needed. This approach puts the burden of generating explanations on the designer when the system is being created, instead of on the tutor at run time, but it is much easier than the approach discussed earlier. First, asking the designer to generate actual English explanations is much easier than asking her to create a knowledge representation that would allow the tutor to generate these same explanations. Any designer familiar with the procedural task being taught should be able to explain quite easily why a particular step is or is not needed in a given task. Second, the hierarchical structure of procedural tasks makes it possible to employ a technique called *explanation inheritance*, which eliminates the need for the designer to generate explanations for each and every step in a task.

Explanation inheritance exploits the hierarchical task/subtask structure of a procedural task model to allow a tutor to maximize the usefulness of the prestored explanations entered by the designer. The technique works as follows. Instead of attaching these prestored explanations to each step in the task model, the explanations for why a particular step is needed or unneeded can be stored either at the step or task level (see Fig. 4.5). By storing the explanations at the task level, the designer can desig-nate that a particular explanation for why a step is needed or unneeded is relevant for all subtasks subordinate to that task in the task model. In

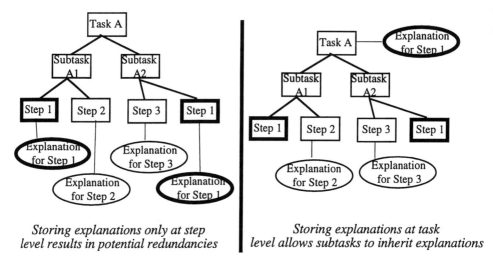

Storing explanations only at step   *Storing explanations at task*
level results in potential redundancies   *level allows subtasks to inherit explanations*

FIG. 4.5.   Annotating procedural task model with explanations at the step
level versus the task level.

other words, this permits the designer to say that the reason a particular
step is needed or unneeded remains the same throughout the task.

Although storing explanations at the task level in a procedural task
model allows for the elimination of redundancies, it still requires that an
explanation be generated by the designer for each step in the task. This
can be especially problematic when there is a wide range of possible steps
a student can take, only a few of which are actually relevant in a given
task. The designer would be required to generate an explanation for why
each of the steps that were not part of the task were unnecessary, a tedious
undertaking. To address this problem, and to further enhance the efficiency of providing explanations, the explanation inheritance technique
also provides a mechanism for the designer to specify default explanations. A default explanation, as its name implies, is a standard reason
why a step is or is not needed in a given task. Default explanations are
used when no specific explanation can be found for a given step. This
allows the designer to specify explanations for only those steps that have
unique reasons why they are needed or unneeded, and have the default
explanation be given for all other steps.

Default explanations can also be stored at the task level. This provides
the designer with the flexibility to specify different default explanations
for different parts of a task. For example, in the BC Server system, the
first thing a student must do is greet the customer. Any other step taken
before this is done is incorrect. Thus, the default explanation for why all
other steps are incorrect at this point is that the customer has not yet been
greeted. After the student greets the customer, the default explanation

changes based on what the customer has ordered. Using default explanations in this way allows the designer to provide explanations for dozens, or even hundreds, of steps without having to actually enter this many explanations by hand.

The specific algorithm used by the explanation inheritance technique to select an explanation for why a given step is needed or unneeded is as follows. Each step of the algorithm is tried in order until an explanation is found:

1. Look for a specific explanation for this step in the task immediately containing this step. If an explanation is found, then give it.
2. Look for a specific explanation for this step in the next higher containing task. If an explanation is found, then give it; otherwise, repeat this step until an explanation is found or no more containing tasks exist.
3. Look for a default explanation for this step in the task directly containing this step. If a default explanation is found, then give it.
4. Look for a default explanation for this step in the next higher containing task. If a default explanation is found, then give it; otherwise, repeat this step until a default explanation is found or no more containing tasks exist.

If Step 4 of this algorithm is completed and no explanation is found, the tutor has no choice but to simply tell the student that no explanation is available. Clearly this is undesirable, and the designer should go back and ensure that, at the least, a default explanation is available for every step. Using this algorithm, the technique of explanation inheritance provides a powerful and flexible mechanism for providing a student engaged in a procedural task with relevant explanations. At the same time, this technique minimizes the number of explanations the designer must generate ahead of time.

TEACHING STRATEGIES FOR PROCEDURAL TASKS

Introduction

The world is full of tasks that require steps to be performed in a given sequence, or a certain procedure to be followed. Even without realizing it, we are constantly explaining to people how to perform various tasks—from how to assemble a wagon to directions for getting to the baseball stadium. What techniques do people use when they are helping someone learn to perform a new procedural task? What questions are most commonly asked when someone tries to perform a procedural task for the first time? This section presents a set of 14 teaching strategies that specify how a tutor helping a student learn a procedural task can recognize student misconceptions and how the tutor should respond in each case. The strategies specify when a tutor should interrupt the student with advice and how the tutor should answer student questions at various points in the task. These teaching strategies were developed for use in the BC Cashier and BC Server systems.

The teaching strategies are divided into five basic categories:

I. Teaching strategies for dealing with incorrect steps,

II. Teaching strategies for tracking the student's performance of the task,

III. Teaching strategies for helping a student who does not know what to do next,

IV. Teaching strategies for helping a student who knows what step to take but does not know how to do it, and

V. Teaching strategies for helping a student who wants an explanation about why a step is necessary or unnecessary.

These five categories reflect the kinds of tutor- and student-initiated tutoring that exist in procedural tasks (Categories I, III, IV, V), along with the kind of bookkeeping the tutor must do to track the student's performance of the task (Category II). A schematic overview of these teaching strategies and how they relate to a student's actions in a procedural task is shown in Fig. 4.6.

Teaching Strategies for Dealing With Incorrect Steps

One of the most common problems a student encounters when learning a new procedural task is taking an incorrect step. In simple procedural tasks, there are at least three ways in which a student can take an incorrect step: by performing a step that is not part of the task, by performing a step too early, or by repeating a step already taken. This section describes three teaching strategies that allow a tutor to recognize each of these types of incorrect steps and respond appropriately. These strategies embody a straightforward approach to helping a student learn a procedural task that reflects the kinds of tasks the teaching strategies were originally developed for. Recall that these teaching strategies were developed for use in computer-based LBD tutors that train fast food restaurant workers on the procedures they need to know to do their jobs. In these kinds of procedural tasks, the main point is to have the student learn to perform the task, as opposed to using the task to teach some other content area.

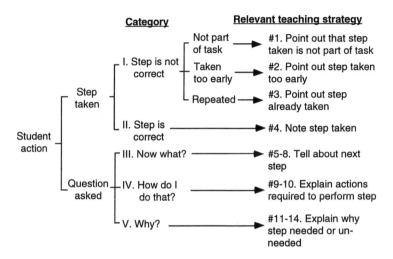

FIG. 4.6. Student actions in a procedural task and the teaching strategies relevant to each type of action.

In straightforward procedural tasks like these, there is often little or no meaningful way for the student to discover the correct step when a mistake is made. Thus, having the tutor delay intervention to let the student discover the mistake on his own is usually an ineffective approach. Instead, the tutor chooses to intervene right away to keep the student on track in the task. This helps the tutor avoid the tricky situation where a student makes several incorrect steps in a row and the tutor must decide which of the steps to remediate, and in which order.

Another use of procedural tasks in LBD tutors is in incidental learning tasks. Unlike straightforward procedural tasks, incidental learning tasks use the procedural task as a way to learn some other material. In these sorts of tasks, it usually makes more sense to allow the student to make mistakes without immediate intervention so the student can be forced to discover the material to be learned for him or herself. In incidental learning procedural tasks, the teaching strategies described in this section would still be applicable, but they would have to be modified to reflect a more wait-and-see approach to intervention by the tutor.

Procedural Teaching Strategy #1: Point Out That Step Taken Is Not Part of Task.

Ben and Michelle are assembling a baby crib.

Ben: This screw doesn't seem to fit here.

Michelle: That's because you aren't supposed to attach the legs with the 1/4-inch screws. You need to use the 3/8-inch screws.

In this example, Ben takes the most basic kind of incorrect step—one that is not part of the task at all. This kind of mistake is most often seen the first few times a student attempts a new procedure, or when there are many possible steps that could be taken at a given point in the task. Whenever the student takes a step, the tutor checks whether that step is part of the current task. In isolated tasks, this is done by comparing the step taken by the student to a list of all the steps in the current task provided by the task model. If the student's step is not found in this list of steps, then the *Point out that step taken is not part of task* strategy is activated. In nonisolated tasks, however, a decision about whether the student's current step is not part of the task cannot be made until the containing task is also checked. This is done by consulting the task model list and comparing the list of steps in the containing task against the step just taken by the student. If the student's step is not contained in that list, the nonisolated version of the *Point out that step taken is not part of task* strategy is activated.

Once this strategy is activated, the tutor must decide whether to intervene immediately. This decision rests on a number of factors:

- *Visibility of consequences*—Will the consequences of the mistake be apparent to the student, or are the effects too subtle to notice?
- *Proximity of consequences*—Will the consequences occur quickly after the mistake is made, or will it take some time for the consequences to manifest themselves?
- *Clear linkage of mistake to consequences*—How obvious will it be to the student that a given mistake is responsible for the observed consequences? Could more than one factor cause the same consequences?
- *Cascading consequences*—Will this mistake lead to other mistakes in such a way that untangling all the mistakes at a later point will be a complex undertaking for the tutor?

In general, it is usually best for the tutor to delay intervention and allow the student to discover mistakes independently. But in the BC Server and BC Cashier systems, this is not the most effective approach. In these systems, correcting a mistake is much easier if the correction can be made before any additional steps in the procedure have been taken. For this reason, the decision is made to intervene immediately every time the student takes a step that is not part of the task, rather than delaying intervention and forcing the student to go through a much more complicated error-recovery procedure.

The next decision that must be made in applying the *Point out that step taken is not part of task* strategy is whether to intervene directly or indirectly.

A direct intervention has the tutor interrupting the student's task to deliver a tutorial response, whereas an indirect intervention might have the tutor change the task environment in a pedagogically useful way. In the case of BC Server and BC Cashier, an indirect intervention would mean having the tutor cause the simulated customer to inform the student he or she had just rung up an item that was not ordered. This type of indirect intervention would have provided the student with the kind of feedback he or she might receive in performing the task in the real world. However, other factors made the choice of direct tutor intervention the option chosen. In particular, there are errors in both the BC Server and BC Cashier tasks that would be unrealistic for customers to notice. For example, in BC Cashier, certain combinations of items can be ordered together for a lower price than if bought individually. Part of the cashier's job is to inform the customer when a combination order would save them money. Thus, it would be stretching reality to switch roles and have the simulated customer tell the student cashier when he had neglected to ring up a combination order in such a way as to give the customer the most savings.

Once the decision is made to intervene directly, the tutor must decide what the tutorial response will actually be. This depends on what the tutor's explanation for the student's mistake is. There are at least two reasons why the student may have taken a step that is not part of the task: (a) he or she mistakenly believes the step is really part of the task, or (b) he or she knows what the correct step is, but inadvertently took the incorrect step. The tutor need not try to single out which explanation is the correct one because in either case the tutor should point out to the student that the step just taken is not part of the current task (i.e., "You don't need to X now"). This response is effective in both cases for the following reasons. Although the tutor intervenes immediately and directly to point out the student's mistake, it would still be nice if the student could figure out *why* the step was a mistake on his or her own. By only saying that the step was incorrect, the tutor leaves the door open for the student to think about why that is and to fix it on his own. If the real explanation for the student's mistake is (a), and the student does not figure out why the step was incorrect on his own, he may ask the tutor for an explanation. However, if the explanation for the student's mistake is (b), then it is likely that simply pointing out that the step is not part of the task will alert the student to the mistake, and allow him or her to correct it on his or her own without further input from the tutor.

Procedural Teaching Strategy #2: Step Taken Too Early.

John and Mary are making stir-fry.
[Mary adds the broccoli to the wok]

John: You don't want to add the broccoli now, it will just get soggy.
               We'll add the broccoli later after we drain the liquid from the beef.

Another common mistake in learning procedural tasks is taking an otherwise correct step, but taking it before the appropriate point in the procedure. This mistake differs from the one handled by the previous strategy, in that it deals with the ordering of the steps in the procedure, and not with the identity of the steps. Mary knows that adding the broccoli is part of the "making stir-fry" procedure (also called a *recipe*), but she performs the step before it is called for, leading to the consequences pointed out by John.

Detecting an opportunity to apply the *Step taken too early* strategy requires the tutor to go through much the same process as in *Point out that step taken is not part of task* strategy earlier. Whenever the student takes a step, the tutor first checks whether the current task is an ordered or unordered procedure. Because taking a step too early has no meaning in unordered procedures, this strategy is only relevant to apply in tasks defined as ordered procedures. Next, the tutor consults the task model to see if the step just taken is one of the steps remaining to be performed in the current task. If it is, but it is not the next step to be performed, the *Step taken too early* strategy is activated.[3]

In addition, there is another set of circumstances that can indicate that the student has taken a step too early. A separate version of the *Step taken too early* strategy is needed for nonisolated tasks to check whether the student has taken a step too early in a containing task. To apply this version of the strategy, the tutor goes through a process similar to that described earlier, but focused on the containing task instead of the current task. This means the tutor must first confirm that the containing task is an ordered procedure. Next, the tutor must check that the step just taken is not part of the current task, but is part of the containing task. Furthermore, the step taken must be one of the remaining steps in the containing task, but not the very next step. Once all these conditions are verified, the nonisolated task version of the *Step taken too early* strategy can be activated.

The tutor must then decide whether to intervene immediately or delay intervention, as well as whether to intervene directly or indirectly. The basis for these decisions is the same as in the *Point out that step taken is not part of task* strategy described previously. Given the constraints im-

---

[3]What about taking a step too late? There is no possible way for this error to occur in ordered procedures. In order for Step a to be taken too late, the student must take another step, Step b, instead. As soon as Step b is taken, the *Step taken too early* strategy will be triggered because Step a, which must be performed prior to b, has been skipped. Thus, the student will be made aware of the error before even getting a chance to perform Step a too late.

posed by the BC Server and BC Cashier tasks, the tutor opts to intervene immediately and directly in response to the student taking a step too early. The tutor must next decide on the tutorial response, which will depend on the explanation for the student's mistake. There are at least three reasons why the student may have taken a step too early: He or she does not know about the skipped step(s), he or she thinks the step just taken is to be performed before the skipped step(s), or he or she simply forgot the correct ordering of the steps.

As was the case in the *Point out that step taken is not part of task* strategy, actually differentiating among these possible explanations may not be worth the tutor's effort. To allow the student a chance to recognize the mistake on his or her own, the tutor's response is to simply point out that the step just taken by the student is not necessary to perform at this point in the task. If the student cannot determine why the step just taken is not correct on his or her own, he or she may follow-up by asking the tutor for an explanation. If the student simply forgot the correct ordering of the steps, or is able to realize the mistake on his or her own, then no further assistance from the tutor is necessary, and the student can continue performing the task without further interruption.

Procedural Teaching Strategy #3: Step Already Taken.

Courtney and Lee are making brownies.
Lee: I'm going to add the baking soda now.
Courtney: You already added the baking soda when you sifted the flour.
Lee: Oh, that's right, I forgot.

A third type of incorrect step a student can take in performing a procedural task is taking a step that has already been done. Although typically due to a simple oversight on the part of the student, this error is not uncommon with novices when the initial complexity of the task overwhelms their ability to remember what steps have already been performed. To detect an opportunity to apply the *Step already taken* strategy, every time the student takes a new step, the tutor checks a list of steps already taken by the student to see if the current step has already been performed. This list is created specifically for this purpose by the tutor recording each correct step taken by the student in a particular task.

Once activated, the decisions about whether to intervene immediately and directly are based on considerations similar to those in the other procedural teaching strategies discussed earlier. In particular, the tutor opts for immediate intervention to reduce the confusion that might result if a number of student mistakes were allowed to collect, uncorrected, until the end of the task.

In deciding to intervene directly or indirectly, the tutor, in the case of the BC Cashier system, has a real choice. The tutor could intervene directly, as in the other teaching strategies, by jumping in and pointing out the mistake to the student. However, because repeating a step that has already been taken is such an obvious mistake, it is plausible to use indirect intervention, in the form of a customer's comment, in responding to this mistake. In the BC Cashier system, the tutor should cause the customer to object to the student's ringing up an item twice because this is the sort of feedback the student would receive in the real world. For practical reasons, however, the actual teaching strategy used in BC Cashier opts for direct tutor intervention, instead of the preferred method of indirect intervention described here.[4]

Although this type of customer feedback is realistic in the BC Cashier system, the same logic does not necessarily apply to the BC Server system. In that system, taking a step that has already been done may mean serving the simulated customer two helpings of a food item or putting two lids on a container. In either of these cases, it seems implausible that the customer would comment on the mistake, especially if it meant getting more food. This means that indirect intervention is not a viable option for making the student aware of a repeated step in BC Server.

The next decision the tutor must make is how to respond directly when the student repeats a step; this decision depends on the tutor's explanation for the student's mistake. There are at least three reasons why a student may have repeated a step already taken: (a) he or she simply forgot having taken the step the first time; (b) he or she confused two similar steps and repeated an already taken step, thinking he or she was performing a different one; or (c) he or she mistakenly thought a step had to be done twice. In each of these cases, the tutor's response is the same: Point out to the student that the step does not need to be taken. The same response is used for two reasons. First, actually determining which explanation is really correct is too difficult and potentially intrusive to the student's task to be worth the tutor's effort. Second, this response is both a simple and effective way to handle any of these possible explanations. If the reason for the student's mistake is (a) or (b), simply alerting the student to the fact that the step need not be taken at this point in the task will most likely suffice to make the student aware of the problem. If the reason for the mistake is really (c), and simply pointing out that the step is not needed does not suffice in

---

[4]To implement indirect intervention for the mistake of repeating a step that has already been taken in the BC Cashier system, it would be necessary to have a video clip of each simulated customer pointing out to the student that an item was rung up twice . . . for every possible item on the menu! The combinatorics of this endeavor made the use of direct tutor intervention a much more attractive option.

helping the student understand why this is the case, then the student can subsequently ask the tutor for an explanation.

In addition to responding directly to the student, the tutor also records the fact that the student took the step again. By doing this, the tutor keeps a record of which steps the student is repeating. If the student continues to repeat a particular step, the tutor would be able to notice this fact, and a special teaching strategy could be written to respond differently to the second, third, or subsequent occurrences of this particular mistake.

Teaching Strategies for Tracking the Student's Performance of the Task

So far, this section has discussed teaching strategies that tell a tutor what to do if the student takes an incorrect step. But noticing and responding to student mistakes is not the only reason a tutor is called into action. For the tutor to notice that the student has made the mistake of taking a step that has already been taken, the tutor must keep track of what steps have already been (correctly) taken. To do this bookkeeping, a separate teaching strategy is employed. Although this strategy is perhaps less glamorous than many of the others discussed herein, it is nonetheless quite necessary. Whenever the student takes a step, the tutor checks that the step is part of the current task, and that the step has not been done before.[5] If both these conditions are met, the tutor records that the step has been taken by updating an internal record of the steps that have been taken so far.[6]

Notice that the tutor's response at this point does not involve communicating with the student at all. This type of response is called a *tutor-internal* response, meaning the only actions taken as a result of triggering the teaching strategy are internal to the tutor. The range of a tutor's repertoire of actions is not limited to those visible by the student. Tutor-internal responses are critical in allowing the tutor to collect information about the student's actions that can affect the tutor's later decision making.

Teaching Strategies for Helping a Student Who Does Not Know What to Do Next

Billy is assembling a new wagon.

Billy: I've got all the wheels on. Now what do I do, Mom?

Mom: You still need to attach the handle.

---

[5]Assuming, of course, that the step is to be performed only once in the task.

[6]Another option is for the tutor to annotate the task model by marking the steps that have been completed. These methods are equivalent.

In learning a new task, one of the most common sources of confusion for a student is what the next step should be. A tutor helping a student learn a new procedural task must be prepared at all times to help the student identify an appropriate next step to take. To make it easier for a student to ask the tutor for help on what to do next, many LBD tutors provide a button labeled "Now what?" in the user interface (Jona et al., 1991). For complex, domain-dependent tasks like diagnosis, the problem of telling the student what to do next can be quite complicated. In procedural tasks like BC Cashier and BC Server, however, things are greatly simplified. Using a task model like the one described earlier, along with a record of the steps the student has performed so far, determining what step should be performed next is fairly straightforward. In general, the tutor subtracts the set of steps already performed from the set of all steps in a task to arrive at the set of steps remaining to be performed. However, the specifics of this operation depend on the nature of the task the student is currently performing.

In procedural tasks, there are two contextual factors that affect what the tutor should tell the student when asked about what to do next. The first is whether the student's current task or subtask is an ordered or unordered procedure. This will affect whether the tutor needs to supply information not just about the steps, but also about the order they must be performed in. The second task characteristic that can affect the tutor's response is whether the current task or subtask is isolated. This determines whether the tutor should mention any remaining floating steps that have yet to be performed. If the student's current task is isolated, no mention is made of any floating steps. However, if the task is nonisolated, the remaining floating steps are added to the set of regular steps remaining, and the tutor tells the student about all of them. The tutor's responses to a student who asks for help about what to do next in each of the four permutations of these task characteristics are captured in the four teaching strategies summarized in Table 4.2.

The tutor's responses encoded in these teaching strategies were designed for procedural tasks like BC Server and BC Cashier. If these teaching strategies were to be used in other systems, where a goal was to have the student determine what the steps in the procedure are, other teaching strategies would have to be created that would give the student hints about the next step, or perhaps engage the student in a Socratic dialogue to help him or her discover the next step on his or her own. But even in these sorts of systems, the four teaching strategies described here would still be useful. If the student was unable to determine what to do next, even after receiving hints from the tutor, the strategies described earlier could be used to help the student identify the next step to take.

TABLE 4.2
Four Teaching Strategies for Responding to a
Student Who Does Not Know What to Do Next

Proc. Teaching Strategy	Context of Question	Tutor's Response	Example
#5	The current task is an unordered procedure. The current task is not isolated.	Tell the student what steps still remain to be performed, including any floating steps.	Student: Now what? Tutor: You need to put a half chicken on the plate, put a cornbread on the plate, and ask the customer if he wants gravy. *[asking about gravy is a floating step]*
#6	The current task is an ordered procedure. The current task is not isolated.	Tell the student what steps still remain to be performed, including any floating steps, and in what order they must be performed.	Student: Now what? Tutor: You need to tell the chicken cutter that you need a whole chicken quartered, then package the mashed potatoes and ask the customer if he or she wants gravy with the potatoes.
#7	The current task is an unordered procedure. The current task is isolated.	Tell the student what steps still remain to be performed in the current task only.	Student: Now what? Tutor: You need to put the quarter chicken dark back in the quarter chicken dark pan. *[no mention of asking about gravy]*
#8	The current task is an ordered procedure. The current task is isolated.	Tell the student what steps still remain to be performed in the current task only, and in what order they must be performed.	Student: Now what? Tutor: You still need to press the size key and the key for the side dish, in that order.

Teaching Strategies for Helping a Student Who Knows What Step to Take, but Does Not Know How to Do It

Mom has just told Billy he still needs to attach the handle to finish assembling his new wagon.

Billy: But how do I do that?

Mom: To attach the handle, you need to put that black bolt through the hole and then screw on the nut, in that order.

In learning a new procedural task, even if the student knows what the next step is, translating that knowledge into the specific actions to be performed can be difficult. Helping students who do not know how to perform a step is an important situation for an LBD tutor to be able to handle. In computer-based LBD tutors, the task to be learned is simulated on the computer, and the student may be confused by the user interface. Even students who have some experience performing a task in the real world may have difficulty knowing what specific actions in the user interface are required to perform a given step. The tutor must be prepared to assist a student who knows what step to take, but is confused about what actions must be performed to execute that step. To this end, LBD tutors often provide a button labeled "How do I do that?" in the user interface, which the student can click on to ask the tutor for help about how to perform a step (Jona et al., 1991).

In responding to a student who has expressed confusion about how to perform a step, the tutor must first have some idea of which step the student is confused about. Because of the limited information bandwidth provided by a "How do I do that?" button press (i.e., what *that* means is not directly specified by the student), the tutor must maintain some conversational context to interpret what step the student is referring to. To do this, the tutor maintains a contextual variable that is updated whenever the student asks the tutor what the next step is (i.e., "Now what?"). The first step mentioned in the tutor's response is assumed to be the current focus of conversation between the tutor and student, whether the task is an ordered or unordered procedure. If the student follows a "Now what?" question with a "How do I do that?" question, the tutor can use this contextual variable to determine what step the student is likely to be asking for help on.

In addition to telling the student what actions must be taken to perform the current step, the tutor may also choose to demonstrate the step for the student. Being able to do this is a useful tutorial option when simply telling the student about the action does not suffice. In doing a demonstration of an action, the tutor might employ an animation of the action the student is to perform, or show a video clip of the action being performed. Either way, the intention is to make the action required by the student extremely explicit. Having the tutor perform a demonstration raises some difficult issues about how the tutor is to exert control over the task environment and user interface. These issues are discussed at length in a later section.

The exact content of the tutor's response to a student who is confused about how to perform the current step depends on the characteristics of the task the student is currently performing; specifically, whether the current task is an ordered or unordered procedure. Ordered tasks require that the tutor inform the student not just what actions to perform, but also about the proper sequence to perform the actions in. The tutor's response to a student who does not know how to perform a step for both ordered and unordered procedures is summarized in Table 4.3.

Teaching Strategies for Helping a Student Who Wants an Explanation About Why a Step Is Necessary or Unnecessary

Billy: Why do I have to put these little red caps on the axles?

Mom: You need to do that to keep the wheels from falling off.

A third common source of confusion that students have when learning a new procedural task is why certain steps in the procedure need to be taken, or why other steps need not be taken. An LBD tutor needs to be ready to provide the student with explanations for why the procedure is structured as it is. These explanations assist the student in developing a more complete understanding of the task and how it is structured.

As in the "Now what?" and "How do I do that?" questions discussed earlier, many LBD tutors provide a button labeled "Why?" in the user interface to provide an easy way for the student to ask the tutor for an explanation (Jona et al., 1991). Because the student does not specify exactly

TABLE 4.3
Two Teaching Strategies for Responding to a Student Who Does Not
Know What Actions Are Needed to Perform a Step

Procedural Teaching Strategy	Context of Question	Tutor's Response	Example
#9	The current task is an unordered procedure.	Explain the actions that must be performed to accomplish the current step.	Tutor: You need to package the chunky chicken salad. Student: How do I do that? Tutor: To package the chunky chicken salad, you need to put an individual container on the tray, fill it with chunky chicken salad, and put a lid on it.
#10	The current task is an ordered procedure.	Explain the actions that must be performed to accomplish the current step, and in what order they must be performed.	Tutor: You need to ring up the coleslaw. Student: How do I do that? Tutor: To ring up the coleslaw, you need to press the INDIV key, then press the COLE SLAW key.

what explanation is desired when pressing the "Why?" button, the tutor must try to infer from the context of the interaction what explanation to give. There are three main contexts in which the student might want an explanation:

- The tutor has just intervened to point out to the student that the step just taken is not correct. The student wants to know why this is the case.
- The student asked what to do next, and the tutor described the next step. The student wants to know why this next step is necessary.
- The student asked how to perform a step, and the tutor described the actions required. The student wants to know why those actions are required.

All of these situations require the tutor to maintain some idea of what the "current step" is so that the appropriate explanation can be given. This is the same contextual variable described earlier. If the contextual variable is empty, the tutor does not have a good idea about what step the student is asking about. In such cases, the tutor has two options. It can either ask the student which step he or she wants an explanation for, or it can simply tell the student that it is not clear what explanation is desired. The first option, although good for obtaining the information required by the tutor directly, has these disadvantages: It further interrupts the student's task, and it requires being able to interpret the student's answer. Telling the student that the tutor does not know what step is being asked about does not give the student the information he or she needs right away. But it does encourage him or her to return to the task and either ask another question or take another step so the tutor can come up with the context needed to answer the question next time. The current versions of the teaching strategies described here opt for this latter response, primarily for its simplicity. A more elaborate response, such as asking the student to clarify the topic of the explanation desired, could be easily substituted.

Returning now to the cases where the tutor does in fact know what step the student is asking for an explanation of, there are three types of explanations the tutor must be prepared to give. These form the types of mistakes and questions a student could conceivably make or ask in a procedural task. First, consider the situation where the tutor has just intervened to point out an incorrect step, and the student wants to know why the step is incorrect. Two kinds of explanations might be needed in this situation, based on the two reasons the step could be incorrect (because the student has already taken that step, or because the step is not part of the task at all). Thus, the tutor must be prepared to explain to the student either that the step is not correct because it has already been performed, or why the step is not part of the task to begin with. This latter explanation will depend on the particulars of the student's task, and on the step being asked about.

Next, consider a situation where the student asks the tutor what to do next or how to perform some step, the tutor tells the student what step or action is required, and the student wants to know why. The third type of explanation required in these situations is why a particular step or action is necessary to take. The particular details of this explanation will depend on the task the student is performing, and on what step is being asked about. Taken together, the three types of explanations described previously (plus the situation where the tutor does not know what the current step is) result in four possible contexts a tutor might find itself in when responding to a student who wants an explanation about why a step is necessary or unnecessary. The tutorial response for each of these four contexts is captured in a separate teaching strategy (see Table 4.4, p. 336).

LEARNING-BY-DOING TUTORS FOR TEACHING DIAGNOSIS TASKS

Introduction

Another skill that can be taught effectively in an LBD environment is diagnostic problem solving. In diagnosis tasks, the student is focused on accounting for phenomena, diagnosing systems, or predicting outcomes. The student is presented with an environment in which to collect evidence and then must formulate and test hypotheses about the underlying cause or causes of the observed symptoms. The student must then articulate a diagnosis, and may also be asked to provide an explanation of the reasoning that led to that conclusion. Finally, the student may be required to recommend or perform some actions to remedy the diagnosed problem.

In general, diagnosis tasks are an effective type of task to use in LBD tutors when the goal is to have the student learn and exercise a causal model of a particular domain. Because diagnosis tasks are very different than the procedural tasks described earlier, LBD tutors that teach such tasks require both a different task model and different teaching strategies to provide effective tutoring. This section describes the Casper system, an LBD tutor that teaches a student how to perform a type of diagnosis task.

Casper: An LBD Tutor for Teaching Diagnosis

The Casper system (Kass, 1994) is a training environment that allows a student to practice being a water utility customer service representative. The student is asked to handle phone calls from various simulated cus-

TABLE 4.4
Four Teaching Strategies for Responding to a Student Who Wants an
Explanation About Why the Current Step Is Needed or Unneeded

Proc. Teaching Strategy	Context of Question	Tutor's Response	Example
#11	No current step has been established as the topic of discussion.	Tell the student that it is not clear what step is being asked about, and what to do to make it clear.	Student: Why? Tutor: Sorry, I can't answer your question because I don't know what it is you are trying to do. If you click the Now What? button, I can help you decide what to do next.
#12	The current step has already been performed.	Explain to the student that the reason the current step is not needed is because it has already been done.	Tutor: You don't need to ring up the small drink. Student: Why? Tutor: You don't need to ring up the small drink because you already did that step.
#13	The current step is not needed.	Explain why the current step is not necessary to take.	Tutor: You don't need to ring up the cranberry walnut relish. Student: Why? Tutor: You don't need to ring up the cranberry walnut relish because it's included when you press the CHIX SALAD COMBO key.
#14	The current step is necessary.	Explain why the current step is necessary to take.	Tutor: You need to put the individual container in the trash. Student: Why? Tutor: You need to put the individual container in the trash because you put the wrong item in it.

tomers, and must ask each customer questions to collect evidence about the likely cause of the problem. Once the student has formulated a hypothesis about the cause of the problem, he or she needs to decide on an appropriate remedy and inform the customer what will be done. The diagnosis task structure was selected for this system because it teaches the skills actually needed to perform the job of a customer service representative for that company.

The student can communicate with a simulated customer by typing responses in English, or by using a set of menus. Customer responses are

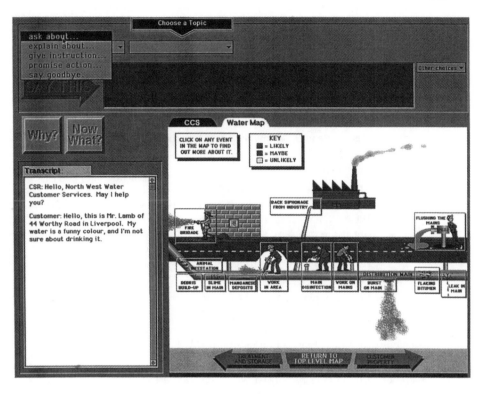

FIG. 4.7. The Casper interface.

heard on the computer's speaker. The interface also provides a transcript of the student's conversation with the customer and a graphical map of the water delivery system that the student can browse through. Both the transcript and the water map can also be used to respond to the tutor's questions. Figure 4.7 shows the main interface screen. At the top of the screen are the menus used to communicate with the simulated customers; the transcript is at lower left, and in the center a portion of the water map is displayed. A transcript of a typical interaction with the Casper system follows.

Tutor:	Welcome to the North West Water Customer Service Representative Tutor. Choose Answer The Phone to take the next call.
Student:	clicks Answer The Phone
Student:	Hello, North West Water Customer Services. May I help you?
Customer:	Hello, this is Mrs. Hughes in Liverpool. I've rung up to complain about bits in my water.
Student:	How long have you had the problem?
Customer:	I've had the problem for a couple of days, now.

Student: Presses "Now what?" button

Tutor: You should be sure to get the customer's name and address at the beginning of each call. These allow you to look up her record and check if she has had previous problems. Choose Return to Customer so you can get that information.

Student: Presses Return to customer

Student: What is your address?

Customer: Yes, I live at 9 Willow's End in Liverpool.

Student: Looks up local works on computer system (finds no relevant information)

Student: Presses "Now what?" button

Tutor: You should try to determine if the customer's problem is North West Water's responsibility or not. To do this, you need to find out if the problem is located within the customer's water system. Choose Return to Customer (or How? to learn how to determine responsibility for the problem.)

Student: Presses "How?" button

Tutor: Let me explain the need to determine whether or not the problem is North West Water's responsibility.

[Video of expert explaining what problems are not North West Water's responsibility and how that can be determined.]

Student: Is it in both the hot and the cold taps?

Customer: I hadn't really noticed which taps are affected.

Student: Can you run the cold tap for a bit and tell me what you see?

Customer: Let me run it a minute . . . The bits only appear in the hot water.

Student: Presses "Now what?" button

Tutor: Before I help you with the next step, you should record the customer's call. Record the contact in the Customer Contact System. Categorize the contact category and contact reason. Then choose Finished Recording Information.

Contact category chosen: WATER-SUPPLY (WATER-SUPPLY-PROBLEM)

Contact category chosen: WATER-QUALITY (WATER-QUALITY-PROBLEM)

Specific contact reason chosen: APPEARANCE (odd coloured water)

Tutor: To help you decide what to do next, I need to understand your current goal. Choose the item at right that best describes your current goal. (Choices: Gather Information, Examine Possible Causes, Narrow Down The Likely Causes, Act On A Diagnosis, I Don't Have A Clue).

Student: Chooses Gather Information

Tutor: Before helping you choose a treatment, I'd like you to show me what your diagnosis for the problem is. Use the map of the water system to choose your diagnosis for Mrs. Hughes' problem. (Choices: I can't figure out a diagnosis, What is a 'diagnosis'?)

Student: Selects deterioration of parts of the hot water system such as the water heater from water map.

Tutor: Let me explain the treatment that should be prescribed if the deterioration of the hot water system is the cause of the problem.

[Video of expert explaining how to deal with deterioration of the hot water system.]

Tutor: Choose from the items at right. (Choices: My diagnosis is: deterioration of parts of the hot water system such as the water heater, I can't figure out a diagnosis, What is a 'diagnosis'?)

Student: Chooses My diagnosis is: deterioration of parts of the hot water system such as the water heater

Student: Return to customer

Student: If the problem is only in your hot water, then it is probably your responsibility to get it fixed.

Customer: Well, what do I need to do about it?

Student: You'll have to call a plumber to sort this problem out.

Customer: Well, if it is not your responsibility then I suppose I'll have to get someone for myself.

Student: Thank you for calling North West Water.

Customer: Good-bye

Tutor: Now that you've finished talking to Mrs. Hughes, let's review her problem and how you attempted to solve it.

Tutor: Do you think you know the cause of Mrs. Hughes' problem? (Choices: Yes, I think I know the cause; No, I need more information before making a diagnosis; No, but I think I should be able to make a diagnosis without more information; The cause can't be determined over the phone in this case.)

Student: Chooses Yes, I think I know the cause.

Tutor: What is your diagnosis? Use the map of the water system to choose your diagnosis for Mrs. Hughes' problem.

Student: Chooses My diagnosis is: deterioration of parts of the hot water system such as the water heater

Tutor: Yes, I think deterioration of parts of the hot water system such as the water heater is the cause of Mrs. Hughes' problem. Now let's talk about how you might have been able to determine that earlier.

Tutor: So you need to try to find the best diagnosis of the problem in order to help the customer effectively. Choose Continue to find out more about diagnosing problems like Mrs. Hughes'.

Student: Chooses Continue

Tutor: Bits in the water is one of the most common water quality problems. When a customer calls with bits in her water, it could be due to any number of causes, from problems in treatment to problems in the customer's own pipework.

Tutor: Things that can cause bits in the water are: Lead pipework, lead
           common supply pipes, incomplete backflushing in treatment, a
           pH failure in treatment, flaking bitumen in the mains, manganese
           deposits in the mains, or a deterioration of the customer's hot
           water system.

Tutor: You did very well on that customer's problem. Specifically you:
           • did a great job of acquiring information about that customer's
             problem.
           Also, you:
           • didn't indicate to the customer or the tutor what the cause of
             the problem was.
           • did a great job of choosing the remedy for that customer's
             problem.

Tutor: I think you are ready for the next customer.

The Uses of Diagnosis Tasks in LBD Tutors

Diagnosis tasks can be used both as incidental learning tasks or complex
domain-dependent tasks. In creating appropriate tutoring to help a student engaged in a diagnosis task, it is important to be clear about which
use is intended. Unlike procedural tasks, both of these types of tasks are
structured so that successful performance depends on knowledge of the
target domain or subject matter. In differentiating an incidental learning
task from a complex domain-dependent task, the key determining factor
is whether a pedagogical goal of the system is for the student to learn
the task.

An incidental learning task is one in which the main pedagogical goal
is to have the student learn about a target domain; the task the student
is to perform is simply used as a means to promote this learning (Schank
& Jona, 1991). To be successful, an incidental learning task must be
structured so that it requires the student to demonstrate knowledge of
the target domain to perform the task. Although almost any kind of task
can be contorted to require domain knowledge for successful performance, tasks that do this in an authentic, engaging, and motivating way
are much rarer.

A good example is asking the student to diagnose and treat a disease
to have the student acquire, refine, and apply biological, physiological,
and pharmacological knowledge (but not necessarily to learn how to be
a good diagnostician). The task of diagnosing and treating diseases is an
authentic one—physicians do it for a living—and can be engaging and
motivating for students. A bad example is a multiple-choice quiz, where
the student must pick the correct answers for a series of questions about
diseases, their causes and treatments. Although this task may indeed rely

on the same knowledge as the prior diagnosis task, it is neither authentic nor engaging (Edelson, 1993).

A real example of using diagnosis as an incidental learning task is Sickle Cell Counselor (Bell, Bareiss, & Beckwith, 1994). In that system, the student plays the roles of a genetic counselor and laboratory technician to advise simulated clients about the likelihood of their offspring inheriting Sickle Cell disease. The student takes a sample of each couple's blood, and must perform a series of genetic tests to determine the genotype and phenotype of each individual. Once the student has determined the probability of the couple having children with Sickle Cell disease, he or she must explain his or her findings to the simulated couple. If the student's reasoning is faulty, or he or she has neglected to perform some important lab tests, the simulated couple asks pointed questions that indicate to the student the need for additional explanations or tests.

Sickle Cell Counselor is a good example of the use of the diagnosis task structure to teach a target domain. It is not trying to actually train its users to be genetic counselors; in fact, the target audience for Sickle Cell Counselor is museum visitors. The diagnosis task structure is used as an engaging way to teach about a topic (Sickle Cell disease) that is often taught in much drier, less exciting ways. The goal of the system is not to teach museum visitors how to be genetic counselors, but to use the genetic counseling task as a way to teach about Sickle Cell. This use of a diagnosis task is very different than in Casper. Casper is not an example of an incidental learning task because teaching students how to perform the task of a customer service representative is a desired goal of the system.

Using diagnosis as an incidental learning task requires a different approach to providing the tutoring needed to assist a student engaged in this type of task. Because learning how to perform the diagnosis task is not a goal, the tutor's focus is primarily on helping the student master background knowledge; less attention needs to be devoted to helping the student learn the proper way to do diagnosis. For example, the tutor may actively guide the student through the steps in the diagnosis process, rather than making those steps the object of study. This allows the tutor to concentrate the student's learning on the subject matter that is the real focus of an incidental learning task.

Modeling the Casper Diagnosis Task

In Casper, asking the customer questions is the primary method used to collect evidence to make a diagnosis about the cause of the customer's problem. Because evidence is collected primarily via a conversation with another person, the task in the Casper system is really a type of diagnosis task called a *diagnostic interview*. Diagnostic interviews are just one version of a diagnosis task. Another version might involve using laboratory equipment to gather evidence, instead of conversing with a person (as in Sickle Cell Counselor). Although many aspects of the diagnosis task are similar across these different versions, there are some variations. Identifying the factors that contribute to these variations is important because the teaching strategies used by a tutor can vary based on the particulars of the diagnosis task.

In formulating the teaching strategies described in the next section, a five-stage model of the diagnosis task was employed. This model serves two important functions. First, it helps serve as a framework for teaching the diagnosis process. Second, the task model makes it easier for the tutor to track the student's progress through the diagnosis process, and to offer advice about what to do next should the student need help. Modeling the diagnosis task is important for these reasons. But it should be made clear that the point of this work is not to present a particular theory of diagnosis. That has been explored in depth by a number of other researchers (e.g., Pople, 1977; Shortliffe & Buchanan, 1975). Rather, the point is to take a model of the diagnosis task and examine how that model can help a tutor recognize when the student is having difficulties, and how the tutor should intervene to help the student through these difficulties.

The five-stage model was designed to capture the main steps in the diagnosis process. It is purposely pared down to the most essential steps to make it easier for the student to adopt and use the model to guide his or her thinking. A simplified model also makes it easier for the tutor to track the student's actions and infer what stage of the diagnosis process is currently being engaged in. The task model consists of the following five stages:

1. Gather initial information (collect evidence)
2. Formulate a set of likely causes
3. Gather more evidence to rule out likely causes until one remains or no more can be ruled out
4. Articulate a diagnosis about the cause of the problem
5. Prescribe an appropriate remedy for the diagnosed cause or set of causes

The student is expected to follow these five stages in sequence. In Casper, gathering information is done primarily by asking the simulated customer questions, or by instructing the customer to perform some test or action and report back on the results. The student can also consult a simulation of the customer database computer screens used by real CSRs on the job.

The nature of the customer service role played by the student imposes several constraints on the diagnosis process as it is realized in the Casper system. First, it is important for the student to diagnose the customer's problem as efficiently as possible. Asking seemingly unrelated questions, or asking the same question more than once, can irritate the customer and make it appear that the CSR lacks competence. Second, it is important that the student tell the customer what the likely cause of the problem is (Stage 4). Most customers want to know what will be done to fix the problem, as well as what is causing it. Finally, one solution always available to the student is to send a systems controller (a water utility technician) to the customer's house. Although this option usually suffices to solve any problem, it is important that the student learn to use it only when no other solutions exist. Not only is it expensive to send out a systems controller, but there are a limited number of them available at any given time. Sending them out needlessly is to be avoided.

Variations in the Diagnosis Task

Despite the simplicity of the five-stage task model used to represent the diagnosis task in Casper, a number of factors (or variables) exist that can have a significant impact on the exact nature of a given diagnosis task. The teaching strategies for diagnosis tasks described in the next section have been shaped by a number of variables that define the kind of diagnostic interview being performed by the student in Casper. In this section, 14 diagnosis task variables that can alter the nature of diagnosis tasks in general, and diagnostic interviews in particular, are presented. These variations, in turn, can change the information that must be incorporated into a model of a diagnosis task, as well as the kinds of decisions that must be encoded into teaching strategies used with such tasks. Before looking at the kinds of teaching strategies required in a diagnosis task, it is important to have a clear idea of the sources of variability in such a task so that one can better anticipate how particular teaching strategies may be affected. The 14 diagnosis task variables are discussed next, presented according to the stage of the diagnosis process each variable most directly affects. Table 4.5 presents an overview of these diagnosis task variables. The majority of the student's time in a diagnosis task is spent collecting evidence, either to generate some initial hypotheses or to help narrow down the set of plausible hypotheses. As such, this phase of the diagnosis task has a large number of variables that can affect the specifics of how evidence is to be collected.

Diagnosis Task Variable #1: Primary Source of Evidence
The primary source of evidence in a diagnosis task can have a large impact on the nature of the task. Evidence may be obtained from a variety of sources, including people—as is the case in diagnostic interviews—or

TABLE 4.5
Summary of the 14 Variables That Can Change the
Structure of Diagnosis Tasks, Grouped According
to the Stage of the Diagnosis Process Each Affects

Collecting Evidence	Making a Diagnosis	Prescribing a Remedy
1. Primary source of evidence	10. Stating a diagnosis required	12. Observable Consequences of incorrect or suboptimal remedy
2. Cost of collecting evidence	11. Cost of an incorrect diagnosis	13. Variability of preferred remedy
3. Importance of diagnostic efficiency		14. Implementing remedies
4. Complexity of collecting evidence		
5. Success rate of queries in providing evidence		
6. Reliability of evidence		
7. Number of ways to obtain evidence		
8. Biasing evidence by format of query		
9. Sequencing of evidence collection		

from laboratory tests or equipment, to name just a few possibilities. When evidence is obtained by asking a person questions, as it is in Casper, the diagnosis task can be affected in a number of ways. First, being as efficient as possible in making a diagnosis will be important. Second, repeating the same questions is to be avoided.

Diagnosis Task Variable #2: Cost of Collecting Evidence

One factor that separates simple diagnosis tasks from more complex ones is whether there is a cost associated with collecting evidence. All other things being equal, if there is no cost associated with asking questions or running tests to collect evidence, there is little motivation to be selective about the evidence-collection process. In diagnosis tasks where there is a cost incurred for each piece of evidence collected, the process of collecting evidence becomes much harder and requires more careful consideration. The cost of collecting evidence can be more than just monetary. If the primary source of evidence is a person (Diagnosis Task Variable #1), the impact of collecting certain types of evidence must be carefully weighed. Specifically, it is probably not acceptable to ask a person to do things that are difficult, time-consuming, or painful to collect evidence. This "social cost" of collecting evidence differs from other types of resource costs that are associated with collecting evidence from lab instruments (i.e., how much money running a particular lab test costs). How the "cost" of collecting a given piece of evidence is calculated, and whether that cost is deemed worth it, will vary depending on the source of that evidence.[7]

When there are costs associated with collecting evidence, the diagnosis task becomes more complex to model. A cost value must be associated with each method of obtaining evidence, and mechanisms for summing the total cost of collecting evidence will have to be built. Furthermore, there is the issue of whether these evidence-collection costs can change during the diagnosis process. In diagnosis tasks where cost changes depend on the context, the student will have to come to understand the factors that cause the cost of collecting certain pieces of evidence to vary. This means the tutor will also have to be able to access information about these factors so that they can be explained to the student.

Diagnosis Task Variable #3: Importance of Diagnostic Efficiency

Related to the issue of the cost associated with collecting evidence is the importance of performing the diagnosis task efficiently. In some diagnostic situations, there can be negative consequences associated with an inefficient diagnosis process that are to be avoided. For example, if there is a high cost associated with collecting evidence (i.e., expensive lab tests), then minimizing the overall cost of evidence collection may be a desired goal in performing the diagnosis task. However, in diagnostic interviews, the emphasis on efficiency may be in minimizing the amount of time needed to make a diagnosis. In Casper, this is particularly true because of the nature of the telephone customer service job. Specifically, there is an emphasis placed on handling as many calls as possible. This emphasis changes the diagnosis task in Casper by requiring the student to try to arrive at a correct diagnosis as quickly as possible. Given these constraints, collecting more information than is necessary to arrive at a diagnosis is to be avoided.

Diagnosis Task Variable #4: Complexity of Collecting Evidence

How complicated the process of collecting a piece of evidence is is another variable that affects how evidence is collected in a diagnosis task. For example, collecting evidence in Casper is very straightforward—the student asks the simulated customer a question, or occasionally looks up information in the company's computer database. Other types of diagnosis tasks might require the use or calibration of complex lab equipment, so learning the procedure for using a piece of equipment to collect evidence may be an integral part of the student's task. If this is the case, a tutor will require additional information about the procedures to be performed so that the student can be given assistance if needed. The task model and teaching strategies for procedural tasks described in the previous sections could be used to create tutoring that would guide the

---

[7]For an example of how cost can affect tutoring in a diagnosis task, see Diagnosis Teaching Strategy #3 in the next section.

student through the mechanics of collecting evidence using laboratory or other types of equipment.

Diagnosis Task Variable #5: Success Rate of Queries in Providing Evidence
A diagnosis task can also be affected by how likely it is that a particular attempt to collect evidence will be successful. In the Casper system, asking the customer a question almost always results in obtaining some information. In other diagnosis tasks, however, actions taken to obtain evidence may not always be successful. This introduces an added level of complexity to the diagnosis task because the student must now learn what factors affect the success rate of particular actions in providing evidence. This added task complexity can have a direct impact on the kinds of tutoring needed as well. For example, in these types of diagnosis tasks, attempting to collect the same piece of evidence multiple times may no longer be regarded as incorrect if prior attempts to gather that evidence have failed. Further, a tutor must be prepared to recognize the situation where the student is aware of the factors that are preventing a particular query or test from yielding any evidence, but nonetheless tries to collect that evidence again while these factors are still present.

Diagnosis Task Variable #6: Reliability of Evidence
In addition to worrying about whether a particular query will provide the desired evidence, another factor that affects the evidence-collection process is how reliable the information obtained really is. In other words, when the customer answers a question, or a lab test provides some results, how accurate is the information? Collecting evidence from sources with dubious reliability affects the structure of the diagnosis task; it requires that the evidence be collected multiple times, or that confirmatory evidence from another source be obtained.

Diagnosis Task Variable #7: Number of Ways to Obtain Evidence
The existence of multiple methods for collecting the same piece of evidence adds considerable complexity to a diagnostic task. Such diagnosis tasks are also more complex to model than those having only a single method for obtaining each item of evidence. When a one-to-one mapping between questions or tests and the evidence those actions provide are not available, more information needs to be maintained about which questions or tests provide what evidence (and, as discussed next, whether there is any preference for which evidence-collection method is best). This information will be needed by a tutor if the student ever needs help understanding how to collect certain pieces of evidence in a diagnosis task.

Diagnosis Task Variable #8: Biasing Evidence by Format of Query
Another related variable that can influence how evidence is collected is whether the way in which a question is phrased, or a test conducted, can bias the evidence obtained, or, in some cases, actually change the evidence collected. Certain ways of performing a test or experiment may

cause the data obtained to be tainted. The possibility that evidence can be affected by the method in which it is obtained can change the nature of a diagnosis task and the kinds of tutoring required. Specifically, the existence of an incorrect way to collect evidence means the student must learn which methods to avoid to not bias the evidence obtained. To guide a student through this process of selecting the correct way to gather evidence, a tutor must have access to information about the various ways in which a piece of evidence can be obtained, which methods of obtaining that evidence can lead to bias, and why. This means the tutor must be able to monitor the student's evidence-collection process and notice when inappropriate methods are being used so that the student can be warned about the possibility that the data may be tainted.

Diagnosis Task Variable #9: Sequencing of Evidence Collection
A final variable that can impose constraints on the evidence-collection process in a diagnosis task is whether the order in which evidence is collected matters. In some diagnosis tasks, each piece of evidence is independent, and whether it is collected first or last in the diagnosis process does not matter. This is the case in the Casper system. In other types of diagnosis tasks, however, the sequence in which evidence is collected can play an important role. Whether the evidence-collection process must be performed in sequence can have an impact on the way in which a diagnosis task is modeled and the kinds of tutoring that needs to accompany that task. If there are constraints on the order in which evidence is collected, these constraints must be represented in the model of the task so that the tutor can detect when the student departs from the required sequence. In addition, new teaching strategies would have to be put into place that direct the tutor to look for any out-of-order steps by the student, and assist the student in understanding the correct sequence for evidence collection. Further, the student is likely to want to know what the consequences are of collecting evidence out of the proper sequence, and the tutor will also have to be prepared to provide this explanation when asked.

Once the evidence-collection process is completed and the set of possible causes has been narrowed down, the next step is to make a diagnosis. There are two diagnosis task variables related to this stage of the process. Each variable can change the specific details of what this stage of the diagnosis process is like, causing changes both in the kind of task model needed and the kind of tutoring required.

Diagnosis Task Variable #10: Stating a Diagnosis Required
A variable that, on the surface, seems to have only a small impact on the structure of diagnosis tasks, but in reality has wide-reaching ramifications, is whether the student (or person doing the diagnosis) is required to explicitly state what the diagnosis is before proceeding to the next stage of the diagnosis task (i.e., prescribing a remedy). Diagnosis tasks that do

not require a diagnosis to be explicitly stated introduce a great deal of additional complexity for a tutor. The tutor must wait until the student has prescribed a remedy and then either work backward to figure out what diagnosis the student has implicitly arrived at or, if that is not possible, ask the student what his or her diagnosis is. "Reverse engineering" a diagnosis from a remedy is difficult, and sometimes impossible, to do. There are two possible situations that can arise, each of which requires an additional teaching strategy to handle: The remedy prescribed by the student indicates an incorrect diagnosis, or it is associated with more than one possible diagnosis, so there is no way to tell which diagnosis has been made. In the first case, the tutor can actually infer which diagnosis the student must have made, and so can intervene to help the student correct the mistake. In the second case, however, the tutor has no choice but to intervene and ask the student which diagnosis he or she arrived at so that appropriate guidance can be provided.

Diagnosis Task Variable #11: Cost of an Incorrect Diagnosis

Another possible variation in a diagnosis task concerns how costly an incorrect diagnosis is. The cost of making an incorrect diagnosis in a particular diagnosis task will affect how thoroughly the set of possible causes must be narrowed down before a diagnosis can be made. In low-cost situations, it may not be worthwhile ruling out every conceivable alternative possible cause, even unlikely ones. This is especially true if there is a cost associated with collecting the additional evidence needed to rule out all the alternatives (Diagnosis Task Variable #2), or if there is a premium on performing the diagnosis process as efficiently as possible (Diagnosis Task Variable #3). However, if the cost of making an incorrect diagnosis is high, then collecting the additional evidence needed to rule out alternative diagnoses, even unlikely ones, may be worth the cost incurred. How thoroughly the set of possible diagnoses must be narrowed down will in turn affect a tutor's decision about when to suggest to the student that it is time to stop collecting evidence and move on to making a diagnosis.

In the final stage of the diagnosis process, the student must prescribe a remedy or treatment for the diagnosed problem. There are three diagnosis task variables related to this stage, each of which can lead to changes in the kind of task model needed and the kind of tutoring required.

Diagnosis Task Variable #12: Observable Consequences of Incorrect or Suboptimal Remedy

If the student prescribes an incorrect or less-than-optimal remedy, will the consequences of this mistake be visible to the student later on, or are the effects of the mistake too subtle to notice? How this question is answered in different diagnosis tasks can have an impact on how the tutor chooses to intervene. In Casper, the consequences of selecting an incorrect or suboptimal remedy are hard for the student to notice. The key factor here is how much feedback on the effectiveness of the student's remedy or treatment is naturally present in a given diagnosis task. If there is a high level of feedback, for example, obvious signs of illness or healing in treating a sick patient, then the tutor need not intervene as much to supply this feedback. In diagnosis tasks with little or no feedback, the tutor may have to intervene to point out to the student why the chosen remedy was not correct.

In diagnosis tasks where a student may prescribe a suboptimal treatment or remedy, the effect of the level of observable feedback becomes even more pronounced. If the student will be able to clearly notice the effects of a suboptimal remedy, the tutor may elect to withhold comment and allow the student to observe the consequences before intervening. However, because the student's remedy will still solve the problem, the negative consequences will have to be fairly severe before the student (or the customer) will notice. In these cases, the tutor may want to intervene immediately to help the student identify and correct what is often a fairly subtle mistake.

Diagnosis Task Variable #13: Variability of Preferred Remedy

In diagnosis situations where there is more than one possible way to treat a diagnosed problem, one remedy is still generally preferred over the others (because it is cheaper, more effective, etc.). In Casper, the preferred solution to a given water problem does not change from customer to customer. This is not true for all diagnosis tasks, however. When there is variability of the preferred remedy, the complexity of a diagnosis task is greatly increased. In selecting the treatment or remedy for a diagnosed problem, the student must now take into account the various factors that dictate which remedy is to be preferred over another and in what context. For the tutor to recognize when the student has selected a less preferred remedy, and to help the student understand the factors that influence which remedy is preferred, the model of the diagnosis task must be extended to include this preference information, and new teaching strategies must be created.

When the variability of preferred remedies is taken to an extreme, the context of the student's diagnosis task can change so greatly that a remedy that is effective in solving a problem in one context does not work at all for the same problem in another context. This situation requires extensions to the diagnosis task model similar to those described earlier, but may require separate teaching strategies to allow the tutor to help the student understand why a solution that worked for him or her before is no longer effective.

Diagnosis Task Variable #14: Implementing Remedies

A final factor that affects the remedy phase of the diagnosis process has to do with who performs the actions required to implement the remedy recommended by the student. There are at least three possibilities: The remedy actions can be done: (a) only by the student, (b) only by another person, or (c) by both the student and another person. In situations where a remedy can only be implemented by the student, there is little additional complexity to worry about. But what about a case where either the student or another person (the customer or a patient) could reasonably be expected to take the steps required to remedy the diagnosed problem? Two issues to be considered are the reliability of asking another person to implement the remedy (they may not do so conscientiously) and the cost or burden that the remedy might impose (e.g., asking the customer not to drink the tap water for 48 hours). In diagnosis tasks where there is a choice of who is responsible for implementing remedies, the complexity of the student's task is increased. Likewise, the task model must be extended to capture additional information about who is to perform each possible remedy, and what cost or reliability issues must be considered by the student in choosing one remedy over another. This additional information, along with new teaching strategies, will be necessary if the tutor is to be prepared to assist the student in understanding the new issues that must be considered when selecting a remedy that is to be implemented by another person.

TEACHING STRATEGIES FOR DIAGNOSIS TASKS

Introduction

This section presents 17 teaching strategies useful for LBD tutors in which the student is engaged in a diagnosis task. A tutor can use these teaching strategies to detect opportunities for tutoring, and to decide how to intervene when such opportunities are recognized. These strategies were created for the diagnosis task in the Casper system. They deal with the most common misconceptions or misunderstandings a student is likely to have while using this system (other types of diagnosis tasks might require a different set of teaching strategies). The strategies described in this section are organized into four sets reflecting fundamental areas of tutorial intervention in diagnosis tasks:

I.   Strategies that deal with misconceptions associated with collecting evidence

II. Strategies that deal with misconceptions associated with articulating a diagnosis

III. Strategies that deal with misconceptions associated with prescribing a remedy

IV. Strategies for helping a student who is confused about what to do
next

This organization reflects the main stages of the diagnosis process, along
with the kinds of questions a student might have while engaged in the
diagnosis task. A schematic overview of the teaching strategies for diagnosis tasks described here, and how they relate to the various phases of
the diagnosis process, is shown in Fig. 4.8.

Teaching Strategies for Misconceptions Associated With Collecting Evidence

Because so much of the diagnosis process involves evidence collection,
there are many opportunities for a student to take a misstep, and consequently for the tutor to intervene with advice. Six teaching strategies were

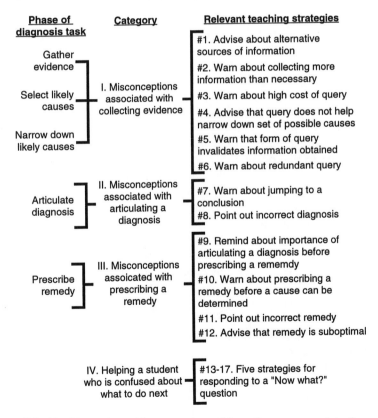

FIG. 4.8. Diagnosis teaching strategies and how they correspond to the
diagnosis process.

developed for dealing with student misconceptions that can arise during the process of collecting evidence. Most of the strategies attempt to help the student become aware of and correct inefficiencies in gathering information about the cause of a problem. In the five-stage model introduced earlier, the student is collecting evidence both in Stage 1 and Stage 3. Because it is often difficult to tell whether the student is collecting initial information, or is narrowing down the set of likely causes, the teaching strategies relevant to both Stages 1 and 3 are grouped together in this section.

Diagnosis Teaching Strategy #1: Advise About Alternative Sources of Information.

An apprentice mechanic is talking to a customer about his car while a supervisor observes.

Apprentice: What seems to be the problem with the air/fuel mixture?

Customer: I don't really know—all I can tell is that the acceleration is gone.

Supervisor [to apprentice]: You can get better information about the air/fuel mixture by hooking up the monitor to the car's on-board computer. Asking the customer about the fuel/air mixture doesn't usually provide useful information because most customers have no way of knowing the answer.

The apprentice mechanic makes a common rookie mistake: He does not realize the information he seeks about the air/fuel mixture can be more easily, and more reliably, obtained via a source other than questioning the customer. In diagnostic interviews, novices can sometimes become so focused on the conversation that they forget to utilize other sources of information in collecting evidence to make a diagnosis. This is more than just an issue of efficiency in collecting information; asking customers questions they cannot answer may make them feel unintelligent.

The *Advise about alternative sources of information* strategy is considered whenever the student asks the customer a question to obtain information. If that evidence has not yet been obtained by the student, and there are better ways to obtain it than by asking the customer, this strategy is triggered. To detect these conditions of applicability, the tutor must be able to access two kinds of information. First, it must have a record of the information the student has obtained up to the current point. Second, it must know, for each piece of evidence, the various ways that evidence can be obtained. Each method of obtaining the information is given a ranking, with the preferred method getting the highest rank. Figure 4.9 shows how the data structures representing queries and evidence are connected with bidirectional links. The links are bidirectional because the

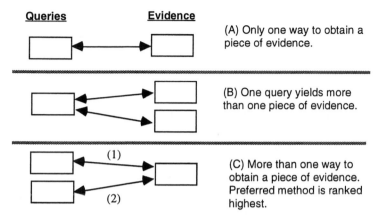

Queries   **Evidence**

(A) Only one way to obtain a piece of evidence.

(B) One query yields more than one piece of evidence.

(C) More than one way to obtain a piece of evidence. Preferred method is ranked highest.

(1)

(2)

FIG. 4.9. Three kinds of relationships between queries and evidence. The links between queries and evidence are bidirectional.

tutor must be able to determine, given a query, what evidence that query can provide, and, given some evidence, what queries can be used to obtain that evidence.

Once the opportunity to apply this strategy has been detected, the tutor must decide whether to intervene. Allowing the student to discover for him or herself what other ways there are to obtain the information apart from asking the customer is best. In the Casper system, this is a remote possibility, so the decision is made to intervene immediately when the student makes such a mistake.

The next decision to be made in applying the *Advise about alternative sources of information* strategy is whether to intervene directly or indirectly. A direct intervention has the tutor interrupting the student's task to deliver a tutorial response, whereas an indirect intervention might have the tutor change the task environment in a pedagogically useful way. In this case, the customer may not always be aware that the student can obtain information from another source. Thus, an indirect intervention— where the tutor causes the simulated customer to point this out to the student—would be unrealistic. Therefore, the decision is made to intervene directly every time.

In other diagnostic interviews, it might be reasonable for the person being interviewed to know that the student should obtain information from another source instead of asking. In such cases, an indirect intervention might be attempted the first time the *Advise about alternative sources of information* strategy is invoked. This would entail the tutor causing the simulated customer to say something along the lines of: "Why are you asking me that? You can get that information from somewhere else."

(Indirect interventions like this require the tutor to control the behavior of the simulated customer.) If the student again asked for information that could be better obtained from another source, then direct intervention, as described here, would be necessary.

Once the decision is made to intervene directly, the tutor must decide what the content of the tutorial response will be. This is determined by the tutor's explanation for the student's mistake. There are three possible explanations that might be considered: The student (a) does not know this particular piece of information can be obtained from other sources, (b) knows about the other sources but forgot to use them this time, or (c) knows about them but does not realize they are preferred over asking the customer for the information. The first explanation is the tutor's default assumption if it is the first time the student has made this particular mistake. To confirm this explanation, the tutor must consult a history of the teaching strategies it has employed so far to see if the student has been tutored on the alternative sources of information available for this query. If no such instance is found, the tutor assumes the student is unaware of the alternative sources available.

The tutorial response in this case is fairly straightforward. The tutor should:

1. Tell the student there are better ways to obtain the information than by asking the customer.
2. Ask the student what information he or she is seeking.
3. Help the student identify a better source for obtaining that information, and explain why it is preferred.
4. Ask the student if he or she would like to retract his or her last question to the customer and obtain the information a different way.

However, if the student has been previously tutored on the alternative sources of information available, the tutor must opt for the other explanations. Because differentiating these two explanations is difficult, the following tutorial response handles both possibilities. The tutor should:

1. Remind the student there are better ways to obtain the information than by asking the customer.
2. Ask the student whether he or she did not use a better alternative because he or she forgot or because he or she did not realize the alternative was actually better.
3. If the student replies that he or she did not realize the alternative was better, explain why it is preferred over asking the customer for the information.

4. Ask the student if he or she would like to retract his or her last question to the customer.

Diagnosis Teaching Strategy #2: Warn About Collecting More Information Than Necessary.

A resident is discussing a case with her supervising physician.

Physician: What's your diagnosis for this case?

Resident: I need to order a complete blood work-up before I can determine what the problem is.

Physician: There's no need for that, you've already got enough information in the patient's chart to make a diagnosis. What do you think it is?

In this exchange between a resident and a more experienced physician, the resident seeks to collect additional information on the patient although enough evidence is available to make a diagnosis. In doing medical diagnoses, making this mistake can not only be costly, but also pose unnecessary risks to the patient. In other kinds of diagnosis tasks, the cost of making this mistake may be only a lack of efficiency. Nonetheless, when the student wants to collect more information than is necessary to make a diagnosis, a tutor is provided with a revealing window into the student's thinking.

Detecting an opportunity to apply the *Warn about collecting more information than necessary* strategy requires the tutor to recognize when enough information is available to determine the cause of the problem. Depending on the domain of diagnosis, determining that enough information is available to decide on the cause of the problem can be an inexact science. In the Casper system, the tutor consults a domain model that links evidence to possible diagnoses. Each of these links is weighted. By summing the weights on the links from all the evidence collected so far by the student, the tutor can get an estimate of how strongly supported a given diagnosis is. When the likelihood weight of any diagnosis exceeds a predefined threshold value, the tutor decides that enough information is available for the student to make a diagnosis. Figure 4.10 depicts the domain model graphically.

Once this strategy is triggered, the tutor must decide whether to intervene. Here the decision is more difficult than in other strategies. Because the tutor's method for deciding whether sufficient evidence has indeed been obtained is imprecise, the tutor cannot be 100% confident that an intervention is necessary. Because of this uncertainty, and to give the student a chance to realize on his or her own that enough evidence has been collected, the student is allowed to ask two extra questions before an intervention is made. To implement this

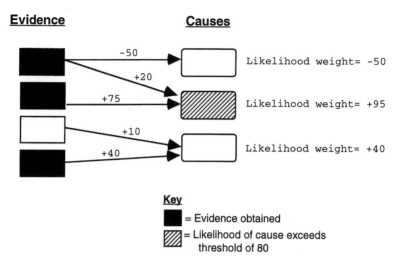

FIG. 4.10. Structure of the model used by the tutor to determine when enough evidence has been collected.

response delay, each time the strategy is triggered the tutor notes that the student has asked a question even after a diagnosis is possible. The third time the strategy is invoked, the tutor will check whether the student has exceeded the two extra question limit and, finding that he or she has, will opt for immediate intervention.

Once the delay is over and immediate intervention has been decided on, the next decision is whether to intervene directly or indirectly. This situation is similar to that encountered in the *Advise about alternative sources of information* strategy. A real customer is usually not sophisticated enough to know that a CSR has collected sufficient evidence to proceed with making a diagnosis. Thus, an indirect intervention—where the tutor causes the simulated customer to point this out to the student—would be unrealistic. Therefore, the decision is made to intervene directly every time an intervention is required.

In choosing a tutorial response, the tutor must consider several possible explanations for why the student collected more information than necessary. These include:

1. The student is too focused on gathering information and simply does not realize it is time to stop gathering information and proceed with the rest of the diagnosis process.
2. The student does not realize enough information has been collected to rule out other causes. The student may not know how some of the evidence collected excludes some potential causes of the problem.

3. The student is not giving enough weight to evidence already collected. The evidence collected points more strongly to the cause of a problem than the student realizes.

4. The student does not know how some of the evidence collected contributes to possible causes. He or she does not realize that some of the symptoms observed give evidence for or against various causes.

5. The student forgot about evidence he or she already collected.

6. The student has an unrealistically high expectation for how much evidence is needed to confirm a particular cause of the problem.

Despite these different explanations for why the student is collecting more information than necessary, the tutorial response is similar in all cases. The tutor should:

1. Tell the student enough information has been collected to make a diagnosis.

2. Ask the student to identify the diagnosis he or she thinks is most likely.

3. Ask the student to identify the evidence he or she thinks contributes to the diagnosis selected.

4. For each piece of evidence identified, give the student feedback on how much it contributes to the likelihood of the diagnosis.

5. If the student has identified a hypothesis in Step 2 that is not the most likely, point out why the evidence does not support the student's hypothesis as strongly, and suggest that the student consider the most likely hypothesis instead. Return to Step 3 to discuss evidence for this hypothesis.

6. For each piece of evidence obtained by the student, but not identified in Step 3, remind the student about that evidence and how much it also contributes to the likelihood of the diagnosis.

Despite these different explanations for why the student is collecting more information, the reason for responding similarly in all cases here is that it is simply not worth the effort required to determine which possible explanation actually accounts for the student's mistake. Regardless of the true cause of the error, the tutorial response described earlier serves reasonably well to get the student back on track. Zeroing in on the student's exact misconception would require the tutor to engage the student in an extended dialogue consisting of questions about the student's mental model of evidence and causes that the student may not even be able to answer.

Diagnosis Teaching Strategy #3: Warn About High Cost of Query.

Resident: I think we should go in and do a biopsy.

Physician: That could be very risky given the fragile state the patient is in.
The information we might get from a biopsy doesn't seem worth
the risk to the patient's health.

The resident may indeed be correct in recommending a biopsy. However,
in neglecting to consider the cost—in terms of risk to the patient—she
has made a mistake commonly seen in novice diagnosticians. In diagnosis
tasks, particularly those that involve obtaining information from another
person, there is usually a cost associated with each query. That cost may
be monetary or social in nature. Whatever the case, the value of the
information gained from a query must be balanced against the cost of
making that query. Factored into evaluating the utility of making a particular query is the likelihood that the query will yield any information
at all. For example, if a particular lab test yields definitive results every
time, it may be worth using even if the cost is fairly high. However,
another lab test that cost the same amount, but had only a 10% chance
of providing usable results, might not be worth the risk.

For a tutor to detect an opportunity to apply this teaching strategy, it
must be able to access the cost and reply likelihood of each query. In the
Casper system, each query or request the student can make is assigned
estimated values for cost and for likelihood of obtaining a useful reply.
Whenever the student makes a query or tells the customer to perform a
test and report back on the results, the tutor examines both cost and reply
likelihood estimates for that query or request and compares them to
threshold values.[8] If the cost estimate is over the threshold for queries
that are too expensive or the likelihood estimate is below the minimum
needed to make the query worth making, the *Warn about high cost of query*
strategy is triggered.

Due to the subtlety of the cost and likelihood factors, the strategy calls
for immediate intervention by the tutor. A direct intervention is made
every time because the nature of the CSR task makes it unlikely that the
student will see any consequences of this mistake first-hand. The explanations for why the student might make high-cost/low-answer likelihood
queries are fairly straightforward. Either the student does not realize the
cost associated with making the query or he or she does not realize the

---

[8]The tutor in the Casper system uses scales of 1 to 10 to estimate both the cost of a query
and the likelihood of obtaining useful information from it. Higher values indicate higher
cost or greater likelihood. Values for cost and likelihood are assigned to each query a priori
by content experts; the values do not change dynamically during the diagnosis process.

low probability of obtaining useful information from the query; a combination of both explanations is also possible.

Diagnosis Teaching Strategy #4: Advise That Query Does Not Help Narrow Down Set of Possible Causes.

Dave and Laura are trying to figure out why their dishwasher will not operate.

Laura: I think it has either a loose belt or a problem with the mechanism that controls the cycles.

Dave: What if it's the fuse? I'll go check that the fuse is still OK.

Laura: That won't tell us anything. We know that we are getting electricity into the unit, so checking the fuse won't give us any new information.

Once a set of possible causes of a problem is identified, subsequent queries should help narrow down that set as much as possible. In the prior exchange, Dave suggests obtaining information about the status of the fuse. Laura points out that information on the fuse will not be useful because it will not help decide between the two causes she has identified as being the most likely.

Whenever the student makes a query, the tutor looks for an opportunity to apply the *Advise that query does not help narrow down set of possible causes* strategy. To trigger this strategy, two additional conditions must first be met: (a) the student must have collected enough evidence up to that point to point to some likely causes of the problem, and (b) the student's query must not give evidence for or against any of these likely causes. To test whether enough information has been collected to identify some likely causes of the problem, the tutor uses the same model described in the *Warn about collecting more information than necessary* strategy. The tutor sums up the contributions of all the evidence collected by the student so far and checks to see if any causes have accrued enough weight to be considered a possible cause at this point. The tutor collects all causes with enough total weight into a set. By testing whether this set is empty, the tutor can determine whether enough information has been collected to identify likely causes of the problem.

Once the tutor has decided there are likely causes, it must test whether the student's query provides any evidence for or against this set of causes. The tutor does this by following the links from evidence to causes to see if the evidence provided by the student's query is linked (with either positive or negative weight) to any causes in the set of likely causes. For example, in Fig. 4.11, Query A would cause this strategy to be triggered because it provides evidence neither for nor against any currently likely causes. Because Query B provides evidence against a likely cause, it would be considered acceptable and would not cause this teaching strategy to be activated.

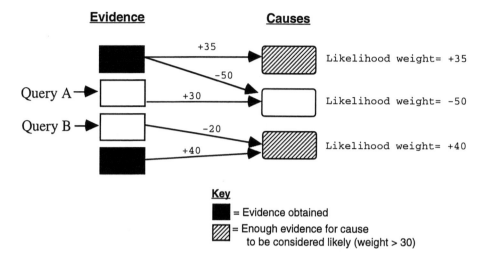

FIG. 4.11. Checking if a query provides evidence for or against any likely causes.

When the tutor has verified that the student has just made a query that does not help narrow down the set of possible causes, it must decide whether to intervene immediately. Two factors point to delaying intervention. First, because the tutor's model of the domain is approximate, the tutor cannot be completely sure it has correctly identified the set of all possible causes. Second, it must recognize that a student will not always select the optimal question to ask in every case. Delaying intervention gives the student a bit of leeway in asking some less-than-optimal questions. Given the opportunity, the student may figure out on his or her own that the questions are not helping to narrow down the set of likely causes and will get back on track without help from the tutor. Because of these factors, the tutor should delay intervention until after the student has made more than two such queries.

Having decided to intervene, the choice between direct and indirect intervention is straightforward. There is little chance the student will see the negative consequences of this particular mistake on his or her own. If a customer knew enough to point out to the student that he or she was asking questions that did not help narrow down a set of possible causes, he or she would know how to solve the problem without assistance. These considerations point to a direct intervention every time this strategy is employed.

Why might a student make a query that does not help narrow down a set of possible causes? There are at least three possibilities:

1. The student is still collecting information to identify additional causes instead of trying to narrow down the set of likely causes.

2. The student does not know what causes are likely. Specifically, the student may think that one or more causes are likely when they are not.
3. The student mistakenly thinks the query will provide evidence for or against one of the likely causes.

The first step in responding to the student in any of these cases is to ascertain what goal the student is pursuing (i.e., gathering information, narrowing down causes, etc.). This will give the tutor a hint if the reason for the student's action is Explanation 1. If the student indicates that his or her goal is to collect information, the appropriate tutorial response would be to inform the student that enough potential causes have already been identified and that he should start trying to narrow down the set of likely causes. If the student indicates that he or she is trying to narrow down the set of likely causes, the tutor should ask the student to identify the likely causes. This will help differentiate between Explanations 2 and 3. If the student identifies some causes that do not have enough evidence to make them likely, the tutor should explain to the student that there is not enough evidence to consider those causes likely. However, if the student identifies a set of causes that are likely, the student probably does not realize that his or her query does not give evidence for or against any of the likely causes. The tutor should explain this to the student and help him or her select a better question to ask next.

Diagnosis Teaching Strategy #5: Warn That Form of Query Invalidates Information Obtained.

An apprentice mechanic is talking to a customer about his car while a supervisor observes.

Customer: The car acts weird when I accelerate.

Apprentice: Does it lurch sporadically when you accelerate quickly?

Supervisor [to apprentice]: You should be careful how you phrase your questions—customers will often tell you what they think you are looking to hear. You might want to phrase the question as, "Could you describe what happens when you accelerate?" so that you don't bias the answer.

The apprentice mechanic does not recognize what political pollsters have long known: The form of a question can influence the response obtained. In many interview situations, the interviewee will provide the answers he or she thinks are being sought by the interviewer. In diagnostic interviews, asking leading questions can result in the interviewee providing inaccurate information and confounding the diagnosis. The more general form of this mistake applies to any diagnosis situation where the method used to obtain some evidence can, if performed incorrectly, taint the reliability of the information collected.

To detect this mistake in diagnostic interviews, the tutor must monitor the way the student phrases questions for the customer. Questions phrased in a leading way cause this strategy to be triggered. In general, leading questions are those that describe a symptom and ask the customer to confirm if he or she has that symptom. In Casper, questions considered leading are tagged, allowing the tutor to quickly recognize the opportunity to trigger this strategy.[9]

Once the tutor recognizes that the student has asked a leading question, the decisions about whether and how to intervene are straightforward. Because this mistake deals with surface-level details of question phrasing, and not with deeper causal understanding, it is fairly easy for students to learn to avoid asking leading questions once they are made aware of it. This points to an immediate and direct intervention by the tutor. Because this mistake is straightforward, the only explanation for why the student might have made it is that he or she is unaware of the concept of leading questions and their effect on the information obtained. Therefore, the tutor's response to a student who asks a leading question should be to:

1. Make a note that the student asked a leading question (for future tutor reference).
2. Point out that the student phrased the question in a leading way.
3. Explain that leading questions can influence the accuracy of the information obtained in response.
4. Ask the student if he or she wishes to retract the last question and ask it in a different way.

Diagnosis Teaching Strategy #6: Warn About Redundant Query.

A resident is interviewing a patient complaining of abdominal pain while a supervising physician watches.

Resident: How long have you had this pain in your abdomen?

Patient: About 2 weeks, I guess.

[. . . later in the interview . . .]

Resident: . . . And this pain has been going on for how long?

---

[9]The technique of tagging all leading questions ahead of time clearly will not work in more open-ended diagnostic interview situations. In such cases, a natural language parsing system could be used to recognize questions phrased in a leading way. Constructing such a system would be an interesting research challenge.

Patient: I already told you—about 2 weeks.

[. . . later still . . .]

Resident: How long have you been experiencing pain there?

Supervising Physician [intervenes]: You've already asked the patient the same question several times, with the same response. Asking redundant questions like that can annoy the patient and give the impression that you aren't really listening to what the patient is telling you.

As the prior exchange shows, being asked the same question repeatedly is not only annoying to the person being interviewed, but can undermine that person's confidence in the question asker. In a complex diagnostic interview, however, the fact that a question has already been asked can be forgotten. Although this happens relatively infrequently, a tutor must be prepared to intervene if the student continues to make redundant queries. Detecting an opportunity to apply this strategy requires the tutor to keep a record of all the questions the student asks the customer. (This is the same history used in the *Advise about alternative sources of information* strategy.) Each time the student makes another query, this record is checked to determine whether it was made before. If so, the strategy is triggered.

Once this strategy has triggered, the next decision is whether to intervene. Several factors point to immediate intervention by the tutor. Asking redundant questions is a mistake that is easily observed by the customer; it will annoy the customer, and it can quickly damage the credibility of the CSR. Finally, because detecting a redundant query is so straightforward, a tutor can be totally confident that this mistake has been correctly recognized.

Once the decision is made to intervene, the next decision is what type of intervention is necessary. In this strategy, unlike some others, a real choice exists between direct and indirect intervention. As a general rule, in LBD tutors, it is best to let a student observe the consequences of his or her mistake. Because the customers in the Casper system are simulated, it is possible for the tutor to control their responses to students' queries. To let the student observe first-hand the consequences of asking redundant questions, the tutor can cause the customer to react angrily, or even to chastise the student CSR, as real customers occasionally do. To drive home the negative consequences of making redundant queries, the first time a student makes this mistake, the tutor should intervene indirectly by causing the customer to respond to the student in a realistic way. If the student continues to make redundant queries, however, the tutor should intervene directly to help the student prevent this mistake from happening again.

Deciding whether to intervene directly or indirectly requires the tutor to track how many times the student has asked a redundant question.

Each time this strategy is triggered, the tutor records that the student has made a redundant query. If the student should make a redundant query again, the tutor can quickly confirm that the student is a repeat offender and opt for direct intervention. Once the decision has been made to intervene directly, the tutor must decide how to best help the student realize his or her error and avoid it in the future. There are at least three reasons a student might have made a redundant query after having obtained the information the first time the query was made. The student either forgot that he or she made the first query, forgot what the information obtained from the query was, or made a different form of the query and did not realize that this yields the same information.

The content of the tutorial response depends on which of these explanations is correct. The first two possibilities are the most common and most easily handled. However, the only way to ascertain that forgetting is indeed the reason for the redundant query is to ask the student if this is the case. The tutorial intervention in these cases should consist of the following actions:

1. Point out the redundancy to the student.
2. Ask the student whether he or she remembers making the query and the evidence obtained from it.
3. If the student does not remember the evidence obtained, tell him or her to go back and find out what it was (by consulting a transcript, if available). Otherwise, remind the student of the evidence obtained.
4. Explain the negative consequences of making redundant queries.
5. Ask the student if he or she would like to retract the redundant query and offer to help him or her select a better query.

To decide whether the third explanation (i.e., that the student made a different form of the query and does not realize that it yields the same information) is plausible, the tutor must have access to a history of the queries the student has made and the evidence each provided. The tutor can check this history to see whether the student's current query yields evidence that is identical to evidence obtained from a prior query. If such a match is found, the student may be unaware of the various queries that yield the same evidence. This might explain the student's mistake. In such cases, a tutorial response slightly different than the one described earlier is necessary. The tutorial response should:

1. Point out that the query just made yields evidence the student has already obtained.

2. Ask the student to point out which prior query provided the evidence he or she seeks to obtain via the current query (by consulting a transcript, if available).
3. If the student is unable to identify the prior query, point out which query it was and remind the student of the evidence obtained from it.
4. Explain that the past and current queries yield the same information.
5. Explain the negative consequences of making redundant queries.
6. Ask the student if he or she would like to retract the redundant query and offer to help him or her select a better query.

Teaching Strategies for Misconceptions Associated With Articulating a Diagnosis

Once the student has collected enough evidence to narrow down the set of possible causes, he or she must articulate a diagnosis about the cause of the problem. Particularly in diagnosis tasks that involve helping another person, this step is important for three reasons. First, the person being helped will invariably want to know what the problem is; understanding the cause of the problem helps clarify why the remedy is needed. Second, insisting that the student articulate a diagnosis is beneficial because it is a way to model the behavior the student should do on his or her own. The student should get into the habit of consciously selecting a diagnosis even when he or she is not required to articulate it to a customer or tutor. This helps the student acquire a model of the diagnosis process that includes this important step. Third, having the student articulate a diagnosis is helpful because it gives the tutor a window into the student's thoughts about the cause of the problem (Clancey, 1982). The strategies described in this section use the opportunity provided by the student stating his or her diagnosis to recognize and respond to two common mistakes: jumping to a conclusion too early and making an incorrect diagnosis.

Diagnosis Teaching Strategy #7: Warn About Jumping to a Conclusion.

An apprentice mechanic is talking to a customer about the problems with his car while a supervisor observes.

Customer: What do you think is the problem with my car?

Apprentice: Looks like you've got a bad carburetor.

Supervisor [to apprentice]: It's too early to decide that the carburetor is the cause of the problem here—you haven't ruled out some other possibilities. For example, have you considered that the problem might be in the fuel line somewhere?

The apprentice mechanic is making one of the most common novice mistakes: jumping to a conclusion about the cause of the problem before enough evidence has been collected. One of the trickiest parts of the diagnosis task is knowing when there is enough evidence to settle on a diagnosis. In terms of the five-stage model of the diagnosis process described earlier, this mistake lies at the boundary between Stage 3 (collecting evidence to narrow down likely causes) and Stage 4 (articulating a diagnosis). Helping the student understand when to make the transition between collecting evidence and the remainder of the diagnosis process is the point of this strategy.

To recognize an opportunity to apply this teaching strategy, the tutor looks for the student to articulate a hypothesis about the cause of the problem to the customer. Anytime the student tells the customer what he or she thinks the problem is, the tutor checks to see if there is enough evidence to determine the cause of the problem. This is done by summing the likelihood weights from all the evidence collected so far and checking if any causes have a total likelihood weight that exceeds the threshold (i.e., the same process used in the *Warn about collecting more information than necessary* strategy). If the student has not collected enough evidence, this strategy is triggered.

Once this strategy is triggered, the tutor must decide whether to intervene immediately and whether the intervention should be direct or indirect. The primary factor that must be considered in making this decision is whether the negative consequences of making an incorrect diagnosis will be directly visible to the student. If the student is able to clearly see the effects of this mistake, the tutor should delay intervention and let the student proceed with the incorrect diagnosis and observe the consequences. If the negative consequences will not be directly visible to the student, or will only be apparent much later on, the tutor should intervene immediately and directly; this will make the student aware of his or her mistake and help correct it.

In the Casper system, the negative consequences of making an incorrect diagnosis are difficult for the student to observe first-hand. The customer does not immediately know whether the student's diagnosis is correct. The only way the student might obtain feedback on a diagnosis is if the customer calls back later and complains that the problem has not been solved. By the time this happens, the student may have already handled a dozen or so other customer problems, and the specifics of the misdiagnosis will have long been forgotten. Because of these factors, the tutor in the Casper system opts for immediate and direct intervention whenever this mistake is recognized.

The essence of the jumping to a conclusion mistake is that a diagnosis should not be made before enough evidence has been collected to rule out other likely causes of the problem. There are at least three explanations why the student may have made this mistake:

1. The student thinks he or she has collected enough evidence for the diagnosis because he or she believes the evidence collected rules out other possible causes.
2. The student thinks he or she has collected enough evidence for the diagnosis because he or she believes the evidence for the chosen diagnosis is much stronger than it actually is.
3. The student does not know what other evidence to obtain and so has proceeded to make a diagnosis based on available evidence.

In each of these cases, the tutor should respond as follows:

1. Ask the student what evidence he or she thinks supports the diagnosis.
2. For each piece of evidence identified by the student, explain how much weight that evidence contributes to the student's diagnosis.
3. Explain to the student that there are other possible causes for the problem.
4. Suggest that the student continue to gather evidence to rule out alternative causes before making a diagnosis.
5. Offer the student the opportunity to retract his or her diagnosis and collect more information.
6. Ask whether the student needs help in deciding what other evidence to collect to rule out other possible causes for the problem.
7. If the student asks for help, suggest something for the student to collect more evidence about.

Diagnosis Teaching Strategy #8: Point Out Incorrect Diagnosis.

A father is helping his son figure out what is wrong with the VCR.

Son: I can't figure it out, Dad. I think there must be something wrong with the video out cable.

Father: I don't think that's it. If that were the problem, we would be getting the same problem even if we weren't playing the tape. From the way the picture looks, I'd say you need to adjust the tracking.

A common student problem in diagnosing is having a misconception about the causal relationship between causes and symptoms in the system being diagnosed. The son trying to fix his VCR probably does not realize that the screen image is only affected when the tape is played; this makes it unlikely that the cable is the cause of the problem. To help a student correct misconceptions like this one, it is important for the tutor to determine the cause of the misconception. To recognize an opportunity to apply this teaching strategy, the tutor looks for the student to articulate a hypothesis about the cause of the problem. Once the student identifies his or her hypothesis, the tutor checks to make sure that enough information is indeed available to make a diagnosis. If insufficient evidence exists, the *Warn about jumping to a conclusion* teaching strategy is invoked instead. If enough evidence is available to make a diagnosis, the tutor checks to see whether the student's diagnosis of the problem is among those it considers plausible. If the tutor finds that another cause is more likely than the one the student selected, the *Point out incorrect diagnosis* strategy is triggered.

The decisions about whether to intervene immediately and whether to intervene directly or indirectly are exactly the same as in the *Warn about jumping to a conclusion* strategy. In the context of the Casper system, there is little chance that the student will have an opportunity to observe the negative consequences of an incorrect diagnosis. Thus, the tutor should intervene immediately and directly whenever this particular mistake is recognized. The tutor's response depends on the explanation for why the student came up with an incorrect diagnosis. Four possibilities are:

1. The student does not realize that some of the symptoms observed give evidence against his or her diagnosis.
2. The student does not realize that some of the symptoms observed give evidence for other possible causes.
3. The student does not know that a particular cause exists at all.
4. The student forgot about some evidence already collected.

The first two explanations deal with situations in which the student is aware of the evidence collected, but he or she is not making the correct causal connections between that evidence and possible causes of the problem. The second two explanations deal with the simpler cases where the student is missing some knowledge: Either the student does not know that a particular cause exists at all, or the student simply forgot about some evidence already collected that would help him or her settle on the correct diagnosis. The following tutorial responses should be effective if any of these four possible explanations for the student's mistake turn out to be on target:

1. Tell the student that his or her diagnosis is not correct.

2. Ask the student what evidence he or she thinks supports his or her diagnosis.
3. For each piece of evidence identified by the student, explain how much weight that evidence contributes to the student's diagnosis.
4. If the student failed to identify any evidence already collected, remind the student about that evidence and how much weight that evidence contributes to the student's diagnosis.
5. Offer the student the opportunity to retract his or her diagnosis and pick a different diagnosis.
6. Ask if the student needs help in figuring out another diagnosis.
7. If the student asks for help, explain how the available evidence points to the correct diagnosis instead of the student's diagnosis.

Teaching Strategies for Misconceptions Associated With Prescribing a Remedy

The final stage in the diagnosis process is taking some kind of action to address the cause of the problem. The person doing the diagnosis may attempt to fix the problem directly, as in a mechanic fixing a car, or he or she may give instructions to someone else about how to fix it, as in a physician prescribing medication to a patient. Both of these cases are grouped under the title of *prescribing a remedy*.

Although arriving at a correct diagnosis is often thought to be the hardest part of diagnoses, selecting an appropriate and effective remedy can be quite challenging in its own right. Conceptually, an understanding of what is causing a problem does not always translate into an understanding of how to fix that problem. This is because understanding how a system works is not necessarily equivalent to understanding how to affect the functioning of that system. This section describes four teaching strategies that deal with prescribing a remedy. The first two strategies are concerned with making sure the student only prescribes a remedy at an appropriate point in the diagnosis process. The second two strategies focus on helping the student select the best possible remedy for the diagnosed problem.

Diagnosis Teaching Strategy #9: Remind About Importance of Articulating a Hypothesis Before Prescribing a Remedy.

An apprentice mechanic is talking to a customer about the repairs that will be needed while a supervisor observes.

Customer: What did you find out?

Apprentice: Well, I took a look at your car and we're going to have to replace the timing belt and the water pump.

Supervisor [to apprentice]:   Before you tell a customer what repairs you plan
                              on making, you should always tell him or her what you think the
                              problem is. That way the customer will understand why the repairs
                              are necessary.

In many diagnosis tasks, and particularly in diagnostic interviews, articulating a diagnosis is essential. As the prior conversation illustrates, the apprentice mechanic skips this important step and proceeds right to prescribing a remedy. Without the supervisor's intervention, the customer most likely would have demanded to know the cause of the problem before authorizing any repairs. In diagnostic interviews, a tutor must act much like the supervisor and ensure that the student articulates a diagnosis to the customer before being allowed to prescribe a remedy.

Detecting an opportunity to apply this strategy is straightforward. The tutor waits for the student to prescribe a remedy; when this occurs, the tutor checks to see whether the student has articulated a diagnosis to the customer yet. Having recognized this mistake, the tutor should intervene promptly because the student has already skipped an important step in the diagnosis process. Waiting until later to discuss this mistake will only confuse the student. In deciding how to intervene, the tutor should consider whether the negative consequences of this mistake will be noticeable and memorable to the student. If so, the tutor should intervene indirectly (e.g., by causing a simulated customer to become upset and ask the student about the cause of the problem). If failing to articulate a diagnosis would not have a noticeable or memorable consequence, the tutor should opt for direct intervention to help the student realize the importance of articulating a diagnosis before prescribing a remedy.

There are three likely explanations for why the student failed to articulate a hypothesis before prescribing a remedy: The student (a) does not know he or she is supposed to articulate a diagnosis before prescribing a remedy, (b) knows he or she should first articulate the diagnosis but forgot to do so at this time, or (c) does not have a diagnosis and is just guessing at a solution. Regardless of the explanation, the tutor's response should seek to achieve two goals. First, it should use the opportunity for intervention provided by this mistake to find out what the student thinks the cause of the problem is. By asking the student for his or her diagnosis, the tutor obtains valuable insight into how the student is going about solving the current problem. The second goal is to teach the student about the importance of articulating a diagnosis before prescribing a remedy. In particular, the tutor should seek to reinforce the model of the diagnosis process by helping the student understand why articulating a diagnosis is important in terms of proper problem-solving procedure. In addition, the tutor should also explain why articulating a diagnosis first is important in terms of helping a customer understand both the cause of the problem and its solution.

Thus, the tutor's response should consist of the following:

1. Tell the student that, before he or she prescribes a remedy, it is important to tell the customer what the cause of the problem is likely to be.
2. Ask the student if he or she thinks he or she knows the cause of the problem and, if so, what it is.
3. If the student does not know what is causing the problem, tell him or her that he or she should identify a likely cause before prescribing a remedy. Help the student identify a possible cause of the problem.
4. If the student's diagnosis is incorrect, follow the *Point out incorrect diagnosis* strategy.
5. If the student's diagnosis is correct, explain why articulating a diagnosis is a good problem-solving technique.
6. If relevant, explain why it is important to inform the customer about the cause of the problem before prescribing a remedy.

Diagnosis Teaching Strategy #10: Warn About Prescribing a Remedy Before a Cause Can Be Determined.

Charles:	My computer's hard drive is corrupted—I can't access any files. I've run a disk utility program and it says that there's nothing wrong with the disk itself. It seems like the only way to fix it is going to be to reformat the drive and lose all my files.
Doug:	Whoa! I wouldn't take that kind of drastic action yet. Have you ruled out the possibility that the directory might be mangled? Try rebuilding the directory file and see if that solves the problem.

By failing to gather enough evidence about the cause of his problem before attempting to solve it, Charles is on the verge of making things worse instead of better. This mistake plagues many people attempting do-it-yourself repairs. In trying a solution before the cause of the problem is well understood, the cure sometimes becomes worse than the disease. A student who prescribes a remedy before a cause can be determined is skipping two important stages of the diagnosis process: gathering evidence and articulating a diagnosis. In responding to this mistake, the tutor must help the student backtrack so that he or she can then proceed through these two stages in the proper sequence. This teaching strategy can be thought of as a complement to the *Warn about jumping to a conclusion* strategy. That strategy is triggered when the student skips parts of the evidence collection phrase, with the tutor helping the student to back up and finish that stage of the diagnosis process. The current strategy helps the student back up to the evidence collection phase as well. Although each strategy is triggered under different circumstances, the tutorial response is largely the same.

Detecting an opportunity to apply this strategy requires that the tutor monitor each time the student prescribes a remedy. When this occurs, the tutor must check whether enough evidence has been collected to arrive at a diagnosis. This check involves the same process used in the *Warn about collecting more information than necessary* teaching strategy (Fig. 4.10). If insufficient evidence exists, the tutor has recognized that the student prescribed a remedy before a cause can be determined and this strategy is triggered.

The decision of whether to intervene immediately is based on whether the negative consequences of making this mistake will be directly visible to the student. As in the *Warn about jumping to a conclusion* strategy, if the negative consequences of an incorrect diagnosis and remedy are directly visible to the student, the tutor should let the student proceed with the incorrect diagnosis and observe the consequences. Because this is not the case in the Casper system, the tutor uses an immediate and direct intervention policy in applying this strategy.

What happens if the student, despite having insufficient evidence to make a diagnosis, happens to get lucky and prescribes the correct remedy anyway? To maximize the pedagogical impact of the student's failure to follow the proper diagnosis process, the student should not be allowed to profit from this type of lucky break. In situations where the tutor has extensive control over the state of the simulated customers, a subtle, but more difficult to implement alternative to direct intervention can be used. Because the student has not collected enough evidence to narrow down the cause of the problem, the possibility must exist that, given the evidence available, more than one cause is possible. If any of the still-plausible causes require a different remedy than the one just prescribed by the student, a crafty indirect intervention available to the tutor would be to change the problem being reported by the simulated customer to one that required a different remedy. As long as the evidence collected by the student so far is consistent with this new problem, the student will never be aware that the tutor changed the customer's problem underneath him or her. The tutor could then make a more pedagogically memorable intervention by showing the student that failing to collect enough evidence led him or her to an incorrect diagnosis and remedy.

The reasons that a student may have prescribed a remedy before collecting enough evidence to make a diagnosis could be any of those discussed in the *Warn about jumping to a conclusion* and *Remind about importance of articulating a hypothesis before prescribing a remedy* strategies. However, it is likely that the misconceptions that led to this mistake are much more basic. In prescribing a remedy before collecting enough evidence to make a diagnosis, the student has skipped over most of the diagnosis process. The tutor should interpret this as meaning that the student is confused about the problem and how to go about solving it. Thus, in addition to the explanations given in the *Warn about jumping to a conclusion* and *Remind about importance of articulating a hypothesis before prescribing a remedy* strategies, the tutor could explain the student's mistake as follows: The student does not have a diagnosis, does not know what other evidence to obtain, and is just guessing at what might solve the problem.

The tutor's response should focus on getting the student to collect more evidence and not on the importance of articulating a diagnosis. If the student proceeds to collect sufficient evidence and again neglects to articulate a diagnosis, the tutor, using the *Remind about importance of articulating a hypothesis before prescribing a remedy* strategy, will have an opportunity to address that error later. The principle of addressing mistakes in earlier steps in the diagnosis process before later steps is an application of the approach identified in Collins and Stevens' (1982, 1983; Stevens & Collins, 1977) work on Socratic tutoring.

Diagnosis Teaching Strategy #11: Point Out Incorrect Remedy.

Mary: Little Susie's got the flu. I'm going to give her some antibiotics.

Beth: That won't help anything. The flu is caused by a virus—antibiotics only work for bacterial infections. Just keep her in bed and give her lots of fluids.

Coming up with a correct diagnosis for a problem is not always a guarantee of taking the right steps to solve that problem. Although Mary has correctly identified Susie's illness, she does not know that antibiotics will not act directly against a viral illness. Picking a good remedy can sometimes be as hard as coming up with the right diagnosis. A tutor helping a student engaged in a diagnosis task must be prepared to assist the student in understanding the various remedies available and selecting one that addresses the cause of the problem.

Recognizing an opportunity to apply this strategy requires that three conditions be met. First, the student must prescribe a remedy for the problem. Second, the student must have already identified a likely cause of the problem. If the student's diagnosis of the problem is not correct, a teaching strategy like *Point out incorrect diagnosis* should be used instead. Third, the remedy prescribed by the student must not be appropriate for the current problem.

To tell whether a remedy is appropriate for the problem identified by the student, the tutor consults a model that associates causes and remedies. Each problem cause is linked to one or more remedies that will solve

Causes   **Remedies**

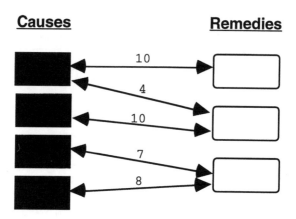

FIG. 4.12. Structure of the model used by the tutor to link causes and remedies. Numbers on links indicate how likely it is (on a 1–10 scale) that a remedy will solve that problem.

that problem. The link between a problem and a remedy is given a number indicating how likely it is that the remedy will solve that problem (Fig. 4.12).[10] If the remedy just prescribed by the student is not linked to the cause of the problem identified, that remedy is not appropriate in treating the problem, and the final condition for triggering this strategy is met.

Once the tutor has recognized that the student has prescribed an incorrect remedy, it must decide whether to intervene immediately or postpone intervention. This decision is largely contingent on whether the negative consequences of prescribing an incorrect remedy will be directly and immediately visible to the student. If the student is able to see first-hand what happens when he or she selects an incorrect remedy, the tutor should withhold comment until the student can see the results of his or her mistake.

In the Casper system, however, the consequences of prescribing an incorrect remedy are not immediately visible to the student. The customer may not realize for several days that the remedy is not working. By the time the customer calls back to complain, the student may already have handled many other calls and forgotten the details of the customer's problem. Furthermore, some water problems will resolve themselves without intervention in a matter of hours or days. The student may be led to think that his or her solution really worked, when in reality it had no effect and the problem actually went away on its own. Because of

---

[10] The current model uses a simple 1 to 10 scale to rank the likelihood that a remedy will solve a problem, with a value of 10 indicating a very high likelihood. Bayesian or other probabilistic models could also be used. The likelihood ratings are used primarily in the *Advise that remedy is suboptimal* strategy.

these factors, the tutor in the Casper system opts for immediate and direct intervention when the student prescribes an incorrect remedy. There are two reasons that the student may have prescribed an incorrect remedy. Either the student thinks his or her remedy is the best available because he or she does not know about other ones or he or she thinks his or hers will solve the problem. In either case, the tutor's response should help the student understand why the chosen remedy does not solve the problem and assist the student in picking a more appropriate remedy. Specifically, the tutor should:

1. Tell the student his or her remedy is not appropriate and explain why the remedy will not solve the problem.
2. Ask the student to select a different remedy to solve the problem.
3. If the student does not know any other remedies, tell him or her about the remedy that will solve the problem and why.
4. If the student picks another inappropriate remedy, go back to Step 1.
5. Ask the student if he or she would like to retract his or her last remedy and prescribe a new one.

Diagnosis Teaching Strategy #12: Advise That Remedy Is Suboptimal.

A resident is talking to a patient about the results of some lab tests while a supervising physician observes.

Patient: Did you get my test results back?

Resident: The culture we took indicates that you have strep throat. I'm going to give you a prescription for amoxicillin to treat it.

Physician [intervenes]: Treating strep throat with amoxicillin will work, but because it's a broad-spectrum antibiotic it can have a number of negative side effects. Tetracycline would probably be a better antibiotic to prescribe in this case.

When more than one method exists to correct a problem, some solutions may be preferred over others. As the resident in the prior exchange discovers, although his or her remedy would have solved the patient's problem, a better treatment exists. One remedy can be preferred over another for a variety of reasons—because it is less expensive to implement, works faster, is simpler to implement, is more likely to work, or fixes the problem for a longer period of time. Unlike the *Point out incorrect remedy* strategy, which comes into play when a remedy does not solve a problem at all, the current strategy deals with situations where the student's remedy will work but is not the optimal solution to the problem.

Detecting an opportunity to apply this strategy is similar to the process used in the *Point out incorrect remedy* strategy. The student must have just prescribed a remedy and must have previously articulated a hypothesis about the cause of the problem. However, in addition to verifying that the remedy prescribed by the student is appropriate for the current problem, the tutor checks to see if another remedy is preferred over the student's remedy. To perform this last check, the tutor compares the ranking of the student's remedy to the rankings of the other remedies for the problem. If the student's remedy is ranked lower than any other remedies, the tutor concludes that the student has prescribed a less-than-optimal remedy and this strategy is triggered.

Once the tutor has recognized that the student has prescribed a less-than-optimal remedy, a decision about whether to intervene immediately must be made. As was the case in the *Point out incorrect remedy* strategy, this decision rests largely on whether the negative consequences of prescribing a less-than-optimal remedy are directly visible to the student. If the student is able to clearly notice the effects of a suboptimal remedy, the tutor should withhold comment and allow the student to observe the consequences before intervening. However, because the student's remedy will still solve the problem, the negative consequences will have to be fairly severe before the student (or the customer) will notice. This suggests that the tutor should intervene immediately to help the student identify and correct what is often a fairly subtle mistake.

There are several possible explanations for why the student may have prescribed a less-than-optimal remedy even after correctly diagnosing the problem:

1. The student is not aware of any better remedies for the problem.
2. The student does not realize his or her remedy has some negative aspects that make it a less desirable option than other remedies.
3. The student mistakenly believes other remedies are less desirable than they really are.
4. The student thinks there are some special circumstances about the problem that make his or her remedy optimal, although in general he or she knows that another remedy would be preferred.

If there are no special circumstances that could change which remedy is considered optimal for a given problem, the last explanation may not make sense in a particular problem domain. If the context of a problem can change in such a way as to make different remedies preferred in different contexts, the tutor will have to determine whether Explanation 4 is in fact the reason for the student's mistake and be prepared to explain why the context of the problem makes a different remedy more preferable than the student's.

In the Casper system, the context of each problem is static so the tutor's response is geared toward addressing the first three explanations for the student's mistake. To help the student resolve any of these three misconceptions, the tutor should:

1. Acknowledge that the student's remedy will solve the problem.
2. Tell the student that a better remedy for the problem exists and hint at why this other remedy is better (i.e., it's simpler, faster, etc.).
3. Ask the student to identify a remedy he or she thinks is better.
4. If the student identifies the optimal remedy, acknowledge that fact and explain what makes that remedy better than the student's original remedy.
5. If the student identifies another remedy that will work, but this is still not the optimal one, return to Step 2.
6. If the student identifies a remedy that is not appropriate at all, execute the response that is part of the *Point out incorrect remedy* strategy.
7. If the student does not know any other remedies, tell the student which remedy is optimal for the current problem and what makes it preferred over the student's remedy.
8. Ask the student if he or she would like to retract his or her last statement prescribing a remedy to the problem and prescribe a different remedy instead.

To execute this response, the tutor must have access to explanations for why certain remedies are preferred over others for a given problem. These explanations are necessary to help the student understand why some remedies are preferred over others. By helping the student understand the factors that make a remedy preferred for a given problem (i.e., low cost, easy to implement), the tutor is giving the student the necessary tools for evaluating potential remedies in other problem situations as well.

Teaching Strategies for Helping a Student Who Is Confused About What to Do Next

Recall that in LBD tutors, the student's activities are centered on the performance of a task. Because of this emphasis on action, one of the most frequently asked questions is what to do next. A tutor must be prepared to help the student find the answer. Because the student might become confused at any point in the task, the tutor must be able to determine where the student is in the task and what the next step should be.

When the student asks the tutor for help, the decisions that must be made by the tutor differ from those that must be made when it decides on its own to intervene. The teaching strategies described in this section have all been tutor-initiated interventions. Teaching strategies used in responding to student questions, like those described in this section, are student-initiated interventions. What makes tutor-initiated interventions different from student-initiated interventions?

Because it is the student who has requested the tutor's intervention by asking a question—in the current case, by pressing the "Now what?" button—there are fewer decisions that must be encoded in the teaching strategies that respond to this question. The decision of whether to delay intervention or respond immediately is irrelevant; when the student asks a question, the tutor should respond immediately. Further, there is no need for the tutor to choose between direct or indirect intervention. The student's question is addressed to the tutor and so the tutor should always respond directly to the student. These two factors simplify the tutor's decision making when the tutor intervenes at the request of the student. As a result, the teaching strategies that encode these decisions are simpler than teaching strategies used in tutor-initiated interventions.

Once the student has pressed the "Now what?" button, the tutor must determine the context in which the student is asking the question so it can decide how best to respond. In recognizing what the student has done so far, and what remains to be done, the tutor must rely on the model of the diagnosis task described earlier. Using the diagnosis task model as a guide, the tutor can deduce what stage of the diagnosis process the student is currently in and what action to suggest the student attempt next. Table 4.6 summarizes the conditions the tutor looks for following a press of the "Now what?" button, the stage of the diagnosis process these conditions indicate the student is in, and what the tutor will tell the student to do next. Each row of the table represents the conditions and response that comprise a separate teaching strategy.

In addition to helping the student through the stages of the diagnosis process, the tutor may also need to assist the student with other procedures that must be performed in conjunction with the diagnosis process. For example, depending on the specifics of the diagnosis task, the tutor might need to help the student fill out forms or guide the student through the steps involved in using a piece of laboratory equipment to collect some evidence needed to make a diagnosis. If there are multistep procedures the student must perform in conjunction with the diagnosis task, the teaching strategies for procedural tasks described earlier could be used to assist the student who is confused about what to do next while performing one of these procedures.

TABLE 4.6
Summary of the Logic Used by the Tutor to Assist a Student
Who Wants to Know What to Do Next in a Diagnosis Task

Diagnosis Teaching Strategy	Conditions Detected Following "Now What?" Button Press	Current Stage of the Diagnosis Process	Suggested Next Step
#13	No likely causes identified yet	Middle of Stage 1—gather initial information	Continue Stage 1. Tell the student to gather more information to identify some potential causes of the problem.
#14	Likely causes exist; no cause determinable	Middle of Stage 3—gather more evidence to rule out likely causes	Continue Stage 3. Tell the student to continue to gather more evidence to narrow down the set of likely causes.
#15	Enough evidence collected to form a hypothesis	Completed Stage 3—gather more evidence to rule out likely causes	Go to Stage 4. Tell the student to articulate a diagnosis about the cause of the problem.
#16	Student has articulated a diagnosis	Completed Stage 4—articulate a diagnosis about the cause of the problem	Go to Stage 5. Tell the student to prescribe an appropriate remedy for the diagnosed cause or set of causes.
#17	Student has prescribed a remedy	Completed Stage 5—prescribe an appropriate remedy for the diagnosed cause or set of causes	Done. Tell the student the diagnosis process is complete.

Note. Each row represents a separate diagnosis teaching strategy.

REPRESENTING TEACHING STRATEGIES

Introduction

To put the teaching strategies enumerated in previous sections to use in building a computer-based tutoring system, two challenges must first be met. Mechanisms must be created for putting teaching strategies into the computer and applying teaching strategies during the student's use of the tutoring system. Putting teaching strategies into a computer system is a two-part problem. A data structure must be created to represent teaching strategies so they can be readily applied to generate tutorial interactions with a student, and a software tool must be built so a user can enter teaching strategies into the computer.

For a computer system to make use of any kind of knowledge, it must have a data structure for representing that knowledge so it can be stored and accessed by the system when needed. Computer-based tutoring systems that use teaching strategies in an explicit way are no exception. Simply creating a computer-usable representation for teaching strategies is only part of the solution. The other problem is: How will those teaching strategies get input into the computer in the first place? The last part of this section describes part of the Teaching Executive system called the *TE toolbox*, an authoring tool designed to allow nonprogrammers to encode teaching strategies into the computer.

Designing a Representation for Teaching Strategies

Designing a representation for teaching strategies requires two things: creating a representation structure and a representation vocabulary. The *representation structure* is an overall framework for organizing the various components of a teaching strategy. It can be thought of in practical terms as a data structure with a number of slots or fields. The representation vocabulary specifies the kinds of items used to fill in each of the various slots in the data structure. Three design criteria shaped the creation of the representation structure and vocabulary for teaching strategies used in the Teaching Executive. The representation must be:

- *Functional.* The data structure must be easy for the computer system to store, retrieve, and apply.
- *Comprehensible.* Because nonprogrammers will be entering teaching strategies into the computer, both the representational structure and vocabulary must be easy to understand and manipulate.
- *Extensible.* To allow for maximum expressivity, the representational vocabulary must be extensible by the user. It cannot be fixed in advance.

In representing any type of knowledge, the most important consideration should be functional (i.e., how that knowledge will be put to use; Birnbaum, 1986). This implies that, to design a data structure for representing teaching strategies, we must look at how these strategies are used. Based on an analysis of the teaching strategies described previously, a tutor observing a student goes through a three-stage decision-making process based on the student's actions:[11]

---

[11]See Shavelson and Stern (1981) for a similar decision-making model.

- recognizing an opportunity to apply a particular teaching strategy,
- deciding whether and how to intervene, and
- delivering the appropriate tutorial response.

Any knowledge representation for teaching strategies must support these three stages of a tutor's decision making in some manner. The Teaching Executive uses a data structure called a *pedagogical knowledge bundle* (PKB) to represent teaching strategies. A PKB is only one solution for representing teaching strategies on a computer. Other solutions may also suffice as long as they support the kinds of decisions a tutor must make.

In creating the representational vocabulary used to fill in the various slots of a PKB, the goal is not to articulate a complete theory of teaching or teach strategy content. Instead, the vocabulary is meant to be both comprehensible and extensible by the user (see the later discussion of the TE toolbox). The representational vocabulary is a means by which the user communicates with the computer to create teaching strategies and is thus akin to the semiformal representations described by Lemke and Fischer (1990).

The design of the PKB structure for representing teaching strategies was modeled after work in the case based reasoning (CBR) paradigm (Jona & Kolodner, 1992; Kolodner, 1993; Riesbeck & Schank, 1989). In looking at the teaching strategies described previously, several observations can be made. First, each teaching strategy is an individual, independent unit; the strategies do not directly rely on, or refer to, each other. Second, the teaching strategies bundle together several related decisions about what the student's misunderstanding is and how best to respond to that misunderstanding. These observations point to the use of a case based approach to representing teaching strategies.

What does it mean to represent teaching strategies using a case based approach? A case is a memory structure used to store an experience in memory (Jona & Kolodner, 1992; Kolodner, 1993; Riesbeck & Schank, 1989). When we have an experience or encounter a situation similar to one we have seen in the past, we are often reminded of that prior situation and use the knowledge in that remembered case to guide us (Schank, 1982). If the current situation is no different than a case already stored in memory, there is no need to create and store another case; we simply re-use the old case. A collection of multiple individual experiences that is abstracted and stored together is called an *ossified case* (Schank, 1982, 1990). Ossified cases are especially parsimonious memory structures because they can be re-used to guide understanding and action any time a particular situation is encountered.

It seems plausible that a teaching strategy—because it is used so many times with so many students—is abstracted away from any one particular teaching experience. Thus, although a PKB does not record any specific details of when it was used, or with which student, it does package together the knowledge needed to interpret and respond to a specific type of teaching situation, whenever that particular situation should arise. Another reason to think of a PKB as a case is that it bundles together in one place all of the decisions relevant to a particular teaching strategy. These decisions are not spread out and stored separately from each other.

Research on teachers' thinking and decision-making processes lends support to conceptualizing PKBs as ossified cases. Scardamalia and Bereiter (1988) framed the problem as follows:

> Real-world problems encountered in teaching are too complex for anyone to grasp fully, so teachers at best work incrementally toward dealing with them. Incremental advance is possible because of processes like *chunking* (Miller, 1956), *composition* (Anderson, 1982), and *recoding* (Case, 1985), which permit whole patterns of information to be treated as single units, thus freeing mental capacity to deal with additional variables. (p. 39)

Shavelson and Stern (1981) characterized teaching decisions as the carrying out of well-established routines. Such routines, they argued, serve to reduce the cognitive information-processing load on the teacher during the teaching process. A similar view is taken by Leinhardt and her colleagues in their research on the performance of skilled teachers (Leinhardt & Greeno, 1986). Leinhardt argued that skilled teachers have large repertoires of activities—also called *routines*—that have become automatic through repeated practice (Leinhardt & Greeno, 1986; Leinhardt et al., 1987). Leinhardt considered these automatic routines a type of situated knowledge (i.e., knowledge that is used to guide a teacher's actions in a specific context; Leinhardt, 1988). This is consistent with the conceptualization of PKBs described here.

The use of PKBs in the Teaching Executive is similar to the use of cases in other CBR systems, but differs in some important ways as well. Most CBR systems store solutions to old problems as cases and try to re-use those solutions when new problems are encountered. One can think of PKBs as being solutions to a type of tutorial problem. In this sense, the Teaching Executive is like other CBR systems in that it re-uses solutions to previously seen problems. The Teaching Executive differs from other CBR systems, however, in that the content of its case base—its library of PKBs—is not modified dynamically. The only PKBs the Teaching Executive knows about are the ones put into it by the user; the Teaching Executive does not have the ability to learn new PKBs on the fly.[12]

---

[12]Building a computer tutor that can learn new teaching strategies dynamically is a difficult but interesting problem (see e.g., Dillenbourg, 1988; O'Shea, 1982). The problem is analogous to building an expert system that can acquire expertise by observation, something that is still considered an open problem in that field (Boose, 1986).

Other researchers represent teaching strategies as a set of if–then rules (also known as *production rules*). This approach is used for representing knowledge for use in expert systems (Davis & King, 1977; Waterman & Hayes-Roth, 1978). Still other tutoring systems have used a production rule formalism for representing teaching strategies. Collins & Stevens (1982; Stevens & Collins, 1977) studied the behavior of human teachers and identified a set of production-style rules that could be used to generate Socratic-style tutoring interactions with a student. These rules were employed in the WHY system, a Socratic-style computer-based tutor that teaches students how to reason about the factors affecting rainfall in different regions of the world (Stevens & Collins, 1977). GUIDON was another intelligent tutoring system (ITS) to represent teaching knowledge as production rules (Clancey, 1982). The quadratic tutor (O'Shea, 1982) also used production rules to explicitly represent teaching expertise. Anderson's research group at Carnegie Mellon University has been a major proponent of the use of a rule-based approach to encoding teaching interventions. Anderson and his colleagues built tutors for teaching algebra, geometry proofs, and Lisp programming, all of which use a production rule approach based on Anderson's ACT theory of cognitive processing (Anderson, 1982; Anderson et al., 1990; Anderson & Corbett, 1993; Anderson & Skwarecki, 1986).

There are several reasons why a rule-based approach was not used to represent teaching strategies in the Teaching Executive system.

- A tutor needs to quickly recognize whether any of its teaching strategies are relevant to apply in a given situation. It is pointless to have the tutor do a lot of work chaining rules together only to find out it has nothing relevant to say. In other words, there is no need for the tutor to reason from first principles every time it needs to decide what to do.

- As the size and complexity of tutoring systems scale up and hundreds of teaching strategies are needed, a tutor cannot be expected to examine every one of its teaching strategies each time a response might be needed (see e.g., Kolodner, 1984). Instead, a tutor needs to label its teaching strategies so the relevant ones can be quickly and efficiently retrieved and applied.

- Each teaching strategy contains many related decisions (i.e., when intervention is relevant, whether to delay intervention, how to intervene). In a rule-based system, each of these decisions would be encoded into a separate rule. To apply a teaching strategy represented in this way, the system would need to search for all the related decisions in a large list of rules. By employing a case based representational approach, all the related decisions that comprise a teaching strategy can be bundled together in one place, eliminating the need for excessive searching.

- Representing teaching strategies as cases makes them easier for the computer to apply and for a human to author (Murray, 1992). Everything is in one place, rather than spread out over separate data structures (i.e., production rules). Because one design goal for the Teaching Executive's representation of teaching strategies is to enable the system designer to extend the representation as needed, bundling the set of decisions that comprise a teaching strategy together in a single case makes it easier for the designer to understand existing strategies and create new ones. Using production rules would mean that each context element and decision would have to be represented in a separate rule (Clancey, 1985, 1986; Woolf & McDonald, 1984).

Another approach to explicitly representing teaching strategies is that taken by Murray (1992). His KAFITS architecture, used to build a physics tutoring system, represented teaching strategies as a variant of augmented transition networks (ATNs; Woods, 1970) called *parameterized action networks* (PANs). PANs are similar to PKBs in that they bundle together a set of related teaching decisions into one strategy. Another advantage of PANs is that they lend themselves to a graphical representation that Murray claimed makes it easy for a system designer to visualize and edit teaching strategies. PANs are much more procedural, whereas PKBs are more declarative. The set of tutorial actions that comprise a PAN are intermingled with contextual decisions that dictate which actions should be taken in a particular situation. As is seen later, PKBs separate decisions about the context in which a teaching strategy is relevant from the tutorial actions that are to be taken if the strategy is executed.

Pedagogical Knowledge Bundles

A PKB bundles together three components of teaching knowledge, two of which are further decomposable into subcomponents. Each component of a PKB is designed to support one of the tutor's three decision-making stages described earlier. The three major components that, taken together, comprise a PKB are: (a) the PKB index, used for recognizing an opportunity to apply a teaching strategy; (b) the diagnosis procedure, used for deciding whether and how to intervene; and (c) the response packets, used for delivering the appropriate tutorial response (see Fig. 4.13). To illustrate how a PKB can be used to represent the content of a teaching strategy, the following sections fill out the PKB for the *Advise that query does not help narrow down set of possible causes* teaching strategy. In the Casper system, whenever the student asks the customer a question to collect some evidence, this strategy is used by the tutor to ensure that the

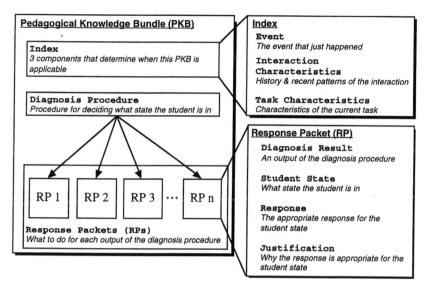

FIG. 4.13. The structure of a PKB.

student's question is really helping zero in on the cause of the problem. Questions that do not provide evidence that helps rule in or out any possible causes of the problem are to be avoided because they unnecessarily prolong the diagnosis process. However, to give the student a chance to get back on track by him or herself, this teaching strategy instructs the tutor to wait until the student asks two unnecessary questions before intervening to help the student ask better questions. The *Advise that query does not help narrow down set of possible causes* teaching strategy is summarized in Fig. 4.14.

The PKB Index

The first thing a tutor must be able to do is recognize when an opportunity for tutoring presents itself. For a tutor whose repertoire of possible interventions is determined by the set of teaching strategies it knows about, this means noticing when one of its teaching strategies is relevant to apply in the current situation. To determine which teaching strategy out of a potentially large set is relevant in a given situation, the strategies must be labeled, or indexed, so an appropriate one can be quickly selected. To support this requirement, the first component of a PKB is the *PKB index*, a label that describes when (i.e., under what conditions) the teaching strategy represented by that PKB is relevant to apply.

The hardest part of labeling or indexing any kind of item for retrieval is deciding what labels will be used—in other words, what the indexing

Triggering event	Student asked a question to obtain information
Context	There is enough evidence to point to some likely causes of the problem -AND- This question doesn't give evidence for or against a likely hypothesis
Intervention criteria	Wait for the student to ask two questions that yield no evidence for or against likely hypotheses before intervening
Intervention type	Direct
Tutorial response	If the student has made two or fewer such queries then record the fact that a poor query was made, otherwise engage the student in a Socratic dialogue to help her ask better questions.

FIG. 4.14. Summary of the *Advise that query does not help narrow down set of possible causes* strategy.

vocabulary will be.[13] This is true in trying to label teaching strategies as well. To decide how teaching strategies should be indexed, we must consider what types of information a tutor would have access to in observing a student engaged in performing a task in an LBD environment. This determines, in large part, the types of labels that may be useful in selecting relevant teaching strategies to apply.

Based on an analysis of the types of information present in an interaction between a computer-based teacher and a student, there are three categories of information that can be used as cues to select an appropriate response: (a) the student's current action, (b) the history of the interaction with the student so far, and (c) the structure of the task being performed by the student. In LBD tutors—where the student is engaged in performing a task—the primary source of evidence that can indicate the need for tutorial intervention is the student's current action. However, the only way for a tutor to decide whether the student's action is cause for intervention is to interpret that action in context. In establishing the context for the student's action, the tutor must consider what task the student is trying to perform and what the student has done so far.

Thus, the PKB index is composed of three parts, reflecting the three types of information that are useful in deciding whether a particular teaching strategy is relevant to apply: triggering events, interaction characteristics, and task characteristics.

---

[13]The problem of how to label items so that they can be retrieved when relevant is known as *the indexing problem*; it has been discussed extensively in the case based reasoning literature (Domeshek, 1992; Jona & Kolodner, 1992; Kolodner, 1993; Schank, 1982). In particular, Owens (1990) examined this problem in the context of retrieving proverbs, Domeshek (1992) for retrieving stories containing social advice, Burke (1993) for retrieving tutorial stories in a social simulation, and Edelson (1993) for retrieving stories of animal form and function.

The most critical piece of information that must be considered in selecting a teaching strategy is the most recent event that occurred in the student's performance of a task. A student's actions and questions are used as windows into the student's thinking, and a good teacher is constantly noticing and evaluating these as evidence of the student's progress or need for assistance. It is rare to see a teacher intervene without an event prompting that intervention.

A *triggering event* can be either an action a student takes or something that happens in the task environment as a *result* of the student's actions (or lack of action). Examples of triggering events having to do with student actions include the student (a) asking the teacher a question, (b) taking some step in performing a task, (c) failing to perform a required step in a procedure, or (d) missing an opportunity to notice an important detail. Because the number of individual events that might occur in a teaching interaction is virtually unlimited, the representation of events has to be done at a general level so the size of the event vocabulary will be tractable. Thus, the representation of some events can be divided into two parts: the event type and the event content. The *event type* describes what kind of event just occurred, whereas the *event content* specifies the particulars of that event. For example, if the student is practicing to be a cashier at a fast food restaurant and has just rung up the customer's burger, the event type would be STEP-TAKEN, whereas the event content would be RING-BURGER. Each type of task will have its own vocabulary of events that best describe the actions a student can take in performing tasks of that type.

Making a distinction between event type and event content allows the event vocabulary for a given type of task to be more general and thus applicable in a wider range of situations. By specifying only the event type and leaving the event content variable, it is possible to create a PKB that is triggered any time the student takes a step, regardless of what particular step is taken. In the cashier example, this might be represented as (STEP-TAKEN *<step-name>*), where *<step-name>* is a variable that matches any step. Without this ability, it would be necessary to create a separate event vocabulary item for each of the potentially hundreds or thousands of individual steps a student might take in an LBD tutoring system. A proliferation of the event vocabulary would make it extremely difficult to create PKBs that were applicable whenever any of a set of related events occurred. Instead of being able to describe a category of events for which a PKB is relevant with a single event type descriptor, each of the perhaps dozens of individual events would have to be listed in the triggering event slot of a PKB.

In filling out the PKB for the *Advise that query does not help narrow down set of possible causes* strategy, the triggering event is the student asking the customer a question to obtain evidence. Every time the student asks the customer a question, the possibility exists that the question just asked does not narrow down the space of possible causes, making this teaching strategy relevant. In filling in the triggering event slot of the PKB index for this teaching strategy, we specify an event type of ASK-QUESTION-OBTAIN-INFO, the event type describing the class of student actions where the student asks the customer a question to collect some evidence. We do not yet care what exactly the student is asking about (that comes later), so the event content is left variable. To handle the situation in which different triggering events might call for the same teaching strategy to be applied, multiple triggering events can be included in a PKB index. This eliminates the need to duplicate an entire PKB when the only difference is the triggering event. When any of the triggering events listed in the PKB index are detected, that PKB will be considered potentially relevant to apply. Table 4.7 shows some examples of the event types used in the teaching strategies for the BC Server and BC Cashier systems. Table 4.8 shows examples of the event vocabulary used in the Casper system.

The second component of the three-part PKB index describes what previous student or teacher actions must have occurred for a particular teaching strategy to be considered relevant. These descriptions are called *interaction characteristics*. They can be used to describe: (a) past teacher actions, (b) past student actions, (c) past task environment or simulation events, and (d) changing aspects of the current problem or task being attempted. These four types correspond to the four entities present in any learning environment where the student is attempting to perform a task or solve a problem.

To allow for a precise specification of the context in which a particular PKB is relevant, several interaction characteristics can be listed together in the PKB index to form a conjunctive description. Combining interaction characteristics in this way not only allows for a wider range of expressivity, but it also allows the vocabulary of interaction characteristics to be represented to be kept relatively small. As was the case for triggering events, different types of tasks (e.g., procedural, diagnosis) will have different sets of interaction characteristics that are relevant in making

TABLE 4.7
Event Types in the BC Cashier and BC Server Systems

Event Type	Description
STEP-TAKEN	The student has taken some step in the current task (e.g., pressing a key on the register or moving a tray to the counter).
BUTTON-PRESS	The student presses one of the buttons used to ask the tutor a question (e.g., "Now what?", "How do I do that?", or "Why?").

TABLE 4.8
Some of the Event Types in the Casper System

Event Type	Description
TELL-PROBLEM-DESCRIPTION	The student has given a description of the general cause of the problem to the customer.
PRESCRIBE-REMEDY	The student prescribed a remedy for the current problem.
PROMISE-ACTION	The student has promised an action to the customer.
PRESCRIBE-ACTION	Tell the customer to take an action.
TELL-INFORMATION-CONDITIONAL	Tell the customer some information that depends on a condition for truth value.
PRESCRIBE-ACTION-CONDITIONAL	Tell the customer to take an action depending on a condition.
ASK-LEADING-QUESTION-OBTAIN-INFO	The student asked a leading question to obtain information.
TELL-PROBLEM-DESCRIPTION	The student described or summarized the description of the problem.
TELL-INFORMATION	Provide information about a characteristic of an object.
TELL-REASONS-FOR-QUESTION	The student explained the reasons it was necessary to ask a particular question.
TELL-PROBLEM-CAUSE	The student expressed the conclusion or hypothesis he or she reached about the cause of the problem.
ASK-QUESTION-REFINE-INFO	The student asked a question to refine some information already obtained.
PRESCRIBE-ACTION-OBTAIN-INFO	The student prescribed an action for the customer to take to obtain information about a factor.
TAKE-ACTION-OBTAIN-INFO	The student took an action to obtain information about some factor.
ASK-QUESTION-OBTAIN-INFO	The student asks a question to obtain information about some characteristic of a factor.

teaching decisions in that type of task. Tables 4.9 and 4.10 list some interaction characteristics from the BC Cashier and BC Server systems, as well as the Casper system.

The next step in filling out the PKB index for the *Advise that query does not help narrow down set of possible causes* strategy is to specify the context in which the triggering event of the student asking the customer a question to collect evidence is not useful in narrowing down the cause of the problem, and is thus worthy of intervention by the tutor. The only way to confirm that a question is not useful in narrowing down the set of possible causes is to look at two factors that are determined by the history of the student's interaction so far. First, the student must have collected

TABLE 4.9
Example Interaction Characteristics From the Casper System

Interaction Characteristic	Description
CUSTOMER-JUST-ASKED-QUESTION	The customer has just asked a question of the student.
QUESTION-ALREADY-ASKED	Has the student already asked this question?
ASKED-REDUNDANT-QUESTIONS-BEFORE	Has the student asked redundant questions before?
QUERY-COST-TOO-HIGH-FOR-ANSWER-LIKELIHOOD	The cost of this query is too high considering the likelihood of a useful answer from the customer.
CAUSE-DETERMINABLE	Is there enough information available to determine the cause of the problem?
QUESTION-GIVES-NO-EVIDENCE	The question gives no evidence for any hypothesis in this problem.
LIKELY-CAUSES	There is enough evidence to point to some likely causes of the problem.
QUESTION-GIVES-EVIDENCE-FOR-LIKELY-HYP	This question does not give evidence toward a likely hypothesis.
INFO-ALREADY-OBTAINED	Has the information obtained from this query been obtained yet?
INFO-BETTER-OBTAINED-VIA-OTHER-ACTION	The information the student is trying to obtain can be better acquired via other actions.
INCORRECT-PROBLEM-INFORMATION-GIVEN	The student has given incorrect information about the problem to the customer.
INCORRECT-DIAGNOSIS	The student has made an incorrect diagnosis.
CAUSE-IDENTIFIED	Has the student chosen a hypothesis about the cause of the problem?
REMEDY-APPROPRIATE-FOR-PROBLEM	Is the remedy prescribed appropriate given the student's current hypothesis about the problem?
REMEDY-PRESCRIBED	Has the student prescribed a remedy for the problem?
OPTIMAL-REMEDY-PRESCRIBED	Has the student prescribed an optimal remedy to the current problem?
STUDENT-HYPOTHESIS-IS-BEST-POSSIBLE-GUESS	The student has a hypothesis and it matches the tutor's best guess about the cause.

enough initial evidence to point to some likely causes of the customer's problem. Without some initial pieces of evidence, there will be no set of possible hypotheses to narrow down—there will not be any hypotheses at all. If there is insufficient evidence available, the student need not worry about narrowing down the set of possible causes and should instead continue collecting evidence to get an idea of which causes may be likely. If this is indeed the case, we do not want the tutor to intervene with

TABLE 4.10
Interaction Characteristics From the BC Cashier and BC Server Systems

Interaction Characteristic	Description
STEP-NOT-REPEATED	This step has not been repeated.
STEP-REPEATED	The student repeated a step in the task.
FLOATING-STEP-REPEATED	The student has repeated a step in a task containing the current task.
EARLY-STEP	The student has taken a step prematurely.
EARLY-CONTAINING-STEP	The student has prematurely taken a step from a task containing the current one.

advice about narrowing down the set of possible causes yet. To indicate that this teaching strategy is only relevant in situations where enough evidence exists to point to some possible causes of the problem, the interaction characteristic LIKELY-CAUSES-EXIST is listed in the interaction characteristics slot in the PKB index.[14]

Once the tutor has verified that enough evidence has been collected, the second factor that must be checked is whether the student's question helps give evidence for or against any of these likely causes. This second interaction characteristic, termed *QUESTION-GIVES-NO-EVIDENCE*, looks at the specific question asked by the student, what evidence that question might provide, and whether that evidence is needed to rule in or out any of the currently likely hypotheses about the cause of the customer's problem.[15] Only when both interaction characteristics, LIKELY-CAUSES-EXIST and QUESTION-GIVES-NO-EVIDENCE, are found to be true does the PKB continue to be considered relevant to the student's current situation.

Task characteristics are the third component of the PKB index. They represent information about the nature and structure of the task or subtask that the student is currently engaged in. This information can range from general characterizations of the type of task (e.g., whether the task is procedural or diagnostic) to more specific information about the task at hand (e.g., what steps the task is comprised of, what order the steps have to be performed in). Thus, the task characteristics specified in a PKB index determine, in part, when (i.e., in what kinds of tasks) that PKB is applicable. The information described by task characteristics differs in an important way from that described by interaction characteristics. Task

---

[14]The specifics of how the LIKELY-CAUSES interaction characteristic checks the available evidence collected by the student are described earlier.

[15]An earlier section describes this process in detail.

characteristics are used to describe features of the student's task that are static (i.e., the features do not vary during the course of performing that task).

Including information in the PKB index about the kind of task the student is engaged in is based on the realization that different tasks, or even different parts of a single task, often lend themselves to different styles of teaching. For example, an exploratory task—where the student's role is to discover things on his or her own—might lend itself to a more passive teaching style—one where the teacher intervenes only when asked to do so by the student. A procedural task—one that requires the student to learn how to perform a highly scripted procedure—might dictate a more active style of teaching—one in which the teacher jumps in whenever the student takes a wrong step. Examples of the vocabulary of task characteristics used in the BC Server and BC Cashier systems are shown in Table 4.11. As was true for interaction characteristics, several individual task characteristics can be listed together in a PKB index to form a conjunctive description of the task for which that PKB is appropriate. By allowing individual task characteristics to be mixed and matched in this manner, it is possible to create descriptions of a task that range from the very general to the very specific while keeping the vocabulary of task characteristics small (see Fig. 4.15).

TABLE 4.11
Task Characteristics Vocabulary Used in the
BC Cashier and BC Server Systems

Task Characteristic	Description
TASK-TYPE	What is the nature of the current task or subtask? Possibilities include: UNORDERED-PROCEDURE, ORDERED-PROCEDURE, SINGLE-STEP, and COMPOSITE-ACTION.
ISOLATED-TASK	Information about the task's containing tasks is not relevant.
NOT-ISOLATED-TASK	Information about this task's containing tasks is relevant.
STEP-PART-OF-CURRENT-UNORDERED-TASK	The current step is part of the current task whose steps are unordered.
STEP-PART-OF-ORDERED-TASK	The current step is the next step in an ordered task.
STEP-NEXT-IN-ORDERED-CONTAINING-TASK	The current step is part of an ordered task containing the current task and all of its prerequisite steps have already been taken.
STEP-NOT-PART-OF-TASK	The current step is not part of the current task (ordered or unordered steps).
STEP-NOT-IN-CONTAINING-TASK	The current step is not part of an ordered task containing the current task.

PKB Index	
Triggering event	ASK-QUESTION-OBTAIN-INFO
Interaction Characteristics	LIKELY-CAUSES-EXIST and QUESTION-GIVES-NO-EVIDENCE
Task Characteristics	

FIG. 4.15. Filling in the interaction characteristics portion of the PKB index.

Due to the dynamic nature of the student's task in the Casper system, no task characteristics were used in the PKBs representing the teaching strategies for diagnosis tasks.[16] Thus, the PKB index for the *Advise that query does not help narrow down set of possible causes* strategy is complete as shown in Fig. 4.15.

Diagnosis Procedure

Once a tutor has recognized an opportunity to apply a particular teaching strategy, the next major step is deciding whether and how to intervene. In particular, the tutor must decide whether immediate intervention is warranted in the current situation, or whether the student would most profit by having the tutor delay intervention until the mistake is made a second time. If immediate intervention is deemed most appropriate, the tutor must decide what type of response to give. Two general possibilities that must be considered are whether to intervene directly, by saying something to the student, or indirectly, by causing some change in the task environment or simulation.

Once a PKB has been deemed relevant, it is still not always a straightforward task to interpret the situation so that a single appropriate response can be made. The diagnosis procedure in a PKB is, as its name implies, a procedural mechanism for further interpreting the situation to select the most appropriate type of response. Not all PKBs have a diagnosis procedure; sometimes the triggering event, interaction characteristics, and task

---

[16]The task characteristic describing the PKBs used in the Casper system as being relevant to diagnosis type tasks was omitted because the type of task never changes within Casper. If some components of the Casper diagnosis task involved procedural elements (see earlier discussion of Diagnosis Task Variable #4), then including a task characteristic in each PKB that indicated whether that PKB was relevant to the diagnosis portion of the task or to the procedural portion might be necessary to help determine which teaching strategies were relevant.

characteristics in the PKB index suffice to unambiguously identify the student's situation and an appropriate tutorial response. Once a PKB is selected as applicable to a given situation, its diagnosis procedure is executed. The diagnosis procedure is used to further refine the interpretation of the state the student is in and to select the specific tutorial action that would be most relevant to respond with given that interpretation.

The diagnosis procedure can be thought of as posing a question about some aspect of the student's current state and providing a mechanism for obtaining an answer. The answer to this question is obtained by executing the diagnosis procedure, and it is used to make a final decision about what state the student is in and how to respond. Each answer supplied by executing the diagnosis procedure corresponds to a part of a PKB, called a *response packet*, which is discussed in greater detail in the next section. For now, all that is important to know about response packets is that each represents an answer to the question posed by the diagnosis procedure and describes the state the student is in and how to respond to the student. Table 4.12 provides some examples of how diagnosis procedures are used in various situations.

There are two classes of diagnosis procedures: one that relies only on information the teacher already has, and one that obtains additional information from the student. The internal information class of diagnosis procedures makes an interpretation based solely on information obtained from the Teaching Executive's databases and record of the interaction. These diagnosis procedures consist of a segment of computer code that accesses the relevant information and returns a value used to select the appropriate response packet. This class of diagnosis procedure is used when all the information needed to refine the interpretation of the current situation so that a response packet can be selected is contained within the Teaching Executive's databases.

In contrast, the external information class of diagnosis procedures uses information obtained from the student to make an interpretation and select the appropriate response packet. This class of diagnosis procedures obtains information from the student by asking the student a question and obtaining an answer. Based on the student's answer to the question, an interpretation is made and a response packet is selected. External information diagnosis procedures are used only when there is insufficient information available in the Teaching Executive's databases to make a reasonable interpretation of the current situation and select a response packet.[17]

What kind of diagnosis procedure is needed in filling out the PKB for the *Advise that query does not help narrow down set of possible causes* strategy? Once the tutor has recognized that the student has indeed asked the

---

[17]The external information class of diagnosis procedures has not been implemented in the current version of the Teaching Executive.

TABLE 4.12
Some Example Diagnosis Procedures

Student's Situation	Question posed by diagnosis procedure	Possible answers
The student forgets to take a needed step.	Why did the student forget to take the step?	(1) The student simply forgot. (2) The student did not know that the step was necessary. (3) The student did not know how to perform the step.
The student presses the button labeled "Why?"	What does the student want an explanation for? Have we just discussed a step with the student? If so, is it a step he or she took that was unnecessary, or a step that he or she needs to take?	(1) No, we have not discussed any steps to take with the student yet so it is not clear what needs explaining. (2) We just told the student to perform a step and so the student is probably asking why he or she should perform that step. (3) We just told the student that his or her most recent step is not necessary so the student is most likely asking why his or her most recent step was unnecessary. (4) The student just repeated a step and was informed of this fact so the student probably wants to know why repeating the step was unnecessary.
The student is trying to diagnosis a problem and has collected enough information to determine the cause of the problem, but has yet to prescribe a remedy to the problem. The student asks what to do next.	Has the student given any evidence that he or she has an idea about a possible cause of the problem?	(1) Yes, the student has some idea of a cause of the problem (so the next step is to find a remedy for the problem). (2) No, the student has not shown that he or she knows what the cause of the problem is (so help the student use the available evidence to decide what the cause of the problem is).

customer a question, the answer to which will not help narrow down the set of likely causes of the problem, the tutor must still decide whether to intervene immediately or let the student try to get back on track. This teaching strategy specifies that the student should be given the leeway to ask two unproductive questions before the tutor intervenes. The diag-

PKB Index	
Triggering Event	ASK-QUESTION-OBTAIN-INFO
Interaction Characteristics	LIKELY-CAUSES-EXIST and QUESTION-GIVES-NO-EVIDENCE
Task Characteristics	
Diagnosis Procedure	
Has the student asked more than two questions that fail to give any evidence toward a likely hypothesis?	
If no, then return "don't intervene yet," if yes, return "intervene now."	

FIG. 4.16. Filling in the diagnosis procedure.

nosis procedure is the place in the PKB where this decision is made and the appropriate response selected.

The diagnosis procedure is a short segment of Lisp code that counts how many times the student has made this particular mistake. If the count is two or less, the diagnosis procedure code returns a "don't intervene yet" value; when the count exceeds two, the diagnosis procedure returns an "intervene now" value. These returned values are used to select the corresponding response packet. The PKB for the *Advise that query does not help narrow down set of possible causes* strategy, with the diagnosis procedure filled in, now appears as shown in Fig. 4.16.

Response Packets

The conditions under which some teaching strategies are to be applied are so specific that only one kind of response is appropriate. But this is not universally true. Other teaching strategies contain a set of related responses and, depending on the particulars of the current situation, a different response may be used. If a PKB were to allow only one response per teaching strategy, a teaching strategy that contained a set of closely related responses would have to be broken up and represented as separate PKBs, one for each possible response. This has two distinct disadvantages. First, except for a different response, the rest of the information in the PKB would have to be duplicated, requiring additional storage space on the computer. Second, breaking up a teaching strategy into separate pieces makes it more confusing for the person authoring the teaching strategies. Instead of being able to write down in one place the entire range of responses contained in a single teaching strategy, this information would

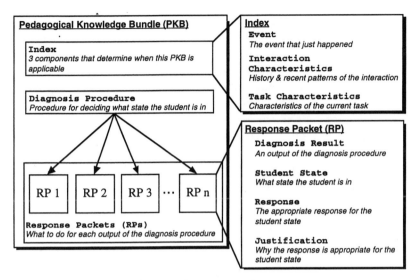

FIG. 4.17. The structure of a PKB.

have to be dispersed across several (similar) PKBs. This greatly increases the potential for mistakes or confusion in encoding teaching strategies on the computer.[18]

For these reasons, each PKB is equipped to represent as many responses as a teaching strategy may specify. Each response is encoded in a data structure called a *response packet* contained within a PKB. The diagnosis procedure acts to select which response packet will be used in a given situation. Thus, the third main component of a PKB is a set of response packets, one for each possible output of the diagnosis procedure. Figure 4.17 depicts this relationship graphically. Response packets package together four types of information that characterize: (a) the result of the diagnosis procedure for which this response packet is relevant, (b) what that result means in terms of the current state of the student, (c) how best to respond to the student's situation, and (d) an explanation of why that response is appropriate for the student's current state. The first element of a response packet (RP) is simply an index that links that RP to one possible output of the diagnosis procedure. There must be one RP for each possible result produced by a diagnosis procedure. This is because it is functionally useless, not to mention wasteful of effort, for a diagnosis

---

[18]A similar approach was employed by Murray (1992) in designing a representation for teaching strategies in the KAFITS system. His use of PANs allowed a system designer to represent many related teaching strategies in a single PAN instead of having to create a separate PAN for each variation.

procedure to interpret student situations for which the tutor has no response.[19]

In analyzing a student's situation and deciding on a response, a tutor is really engaging in an inferential process about the student's cognitive, emotional, or motivational state. Based on this assessment, the tutor decides what kind of intervention would be most helpful. In an attempt to make this inferential process more explicit, each RP contains a slot for specifying the student's current state. The student state slot is used for purely descriptive purposes only; it is not used in either recognizing or responding to the student during the course of a tutorial interaction.[20]

Although student states are not used directly in the process of making teaching decisions, they are useful in summarizing what the essence of the student's current cognitive, motivational, or emotional state is. Explicitly articulating the student state helps clarify what kind of tutorial response would be most effective in addressing that state. Based on this realization, the software tool for authoring PKBs uses the student state to suggest responses that might be appropriate for that student state. Thus, although the student state slot plays no role in responding to the student at run time, it is used by the authoring tools to assist a user in the process of creating new teaching strategies.

Although describing what is going on in the student's mind is an inexact science, it is still possible to make an educated guess. In the *Advise that query does not help narrow down set of possible causes* strategy, there are at least three explanations for why the student tried to collect evidence that does not serve to narrow down the cause of the problem:

1. The student is still collecting information to identify additional causes instead of trying to narrow down the set of likely causes.
2. The student does not know what causes are likely. Specifically, the student may think one or more causes are likely when they are not.
3. The student mistakenly thinks the query will provide evidence for or against one of the likely causes.

Deciding which of these possible explanations is actually the correct one may not be possible without some additional information. The initial assumption in this teaching strategy is Explanation 1. This assumption is

---

[19]This idea has also been articulated by Ohlsson (1987). His "Principle of Pragmatic Diagnosis" states "The purpose of the diagnostic component of an intelligent tutoring system is to support the execution of its instructional plan" (p. 214).

[20]One reason that the student state is not a functional part of a PKB is that it is extremely difficult, if not impossible, for a tutor to know for sure what exactly is going on in the student's head. Moreover, the extra effort a tutor would need to make to figure this out with any certainty would likely not be worth the trouble.

reflected in the decision, made in the earlier diagnosis procedure, to wait for the student to ask two unproductive questions before intervening. After two such questions, it becomes more likely that the real explanation is either 2 or 3, and these possibilities are dealt with in the response. Table 4.13 lists examples of student states from the PKBs used in the Casper system.

The most important component of an RP is the response slot. It specifies what action or actions the tutor will take in responding to the student's current situation. This response may entail communicating with the student, altering the curriculum to be presented to the student, or simply modifying a database about student performance and preferences. Responses may consist of a single action to take or may specify a multiple-step response. There are three basic classes of responses a tutor might employ: (a) *communicative acts*, meaning responses that entail some communication with the student; (b) *curriculum management and task environment control responses*, concerned with the changing current and upcoming activities the student is engaged in; and (c) *tutor-internal responses*, which involve storing or retrieving information about the student's actions or history of the interaction.

The most common class of responses, communicative acts, involves the tutor communicating some information to the student. For example, the tutor might interrupt the student's task to tell, ask, remind, demon-

TABLE 4.13
Some student states listed in the PKBs for the Casper system

Student States
The student does not know what to do.
The student forgot that an action was already performed.
The student does not understand the serious implications of his or her action.
The student does not realize what information he or she has already obtained.
The student does not understand that the information he or she has obtained is sufficient to allow him or her to draw a conclusion.
The student does not know the best way to obtain some information.
The student's causal understanding of the domain is inefficient.
The student does not understand that asking this question will not give him or her any evidence toward a likely hypothesis.
The student does not understand why an event just happened (what could cause it to happen, etc.).
The student does not realize that the remedy prescribed does not address the current problem.
The student jumped to a conclusion about the cause of the problem.
The student failed to identify a possible hypothesis about the cause of the problem before taking subsequent actions.
The student does not understand the current material.
The student is not aware that a better remedy exists for the problem.

strate, suggest, or explain something to the student. These types of responses were used often in the BC Server and BC Cashier systems (see Table 4.14). Also included in this class of responses are Socratic dialogues. These are a more complex form of response that consists of having an extended question-and-answer dialogue with the student about a particular topic (similar in some respects to Clancey's, 1982, dialogue procedures). Table 4.15 lists some of the responses used in the Casper system, including examples of Socratic dialogue responses.

Curriculum management and task environment control responses deal with issues related to the task the student is currently engaged in and the set of activities planned for the future. Also included in this group are responses by the tutor to control the task environment or simulation the student is using. These responses are examples of indirect interventions by the teacher. That is, the teacher is intervening in ways that do not involve communicating directly with the student. In cases where the teacher's response is to cause something to happen in a simulation, it may not even be obvious to the student what the teacher's response is.

Tutor-internal responses deal with annotating an internal database of information about the student's actions. The responses in this group are also indirect interventions. A tutor may want to note certain actions a student takes for a number of reasons. For example, determining whether

TABLE 4.14
Responses Used in the BC Server and BC Cashier Systems

Response	Description
TELL-STEP-INCORRECT	Tell the student that the step he or she just took is not a correct one.
TELL-NEXT-STEP	Tell the student what the next step(s) is/are in a task.
TELL-WHY-DO-NEXT-STEP	Tell the student why he or she needs to perform the next step.
EXPLAIN-STEP	Explain how to execute the current step in a task.
EXPL-REASON-STEP-UNNEEDED	Explain to the student why the step he or she just asked about is not necessary.
EXPLAIN-SUBSTEPS	Explain all substeps needed to complete higher level step.
TELL-STEP-ALREADY-DONE	Tell the student that the step has already been done.
TELL-NO-STEP-DISCUSSED	Tell the student we cannot answer his or her question because there is no context—we have not discussed any steps with him or her yet.
DEMONSTRATE-STEP	Demonstrate a step in the task environment.
NOTE-STEP-TAKEN	Record that the student has taken a particular step in a task.

TABLE 4.15
Responses Used in the Casper System

Response	Description
REMIND-INFO-OBTAINED-VIA-AGENT	Have the agent in the task environment remind the student that he or she has already volunteered that information.
REMIND-REPEATED-QUESTION-VIA-AGENT	Have the agent in the task environment remind the student that he or she repeated a question.
WARN-AGAINST-LEADING-QUESTIONS	Tell the learner that leading questions are usually a bad idea.
TUTOR-INCORRECT-PROBLEM-INFORMATION-GIVEN	Show the student that what he or she has told the agent is not correct.
TUTOR-INCORRECT-CAUSE-IDENTIFICATION	Show the student that his or her diagnosis is incorrect.
TUTOR-EARLY-CAUSE-IDENTIFICATION	Show the student that there are other possible causes for the problem.
TELL-GATHER-INFO	Tell the student that he or she should get more information and assist him or her in how to do that.
TUTOR-SUBOPTIMAL-TREATMENT	Tell student that treatment prescribed is not the best one available for the current problem.
TUTOR-INCORRECT-REMEDY	Confirm what the student's working hypothesis is, check if it is plausible, and explain why the remedy is not appropriate given that hypothesis.
INFO-BETTER-OBTAINED-VIA-OTHER-SOURCE	Tell the student that there are better ways to obtain the information being sought and help him or her select a better method to obtain that information.
TELL-REPERCUSSIONS	Tell the student about the potential repercussions of his or her actions.
TELL-CAUSE-DETERMINABLE-AND-PROMPT-FOR-CAUSE	Tell the student that a cause is determinable given current information and prompt him or her to identify a hypothesis about the cause.
HANDLE-CAUSE-AFTER-TREATMENT	Point out that the student needs to identify a possible cause of the problem before prescribing a remedy.

the student has repeated a step requires that the tutor make a note of which steps the student has taken so far. Further, a tutor may want to respond differently the first time the student makes a particular mistake than when the same mistake is repeated later. This means that the tutor must note the kinds of mistakes the student makes and perhaps record how many times each has occurred. This is exactly the kind of situation that occurs in the *Advise that query does not help narrow down set of possible causes* strategy.

Although often overlooked, tutor-internal responses are an important part of a tutor's repertoire of actions. In particular, they play a key role in providing the data on which future teaching decisions are based. Thus, it is usually the case that a tutor-internal response has a corresponding interaction characteristic that checks the data stored by that response. Some examples of tutor-internal type responses from the Casper system that store information later checked by interaction characteristics are shown in Table 4.16.

To specify the tutor's response in the PKB for the *Advise that query does not help narrow down set of possible causes* strategy, we must fill in the response slot for each of the two RPs. In the first RP, corresponding to the do-not-intervene-yet decision provided by the diagnosis procedure, the tutor's response is simply to note that the student's question does not contribute evidence to any currently likely hypothesis. This tutor-internal response stores a message in the tutor's database indicating that the student has asked one such unproductive question. In the second RP, corresponding to the intervene-now decision provided by the diagnosis procedure, the tutor's response is to engage the student in a Socratic dialogue to help him or her recognize the mistake, identify the misconceptions that led to it, and help identify a better question to ask instead.

The slot in an RP is a justification that explains why a particular response is appropriate for the student state, to which it is a reaction. Thus, every student state/response pair in an RP has associated with it a justification of why that response is pedagogically valid given that

TABLE 4.16
Some Example Tutor-Internal Responses That Store
Information Used to Make Subsequent Teaching Decisions

Response	Description	Example
NOTE-STEP-TAKEN	Record that the student has taken a particular step in a task.	Record that the student has asked the simulated customer what his water tastes like.
NOTE-IRRELEVANT-QUESTION	Make a note that the student has asked an irrelevant question.	Record that the student just asked the simulated customer a question that has no relationship to any likely hypothesis at this point.
NOTE-LEADING-QUESTION	Make a note that the student asked a leading question.	The way a question is phrased can influence how the customer answers it. Record that the student asked the simulated customer a question that was phrased in a leading way.
NOTE-REDUNDANT-QUESTION	Make a note that the student asked a redundant question.	Record that the question just asked is redundant to those asked before. Customers get annoyed if asked too many redundant questions.

student state. These justifications are not used directly in making teaching decisions. Rather they are intended to capture the PKB author's beliefs about why responding to the student in a particular way will be effective. Almost every human teacher can supply an explanation for why he or she responded to a student in a certain way. To date, however, few computer-based tutors have had this ability. One notable exception is the instructional design environment (IDE; Russell et al., 1988)—a system that contained a justification mechanism similar to that described here. Recording justifications for every response allows the Teaching Executive to provide the rationale for each response it makes during the course of an interaction with the student.

The final step in filling in the response packets for the PKB representing the *Advise that query does not help narrow down set of possible causes* strategy is to fill in the justification slots. By the time the student has asked a third question that provides no useful evidence, it has become clear that the student does not have a well-formed domain theory, so it is time for the tutor to jump in and help clarify things. This is what gets put in the justification slot of the second RP (see Fig. 4.18).

The TE Toolbox: A Tool Set for Authoring Teaching Strategies

A second critical challenge in creating a system that represents and applies teaching strategies is constructing a graphical user interface that makes it easy for nonprogrammers to encode these teaching strategies into the system. The TE toolbox is the suite of interfaces and tools that have been developed to address this challenge. The TE toolbox provides a friendly, usable way for nonprogrammers to browse, edit, and create teaching knowledge that can be directly used by the TE engine and incorporated into new educational software systems.

One of the primary design goals of the Teaching Executive is to make it possible for teachers or other content experts with little or no programming ability to be included in the process of creating educational software. Specifically, the goal is to allow these experts to be active participants in authoring the teaching strategies that create the tutorial interventions a student will encounter while using a computer-based learning environment. If the system is to be used by experts who are not programmers, programming abilities must not be a requirement for using the system.

Despite this goal, the current reality of building a flexible and powerful tool is such that the need for programming cannot be entirely eliminated. This poses an interesting dilemma in the quest to allow teachers without extensive programming abilities to use the tool. The compromise reached in the design of the TE toolbox is to separate the conceptual part of

PKB Index		
Triggering Event	ASK-QUESTION-OBTAIN-INFO	
Interaction Characteristics	LIKELY-CAUSES-EXIST and QUESTION-GIVES-NO-EVIDENCE	
Task Characteristics		

Diagnosis Procedure
Has the student asked more than two questions that fail to give any evidence toward a likely hypothesis?
If no, then return "don't intervene yet," if yes, return "intervene now."

Response Packets		
	Response packet #1	**Response packet #2**
Diagnosis result	"don't intervene yet"	"intervene now"
Student state	• The student is still collecting information to identify additional causes instead trying to narrow down the set of likely causes.	• The student does not know what causes are likely. Specifically the student may think that one or more causes are likely when they are not. -or- • The student doesn't understand that asking this question won't give any evidence toward a likely hypothesis.
Response	Note that the student's question does not contribute evidence to any currently likely hypothesis.	Engage the student in a Socratic dialogue to help the student recognize the mistake, identify the misconceptions that led to it, and help identify a better question to ask instead.
Justification	Give the student some latitude before jumping in with tutoring.	It's clear that the student doesn't have a well-formed domain theory, so jump in and help clarify things.

FIG. 4.18. The completed PKB for the *Advise that query does not help narrow down set of possible causes* teaching strategy.

authoring teaching strategies from the underlying programming needed to implement those strategies. Under this scheme, authoring teaching strategies becomes a two-pass process. The first pass consists of a teacher or other user authoring teaching strategies using either predefined vocabulary elements (i.e., triggering events, interaction characteristics, responses, etc.) or creating new vocabulary elements on an as-needed basis. The second pass consists of a programmer going through the newly authored rules and writing a small segment of code to accompany every new vocabulary element added by the user. This two-pass process effectively frees the user from having to worry about coding details, allowing him or her to focus entirely on the conceptual aspect of crafting teaching strategies for a particular LBD tutor.

A collection of PKBs used together for a particular LBD tutor are stored in a PKB library. A PKB library is stored as a separate file on the computer, much like a document created by a word processing program. The tool that provides access to these libraries is the PKB library manager. It allows a user to inspect the PKBs in a library, edit individual PKBs, merge the contents of two libraries together, and move PKBs from one library to another. The PKB library manager interface, shown in Fig. 4.19, consists primarily of a list of the PKBs that comprise the library. The name of each PKB and a brief description of its contents are shown, along with a check box indicating whether that PKB is active. For example, in Fig. 4.19 PKB.30 has been deactivated. A user can tailor the teaching behavior of an LBD tutoring system by activating or deactivating certain PKBs and observing the effect on the style of teaching until the desired effect is achieved.

How can an interface be designed that allows a user to gain an overall view of a complicated data structure with many specialized components while allowing the user to easily edit each of those components? Because the PKB is a complex data structure, it is difficult to present the contents of one to a user in an understandable way. Furthermore, each component of a PKB has its own structure, making it even harder to design a way for the user to edit each part in its own specialized editor. The solution adopted in designing the PKB editor, the interface used to edit individual PKBs, is to first provide the user with a display specialized to make it easy to gain an overall picture of the contents of the PKB. Once the user can visualize the structure of a PKB, simply clicking the mouse on the part of the screen displaying the part of the PKB to be edited brings up a specialized interface for editing that component. When the user is done editing that component, the specialized editor is hidden, leaving the screen as uncluttered as possible. Thus, the big picture view of the PKB data structure is given precedence, with specialized editors for the components accessible via one or two mouse clicks. This design is intended to maximize the user's ability to visualize the data while providing relatively

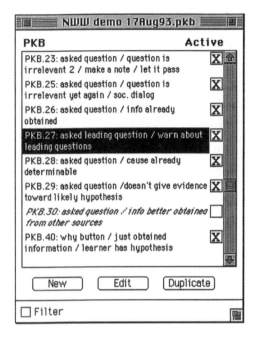

FIG. 4.19. The PKB library manager.

easy access to editing and minimizing the amount of clutter on the screen at any one time.

The PKB editor interface is shown in Fig. 4.20. The user is editing the PKB for the *Advise that query does not help narrow down set of possible causes* teaching strategy. Section A of the screen contains summary information about the PKB, Section B displays the PKB index, Section C the diagnosis procedure, and Section D the RPs.

The third main interface screen used in creating PKBs with the TE toolbox is the response packet editor. Each RP is composed of four components (diagnosis result, student state, response, justification), and each of these has a corresponding section in the response packet editor window (labeled A–D in Fig. 4.21). One notable feature of the response packet editor is the "See others" button located under the field for specifying student states. As described later, although the student state slot plays no role in responding to the student at run time, it is useful in assisting a user in the process of creating new teaching strategies. In particular, the response packet editor uses the student state to suggest responses that might be appropriate for that student state. After the user specifies the student state, pressing the "See others" button causes a list of the response packets with similar student states to be displayed (see Fig. 4.22). Clicking on any entry in this list will immediately display that response packet, allowing the user to compare what response was given to that particular student state in other response packets.

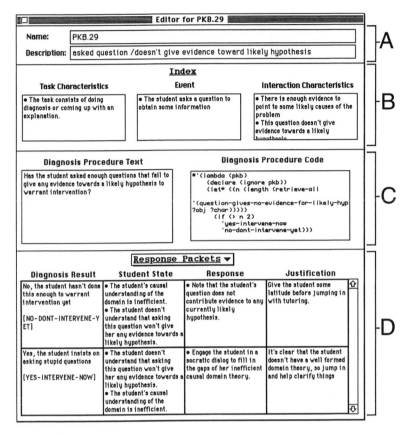

FIG. 4.20. The PKB editor window showing a completed PKB used in the Casper system.

The TE toolbox was used to create PKBs representing the teaching strategies for the BC Cashier, BC Server, and Casper systems (and other systems not described here). All told, approximately 50 actively used PKBs have been created using this tool set. Although the interface can be daunting to a beginner, an experienced user can create a new PKB using the TE toolbox in a minute or two.

MONITORING THE TASK ENVIRONMENT

Introduction

Regardless of the kind of tutoring system being built, it must be able to look over the shoulder of the student while he or she engages in the learning activity. Without this ability, a tutoring system will not be able

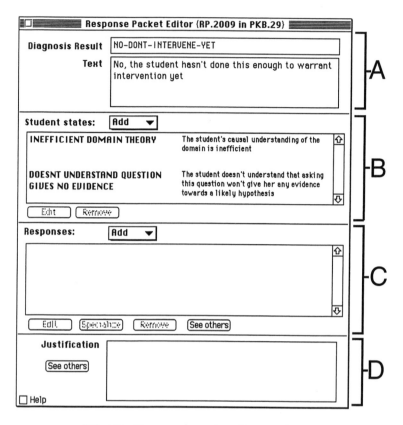

FIG. 4.21. The response packet editor interface.

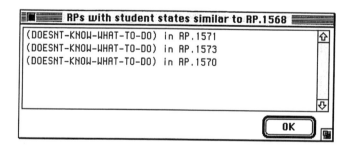

FIG. 4.22. A list of other RPs that specify the same student state as the one currently being edited. This display is brought up by the "See others" button.

to decide whether and when to intervene, or what to say. No tutor can function without being able to observe what the student is doing. The Teaching Executive is the tool used to add tutoring to task environments created with the MOPed authoring tool (Ohmaye, 1992). For the Teaching Executive to provide appropriate tutoring for task environments built using MOPed, it must be kept informed of the kind of task the student is engaged in, what actions the student is taking, and what consequences those actions have in the task environment.

The Communication Problem in LBD Tutors

The term *communication problem* is used here to refer to the general problem of ensuring that a tutor can both receive information about the student and execute its tutorial responses. Understanding how this problem arises requires one to look at the architecture of computer-based LBD environments. A computer-based LBD tutor consists of three layers: the interface, the task environment, and the tutoring. The task environment layer consists of a simulation or other mechanisms that allow the student to actually engage in a task. The tutoring layer implements any guidance the student is to receive while interacting with the task environment. Some example forms of guidance that might be part of the tutoring layer are storytelling, coaching, or Socratic dialogues. The interface layer presents a graphical user interface of the task environment and means for displaying any tutorial guidance to the student.

Separating the development of LBD tutors into these three layers helps manage the complexity of developing such systems. Also, specialized authoring tools can be used to create each layer. The general organization of these three layers in an LBD tutor, and the authoring tools used to create each layer, is shown in Fig. 4.23.

The communication problem arises when the construction of the task environment, interface, and tutoring layers are separated and different authoring tools are used for each. When this occurs, the tutor may not be able to track and interpret the student's actions in the task environment. Moreover, the tutor may not be able to control the task environment in pedagogically useful ways. The communication problem, then, is essentially twofold: informing the tutor when pedagogically relevant events occur in the task environment and enabling the tutor to implement tutorial responses that require exercising control over the task environment or communicating with the student via the user interface.

By incorporating the Teaching Executive system into the MOPed tool for building task environments, it became possible to implement a solution to the problem of building a tutor that can function in a range of different task environments. MOPed provides a system designer with building

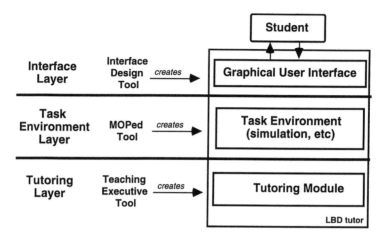

FIG. 4.23. The three conceptual layers in a computer-based LBD environment.

blocks out of which many different task environments can be constructed. By extending this set of standard building blocks with specialized ones that provide a standardized communication channel to the Teaching Executive, it became possible for the Teaching Executive to function as the tutoring layer for any task environment built using MOPed.

The key element in the Teaching Executive addressing the communication problem is having the person creating the LBD tutor (the system designer) use these specialized building blocks to incorporate the necessary communicative links into the task environment as it is being constructed. In other words, the system designer manually indicates which student actions or other events in the task environment need to be communicated to the Teaching Executive. This special set of building blocks allows the Teaching Executive to monitor the task environment, keeping informed of student actions and other important events that might require tutorial intervention. To create a communication channel to the Teaching Executive, MOPed was extended by providing a system designer with three mechanisms for communicating the necessary information to the Teaching Executive. The three mechanisms are node annotations, TE nodes, and MOP annotations. Which mechanism is used depends on the nature of the communication needed at that point in the task environment.

Annotating Nodes With Triggering Events

The key problem in establishing a communicative link between a task environment created with MOPed and the Teaching Executive is enabling the Teaching Executive to understand what actions the student is taking and what effects those actions have. The solution adopted here is to ask the

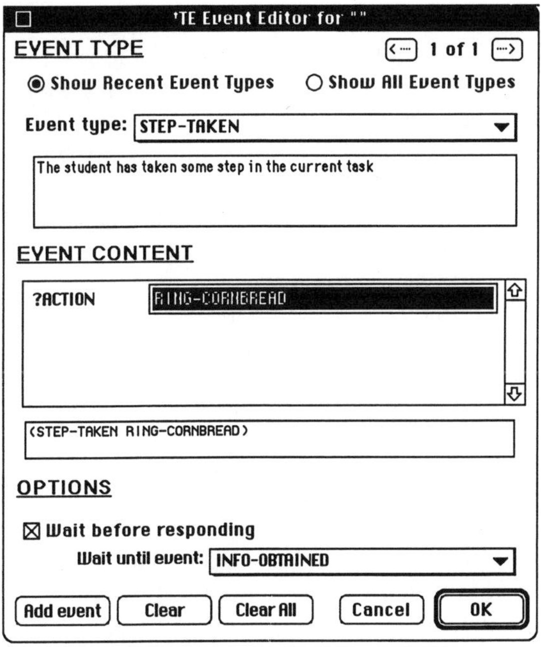

FIG. 4.24.   The TE event editor window.

system designer to translate what happens in the task environment into a language the Teaching Executive can understand. To implement this translation process, the system designer labels the parts of the task environment that represent important student actions and repercussions of those actions with a triggering event (from the Teaching Executive's representational vocabulary described earlier). The triggering event describes the action or repercussion in terms the Teaching Executive can understand.[21]

A system designer can communicate that an important event or student action occurred by annotating a node with one or more triggering events. This is a way to indicate that the student action or other event represented by that node is pedagogically relevant, and hence should be communicated to the Teaching Executive. To annotate nodes with triggering events, MOPed was extended by creating the special TE tool. Clicking on a node with the TE tool brings up a window that allows a system designer to specify one or more triggering events to attach to that node (see Fig. 4.24). Nodes that have been annotated with triggering events display a special badge indicating this fact in a graphical fashion. When viewing a MOP,

---

[21]This mechanism is analogous to the parasitic rules used by the SPIEL system in communicating with the GuSS task environment (Burke, 1993).

it is important for two reasons for the system designer to be able to identify those nodes with triggering event annotations. First, without this ability, the system designer will most likely quickly forget which nodes have been annotated. Thus, to edit or delete any annotations, the system designer would have to click on each node with the TE tool until the desired node is found. Second, the graphical interface provided by MOPed has the ability to look at a MOP and quickly understand what that MOP does. Because nodes with triggering event annotations represent pedagogically significant parts of the task environment, it is especially important that they be immediately identifiable.

Now that we have seen how a system designer goes about the process of annotating a node with triggering events, the next issue to address is how this annotation is processed at run time to actually communicate that event to the Teaching Executive. When the MOP applier encounters an annotated node at run time, the following procedure is followed. First, the actions specified by that node are run as usual, then the execution of the MOP applier is temporarily suspended, and the Teaching Executive is invoked with the events the system designer has attached to the node. If the Teaching Executive determines that one or more responses are needed, those responses are executed. Once the execution of the responses is completed, or if no responses were deemed necessary, the MOP applier resumes exactly at the point where it was suspended (see Fig. 4.24). This means it continues processing immediately after the annotated node. The Teaching Executive intervenes on the link that is taken when flow of control leaves the node.

Annotating a node with a triggering event is used to communicate with the Teaching Executive only in situations where no change in the flow of control in the task environment is needed. Because the Teaching Executive interrupts the flow of control in the task environment, and then resumes it exactly where it left off, there is no way for the Teaching Executive to alter the flow of control. If such a change in flow of control is desired, the designer must use a different communication mechanism. This mechanism is a TE node.

TE Nodes

The system designer must place a TE node in a MOP at the point at which a change in the flow of control is desired. Although the main purpose of the TE node is to allow the tutor to implement indirect interventions, it is also important in a discussion of how events in the task environment get communicated to the Teaching Executive. Any triggering event sent to the Teaching Executive that might lead to a response calling for the tutor to cause a change in the task environment must be communicated to the Teaching Executive via a TE node instead of a node annotation. Thus, in deciding whether to use a node annotation or a TE node to communicate a triggering event to the Teaching Executive, the system designer must consider whether that triggering event might require the tutor to execute an indirect intervention response. If such a response might be required, a TE node must be used to communicate the necessary triggering events in anticipation of providing the Teaching Executive with the means to execute any indirect intervention tutorial responses.

A TE node is used as follows to communicate a set of one or more triggering events to the Teaching Executive. A TE node is a specialized kind of branching node, meaning it can have both in-terminals and out-terminals. Like other branching nodes, the TE node uses its in-terminals to specify input to the node and its out-terminals to provide different paths that flow of control can take when processing of that node is completed. More specifically, the in-terminals of a TE node specify what triggering events should be sent to the Teaching Executive, and the out-terminals represent the different branches that might be followed depending on the response selected by the Teaching Executive. Figure 4.25 shows what a TE node looks like in a MOPed window. In Fig. 4.26, the in-terminals on the left side specify triggering events, and out-terminals on the right side of the node specify the various branches in flow of control that may be taken.

A TE node can obtain the set of triggering events to send to the Teaching Executive two different ways: either directly from the in-terminals of the TE node or from a MOPed record. Which option is used depends on the particulars of the task environment being built and the kind of triggering event being communicated to the Teaching Executive by the TE node. In situations where a static set of triggering events must be sent to the Teaching Executive at a particular point in the task environment, those events may be specified using the in-terminals of a TE node. As discussed earlier, these are a mechanism for supplying input to the processing to be done by that node. In the case of the TE node, the input required is one or more TE events. Thus, the in-terminals of a TE node each contain one or more triggering events. When flow of control enters a TE node via an in-terminal, the triggering events contained by that in-terminal are sent as input to the Teaching Executive for processing.

In other situations, however, the triggering event that needs to be communicated changes depending on the student's most recent action. In such cases, it is both difficult and unwieldy to create a separate in-terminal for each of the potentially large number of triggering events required. How do such cases arise? With the addition of records and looping constructs to MOPed, it has become more common to design a task environment in a way that allows the re-use of the same MOPs to parse and respond to the student's input. This technique allows the same MOPs to be used to handle nearly all of a student's actions, saving a great deal of development time.

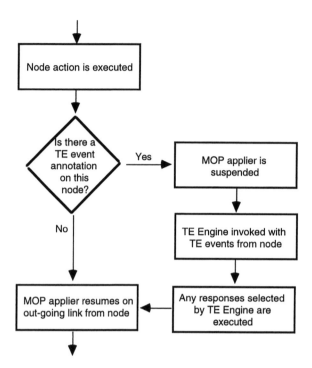

FIG. 4.25. Flowchart of run-time processing for nodes annotated with triggering events.

FIG. 4.26. A TE node with two in-terminals representing two triggering events and four out-terminals representing four possible branches that might be taken based on the response selected by the Teaching Executive in processing the triggering events.

One ramification of this technique is that the student's action is no longer represented by a specific node somewhere in a MOP network, but rather is represented by a record that contains information about that action. As a result, annotating nodes with triggering events no longer suffices as a means for allowing the Teaching Executive to track the student's actions. Instead, because student actions are represented by records, it is necessary to associate triggering events with these individual records, analogous to annotating nodes with triggering events. Of course, once triggering events can be associated with MOPed records, a mechanism for accessing those triggering events and sending them to the Teaching Executive must be created.

To support this need, the TE node is capable of obtaining triggering events from a specified record instead of from its in-terminals. The designer must indicate for each TE node whether triggering events are to be obtained from the in-terminals or from a record; if the latter, it must also specify the particular record from which triggering events are to be obtained. To accomplish this, the system designer is provided with a TE node editor window that can be accessed by double clicking on a TE node in a MOP window, just as editors for other nodes are accessed. An example TE node editor is shown in Fig. 4.27. The controls at the top of the window allow the system designer to specify where triggering events are to be obtained; the bottom of the window is concerned with specifying the out-terminals of the node (discussed in more detail later).

Annotating MOPs With Task Characteristics

In addition to obtaining information about the student's actions and other events that occur in the task environment, a tutor must also keep informed

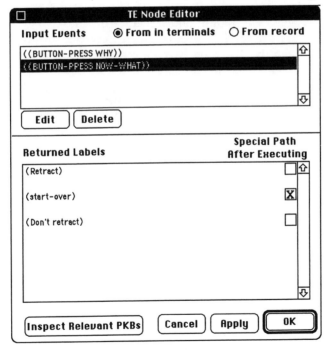

FIG. 4.27. The TE node editor window.

of the kind of task the student is engaged in. In terms of being able to intervene with appropriate tutoring, it is important for a tutor to know not just about the student's individual actions, but also about the structure of the task. For instance, information about a task that can be relevant to tutoring includes such things as what steps make up the task, whether there is more than one way to perform the task correctly, or if there are any special explanations for why a particular step is necessary or unnecessary. As described earlier, this type of information is represented by the Teaching Executive as task characteristics.

What is needed, then, is a way for the Teaching Executive to obtain information about the kind of task represented by a particular MOP. Recall that an MOP packages together a set of nodes that captures the student's actions during some part of a task. To support this need, MOPed was extended with a third communication mechanism that allowed an MOP to be annotated with task characteristics describing the nature of the task represented by that MOP. This is similar to the idea of annotating nodes with TE events discussed previously.

How are task characteristics attached to an MOP communicated to the Teaching Executive at run time? When an MOP is encountered during execution, the task characteristics attached to that MOP, if any, are sent to the Teaching Executive. Because task characteristics only convey information about the nature and structure of a task, they are treated differently than triggering events when received by the Teaching Executive. When the Teaching Executive receives task characteristics, it simply stores them in its internal database; it does not attempt to interpret them using the PKB library as it does when events are received. During the time that the nodes packaged by a particular MOP are being executed, the task characteristics attached to that MOP are used by the Teaching Executive to select the appropriate PKB for any events received.

Summary

The three mechanisms that permit an MOPed-based task environment to communicate with the Teaching Executive at run time are summarized in Table 4.17.

RETRIEVING AND EXECUTING TEACHING STRATEGIES

Retrieving Teaching Strategies

The algorithm used by the Teaching Executive to retrieve teaching strategies is loosely based on the algorithm employed by many case based reasoning (CBR) systems (Jona & Kolodner, 1992; Kolodner, 1993; Ries-

TABLE 4.17
The Three Mechanisms Used to Communicate Information
From the Task Environment to the Teaching Executive
and the Communicative Role Each Fulfills

Communication Mechanism	Description	Communicative Role
Node annotations	MOPed nodes are annotated with TE events. When an annotated node is encountered at run time, the MOP applier is suspended and the Teaching Executive is invoked with those events.	Used to inform the Teaching Executive of student actions or other relevant events that occur in the task environment when either no response is expected or no change in the flow of control is required.
TE nodes	A special type of branching node whose out-terminals represent different possible responses that might be selected by the Teaching Executive.	Implements bidirectional communication between the task environment and the Teaching Executive. Used primarily when the Teaching Executive needs to change the flow of control in response to some student action or other event.
MOP annotations	MOPs are annotated with task characteristics that describe the nature of the task implemented by that MOP. The task characteristics are stored in the Teaching Executive's database when the MOP is executed at run time.	Used to keep the Teaching Executive updated about the nature of the task the student is currently engaged in.

beck & Schank, 1989). The essence of this algorithm is to match the current situation to a library of previously encountered situations stored as cases in memory. The case in memory that most closely matches the current situation is then used to guide the understanding of, and response to, the current situation. Similarly, the Teaching Executive attempts to retrieve the teaching strategy that matches the current situation to use that teaching strategy to determine the tutorial response most appropriate for that situation. The Teaching Executive's algorithm for retrieving teaching strategies in the form of PKBs is divided into four distinct phases: retrieval, selection, interpretation, and execution. Figure 4.28 provides an overview of these phases.

The goal of the retrieval phase is to quickly find a set of relevant PKBs. To do so, the Teaching Executive retrieves all PKBs indexed under the triggering event just received. Recall from earlier in the chapter that all PKBs are indexed by one or more relevant triggering events. If no PKBs are indexed under the triggering event just received, the Teaching Execu-

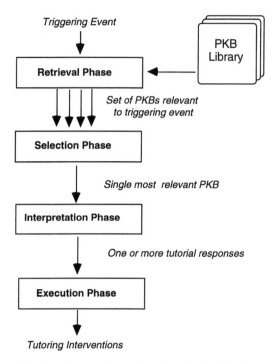

FIG. 4.28. The four phases of processing done by the Teaching Executive in interpreting an event.

tive is not able to respond to the current situation and the retrieval process is aborted. By the end of the retrieval phase, the Teaching Executive has obtained a set of one or more potentially relevant PKBs. This initial retrieval constitutes the first of a two-pass process for finding relevant PKBs to apply. Figure 4.29 shows the transcript produced by the Teaching Executive as it receives a triggering event from the Casper system and begins the retrieval phase.

Because a PKB index is composed of three parts (i.e., triggering event, interaction characteristics, and task characteristics), PKBs retrieved in the retrieval phase are only one third of the way to being confirmed as relevant to the current situation. In the selection phase, the PKBs that match the input event are checked to see whether the remainder of their indexes also match.

Processing in the selection phase proceeds as follows. For each PKB in the set of potentially relevant ones retrieved in the retrieval phase, the task and interaction characteristics of that PKB are checked to see if they match the current situation. To implement this matching process, each element of the task and interaction characteristics representational vocabulary has associated with it either a database query form or a short

```
Received event: (ask-question-obtain-info pipes lead)
_____

Beginning retrieval phase
_____



Retrieving PKBs...


Found seven PKBs matching event: (ask-question-obtain-info pipes lead)
```

FIG. 4.29. Transcript produced by the Teaching Executive during the retrieval phase.

segment of Lisp code.[22] A task or interaction characteristic matches the current situation when either of following is true: the database query form is found in the contents of the Teaching Executive's internal database or the segment of code is executed and returns a true value. The Teaching Executive employs a caching scheme that allows it to minimize the amount of processing required in selecting relevant PKBs by eliminating any redundancy in computing the value of task and interaction characteristics. Because PKBs often reference the same task and interaction characteristics, and the code used to compute the value of that characteristic may be expensive to execute, it makes sense to only compute the value for a particular characteristic once. This is the underlying motivation for the caching scheme.

The caching scheme works as follows. When the Teaching Executive needs to check the value of a characteristic, it first tries the database query associated with that item. If no query exists, or the query fails to find the matching form in the database, a check is made to see if there is a code segment available. If one exists, the Teaching Executive, instead of simply executing the code, first checks to see if the value of the characteristic has already been computed and stored in the cache. If so, the cached value is used and no further computation is needed for that characteristic. Only when the Teaching Executive fails to find the characteristic in the cache is the code segment executed. After the code segment is executed, the characteristic is stored in the cache, along with the true or false value returned by the code. Any subsequent references to that characteristic can be checked without having to re-execute the code segment.

_____

[22]The database query form or code segment associated with each task or interaction characteristic is filled in by a programmer and is typically hidden from the (nonprogramming) system designer who does the work of authoring PKBs.

Many task and interaction characteristics have an inverse (i.e., another characteristic that represents the opposite of a particular feature). Characteristics with inverses present an additional opportunity for the Teaching Executive to use its caching scheme to be even more efficient in avoiding redundant computation. To capitalize on this opportunity, each task or interaction characteristic can be paired with its inverse or opposite, and this pairing is used as follows. When the code segment associated with a paired characteristic is executed, the Teaching Executive stores the *inverse* of the characteristic in the cache. Therefore, if any subsequent PKBs reference the second or subsequent attempt interaction characteristic, its value can be obtained directly from the cache without any additional computation. With this inverse caching scheme, even characteristics that have not been computed directly before can be found in the cache.

Due to the dynamic nature of a teaching interaction, the task and interaction characteristics in the cache are maintained only for the duration of processing one triggering event. When the next triggering event is received by the Teaching Executive, the cache is cleared and all characteristics must be recomputed from scratch. To maintain the cache any longer would run the risk of maintaining characteristics that no longer accurately reflected the student's current situation. This would create two serious problems for the Teaching Executive. First, there would be the possibility of selecting PKBs on the basis of characteristics, confirmed via the cache, that could no longer be confirmed if recomputed from scratch, resulting in inappropriate responses being executed. Second, PKBs that were indeed relevant to the current situation would not get selected, nor their responses executed, for the opposite reason. In the meantime, task or interaction characteristics with false values stored in the cache may have become true if recomputed.

By the end of the selection phase of processing, then, the set of potentially relevant PKBs has been filtered down to only those whose entire index has been matched to the current situation. Should there be more than one PKB left at this point, a decision process is invoked to choose the single best PKB among the set of remaining ones. This decision could be based on the performance history of each of the candidate PKBs (i.e., which PKB has been most successful in the past).[23] Figure 4.30 shows the transcript of processing done during the selection phase.

Once the best PKB has been selected, the interpretation phase begins. During this phase, the diagnosis procedure of the selected PKB is run. The diagnosis procedure is a small segment of code that further refines the interpretation of the current situation. The output returned by the

---

[23]The performance history selection criterion is not implemented yet. Currently, the first PKB that is found to be relevant is the one used.

Beginning selection phase

Confirming relevance of retrieved PKBs . . .

Checking Interaction Characteristics of PKB.21 . . .
  The student already asked this question . . . [not confirmed]
→ PKB.21 not relevant

Checking Interaction Characteristics of PKB.20 . . .
  The student already asked this question . . . [not confirmed]
→ PKB.20 not relevant

Checking Interaction Characteristics of PKB.29 . . .
  There is enough evidence to point to some likely causes of the problem . . .
    [computed]
  This question doesn't give evidence toward a likely hypothesis . . . [computed]
→ PKB.29 relevance confirmed

Checking Interaction Characteristics of PKB.26 . . .
  There is enough information available to determine the cause of the problem . . .
    [not confirmed]
→ PKB.26 not relevant

Checking Interaction Characteristics of PKB.2 . . .
  The learner has not greeted that agent. . . . [not confirmed]
→ PKB.2 not relevant

FIG. 4.30. Processing transcript during selection phase.

diagnosis procedure is used to select among the RPs in the selected PKB, with each RP being labeled by one possible output of the diagnosis procedure. Figure 4.31 shows the transcript of processing during the interpretation phase.

It should be pointed out that one PKB with, say, four RPs could be divided into four PKBs each with one RP and no diagnosis procedure. The conditions tested for by the original diagnosis procedure could be moved into the PKB index; from a purely functional perspective, the two alternatives would be equivalent. Given this observation, why have a diagnosis procedure at all? Although both alternatives may be functionally equivalent, they are not at all the same from the perspective of usability. By grouping sets of related interpretations together in the RPs of one PKB, the human user authoring the PKB can focus on the entire set of interpretations together. Interpretations of the situation that are

There are two possible interpretations of the current situation:

(1) The student's causal understanding of the domain is inefficient and the student doesn't understand that asking this question won't give him or her any evidence towards a likely typothesis.

(2) The student doesn't understand that asking this question won't give him or her any evidence towards a likely hypothesis and the student's causal understanding of the domain is inefficient.

Running diagnosis procedure to select between them . . .

→ Asking:
Has the student asked enough questions that fail to give any evidence toward a likely hypothesis to warrant intervention?

→ Result of diagnosis procedure: YES-INTERVENE-NOW

→ Answer:
Yes, the student insists on asking stupid questions.

Student state interpreted as:
DOESNT-UNDERSTAND-QUESTION-GIVES-NO-EVIDENCE
Meaning: The student doesn't understand that asking this question won't give her any evidence towards a likely hypothesis.
INEFFICIENT-DOMAIN-THEORY
Meaning: The student's causal understanding of the domain is inefficient.

Selecting response:
(1) (TELL INEFFICIENT INVESTIGATION)
Engage the student in a Socratic dialogue to help her ask better questions.

Justification for response:
It's clear that the student doesn't have a well-formed domain.

FIG. 4.31. Processing transcript during interpretation phase.

only slightly different than each other will tend to have similar student states, responses, and justifications. Being able to quickly visualize the RPs that represent the other interpretations helps the user see how the other interpretations were handled and which interpretations still need to be handled. Furthermore, having all the RPs in one place facilitates the authoring of new RPs by allowing the user to copy and paste useful portions of other RPs instead of authoring them from scratch. If each interpretation were stored in a separate PKB, it would be much harder for the user to find the related interpretations and use them as a basis for authoring new ones.

Finally, separating the interpretations into different PKBs would mean a large overlap in the index of each PKB. The user would have to duplicate the contents of the index in several different PKBs—a tedious and annoying task. By grouping all related interpretations in the RP of a single PKB, the user is freed from having to re-create the PKB index multiple times and can easily visualize and edit the set of interpretations represented by that PKB.

The execution phase is the final phase the Teaching Executive goes through in processing a triggering event. The RP selected in the interpretation phase specifies what state the student is believed to be in, what responses to make, and a justification for why those responses are appropriate. In the execution phase, two operations are performed on the selected RP. First, the student state stored in the RP is stored in the Teaching Executive's internal database. This is done so that other PKBs can use the current student state as a basis for determining future responses. The second operation is to queue up the responses it contains for execution. Each response is executed using a response delivery method. Once the execution of all responses in the response queue is completed, the Teaching Executive exits and control is returned to the point in the task environment where the Teaching Executive was originally invoked. The transcript of processing during the execution phase is shown in Fig. 4.32.

Instantiating Tutoring Using Response Delivery Methods

To be fully functional, a tutor must be able to keep informed of a student's actions and other important events that occur in the task environment, as well as able to cause tutoring to be delivered to the student. Simply selecting an appropriate tutorial response is not enough; that response must actually be executed, and the text, video, or other feedback specified by the response must be presented to the student. As obvious as this

---

Beginning response execution phase

Beginning execution of 1 response:

Executing (tell inefficient investigation) ... Using Extended Dialog Response Method "tell inefficient

investigation"

FIG. 4.32. Transcript produced by the Teaching Executive during the execution phase.

might seem, the success of a tutoring module heavily depends on creating mechanisms that allow the tutoring module to deliver tutoring in a variety of task environments.

The Teaching Executive employs a variety of mechanisms when communicating with the task environment for the purpose of implementing tutorial responses. The mechanism employed depends on the kind of tutorial response to be delivered. In general, the various mechanisms can be divided into three categories reflecting three basic types of tutorial responses: direct intervention responses, indirect intervention responses, and tutor-internal responses.

Most tutorial responses involve communicating directly with the student (e.g., giving a hint or answering a question). For these kinds of responses, the Teaching Executive provides response delivery methods (RDM), which allow the designer to cause text, video, or other media to be presented to the student. These comprise the direct intervention category of RDMs. In other situations, the appropriate response does not involve explicit intervention by the tutor, but rather calls for the tutor to change what happens in the task environment in a pedagogically useful way. To provide for this, the Teaching Executive employs RDMs that communicate with the task environment to alter the flow of control or change the state of a simulation. These are part of the indirect intervention category of RDMs. Finally, in addition to direct and indirect interventions, a tutor frequently needs to store information about the student or other aspects of the interaction for later reference. To support this requirement, the Teaching Executive provides a third category of RDMs called *tutor-internal*. Table 4.18 summarizes the RDMs provided by the Teaching Executive. The rest of this section describes the RDMs in each of the three categories in detail.

Many tutorial responses involve conveying particular pieces of information to the student. What this information is (e.g., a hint, suggestion, general principle, etc.) and how it is to be conveyed to the student (e.g., via text, video, etc.) depends on the nature of the tutorial response and the type of LBD tutor. To accommodate the range of response types and means for delivering them, the Teaching Executive provides constructs called RDMs. An RDM is a mechanism that allows a nonprogrammer to instantiate the general responses contained in a PKB into the text, video, or other media that the student actually sees on the screen. In a sense, RDMs are the mechanism the Teaching Executive uses to translate a decision about how to intervene into concrete actions. Any tutoring system that seeks to allow nonprogrammers to directly author the system's tutorial responses must have RDMs or equivalent constructs.

Consider the following example of how RDMs are used to instantiate tutorial responses. When the student does not succeed at part of a task, the tutor may select the response TELL-TRY-AGAIN, specifying that the

TABLE 4.18
An overview of the seven types of response delivery methods that can
be used to implement responses selected by the Teaching Executive

Name	Description
Direct intervention response delivery methods	
Text template	Displays text on the screen
Video	Plays a video clip on the screen
Audio	Plays an audio clip on the speaker
Extended dialog	Conducts an extended dialogue with the student
Code	Executes specified piece of code to communicate information to the student
Indirect intervention response delivery methods	
Code	Executes specified piece of code to change state of a simulation
Task environment control	Used in conjunction with TE nodes to change flow of control in the task environment
Tutor-internal response delivery methods	
Tutor-internal	Stores information in the Teaching Executive's databases for later use

tutor should tell the student to try that part of the task again. Once the Teaching Executive has determined that the TELL-TRY-AGAIN response is appropriate at a particular point, its job is not yet complete. The Teaching Executive must have some way of causing that response to be delivered to the student. RDMs are the mechanism the Teaching Executives uses to do this.

Every response defined in the Teaching Executive has associated with it one or more RDMs. A system designer selects the RDM best suited for the task environment being built or, if no suitable one exists, defines a new one. Only one RDM is active for each response in a given task environment. By storing the RDMs used to implement responses in other task environments, the Teaching Executive acts as a repository for the various ways in which a particular response has been implemented in other systems. This repository of RDMs assists the system designer in two ways. First, it serves as a vehicle for re-use, allowing a system designer to use previously authored RDMs instead of creating them from scratch each time a new task environment is built. Second, if the designer decides to create a new RDM, the repository of existing RDMs can serve as a guide, illustrating how a particular response has been implemented in other systems.

The Teaching Executive contains seven types of RDMs, each representing a different medium for instantiating a response. The system designer's decision about which RDM to use depends on what kind of response is being implemented and, if it is a response that involves communicating with the student, what kind of media will be used for that communication. RDMs are not intended to be a theory of which type of media is best for which type of tutorial response (although they could serve as the basis for such research in the future). Other researchers have examined the relative merits of different media used in tutoring interactions (e.g., Kozma, 1991; Recker & Ram, 1994). The Teaching Executive provides RDMs as tools that allow a nonprogrammer to instantiate the general responses contained in PKBs. It is up to the system designer to select which RDM is associated with a particular response. The Teaching Executive does not dynamically decide which RDM should be used during the course of a tutoring interaction.[24]

Some responses, particularly direct interventions, can be implemented via a number of different RDMs, whereas other responses have only one RDM that makes sense to use. For example, a response like TELL-TRY-AGAIN could reasonably be delivered using a variety of media, and thus any of the text, audio, or video RDMs would be appropriate. For a response like REPEAT-TASK-AGAIN, which specifies that the student should repeat a task he or she is having difficulty with, only the task environment control RDM would make sense to use as a means for implementing it. No other RDMs provide a means to control the task environment, which is the essence of what the REPEAT-TASK-AGAIN response is all about.

Instantiating Direct Intervention Responses

To implement responses that communicate directly with a student, the Teaching Executive provides six types of direct intervention RDMs. These are enumerated next, along with a discussion of the particular strengths and weaknesses of each type of RDM. In addition, the specific mechanisms that each RDM uses to generate output is discussed in detail. The text template RDM is used to display a textual response to the student. It is called a *text template* because it can contain both static elements of text, as well as text elements that are spliced in dynamically at run time. Some example text templates and the output they produce as seen by the student are shown in Table 4.19. Figure 4.33 shows how the output of a text template RDM appears to the student in the BC Cashier system.

---

[24]A tutor could be equipped to reason about which type of RDM to use at a particular point in a tutoring interaction. Research into this issue has been done in other contexts (see e.g., Kozma, 1991; Recker & Ram, 1994). That type of reasoning is beyond the scope of the work reported here.

TABLE 4.19
Some Example Text Template Response Delivery Methods
and the Output They Produce At Run-Time

Text Template	*Output Produced at Run-Time*
In order to :**step** you need to :**action**.	In order to ring up the corn bread you need to press the "CORNBREAD" key.
You don't need to :**step** because :**explanation**.	You don't need to ring up the coleslaw because it's included when you ring up the Boston Basics.

Note. Template variables are indicated in boldface font and begin with a colon. All other text in a template is static.

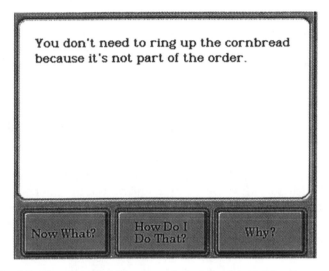

FIG. 4.33.   Appearance of the output of a text template RDM as it appears in the BC Cashier system.

Despite the apparent simplicity of the text template mechanism, it can be used to produce relatively rich tutorial responses when combined with a careful analysis of the domain being taught and the information needed to provide tutoring in that domain. Why is this the case? Although text is often considered an impoverished media compared with audio or video, it provides a level of generativity that is difficult to match. *Generativity*, in the sense used here, means the ability to dynamically assemble content for output based on the changing conditions that exist at run time (see e.g., Clancey, 1982). High-quality computer-based learning environments tend to be richly interactive, and students come to expect the system to respond dynamically to their actions. If the tutor that accompanies this kind of learning environment produces the same text response in a variety of different situations, it will appear to not be following what the student is doing, and the student will quickly lose confidence in the tutor's advice. Therefore, the generativity provided by text template RDMs is an important tool in allowing the Teaching Executive to adapt its output to the student's current actions and, in so doing, maintain the student's confidence in its tutoring abilities.

Some types of tutorial responses call for conducting an extended dialogue with the student (see e.g., Carbonell, 1970; Clancey, 1982; Collins, 1977; Collins & Stevens, 1982, 1983; Stevens & Collins, 1977), for some early examples of this technique). The best example of these types of responses are Socratic-style dialogues, where the tutor engages the student in an extended question-and-answer exchange designed to lead students to realize and correct their own misconceptions. These dialogues tend to have a complex structure, with earlier portions of the dialogue affecting the course of later portions of the dialogue. In some cases, they involve repeated loops through parts of a dialogue until the student comes to an adequate understanding of the topic being discussed. Due to their complex nature, a special RDM was created to make it easier for a designer to author these types of dialogues.

The extended dialogue RDM exploits the strength of MOPed's graphical representation of control structures. By using a special set of nodes and MOPs, it allows the designer to craft extended dialogues in much the same way that regular MOPed control structures are authored. The extended dialogue RDM works by allowing the designer to create and edit a set of MOPs that implement a dialogue and, at run time, causes those MOPs to be executed to conduct that dialogue with the student.

Why is it necessary to have a different RDM for implementing extended dialogues instead of using other existing RDMs? There are two main answers to this question. The first answer is essentially one of ease of use. Although it would be technically possible to create an identical dialogue with a set of PKBs that used text template and other RDMs, the complexity of managing the interactions between the individual PKBs would quickly become untenable. By using MOPed's graphical representation of control structures, the extended dialogue RDM makes it easier for a designer to visualize the contingencies in the dialogue being authored. Although the flow of control among a set of PKBs is not easily identifiable at design time, the contingencies between various components of a dialogue created using MOPed's interface are explicitly represented and can be visualized on the screen in one glance.

The second reason a special RDM for extended dialogues is required is that these dialogues almost always require prompting the student for some type of input. Getting input from the student entails categorizing the input and causing subsequent parts of the dialogue to be altered based

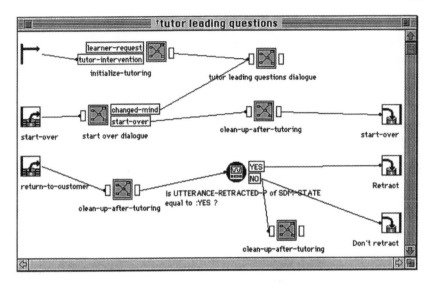

FIG. 4.34.   An example dialogue MOP used in the Casper system.

on the input provided by the student. To simplify the complexity of obtaining and analyzing student input, the designer is provided with a Q&A node. A Q&A node localizes the process of prompting the student for input, categorizing that input, and causing the dialogue to branch depending on the category of the student's input. This localization greatly simplifies the process of categorizing student input because only those responses that make sense for a student to provide in that context need to be handled. The extended dialogue RDM provides a system designer for using Q&A nodes, as well as other mechanisms, for obtaining and classifying student input in the context of a tutorial dialogue. The Casper system makes heavy use of extended dialogue RDMs.[25] For example, if the student asks a leading question, the tutor intervenes with an extended dialogue that explains why asking a question in a leading way is problematic. At the end of this dialogue, the student is offered the opportunity to retract the leading question and go back and ask the question in a nonleading way. Figure 4.34 displays the extended dialogue MOP that implements part of this dialogue.

The video RDM, as its name implies, is used to display video clips to the student. Although lacking the generativity of text, video can be an effective means to deliver certain types of tutoring, particularly stories or anecdotes told by experts. Video can also be effective when used to deliver

[26]The Socratic dialogues for the Casper system were initially authored by Scott Dooley and Noreen Burke.

complex explanations that are difficult to convey in text, especially explanations that use visual or spatial elements. The video RDM supports video stored in digital format as a file on the computer's disc drive.[26]

The audio RDM is identical to the video RDM in almost every respect; the main difference is that audio is played instead of video. Audio RDMs are effective when displaying visual information on the screen (in either text or video formats) is impractical or undesirable. Audio responses can be useful if, in the real-world version of the task the student is practicing, advice will come through an auditory medium, such as a loudspeaker, telephone, or headphone. In such cases, it is usually advisable to accustom the student to getting auditory feedback. Finally, because audio tends to be easier to acquire and store on a computer than video (although this is changing quickly as desktop video acquisition technology improves), audio responses are often used in place of video during the development of a system. If any changes are needed, they are much less costly to make when using audio than when using video. When the final decisions about the kinds of feedback needed are made, the audio can be replaced with video RDMs.

The last type of direct intervention RDM is also the least glamorous. The code RDM provides a fallback option when none of the other RDMs can adequately implement a particular response. By allowing a designer to write arbitrary code to implement a response, this RDM provides the ultimate in flexibility. But this flexibility comes at the expense of usability. All other RDMs are usable, at least in their basic forms, by system designers who do not know how to program. In fact, this was one of the underlying motivations for the creation of those RDMs. However, the code RDM is usable only by designers who know how to program. The functioning of code RDMs is straightforward. The designer is provided a window in which to enter code; at run time, that code is executed.

This RDM is useful for direct intervention for two primary reasons (its use is discussed as an indirect intervention RDM later). First, as mentioned earlier, it is useful when a response cannot be implemented using any other RDM provided by the Teaching Executive. This might be the case for a variety of reasons, but usually it is because the information needed to create the output for the response is embedded in Lisp data structures or must be assembled via some complex function call. The second reason for the usefulness of the code RDM is because it provides a mechanism for evolutionary prototyping of a response during the course of system development. The process of deciding what information will be needed to provide tutoring in a particular task environment, organizing it, and

---

[27]Video RDMs employ the QuickTime™ digital video capabilities on Macintosh computer systems.

actually entering all of it into the computer in a usable form can be extremely difficult and time-consuming. Although this process is under-way, the code RDM provides a mechanism (at least for adept programmers) to implement responses using whatever information is currently available in the computer. Once the content and the organization of that content have been identified, other RDMs can be used to replace a code RDM.

Instantiating Indirect Intervention Responses

In addition to responding directly to a student, a computer tutor can also assist a student's learning by controlling the task environment in peda-gogically useful ways. This kind of control can be as straightforward as causing the student to repeat the same task again or as sophisticated as altering the internal state of a simulation to cause a situation to arise that might help the student realize the misconception. Responses of this type require the tutor to change some aspect of the task environment. The Teaching Executive provides two types of indirect intervention RDMs that can cause changes in the task environment.

The task environment control RDM is used in conjunction with TE nodes to cause a change in the flow of control in MOPed. It implements a response by returning a label to a TE node. A decision about what to do next can then be made on the basis of which labels are returned to the TE node. Recall that a TE node, as a type of branching node, contains out-terminals. The job of the TE node is to select which out-terminal the flow of control will take after the TE node is exited. The out-terminals on a TE node correspond to the labels that might be returned after the Teaching Executive processes the triggering events supplied by that TE node. When a response implemented by a task environment control RDM is executed at run time, it returns a label to the TE node. This label is matched against the out-terminals of the TE node. If a match is found, flow of control exits the TE node via that out-terminal. If no match is found, flow of control exits the TE node via the STANDARD-PATH out-terminal. This mechanism permits responses executed by the Teaching Executive to change the flow of control in the task environment.

An example of the use of task environment control RDMs to implement an indirect intervention comes from the Casper system. When the student asks the customer for information he or she has already obtained, the tutor must decide whether to intervene directly or indirectly. In that system, the decision was made to intervene indirectly the first time the student makes that kind of mistake by having the simulated customer inform the student about the redundant question. On subsequent occur-rences of a redundant question by the student, direct intervention in the form of a story would be used.

To implement this, a TE node is used in conjunction with responses using task environment control RDMs. First the designer specifies that the response REMIND-REPEATED-QUESTION-VIA-AGENT should be implemented using a task environment control RDM. The next step is to create a TE node and link its out-terminals appropriately. An example of this is shown in Figure 4.35. There the TE node used has a number of out-terminals indicating that various changes in the flow of control in the task environment may be affected. Most relevant to our discussion here, the second to last out-terminal on the TE node is labeled REMIND-RE-PEATED-QUESTION-VIA-AGENT and leads to a node that causes the simulated customer to say, "You already asked me that question." The other out-terminals are used to implement other tutorial responses—in particular, those that allow the student to decide whether he or she wishes to retract the last question to the customer. The STANDARD-PATH out-terminal is taken when no task environment changes are specified by the tutorial responses selected by the Teaching Executive.

In addition to its use in implementing direct intervention, the code RDM is also useful in creating indirect interventions. Its main use is to allow designers to implement responses that change the state of a simulation that is part of the task environment. The code RDM works as it does when used for direct interventions, except that, instead of writing code to produce output, the designer writes the code to access and change relevant variables used by a simulation. The purpose of this type of

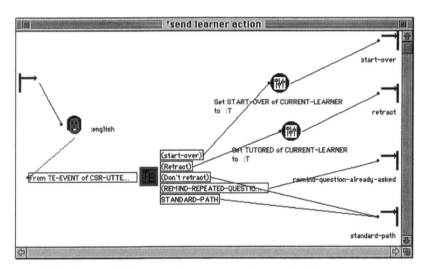

FIG. 4.35. A MOP from the Casper system showing the TE node used to decide, among other things, whether the student will be given feedback directly by the tutor or indirectly via the task environment.

intervention is to provide feedback to the student through his or her interaction with the task environment rather than by a direct statement by the tutor. This is especially effective if a simulation can be altered in such a way that a situation arises in the simulation that forces the student to confront an important misconception.

Instantiating Tutor-Internal Responses

The third category of RDMs is tutor-internal. These methods are used to implement responses that modify the internal state of the tutor. This makes them different than either direct or indirect intervention RDMs in that they are not intended to have a direct effect that is visible to the student. Two examples of things a tutor might want to keep track of are whether a particular step has been taken by the student and how many times a particular kind of mistake has been made. Currently there is only one type of tutor-internal RDM. It provides a mechanism that allows the designer to easily update the Teaching Executive's internal database by specifying a form that is to be stored. When this RDM is executed, the form is stored in the Teaching Executive's database for later reference.

CONCLUSION

Evaluating the Utility of the Teaching Executive

No formal evaluations of the Teaching Executive's efficacy in facilitating development of educational applications were done; the evaluation information reported here comes from informal comments and observations of those who used the Teaching Executive to build real teaching applications. An example of a more formal evaluation process for a system similar to the Teaching Executive may be found in Murray (1992). The Teaching Executive was extremely effective in facilitating the construction of tutoring systems that teach procedural tasks. The teaching strategies described herein have been, at the time of this writing, used (and re-used) in building four training applications (the BC Cashier and BC Server applications described earlier and the 411/Directory Assistance and NOTIS applications described elsewhere; Guralnick, 1996). These systems have all been built by Guralnick as part of his Ph.D. research.

Based on estimates provided by Guralnick, the following figures give a rough idea of the extent to which the Teaching Executive facilitated the development of tutoring component of these systems.

- The teaching strategies for the BC Cashier system took approximately 2 weeks to build using the Teaching Executive. It is estimated that hard-coding the teaching decisions in the traditional manner would have required approximately 6 weeks.

- In developing the BC Server system, the teaching strategies created for BC Cashier had to be slightly modified to handle this new task. This required about a week's worth of time. Without the existing teaching strategies and the Teaching Executive tool, approximately 6 weeks may have been needed to create the desired tutoring behavior in the system.

- The NOTIS system, built to train library personnel how to use the library computer catalogue software, required no changes to the library of teaching strategies. No additional work was needed to create the necessary teaching interventions for this system.

- Developing the 411/Directory Assistance system required a few additional changes to the teaching strategies. These modifications required approximately 1 week to implement. Building the tutoring for this system would have required at least 6 weeks if it were necessary to create it from scratch.

From these rough figures, a picture of the utility of the approach embodied by the Teaching Executive begins to emerge. The library of teaching strategies for procedural tasks, along with the infrastructure and authoring tools provided by the Teaching Executive, appear to be quite effective at facilitating the development of training software to teach this type of task.

The effectiveness of the Teaching Executive in building systems to teach diagnosis tasks is a little less clear-cut. Because only one system that teaches a diagnosis task has been built (i.e., Casper), judging the extent to which the library of teaching strategies described herein can be re-used is tricky. However, there are at least two reasons to be encouraged by the results so far. First, the Teaching Executive does provide a benefit in terms of intra-application re-use of teaching strategies. In other words, because the same teaching strategies apply whenever the student makes a particular mistake, it is not necessary to change or add tutoring when a new simulated customer is added to the system. This allows the system to be extended without requiring any additional work on the teaching strategies. Second, because the tutoring in Casper is more complicated than in the BC systems, the potential payoff of re-usability is much larger should a second or subsequent systems ever be built.

Lessons Learned

Over and above the specific solutions discussed here, there are a few general lessons that transcend the present work and may be useful for those working on related problems. In retrospect, the key to the effectiveness of the Teaching Executive was not any specific architectural feature, but rather the structure and content of the knowledge encoded in the libraries of teaching strategies. Although creating a standard, re-usable architecture for retrieving and applying teaching strategies was important to the overall success of this research, any software engineering that took place was strictly in service of the knowledge engineering required to develop the teaching strategies. The primacy of knowledge in providing the system's power is an important lesson to keep in mind when building knowledge-based systems whose role is similar to that of the Teaching Executive.

A second lesson that came out of building the Teaching Executive is the importance of relying on a human user to provide the background knowledge and inferencing that would be difficult to have the system provide. This lesson manifested itself in the solution to the communication problem between task environment and tutoring module discussed earlier. To apply general teaching strategies, the Teaching Executive must be able to recognize specific student actions in the task environment. In general, the problem of recognizing specific instances of general descriptive categories requires a good deal of knowledge and inference capability.

Instead of attempting to have the Teaching Executive recognize student actions in the task environment autonomously, as was the case in the SPIEL system (Burke, 1993), the solution adopted here was to have the system designer do the recognition process by annotating the task environment with triggering events from the Teaching Executive's representational vocabulary. This freed the Teaching Executive from having to perform a knowledge-intensive recognition task. Building the Teaching Executive as a system that works cooperatively with a human user allowed for the creation of a total system that is more powerful and flexible than if the Teaching Executive were to try to handle everything itself.

The Teaching Executive represents but one stage in a larger process of creating powerful authoring tools for the creation of educational software. A key to the success of the Teaching Executive as a practical, usable, and effective tool was layering it on top of the MOPed tool for building task environments.[27] This linkage allowed relatively more attention to be given to the knowledge engineering involved in creating teaching strategies and less to the endless software engineering issues that arose in trying to incorporate the Teaching Executive into existing tutoring systems.

Moreover, the combination of the Teaching Executive and MOPed is not the final stage of the process. Work continues to be done in layering even more powerful tools on top of the Teaching Executive. Although the Teaching Executive was successful in addressing some of the problems hindering the development of educational software, it also turned out to be

---

[28]The original idea to make the Teaching Executive a part of MOPed came from Alex Kass.

a stepping stone into new areas that were not envisioned at the outset of the work.

Future Directions

There are at least two promising directions in which the research described here could be developed. First, it would be useful to attempt to apply the Teaching Executive to building LBD tutors for other types of tasks in addition to the two described here. The more types of tasks for which libraries of teaching strategies have been created, the greater the chance that any new LBD tutor will be able to use one (or more) of these existing libraries. Second, once the teaching strategies for a particular type of task have been identified, it would make sense to use those strategies to assist the system designer through the process of building a new LBD tutor. The research reported here could be extended to applying the Teaching Executive to other types of LBD tasks. Four types of tasks that have been used in other tutoring systems are described next, along with the types of skills each is useful for teaching. They are also examined to see how well the Teaching Executive might be applied in each.

1. *Exploration Tasks.* In exploration tasks, the student is provided with a simulation or microworld within which to operate. The student's task is to infer the laws governing that microworld or perhaps to notice opportunities for participating in the activities within the simulated world. This type of task is valuable when the skill to be taught is the ability to explore a complex environment or system and determine how it works. It is also effective for teaching students how to recognize important events out of a background of less important ones. An example of an LBD tutor that employs this type of task is YELLO (Kass, Burke, Blevis, & Williamson, 1993), which teaches beginning account executives how to sell Yellow Pages advertising. A difficult aspect of exploration tasks, from the perspective of tutoring, is dealing with the student's failure to discover or capitalize on an opportunity. Clearly, having a teaching strategy that intervened whenever the student missed an opportunity would defeat the whole point of having the student recognize the opportunity on his or her own. What would be needed is a mechanism that allowed the tutor to delay intervention in these cases and, once the student completed the task, to review the missed opportunities and discuss how the student could have better taken advantage of them.

2. *Control Tasks.* Another type of task that can be used in LBD tutors is control. In control tasks, the student runs an organization or operates a system. Typically, the student is given an operational system and must maintain or improve its operating efficiency. The control task structure

can be used to teach the student how a particular organization, machine, or system works as well as how to notice features that indicate impending or actual problems that need to be rectified. An example of a learning environment that employs the control task structure is HRM, a human resources management trainer (Feifer & Bell, 1991). In that system, the student plays the role of a human resource manager in a simulated company. The student must use the information in the employee files, as well as good judgment, to decide whether to promote or fire various employees to maximize productivity and maintain the company's profitability. Bad decisions by the student result in less productivity from the employees, and in some cases even good employees will quit in frustration.

The control task structure is particularly useful in teaching students how to operate complex equipment or other industrial machinery. Because many control tasks deal with operating equipment, they often look like procedural tasks. Although control tasks may resemble procedural tasks, a key difference between the two is that procedural tasks require little or no background knowledge to perform successfully, whereas control tasks rely on such knowledge. Thus, a task would fall into the category of control if the student needed to reason about the state of a process or piece of equipment to know how to operate that equipment.

Two classic examples of learning environments used to teach this type of task are STEAMER (Hollans, Hutchins, & Weitzman, 1984) and Recovery Boiler Tutor (Woolf, Blegen, Jansen, & Verloop, 1987). In the latter system, the student is asked to operate a type of boiler used in pulp mills. The student can select from 20 training scenarios in which he or she must operate the boiler properly in both normal and emergency situations. The student is encouraged to change the settings of various controls and observe the effects of his or her actions. The tutor provides hints or guidance as needed by the student. Because of the large overlap between procedural and control tasks, it is likely that many of the procedural task strategies described herein would be applicable, in some form, to control tasks as well. One key difference in creating teaching strategies would be the decision about whether to intervene immediately. Because control tasks have a nontrivial set of background knowledge the student needs to master, there might be reason to delay intervention when the student makes an error to allow the student to observe the consequences of that mistake. This would present the opportunity for the tutor to explain the misunderstanding that led the student to make the mistake.

3. *Design Tasks.* In design tasks, the student's principal activities are creating an artifact or specifying how a system should be organized. Design tasks are engaging because they tap into the intrinsically motivating sense of ownership that comes with creating one's own artifact (Edelson, 1993). Typically, design tasks used in LBD environments have

two phases. First, the student designs and builds the artifact. Second, he or she has the opportunity to test the design to see how well it performs. This two-phase design and test process gives the student an excellent chance to learn from failures and provides many opportunities for a tutor to provide advice and assistance.

An example of the use of a design task structure in an LBD environment is Broadcast News (Kass et al., 1993). Broadcast News teaches high school students a variety of social studies topics, such as history, political science, international affairs, economics, and current events, by allowing them to produce (i.e., design) their own news show. In this system, the student plays the role of an assistant producer of an evening network news show; the student must write, edit, and organize the stories that will appear on the newscast for a given night. Once the student has completed writing or editing a story, he or she must submit it to a simulated executive producer for approval. The executive producer responds by giving the student feedback on the story, which the student must address. This is how the design and test cycle is realized in the system. By allowing the student to create his or her own newscast and get feedback on its structure and content, the student is confronted with a variety of complex issues that must be dealt with. The student is forced to evaluate current events and their context in a critical fashion. The system provides an engaging format for students to think critically about a wide variety of social studies and current events topics.

4. *Analysis Tasks.* Analysis tasks require the student to collect and analyze information to make a decision, recommendation, report, presentation, and so on. In analysis tasks, the student is typically presented with an environment that provides the sources of information needed to perform the analysis, although in some cases the student must actively seek out the information from sources that are not immediately apparent. Either way, the crux of the student's task is to critically analyze the information and then take some action based on this analysis. What this action is depends on the particular context of the task. The student may be asked to prepare some documents that summarize his or her analysis and the reasoning that went into it, or he or she may have to make a recommendation or decision in some simulated world.

An example of the use of the analysis task structure in an LBD tutor is financial report analysis (FRA; Foster, 1996). Here the student plays the role of a banker who must analyze a company's financial reports to recommend whether to approve a loan to that company. All of the required information is provided to the student in the form of company financial reports. The student must fill out a loan recommendation form that captures his or her analysis of the company's finances. Another system that uses the analysis task structure is Advise the President (Bareiss & Beckwith, 1993). In this case, the student plays the role of an advisor to the president of the United States at some point in recent history. The student is asked to recommend a course of action on a critical domestic or foreign relations issue. To make this recommendation, the student can browse through a hypermedia database of video clips of news stories and interviews with prominent figures of the time. For example, the student might be asked to advise President Carter on the Iran hostage crises or President Kennedy on the Bay of Pigs invasion. For a tutor to assist a student engaged in an analysis task, the tutor must be able to track the kinds of information available to the student, how that information is to be used in the analysis, and what the result or product of the analysis should be. To the extent that the analysis task can be reified in concrete actions, the easier it will be for the tutor to follow what the student is doing and to recognize any mistakes. For example, in both the FRA and Advise the President systems, students are asked to encode their analysis in the form of a final document or report. By tracking what information students include in the report, and how they use that information to justify a recommendation or decision, the tutor can gain a clearer picture of how well or poorly students considered the information available to them, as well as how well they were able to apply that information as support for their position.

Now that libraries of teaching strategies for two types of tasks have been created, it would make sense to use those strategies to further facilitate the process of developing educational software. The most straightforward way to leverage the power of the existing strategies would be to use them to guide the system designer through the process of annotating the task environment with triggering events. A more proactive, knowledge-rich authoring tool could be built by incorporating the libraries of teaching strategies into the tool. Armed with the knowledge of the kinds of teaching decisions that needed to be made, such a tool could help the system designer decide which triggering event to use as an annotation based on the part of the task environment being built.

A slightly more sophisticated way to use the teaching strategies to facilitate the development of educational software would be to create an authoring tool that automatically linked the task environment to the Teaching Executive as the task environment is built. This would mean that all the necessary annotations would be added automatically, freeing the system designer from having to perform this task at all. This would require an authoring tool that knew much more about the kind of task environment that was being built than MOPed currently does (which is to say, not at all). Based on its knowledge of the type of task environment being built and the library of teaching strategies needed for that kind of task environment, the authoring tool would be able to automatically generate the required tutoring. This approach is currently being pursued by Guralnick (1996) and others at the Institute for the Learning Sciences.

REFERENCES

Anderson, J. R. (1982). Acquisition of cognitive skill. *Psychological Review, 89*, 369–406.

Anderson, J. R., Boyle, C. F., Corbett, A. T., & Lewis, M. W. (1990). Cognitive modeling and intelligent tutoring. *Artificial Intelligence, 42*, 7–49.

Anderson, J. R., & Corbett, A. (1993). Tutoring of cognitive skill. In J. R. Anderson (Ed.), *Rules of the mind* (pp. 235–255). Hillsdale, NJ: Lawrence Erlbaum Associates.

Anderson, J. R., & Skwarecki, E. (1986). The automated tutoring of introductory computer programming. *Communications of the ACM, 29*(9), 842–849.

Augusteijn, M. F., Broome, R. W., Kolbe, R. W., & Ewell, R. N. (1992). ITS Challenger-A domain independent environment for the development of intelligent training systems. *Journal of Artificial Intelligence in Education, 3*, 183–205.

Bareiss, R., & Beckwith, R. (1993). *Advise the President: A hypermedia system for teaching contemporary American history.* Paper presented at the annual meeting of the American Education Research Association.

Bell, B., Bareiss, R., & Beckwith, R. (1994). Sickle Cell Counselor: A prototype goal-based scenario for instruction in a museum environment. *Journal of the Learning Sciences, 3*(4), 347–386.

Berliner, D. C. (1987). Ways of thinking about students and classrooms by more and less experienced teachers. In J. Calderhead (Ed.), *Exploring teachers' thinking* (pp. 60–83). London: Cassell.

Birnbaum, L. A. (1986). *Integrated processing in planning and understanding.* Unpublished doctoral dissertation, Yale University.

Bloom, B. S. (1984). The 2 sigma problem: The search for methods of group instruction as effective as one-to-one tutoring. *Educational Researcher*, pp. 4–16.

Bonar, J., Cunningham, R., & Schultz, J. (1986). An object-oriented architecture for intelligent tutoring systems. *OOPSLA-86.*

Boose, J. H. (1986). *Expertise transfer and expert system design.* New York: Elsevier.

Burke, R. D. (1993). *Representation, storage, and retrieval of stories in a social simulation.* Unpublished doctoral dissertation, The Institute for the Learning Sciences, Northwestern University. Technical Report #50.

Burton, R. R., & Brown, J. S. (1982). An investigation of computer coaching for informal learning activities. In D. Sleeman & J. S. Brown (Eds.), *Intelligent tutoring systems* (pp. 79–98). New York: Academic Press.

Calderhead, J. (1988). The development of knowledge structures in learning to teach. In J. Calderhead (Ed.), *Teachers' professional learning* (pp. 51–64). London: Falmer.

Carbonell, J. R. (1970). *Mixed-initiative man-computer instructional dialogues.* Unpublished doctoral dissertation, Massachusetts Institute of Technology.

Chi, M., Feltovich, P., & Glaser, R. (1981). Categorization and representations of physics problems by experts and novices. *Cognitive Science, 5*, 121–152.

Chi, M. T. H., Glaser, R., & Rees, R. (1982). Expertise in problem solving. In R. Sternberg (Ed.), *Advances in the psychology of human intelligence* (pp. 7–76). Hillsdale, NJ: Lawrence Erlbaum Associates.

Clancey, W., & Joerger, K. (1988). A practical authoring shell for apprenticeship learning. In *ITS-88* (pp. 67–74). Montreal, Canada.

Clancey, W. J. (1982). Tutoring rules for guiding a case method dialog. In D. Sleeman & J. S. Brown (Eds.), *Intelligent tutoring systems* (pp. 201–226). New York: Academic Press.

Clancey, W. J. (1985). Representing control knowledge as abstract tasks and metarules. In Coombs & Bolc (Eds.), *Computer expert systems*. New York: Springer-Verlag.

Clancey, W. J. (1986, August). From GUIDON to NEOMYCIN and HERACLES in twenty short lessons: ONR final report 1979–1985. *AI Magazine*, pp. 40–60.

Clark, C. M., & Peterson, P. L. (1986). Teachers' thought processes. In M. C. Wittrock (Eds.), *Handbook of research on teaching* (pp. 255–296). New York: Macmillan.

Collins, A. (1977). Processes in acquiring knowledge. In R. C. Anderson, R. J. Spiro, & W. E. Montague (Eds.), *Schooling and the acquisition of knowledge* (pp. 339–363). Hillsdale, NJ: Lawrence Erlbaum Associates.

Collins, A., Brown, J. S., & Newman, S. E. (1989). Cognitive apprenticeship: Teaching the crafts of reading, writing, and mathematics. In L. B. Resnick (Eds.), *Knowing, learning, and instruction: Essays in honor of Robert Glaser*. Hillsdale, NJ: Lawrence Erlbaum Associates.

Collins, A., & Stevens, A. L. (1982). Goal and strategies of inquiry teachers. In R. Glaser (Ed.), *Advances in instructional psychology II* (pp. 65–119). Hillsdale, NJ: Lawrence Erlbaum Associates.

Collins, A., & Stevens, A. L. (1983). A cognitive theory of inquiry teaching. In C. Reigeluth (Ed.), *Instructional design: Theories and methods* (pp. 65–119). New York: Academic Press.

Davis, R., & King, J. J. (1977). An overview of production systems. In E. Elcock & D. Michie (Eds.), *Machine intelligence 8* (pp. 300–332). Chichester, England: Ellis Horwood.

Dillenbourg, P. (1988). Self-improving tutoring systems. *International Journal of Educational Research, 12*(8), 851–862.

Domeshek, E. A. (1992). *Do the right thing: A component theory for indexing stories as social advice*. Unpublished doctoral dissertation, Yale University. Reprinted as Technical Report #26, The Institute for the Learning Sciences, Northwestern University.

Edelson, D. C. (1993). *Learning from stories: Indexing and reminding in a Socratic case-based teaching system for elementary school biology*. Unpublished doctoral dissertation, Northwestern University. Reprinted as Technical Report #43, The Institute for the Learning Sciences, Northwestern University.

Elsom-Cook, M T. (1991). Dialogue and teaching styles. In P. Goodyear (Ed.), *Teaching knowledge and intelligent tutoring* (pp. 61–83). Norwood, NJ: Ablex.

Elsom-Cook, M. T., & Spensley, F. (1987). Using multiple teaching strategies in an ITS. In *Intelligent tutoring systems* (pp. 286–290). Montreal, Canada.

Feifer, R. G., & Bell, B. L. (1991). Design principles for computer-based instruction: Integrating theory and practice for corporate training. In R. B. Loftin & D. F. Cupitt (Eds.), *Proceedings of the Contributed Sessions 1991 Conference on Intelligent Computer-Aided Training, 2* (pp. 276–288). Houston, TX: NASA.

Foster, D. (1996). *Financial report analyst: A goal-based scenario for teaching financial statement analysis*. Unpublished doctoral dissertation, The Institute for the Learning Sciences, Northwestern University.

Goodyear, P. (1991). Research on teaching and the design of intelligent tutoring systems. In P. Goodyear (Ed.), *Teaching knowledge and intelligent tutoring* (pp. 3–24). Norwood, NJ: Ablex.

Guralnick, D. (1996). *Training systems for script-based tasks*. Unpublished doctoral dissertation, The Institute for the Learning Sciences, Northwestern University.

Hollans, J. D., Hutchins, E. L., & Weitzman, L. (1984). STEAMER: An interactive inspectable simulation-based training system. *AI Magazine*.

Jona, M., Bell, B., & Birnbaum, L. (1991). Button theory: A taxonomy of student-teacher communication for interface design in computer-based learning environments. In *Proceedings of the thirteenth annual conference of the Cognitive Science Society* (pp. 765–769). Chicago, IL.

Jona, M. Y., & Kolodner, J. L. (1992). Case-based reasoning. In S. C. Shapiro (Ed.), *Encyclopedia of artificial intelligence* (pp. 1265–1279). New York: Wiley.

Kass, A. (1994). *The Casper project: Integrating simulation, case presentation, and Socratic tutoring to teach diagnostic problem-solving in complex domains* (Tech. Rep. No. 51). Evanston, IL: The Institute for the Learning Sciences, Northwestern University.

Kass, A., Burke, R., Blevis, E., & Williamson, M. (1993). Constructing learning environments for complex social skills. *Journal of the Learning Sciences, 3*(4).

Kass, A., Dooley, S., & Luksa, F. (1993). *The Broadcast News Project: Using broadcast journalism as a vehicle for teaching social studies* (Tech. Rep. No. 40). Evanston, IL: The Institute for the Learning Sciences, Northwestern University.

Kass, A., & McGee, S. (1993). *The Road Trip Project: Learning geography through simulated travel* (Tech. Rep. No. 42). Evanston, IL: The Institute for the Learning Sciences, Northwestern University.

Kolodner, J. L. (1984). *Retrieval and organizational strategies in conceptual memory.* Hillsdale, NJ: Lawrence Erlbaum Associates.

Kolodner, J. L. (1993). *Case-based reasoning.* San Mateo, CA: Kaufmann.

Kozma, R. (1991). Learning with media. *Review of Educational Research, 61*(2), 179–211.

Leinhardt, G. (1988). Situated knowledge and expertise in teaching. In J. Calderhead (Ed.), *Teachers' professional learning* (pp. 146–168). London: Falmer.

Leinhardt, G., & Greeno, J. G. (1986). The cognitive skill of teaching. *Journal of Educational Psychology, 78*(2), 75–95.

Leinhardt, G., Weidman, C., & Hammond, K. M. (1987). Introduction and integration of classroom routines by expert teachers. *Curriculum Inquiry, 17*, 135–176.

Lemke, A. C., & Fischer, G. (1990). A cooperative problem solving system for user interface design. In *Proceedings of the eighth annual conference on Artificial Intelligence* (pp. 479–484). AAAI Press.

Lesgold, A., & Lajoie, S. (1991). Complex problem solving in electronics. In R. J. Sternberg & P. A. Frensch (Eds.), *Complex problem solving: Principles and mechanisms* (pp. 287–316). Hillsdale, NJ: Lawrence Erlbaum Associates.

Merrill, D. C., Reiser, B. J., Merrill, S. K., & Landes, S. (1993). *Tutoring: Guided learning by doing* (Tech. Rep. No. 45). Evanston, IL: The Institute for the Learning Sciences, Northwestern University.

Merrill, D. C., Reiser, B. J., Ranney, M., & Trafton, J. G. (1992). Effective tutoring techniques: A comparison of human tutors and intelligence tutoring systems. *Journal of the Learning Sciences, 2*(3), 277–305.

Murray, T. (1992). *Facilitating teacher participation in intelligent computer tutor design: Tools and design methods.* Unpublished doctoral dissertation, University of Massachusetts.

Murray, T., & Woolf, B. P. (1990). A knowledge acquisition framework facilitating multiple tutoring strategies. In *Proceedings of the AAAI Spring Symposium on Knowledge-Based Environments for Learning and Teaching.* Stanford, CA.

O'Shea, T. (1982). A self-improving quadratic tutor. In D. Sleeman & J. S. Brown (Eds.), *Intelligent tutoring systems* (pp. 309–336). New York: Academic Press.

Ohlsson, S. (1987). Some principles of intelligent tutoring. In R. W. Lawler & M. Yazdani (Eds.), *Artificial intelligence and education* (pp. 293–326). Norwood, NJ: Ablex.

Ohlsson, S. (1988). Computer simulation and its impact on educational research and practice. *International Journal of Educational Research, 12*(1), 5–34.

Ohmaye, E. (1992). *Simulation-based language learning: An architecture and a multimedia authoring tool.* Unpublished doctoral dissertation, Northwestern University. Reprinted as Technical Report #30, The Institute for the Learning Sciences, Northwestern University.

Owens, C. C. (1990). *Indexing and retrieving abstract planning knowledge.* Unpublished doctoral dissertation, Yale University.

Polson, M. C., & Richardson, J. J. (Eds.). (1988). *Foundations of intelligent tutoring systems.* Hillsdale, NJ: Lawrence Erlbaum Associates.

Pople, H. E. (1977). The formation of composite hypotheses in diagnostic problem solving—an exercise in synthetic reasoning. In *Proceedings of the fifth international joint conference on Artificial Intelligence* (pp. 1030–1037).

Recker, M., & Ram, A. (1994). Cognitive media types as indices for hypermedia learning environments. In *Proceedings of the AAAI-94 workshop on indexing and reuse in multimedia systems.* Seattle, WA.

Riesbeck, C. K., & Schank, R. C. (1989). *Inside case-based reasoning.* Hillsdale, NJ: Lawrence Erlbaum Associates.

Rosenshine, B., & Stevens, R. (1986). Teaching functions. In M. C. Wittrock (Ed.), *Handbook of research on teaching* (pp. 376–391). New York: Macmillan.

Russell, D. (1988). IDE: The interpreter. In Pstoka, Massey, & Mutter (Eds.), *Intelligent tutoring systems: Lessons learned.* Hillsdale, NJ: Lawrence Erlbaum Associates.

Russell, D., Moran, T. P., & Jordan, D. S. (1988). The instructional design environment. In Pstoka, Massey, & Mutter (Eds.), *Intelligent tutoring systems: Lessons learned.* Hillsdale, NJ: Lawrence Erlbaum Associates.

Scardamalia, M., & Bereiter, C. (1988). Conceptions of teaching and approaches to core problems. In M. C. Reynolds (Ed.), *Knowledge base for the beginning teacher.* New York: Pergamon.

Schank, R. C. (1982). *Dynamic memory.* New York: Cambridge University Press.

Schank, R. C. (1990). *Tell me a story: A new look at real and artificial memory.* New York: Scribner's.

Schank, R. C., & Abelson, R. (1977). *Scripts, plans, goals, and understanding.* Hillsdale, NJ: Lawrence Erlbaum Associates.

Schank, R. C., & Jona, M. Y. (1991). Empowering the student: New perspectives on the design of teaching systems. *Journal of the Learning Sciences, 1*(1), 7–35.

Self, J. A. (1988). Bypassing the intractable problem of student modeling. In *Proceedings of the Conference on Intelligent Tutoring Systems–88* (pp. 18–24). Montreal, Canada.

Shavelson, R. J., & Stern, P. (1981). Research on teachers' pedagogical thoughts, judgements, decisions, and behavior. *Review of Educational Research, 51,* 455–498.

Shortliffe, E. H., & Buchanan, B. G. (1975). A model of inexact reasoning in medicine. *Mathematical Biosciences, 23,* 351–379.

Shulman, L. S. (1986). Paradigms and research programs in the study of teaching: A contemporary perspective. In M. C. Wittrock (Ed.), *Handbook of research on teaching* (pp. 3–36). New York: Macmillan.

Sleeman, D. (1987). PIXIE: A shell for developing intelligent tutoring systems. In R. W. Lawler & M. Yazdani (Eds.), *Artificial intelligence and education* (pp. 239–265). Norwood, NJ: Ablex.

Sleeman, D., & Brown, J. S. (1982). *Intelligent tutoring systems.* New York: Academic Press.

Stevens, A. L., & Collins, A. (1977). The goal structure of a Socratic tutor. In *Proceedings of the Association for Computer Machinery national conference.* Seattle, WA.

VanLehn, K. (1988). Student modeling. In M. C. Polson & J. J. Richardson (Eds.), *Foundations of intelligent tutoring systems* (pp. 55–78). Hillsdale, NJ: Lawrence Erlbaum Associates.

Waterman, D. A., & Hayes-Roth, F. (Eds.). (1978). *Pattern-directed inference systems.* New York: Academic Press.

Wilson, S. M., Shulman, L. S., & Richert, A. (1987). "150 different ways" of knowing: Representations of knowledge in teaching. In J. Calderhead (Ed.), *Exploring teachers' thinking* (pp. 104–124). London: Cassell.

Woods, W. A. (1970). Transition network grammers for natural language analysis. *Communications of the ACM, 13*(10), 591–606.

Woolf, B., Blegen, D., Jansen, J. H., & Verloop, A. (1987). Teaching a complex industrial process. In R. W. Lawler & M. Yazdani (Eds.), *Artificial intelligence and education* (pp. 413–427). London: Chapman & Hall.

Woolf, B., & McDonald, D. (1984, September). Building a computer tutor: Design issues. *IEEE Computer,* pp. 61–73.

Author Index

Subject Index